New Frontiers in American– East Asian Relations

Studies of the East Asian Institute,

Columbia University

New Frontiers
in American–
East Asian Relations

ESSAYS PRESENTED TO DOROTHY BORG

Edited by Warren I. Cohen

Columbia University Press · New York · 1983

Library of Congress Cataloging in Publication Data
Main entry under title:

New frontiers in American–East Asian relations.

(Studies of the East Asian Institute, Columbia
University)
"This volume derives from a conference held at the
Wilson Center, Washington, D.C., in May 1981"—P.
Includes bibliographical references and index.
1. East Asia—Foreign relations—United States—
Congresses.   2. United States—Foreign relations—
East Asia—Congresses.   I. Borg, Dorothy, 1902–
II. Cohen, Warren I.   III. Series: Studies of the East
Asian Institute.
DS518.8.N44   1983   327.7305   82-19903
ISBN 0-231-05630-3
ISBN 0-231-05631-1 (pbk.)

Columbia University Press
New York   Guildford, Surrey

Copyright © 1983 Columbia University Press
All rights reserved
Printed in the United States of America

Clothbound editions of Columbia University Press books are Smyth-sewn
and printed on permanent and durable acid-free paper.

Contents

Acknowledgments

THE CONFERENCE FROM which this volume derives was funded by the Woodrow Wilson International Center for Scholars, Washington, D.C. It was cosponsored by the Wilson Center's East Asia Program and the Committee on American–East Asian Relations of the Society for Historians of American Foreign Relations (SHAFR). We are grateful to Harry Harding and to Ronald A. Morse, successive directors of the Wilson Center's East Asia Program, for their advice and support. Lisa Wilson was especially helpful with arrangements for and around the conference, which was held May 29–30, 1981, in the Smithsonian Institution Building.

Sheila Driscoll, coordinator of the Committee on American–East Asian Relations, provided essential administrative and moral support. The Asian Studies Center of Michigan State University contributed the services of Catherine Burt for typing, copying, and mailing. Lee Sligh, supported by an undergraduate assistantship from the Asian Studies Center at Michigan State University, prepared a bibliography of works published in the last decade.

The East Asian Institute at Columbia University offered essential financial guarantees when we threatened to exceed our budget and the editorial services of Anita O'Brien, who also did the index, and Deborah E. Bell. We are indebted to Bernard Gronert of Columbia University Press for publishing so many superb volumes in American–East Asian relations, a number of which are discussed in the essays that follow.

Ernest R. May, James W. Morley, and Allen S. Whiting graciously consented to offer a special open seminar at the Wilson Center on "History and the Policy Makers" in the context of the conference. Other than those whose work appears in this book, the following scholars also participated in the conference: A. Doak Barnett (Brookings Institution), Michael Baron (Columbia University), Robert Beisner (American University), Russell D. Buhite (University of Oklahoma), Roger Dingman (University of Southern California), Harry Harding (Stanford University), Igarashi Takeshi (University of Tokyo), Bradford A. Lee (Harvard University), Steven I. Levine (American University), Charles Lilley (North Virginia Community College), Roderick MacFarquhar (Wilson Fellow), Gary May (University of Delaware), Ray Moore (Amherst College), Ronald A. Morse (Wilson Center), Stephen E. Pelz (University of Massachusetts), Mordecai Rozanski (Pacific Lutheran University), Michael Schaller (University of Arizona), Nancy Bernkopf Tucker (Colgate University), Peter Van Ness (University of Denver), Russell F. Weigley (Temple University), Larry Weiss (Friends World University), Samuel Wells (Wilson Center), and Yao Wei (Ministry of Foreign Affairs, PRC).

And finally, Dorothy Borg was wonderfully tolerant of this violation of her privacy.

Contributors

WARREN I. COHEN Professor of History and Director of the Asian Studies Center, Michigan State University. He has written several books on the history of America's foreign relations, most recently *Dean Rusk* in the *American Secretaries of State* series.

BRUCE CUMINGS Associate Professor, International Studies, University of Washington. He is the author of *The Origins of the Korean War: Liberation and the Emergence of Separate Regimes, 1945–1947* and editor of *Child of Conflict: The Korean-American Relationship, 1945–1953*.

CAROL GLUCK Assistant Professor of Modern Japanese History, Columbia University. She is the author of *Japan's Modern Myths: Ideology in the Late Meiji Period* and studies in Japanese historiography.

WALDO HEINRICHS Professor of History, Temple University. He wrote *American Ambassador: Joseph C. Grew and the Development of the U.S. Diplomatic Tradition* and, with Dorothy Borg, edited *Uncertain Years: Chinese-American Relations, 1947–1950*.

MICHAEL H. HUNT Associate Professor of History, University of North Carolina at Chapel Hill. He is the author of *Frontier Defense and the Open Door: Manchuria in Chinese-American Relations, 1895–1911* and *The Making of a Special Relationship: The United States and China to 1914*.

AKIRA IRIYE Professor of History, University of Chicago. He is the author and editor of many books, especially in the field of American–East Asian Relations. His most recent work is *Power and Culture: The Japanese-American War, 1941–1945*.

JIANG XIANGZE Professor of History, Zhongshan (Sun Yatsen) University, Guangzhou, People's Republic of China. He has written several studies in the history of international relations, but is best known to American scholars for his *The Nien Rebellion,* written while he was at the University of Washington in the early 1950s.

LUO RONGQU Associate Professor of History, Beijing University. He has written widely in the fields of comparative history and Chinese-American relations. His most recent book is *Weidade fan faxisi zhan-zheng* (The Great Anti-Fascist War).

ERNEST R. MAY Charles Warren Professor of History, Harvard University. He is the author of a variety of studies on the international relations of the United States and editor, with James C. Thomson, Jr., of *American–East Asian Relations: A Survey.*

Introduction

THIS VOLUME DERIVES from a conference held at the Wilson Center, Washington, D.C., in May 1981. Several of us were conspiring to put together a volume of essays in honor of Dorothy Borg, the guiding spirit of the field of American-East Asian relations. She in turn wanted us to hold a workshop to examine our field, with particular reference to the achievements of the 1970s. As always, her views prevailed.

Although much had been written before on American relations with East Asia, the field as now conceived dates back only to the early 1960s. At Harvard a small group of historians—John King Fairbank, Ernest R. May, and Oscar Handlin—formed a committee, which was headed by May. Dorothy Borg lived in Cambridge from 1960 to 1962 and helped that committee formulate its program. Its goal was to develop scholars who would have a dual competence, in American and East Asian history—scholars able to use sources written in the languages of both sides of the Pacific. These scholars would transcend ethnocentrism and see issues as they were perceived by Americans and Asians alike. The quality of their work would surpass that of the more narrowly conceived works of the past *and* might lead to a more enlightened foreign policy. In retrospect, the committee was overly optimistic about the possibility of training people who could handle two or more languages readily. Such scholars, however, were found eventually, as the essays herein by Akira Iriye, Michael H. Hunt, and Bruce Cumings will reveal.

In 1968 the American Historical Association, on the advice of a group of American diplomatic historians and specialists in Chinese and Japanese history, appointed the Committee on American-East Asian Relations (AEAR), to be chaired by Ernest May.* That same

* The committee is now affiliated with SHAFR (the Society for Historians of American Foreign Relations).

year John Fairbank used his presidential address to the AHA to declare the study of American-East Asian relations to be our "Assignment for the '70s." Support from the Ford Foundation allowed the AEAR Committee to maintain a modest program of graduate fellowships, research grants, and conferences.

Borg found May to be a kindred soul, a man who shared her penchant for historiography. One of the first actions of the committee was to convene a conference to survey the work of the past: to identify the most valuable writings, analyze interpretations, and chart a course for the future. Out of that conference, held in Cuernavaca, Mexico, in 1970, came *American-East Asian Relations: A Survey,* edited by May and James C. Thomson, Jr.

Comparable to the Cuernavaca conference in importance was a conference that Borg helped organize at Kawaguchiko, Japan, a few months earlier. Here a second approach to the field emerged. Focusing on the years 1931 to 1941, Japanese scholars and their American counterparts wrote parallel papers examining institutions in their own countries. After a week of intense discussions, facilitated by simultaneous translations by day, liquid refreshment and a few bilingual participants in the evenings, everyone present gained new insight into the problems of the 1930s. Perspectives never before considered became apparent. The result was the superb, prize-winning volume, *Pearl Harbor as History,* edited by Borg and Shumpei Okamoto.

A third approach was evident in a conference Borg organized in 1978, at Seven Springs in Mt. Kisco, New York. On this occasion American scholars who were specialists in American foreign policy joined with other Americans specializing in Chinese policy to examine Chinese-American relations in the Truman era. From that conference came Borg and Waldo Heinrichs, *Uncertain Years: Chinese-American Relations, 1947–1950.*

All of these approaches—the ideal of dual competence, the binational or multinational conference, and the bringing together of Americanists and Asianists—have led to an explosion of new work and new interpretations in the field of American-East Asian relations. Behind much of this activity has been Dorothy Borg. Fairbank, Iriye, May, James Crowley at Yale, and others have launched a variety of similar efforts. In the late 1970s generous support from the Henry

Luce Foundation fueled many AEAR projects. The May 1981 conference was designed to assess these accomplishments.

    To comprehend historiographic developments of the last quarter century, it is worth recalling how long prewar works by Tyler Dennett and A. Whitney Griswold dominated the field.* Few realize the impact of Griswold in particular on George Kennan and Tang Tsou, men whose ideas were enormously influential in the 1950s and 1960s. One of Dennett's books, first published in 1922, was reprinted as recently as 1963. Griswold's book, published in 1938, was reprinted in 1964. The point, stated most simply, is that apart from intrinsic merit, works as many as forty years old had to be used because nothing else was available—despite an enormous wealth of new material and a radically changed climate of opinion.

    Dennett wrote when the study of diplomatic history was relatively new. There had been but a handful of general accounts of American foreign policy, and, in the absence of a scholarly history of American activity in East Asia, anyone interested was forced to rely on John W. Foster's apologia, *American Diplomacy in the Orient* (1903). Dennett undertook the first systematic survey of the documentary record, intending to edit a book of source materials on American relations with China to 1870. The Department of State interrupted his work with an offer he found irresistible: privileged access to its archives to prepare a history of American policy in East Asia for the use of the American delegation to the Washington Conference (1921–1922). The resulting study, an extraordinary job of controlling a great mass of material, provided the basis for Dennett's *Americans in Eastern Asia,* which carried the story to the close of the nineteenth century.

    Dennett reported in that book that the United States had demonstrated a single consistent goal—the expansion of trade, especially with China. To achieve this goal, Americans had since the 1840s

*The following discussion of Dennett and Griswold is based upon Dorothy Borg, "Two Historians of the Far Eastern Policy of the United States: Tyler Dennett and A. Whitney Griswold," in Borg and Okamoto, eds., *Pearl Harbor as History* (New York: Columbia University Press, 1973).

demanded most-favored-nation treatment for its merchants and had supported the development of independent Asian states strong enough to protect American rights. The only issue argued in the nineteenth century was strategic: should the United States act alone or in concert with other powers? For Dennett, the answer was manifest. On the eve of the Washington Conference, he demonstrated that past American activity in East Asia had succeeded only when the United States pursued a cooperative policy. The book was an appeal for cooperation with Great Britain and Japan as the best means of serving American interests, of expanding trade and preserving the peace of the Pacific.

Dennett's thoughts about the open door policy and America's role in world affairs underwent rapid transformation in the years that followed. By 1933, when his prize-winning biography of Hay was published, the collapse of the interwar peace system and the miseries of the Great Depression had thoroughly embittered him. Events around the world, and especially in Manchuria, had led to widespread disillusionment in the United States and a determination to avoid involvement with foreigners determined to plunge the globe into another world war. Even in the peace movement, there was greater emphasis on keeping America out of war than on working for world peace. Peace activists and historians, like most other Americans, became more nationalist, less internationalist. Charles Beard's *The Idea of National Interest* (1934), *Open Door at Home* (1934), and many of his other writings in the 1930s articulated the prevailing view that involvement in foreign affairs benefitted a privileged few but was contrary to the national interest. For Beard the answer was to stay at home, forget foreign trade in particular, and practice autarky. To hell with all those Asians and Europeans who wanted to kill each other.

Dennett's work reflected similar sentiments. Hay had endangered the nation by involving the United States in an area of peripheral interest. Dennett depicted past American policy in East Asia in cycles of coercion and retreat. Intervention was wrong, and his growing mistrust of Franklin Roosevelt led him to fear that the United States was entering a new cycle of coercion, of unnecessary and mistaken involvement in East Asian affairs. Work by A. L. P. Dennis and Paul Clyde, sympathetic to Japan's role, may have helped persuade him that it would be wrong for the United States to oppose Japan.

Dennett's writings of the 1930s had less direct influence on post-World War II scholarship than *Americans in East Asia* but were nonetheless of tremendous importance for their influence on Samuel Flagg Bemis and A. Whitney Griswold—and through them, on George Kennan and Tang Tsou. Here were the seeds of the "great aberration," of the muddle-headed Hay who betrayed American interests to the British.

Griswold was a Yale graduate who went off to Wall Street to seek his fortune in 1929. It was quickly apparent that he was safer at Yale, to which he returned in 1930, never to leave again. The history department provided shelter and Bemis, who arrived in New Haven a few years later, taught him about the great aberration: the series of events between 1898 and 1905 that allegedly involved the United States needlessly and dangerously in the affairs of East Asia.

Once an ardent supporter of the League of Nations, Griswold shared the widespread disillusionment with that organization after it failed to stop Japan in Manchuria. Like many other liberal intellectuals in the mid-1930s, he concluded that avoidance of war had to be the highest priority of American foreign policy. As the war clouds gathered, first in East Asia and then across the Atlantic, he argued against American involvement in foreign quarrels. He was attracted to Dennett's writings of the early 1930s, which, like Bemis' text, argued implicitly against a new cycle of American assertiveness in Asia. Why not give up the foolish defense of ephemeral interests in China and seek accommodation with Japan? As the popular imagination was captured by revisionist writers and congressional investigations which suggested that the British had maneuvered the United States into war in 1917, Griswold worried about British machinations that might lead his country into a new conflagration, perhaps through the "back door" in Asia.

In 1935 Griswold decided to write a history of American-East Asian relations. He wanted to examine the past as a guide to coping with current problems. He was seeking a useable past—and he found one.

Griswold adopted Dennett's thesis uncritically as his own. American policy, at least since the Spanish-American War, had aimed consistently at the expansion of American trade with China by maintaining the open door policy, especially as that policy was defined by

Hay in 1899 and 1900. Griswold was troubled particularly by the alleged commitment to preserve the territorial integrity of China. Periodically, he found, each American administration would assert itself in East Asia, generally against Japan, and then be forced to retreat because it was unwilling to use force to accomplish its ends. The open door policy became an end instead of a means, and every American president from McKinley to Franklin Roosevelt was committed to upholding it. Moreover, Hay's initial burst of note-writing had resulted from a sly British plot, perpetrated by Alfred Hippisley of the Chinese Imperial Maritime Customs Service in collusion with William Rockhill, to have the United States front for British interests. Hay was a foolish Anglophile and Hippisley was perceived as a British agent.

Griswold found American leaders from 1900 to 1937 committed to support of China, invariably in opposition to Japan. Despite evidence that American economic interests, trade and investment, were greater with Japan than with China and best served by cooperation with Japan, American leaders persisted on a course that would lead to war with Japan. The message was clear enough: to avoid war, the United States had to resist British manipulation, discard its unrealistic concern for China, and seek accommodation with Japan. The influence of Charles Beard's conception of "realism," as expressed in *The Idea of National Interest* and *The Open Door at Home*, was evident.

Griswold was the first scholar to use Rockhill's papers and particularly the correspondence with Hippisley. There is general agreement among historians today that he misused that correspondence and that, in any event, his analysis of the origin of the open door notes rested too heavily on one source. Nonetheless, the section covering 1898–1900 is the best part of the book. From there on, the sources grow thinner and the analysis less credible. Unlike Dennett, he had no privileged access to Department of State documents, lacked any manuscript materials of consequence for the 1914–1937 period, and made inadequate use of materials for 1900–1914. His discussion of the policies of Theodore Roosevelt, Woodrow Wilson, Charles Evans Hughes, Frank Kellogg, Henry Stimson, and Franklin Roosevelt has been revealed as deficient by dozens of monographs written since

1945. Nonetheless, the book went through several printings in 1964 and dominated reading lists in the field at least until the end of the decade. Two generations of students learned about American policy either from Griswold's book (of which about 12,000 copies were sold) or from teachers influenced by him. George Kennan, Robert Osgood, Hans Morgenthau, and Tang Tsou each wrote books of enormous importance in the 1950s—and each learned about American policy in East Asia from Griswold's book.

The worst offender was probably Kennan, an occasionally brilliant diplomatist and magnificent memoirist, with rather more modest achievements as a student of American diplomatic history. He swallowed Griswold's tale of the open door notes and used them to ridicule the secretary of state and the lack of realism in American policy. His *American Diplomacy, 1900–1950* was probably the single most important book on foreign policy in the 1950s, used as a text in university and high school classrooms across the country. The prevailing theme in the work of Kennan, Osgood, Morgenthau, and Tsou was the need for greater realism in American policy. Notes, reliance on principles like the open door, and moral suasion were of little avail. The American people had to appreciate the role of power in world affairs. Tsou brought all the pieces together in his *America's Failure in China, 1941–1950,* in which he set forth the thesis that unwillingness of the United States to use force in East Asia in support of its principles resulted in the loss of China to the communists. Tsou's work in particular, but the Griswold thesis as used by Kennan and the others, was often cited as justification for the use of force in Vietnam in the mid-1960s—not quite what Griswold had intended.

In the post-World War II era, new sources became available to American scholars. An enormous amount of documents from the U.S. government, manuscript collections, diaries, captured Japanese documents, and Chinese documents permitted scholars to provide new answers to questions posed by Dennett and Griswold—and, increasingly, to ask new questions. At the center of much of this effort was Dorothy Borg.

Borg graduated from Wellesley in 1922 and worked for much of the 1920s as a reporter for the *New York World*. She had been affected by the horrors of the world war and sought to learn about its causes and, more to the point, the way to avoid future wars. After a few years the glamour of journalism wore off and she enrolled in a Ph.D. program at Columbia, seeking an academic career and a lifetime of study devoted to the fundamental issues of international affairs.

Borg and Griswold were in graduate school at roughly the same time and both were affected by the climate of disillusionment with the world war. Both conceived of their work as a search for the means to avoid war. Neither had any previous association with Asia or any manifest interest in that part of the world. Borg came from a family of German Jewish origin whose horizons stretched from the cultural centers of Western Europe to New York, and maybe Boston. But there were major differences in Borg's and Griswold's approaches to international relations and to avoiding war. Borg was essentially a product of the Columbia group of scholars who in the interwar years thought in terms of international cooperation. Such a viewpoint was far from the kind of isolationism Griswold maintained until the eve of World War II.

In the late 1930s, after passing her Ph.D. orals, Borg joined the staff of the American Council of the Institute of Pacific Relations as a research associate. For the first time, she met a wide range of Americans with close ties to China—government officials, missionaries, businessmen, journalists and academic specialists. She had extensive contact with Asians interested in Pacific affairs. And she began to study Chinese-American relations.

Borg's dissertation, written during the war, was published in 1947 as *American Policy and the Chinese Revolution, 1925–1928*. Although she had access to little more evidence than had been available to Griswold, it is difficult to believe that they wrote in the same century. In its systematic study of congressional and public opinion—newspapers and special interest groups—Borg's book revealed the climate of opinion in which Kellogg functioned. She demonstrated that rather than pursuing a policy rigidly committed to the open door, a policy peculiar to China, Kellogg and his advisers adapted policy toward China to the same considerations that affected American policy generally. The 1920s were years in which the peace movement dominated policy considerations, in which Americans abhorred the use of force in world affairs, in which a retreat from cruder forms of imperialism was necessary, in which the United States government had no choice but to accept nationalistic revolutions in Mexico and Turkey. No preoccupation with the China market or with China's integrity was evident; nor was the United States victimized by British machinations or undertaking a crusade to thwart Japan. Borg concluded that Kellogg's policy, based on the assumptions that the Chinese revolution was independent of Soviet control and that the Chinese were entitled to determine their future by themselves, was "bold and imaginative." And not least, Borg provided readers with an understanding of the Chinese context, especially the May Thirtieth Movement, without which much of Chinese-American relations in the 1920s is incomprehensible.

The book was finished as another revolution loomed large in China, and Borg's praise for Kellogg was not without implicit advice for the Truman administration: let the Chinese fight their own civil wars and revolutions. In late 1946 she went to China for the first time, representing the IPR in Shanghai and Peiping for almost two years. While in Peiping she taught for one semester at Peking National University. She learned much about China and about why Chinese intellectuals, faculty and students, were turning against the Kuomintang. Perhaps most of all she recognized the extraordinary difficulty Americans had in understanding life in China, of cross-cultural understanding generally.

Borg discovered something else in China that confirmed a growing suspicion of how deeply rooted and inbred America's China hands were. American missionaries she met in China had often spent their whole careers there and had raised their children there. The children then went on to become academics or journalists or government officials, but frequently specializing in Chinese affairs. Businessmen in Shanghai were deeply rooted, unwilling to surrender a standard of living not available at home. Foreign service officers and journalists, unlike their colleagues stationed elsewhere, seemed exempt from rotation and spent unusually large parts of their careers in China. This perception fit well with the sense she had developed since the beginning of her association with the IPR that long residence in China and insulation from the United States and the rest of the world had allowed these people to develop and disseminate an unrealistic idea of Sino-American relations. They had nurtured a concept of a special relationship between China and America, that Americans felt particularly close to China and obligated to assist and protect the Chinese. Borg was persuaded that most Americans, in or out of government, were indifferent to China, that China was a peripheral concern of Americans. This idea permeates her work and that of a generation of scholars influenced by her.

Before Borg was able to get very far with her next research project, Senators Joe McCarthy and Pat McCarran interceded. With help from Alfred Kohlberg, "the China Lobby man," the McCarthyites promoted the idea that Chiang Kai-shek had lost China because of the activities of the IPR. In particular the McCarran Committee went after Owen Lattimore, a close friend of Borg's. She put her work aside and devoted much of her time in the early 1950s to preparing materials for the defense of Lattimore and other friends. So incredible were those days that she was herself denied access to historical records of the Department of State that any bona fide graduate student could have used. Although she has often spoken of the profound influence of World War II on her thought, it is clear that McCarthyism also left its impact. In her second book she carefully omitted the name of a foreign service officer she praised cautiously for his careful reporting of the rise of the Chinese Communist movement—lest he, O. Edmund Clubb, be victimized again. Years later when I was outraged by the moral insensitivity of a published history of the IPR that appeared to find McCarran no more culpable than the IPR itself, Borg was mildly surprised. Anything less vile than the usual McCarthyite attack seemed a blessing.

Her second book was the Bancroft prize-winning *The United States and the Far Eastern Crisis of 1933–1938.* In that densely textured monograph, she revealed the climate of public opinion in which Franklin Roosevelt and his advisers worked. She demonstrated the constraints imposed on foreign policy by the primacy the administration had to give to coping with the depression and by the pacifist and neo-isolationist sentiment that followed the inability of the United

States or the League to respond adequately to Japan's seizure of Manchuria. Intending to write a book on Chinese-American relations, she found China a marginal concern of the Roosevelt administration. At least from 1934 through 1937, avoidance of war with Japan was the cardinal principle of the administration's East Asian policy. Although Borg avoided the harsh word "appeasement," others using her evidence and argument have insisted that Roosevelt appeased Japan. The view that prevailed in Washington was that the Chinese had to learn to take care of themselves. Suggestions of American responsibility to help China were met with indignation. Neither Roosevelt nor his advisers showed much interest in trade or in China's territorial integrity. They were concerned with American interests, which they concluded were best served by conciliating Japan—precisely the policy Griswold advocated. When policy began to shift in 1938 it was because of a growing apprehension about a threat to the American stake in the existing world order. Even then, Europe, rather than Asia, was central to the renewed movement for collective security.

For most of the 1960s and 1970s Borg devoted herself to historiographic concerns and development of the field. In 1966 she persuaded the Association of Asian Studies to hold a session on "Historians and American Far Eastern Policy" at its annual meeting. She compiled the papers and comments and had them published later that year by the East Asian Institute at Columbia. John A. Garraty surveyed the field and Iriye discussed East Asian scholarship, but the focus was on the work of Dennett and Griswold. In her introductory remarks, Borg left no doubt she thought these works needed replacing, indicated her doubts about Griswold in particular, and urged American diplomatic historians and East Asian specialists to work more closely together. She called on diplomatic historians to learn to use Asian sources and East Asianists to work on relations between the United States and Asia. In 1969 she presented detailed critiques of both Dennett and Griswold in her paper for the Kawaguchi conference. For the past few years she has been engaged in a survey of more recent studies such as the revisionist writings on America's cold war policy, the general works on imperialism and modernization, and the monographs by China specialists in various disciplines that raise fresh questions about the history of China's contact with the West.

The ultimate aim is to stimulate a wider consideration of the extent to which the newer research could be applied to the study of Chinese-American relations.

The net result of Borg's efforts, in which she has been assisted by scores of other scholars, has been the demise of the Dennett and Griswold theses. Current textbooks rarely cite Griswold—and then only for a particularly felicitous phrase, of which his book contains many. Bemis' "great aberration" is no longer taken seriously, although some disciples of William Appleman Williams remain sympathetic. Iriye's *Across the Pacific,* my *America's Response to China,* and Charles Neu's *The Troubled Encounter* are the general works most often cited. A host of finely researched and crafted monographs by Borg, Raymond Esthus, Heinrichs, Hunt, Christopher Thorne, Paul Varg and Marilyn Young, and others like them are available. Hunt's *The Making of a Special Relationship* will likely put Dennett's book to rest. All of these authors have raised the kinds of questions Borg, Fairbank, and May have demanded. They analyze business interests, cultural contacts, the role of immigrants, and mutual perceptions, and they are rarely oblivious to bureaucratic politics or the larger international context. Some use East Asian language materials and all are more understanding of the Asian context than was an earlier generation of scholars. Generalists such as Robert Dallek, Lloyd Gardner, Walter LeFeber, and Thomas Paterson have worked with AEAR Committee members and participated in conferences with Asian scholars and with American Asia specialists. Much has been accomplished, but Borg would be the last to argue that our work is done.

The conference for which the initial versions of these essays was prepared was the first occasion in which scholars from the People's Republic of China participated in the work of the AEAR Committee. Jiang Xiangze of Zhongshan University and Luo Rongqu of Beijing University both examined work in China since 1949. Yao Wei, a member of the Ministry of Foreign Affairs in residence at the Wilson Center, attended the sessions and contributed to the discussions. The papers by Jiang and Luo indicate striking new developments in the study of the history of Chinese-American relations in their country.

Michael Hunt's essay voices his disappointment with much recent work on the nineteenth century. Too little of the new work on this era reveals "new vistas." Too much of it relies on old formulas—familiar questions and familiar answers. But Hunt does have some ideas for new approaches that suggest opportunities for exciting research.

One new tack urged at Cuernavaca has brought magnificent results, as Akira Iriye demonstrates. A wide range of scholars have looked at cultural relations between the United States and East Asian countries and have added greatly to the texture of our understanding of crosscultural contacts. Some of these cultural relationships were clearly of political and economic consequence. In other instances, the connections are yet to be established, but no one who reads Iriye's essay will ever question the importance of cultural contacts for diplomatic historians.

Waldo Heinrichs not only reviews the literature on political and economic affairs from 1900 to 1945, but offers a superb analysis of old and new methods of tackling the problems of the period. He notes the areas in which grand theories have contributed to our understanding—and the areas in which approaches like those of William A. Williams or Immanuel Wallerstein are likely to run aground on the facts.

Reflecting on his assignment to discuss military affairs, Ernest May is struck by the emphasis on work on the 1960s, the decline of polemic in writings about the period 1919 to 1952, and the increased attention given to the military in the work of the last decade. Much of the most exciting scholarship he describes analyzes the activities of the American and Japanese navies, but he does not ignore the army (or the air force) as he considers the rise of militarism in the United States.

My essay focuses more narrowly on the United States and China since 1945, with particular attention to the "lost chance" idea so prominent a decade ago. Restrained by my colleagues from including a history of Chinese-American relations in the 1950s, I merely discount those already written and go to the unusually large body of material already available on the 1960s.

Carol Gluck concentrates on occupation history, clearly the live-

liest subject among students of postwar Japanese-American relations. A new recruit to the field of AEAR, Gluck electrified the conference with her energetic presentation. Her sharply focused paper,
printed here, contributes enormously to our understanding of the work
of Japanese scholars in an excruciatingly sensitive area.

Finally, we asked Bruce Cumings to do something a little different. At Cuernavaca, no one spoke or wrote of Korean-American
relations—in part because so few people could. In Cumings we have
one of the rarest of AEAR specialists, a scholar who meets the ideal
of a dual competence in American and Korean history, able to use
Korean as well as English-language sources. Cumings surveys the
entire field of Korean-American relations, providing a base point from
which scholars of the future may proceed.

All of which brings us back to the original purpose of this volume—our desire to honor Dorothy Borg. There are two attributes of
hers that should be recorded—as appropriately here as anywhere. First
is her extraordinary, continuing interest in young scholars. She is
constantly looking for bright young men and women to recruit to the
field, constantly reaching out to encourage them—as she did Heinrichs and Iriye, Marilyn Blatt Young and me fifteen or twenty years
ago. Her interest is clearly proprietary, but it is not exclusive. Second
is her unending search for new questions to ask, new methods to use.
Indeed, in recent years her focus on methodology has been painful
for those of us without time for all the strange books she felt we
should read. If the essays that follow lack complacency, it is primarily because several guilt-ridden authors surrendered to her demand
for a guide to possible new approaches. I can only assume that long
after we have retired to defend the interpretations of our youth against
the next generation, Dorothy Borg will be urging our grandchildren
to answer the questions we never asked, using the methods we never
mastered.

New Frontiers
in American–
East Asian
Relations

ONE

Research in Sino–American Relations in the People's Republic of China

by LUO RONGQU and JIANG XIANGZE

IN THE LAST thirty years research in China on the history of Sino-American relations and the history of the United States has progressed along a bell-shaped curve. In the decade after 1949, study of Sino-American relations flourished. Then, in the 1970s, especially during the Cultural Revolution, there was a temporary falling off of such research, to be revived only toward the end of the 1970s. In the last few years a new wave of eagerness to understand the United States has again propelled the study of Sino-American relations and American history. To use a contemporary Wall Street analogy, work on Sino-American relations and American history is in great demand and its prospects are bullish for the moment.

From the founding of the People's Republic of China to the early 1960s, China and the United States were in a state of bitter confrontation. In August 1949, on the eve of the founding of the republic, the U.S. Department of State published the notorious China White Paper, *United States Relations with China,* a historical survey of U.S. policy toward China and a compilation of a carefully selected collection of documents from State Department archives. Naturally this survey defended the traditional China policy of the U.S. government. At that crucial time in our history, its one-sided emphasis on the friendship of the United States toward China was unacceptable to most Chinese, regardless of political background. Subsequently Chairman Mao published a number of editorials in *Renmin ribao* on the White Paper. Mao repudiated official U.S. statements in the White Paper concerning its policy toward China and declared that the U.S. government had never been the friend of the Chinese people, but rather their enemy.

In one article Mao suggested that Chinese historians should compile a narrative history to detail American imperialist aggression in China for younger generations. Mao's articles have since been adopted as the guiding ideology for Chinese historians. In accordance with Mao's tenets, Chinese historians have developed their own framework for the history of Sino-American relations and the history of the United States. Especially after the outbreak of the Korean War, tension between China and the United States increased. Consequently—and not surprisingly—almost all Chinese research on Sino-American relations and U.S. history has focused on American imperialist aggression. These studies have contributed significantly to scholarship in the field.

In China, publications on Sino-American relations were abundant during the 1950s. The two most popular works were *Meiguo qin Hua shi* (A history of U.S. aggression against China), by Liu Danian, head of the Institute of Modern History of China, and another book of the same title written by Qing Ruji, also a historian.

Liu's work, originally written in the late 1940s, came out in an enlarged and revised edition with a new title in 1951. According to him, prior to the Opium War Sino-American relations had been peaceful. From the Opium War through the Russo-Japanese War, however, the United States carried out a policy of aggression toward China, following the example of other powers, namely Great Britain. From the Russo-Japanese War onward the United States gradually moved toward a policy of exclusive domination over China. In the period between the two world wars the United States contended with Japan for hegemony over China. After World War II the United States pursued this policy of hegemonism alone, a strategy which resulted in failure. The author points out that one of the chief characteristics of U.S. aggression in China has been to stay closely in step with Japanese aggression. He suggests, in other words, that U.S. policy toward China was copied from that of other nations—first Great Britain and then Japan. Liu's work is probably the first narrative history of U.S. aggression against China written by a native Chinese. It was very popular in the 1950s.

Qing Ruji's scholarly work was published in two volumes. The first, covering the period 1784 to 1860, was published in 1953. The second, focusing on the years 1861–1899, was published in 1956. Unfortunately, Qing died before subsequent volumes were finished. As a result the most crucial period of Sino-American relations, the twentieth century, was left untouched.

From Qing's point of view the history of Sino-American relations is nothing but the history of imperialist aggression, oppression, and exploitation. Qing divides the process of American aggression into five phases: (1) from the founding of the United States through the mid-nineteenth century, when U.S. aggression was characterized as "an exploitation by commercial capitalism in the style of piratical looting"; (2) from the signing of the Treaty of Wangxia in 1844 to the second Opium War in 1856–1860, when Sino-American relations were perceived of as aggression by means of collusion with other powers, an international joint management which used the principles of "equitable sharing of benefits" and "international condominium"; (3) from 1861 through 1899, the year of the declaration of the open door policy, when the United States began a new policy of claiming American hegemony over China; (4) from 1900 (the signing of the Sino-American Friendship and Commercial Treaty) through 1946, when the U.S. developed and established a policy of domination over China; and (5) from 1946 onward, when we see the epilogue of American imperialism in China.

In Qing's work a number of basic historical events are treated differently than in Liu's. In fact, many of Qing's statements contradict those of Liu. For example, Qing rejects the idea that U.S. aggression was a copy of Britain's and Japan's. In contrast, he writes that from 1860 onward the goal of U.S. policy toward China was to keep China totally under U.S. domination; that is, the United States wished to make China an American colony. The open door policy marked the first milestone of such a policy. The author deals not only with political and military aspects of American aggression, but with various economic, cultural, and religious ones as well. This book is a typical scholarly work from the period.

Along with these two general narrative histories, typical Chinese research focuses on American economic and financial penetration in

China. In this field *Meiguo jingji qin Hua shi* (A history of American economic aggression toward China) by Qin Benli is a pathbreaking work.

During this period the work of compiling and translating archival materials was also underway. The most valuable source book in this regard is *Shijiushi ji Meiguo qin Hua dangan shiliao xuanji* (A selection of archival documents on American aggression against China in the nineteenth century), selected and translated by Zhu Shijia, formerly of the Library of Congress. Another source book, *Meiguo pohai Hua gong shiliao* (Some resources and materials relating to Chinese laborers persecuted in the United States), selected and translated by Zhu, was also made available to Chinese readers.

As Sino-American confrontation continued through the 1950s, writings focusing on U.S. imperialism gradually gave way to long-term academic research. In 1961 the first volume of *Diguozhuyi qin Hua shi* (A history of foreign imperialist aggression against China) was published. It was written by a research group established in the Institute of Modern History of the Academy of Sciences in China, under the direction of professors Liu Danian and Shao Xunzheng. In this book, which covers the period 1840–1895, the background of U.S. aggression against China is described succinctly. Unlike previous works, however, it is based principally on primary sources. The treatment of historical materials is far more rigorous, and the writing style is simpler. It is consequently regarded as the definitive work in this field.

One publication from this period worth mentioning is *Fan Mei Hua gong jin yao wenji* (An anthology of literature on the movement to oppose U.S. laws against Chinese labor), published in 1962. Edited by A Ying, a learned scholar and writer, this is a collection of Chinese historical accounts, fragments of reminiscences, and passages from novels that record the lives and suffering of Chinese coolies in the United States at the turn of the twentieth century. The book is a significant contribution in this field. Its focus, of course, is emphatically on anti-U.S. feelings of Chinese nationalism.

From the mid-1960s, when the Cultural Revolution took place, all academic research, teaching, and textbook writing was interrupted for about ten years.

Following the Cultural Revolution the fundamental condition of Chinese studies on Sino-American relations and American history did not improve until the end of the 1970s. With the normalization of Sino-American relations in 1979 and the increased contact that resulted, both the Chinese and American people needed to understand each other better. As a result, historians have undertaken the extremely important task of promoting real mutual understanding between our two peoples. In January 1979, when our two nations resumed diplomatic relations, I wrote an essay entitled "Mantan Zhong Mei liangguo renmin di zaoqi jiaowang" (Notes on early contact between the Chinese and American peoples), published in *Renmin ribao*. This essay was among the first—if not the first—to argue for a reexamination of the history of Sino-American relations.

A few months later Wang Xi, a professor at Fudan University in Shanghai, published an article entitled "Luelun Zhong Mei guanxi shi shang di jige wenti" (A brief discussion of several questions on the history of Sino-American relations) in the periodical *Shijie lishi*. Wang proposed that the relationship between China and the United States be reassessed, based on realistic analysis. As he pointed out, among the imperialist powers, the United States was the only one that did not occupy Chinese territory. He maintained that the open door policy embodied two things. One was the recognition of spheres of influence by the imperialist powers in China and, on this premise, the demand of equal opportunity for U.S. trade. The other principle supported respect for China's territorial integrity and sovereignty. This policy played a definite role in restraining or delaying imperialist aggression against China. He also argued that U.S. policy decisions should be analyzed not only from the Chinese side, but from the American side as well, taking into account the inner contradictions in U.S. society. The author reviewed the role of American missionaries and pointed out that aside from their negative impact, they were of some educational and medical benefit to China. He also acknowledged the contributions of Chinese laborers in building railroads in the western United States as well as the friendship of the American people toward China's revolution. As one might expect, such arguments had never been published before. Thus it is not at all surprising that Wang's article immediately provoked strong repercussions in academic circles. Among those who strongly opposed the article were Ding Mingnan and Zhang Zhenkun of the Institute of Modern History in China. Their rebuttal, "Zhong Mei guanxi shi yanjiu: xiangqian tuijin, haishi xianghou daotui?" (Research on the history of Sino-American relations: A step forward for a step backward?), in *Jindaishi yanjiu,* was typical of Wang's opponents. Ding had assisted Liu Danian in revising his *A History of the U.S. Aggression in China* and was one of the chief authors of the authoritative work *A History of Foreign Imperialist Aggression Against China.* Ding and Zhang held that Wang's article was ambiguous and vague about the essence of the open door policy. They suggested that the several major incidents listed by Wang Xi as playing a restraining or delaying role were mostly deliberate exaggerations and overestimations not in accordance with historical facts. They pointed out sharply that the arguments raised in Wang's article were nothing but a repetition of the worn-out bourgeois views of Dr. Hu Shi and Dr. Jiang Tingfu. In contrast, Ding and Zhang asserted that the established postliberation arguments were tenable and unrefutable. In conclusion they warned against the academic trend to ignore the study of imperialist aggression against China and called on all readers to overcome "all obstructions."

In June 1980 I wrote an article, entitled in English "Some Questions of the History of Sino-American Relations and Research on American History," published in *Lishi yanjiu.* In it I hold that previous researchers in both our countries had been far from compatible with the needs of the development of history as a science and had failed to account for new circumstances. On the Chinese side, although we have made some achievements in our research on Sino-American relations and American history since 1949, our studies have been too narrow in scope and unsystematic. This is due both to the scanty information available and to the narrow focus we have taken, which aims at exposing U.S. imperialist aggression against China and criticizing the imperialist aspect of American foreign policy. I suggest that today issues exist that should be reexamined in their proper historical perspective. Furthermore, a wide range of problems that have not yet been considered should now be taken up. A critical study of the comprehensive historical development of Sino-American relations, especially the evolution of the controversial open door policy, is urgently needed. While in the past our perspective has been limited solely to the Chinese point of view, I propose that we now also observe China from the world's perspective. Aggression and suffering from aggression by foreign powers are a very important aspect of our foreign relations. Indeed, they may be a dominant theme in current history. But aside from the conflict between colonialist aggression and the Chinese people's opposition to aggression, other topics await investigation: for example, the conflict between the advanced capitalist mode of production and the backward feudal mode of production, the conflict between western civilization and tradition, and so forth. These conflicts were very often intertwined in a complicated manner, so oversimplification of them always draws one-sided conclusions. Only through a comprehensive understanding of Sino-American relations can correct judgments be made. I also talk about the problems of adopting a scientific approach to the open door policy.

Turning to U.S. history, I believe that every nation has its national strengths—if not, how could it survive? How could it progress? Hence it is possible for one country to learn from other countries, and for nations to cooperate with each other. We can learn from the strong points of our friends, and even our enemies, and use their experiences to benefit ourselves. With respect to the United States, we know that when the Ming dynasty fell, North America was still a wilderness only beginning to be colonized. When our country was at the heyday of its prosperity under the rule of the Qianlong emperor of the Qing dynasty, the thirteen states of North America had just won independence and consisted only of a narrow strip of land along the Atlantic coast. Yet in the short span of two hundred years this newborn republic quickly developed and accomplished in a few decades the same transformation it had taken Great Britain several hundred years to achieve. No other nation has grown as fast as the United States. Such a fact has universal historical significance worthy of in-depth research by Chinese historians. Studying this question clearly will greatly help our understanding of American history and the characteristics of the nation. Yet most of the theses concerning this question published in China have only been relatively general discussions. Marxists hold that practice develops continuously and that theory will definitely develop alongside it. Since the deaths of Marx and Lenin considerable changes have taken place in American economics, class structure, social life, foreign policy, ideology, and so on. Hence we need to explore these problems anew. The United States as a "model" of modern capitalism provides a clear clue through which we can more easily examine the development and prospects of modern capitalism. In the conclusion of my article I appeal for an upgrading of our knowledge of and research on the outside world to correspond with the new status of our country in international society.

The controversy is still going on. In *Shijie lishi* last October, two articles with basically opposing viewpoints were published. The focus of the controversy was a reassessment of the open door policy. One article points out that this policy was essentially one of aggression, arguing that if we did not discuss the nature and effects of such aggression and confine our discussion to its restraining or delaying role, then we would come to the wrong conclusion. Moreover, at the time the policy was put forth, the United States was still very weak and could not possibly have had the slightest restraining effect on the big powers who blindly followed a policy of "actual strength." The other article holds that, under given conditions, it is possible for an imperialist power to do something objectively beneficial to an oppressed nation. The author also offers some concrete suggestions aimed at facilitating a complete assessment of Sino-American relations. These arguments are good signs for free contention among different schools in social science. Such academic criticism should be promoted and not suppressed.

Aside from some new trends in studying the history of Sino-American relations, there has also been an increasing interest in studying American history and understanding U.S. reality in general. In recent years groups for the study of Sino-American relations and American history have been established in several universities (Wuhan, Nankai, Fudan, Nanjing, Jilin, Zhongshan, Beijing, and in the Institute of World History). In November 1979 the inaugural meeting of the American History Research Association of China (AHRAC) was held in Wuhan. This was possibly the first time that Chinese scholars of American history have met together. During the meeting participants exchanged opinions about how to improve teaching of and research on U.S. history and Sino-American relations. The questions raised for reexamination included the open door policy, the periodization of U.S. history, the causes of the high growth rate of the American economy, the assessment of the New Deal (focusing especially on whether or not Franklin D. Roosevelt was an isolationist), and current American historiography. Recently a book entitled *Meiguo shi lun wenji* (Selected essays on U.S. history) was published, containing twenty-seven essays presented at the meeting.

The first volume of *Hua gong chuguo ji* (Chinese laborers abroad) came out not long ago. This is the first publication of Chinese archival materials on the topic, and it was edited by Professor Chen Hansheng, a well-known Chinese economist and historian. It should prove a very interesting and useful source.

Under these new circumstances, a massive fervor to study Sino-American relations has emerged among students in China. To use American imagery, many students have jumped on the bandwagon, exploring the "West." Many students have also sat for the qualifying examinations to become graduate students in these fields. This has put great demands and pressures on teaching and research in China's universities and institutes, and will become a driving force to improve our work. American studies in China are at present in a new exploration stage. We are just now surveying the ground, deciding where to drill and what is the best way to go about it. Whether we strike oil or not will depend chiefly on our own efforts.

In brief, Chinese studies of Sino-American relations and American history have made much more progress in the past thirty years than before Liberation. Nevertheless, the abnormal state of Sino-American relations has impeded our overall progress. Second, the state of American studies in China lags far behind that of Chinese studies in the United States. In order to change such a state quickly, we must dare to break through the stereotypes and advocate a realistic scientific and comprehensive approach. In recent years quite a few American historians have started to revise their assessment of China, on the basis of new insights and against the backdrop of new developments. So, too, should we improve our study of the United States and its relations with China. American historian John K. Fairbank has stressed the importance of "seeking at all costs a realistic perspective." I sincerely applaud such an attitude. I believe that efforts like this will help increase mutual understanding and strengthen the economic and cultural ties between our two peoples.

Editor's note: Professor Jiang prepared a long, detailed review of work on Chinese-American relations in China since 1949. His paper was translated by Sheila O'Brien of Michigan State University. What follows is a summary with excerpts from O'Brien's translation.

Jiang explains that work done before 1976 focuses on the history of American aggression in China and is "critical of American imperialism and Chinese compradors." This work, however, lacks concrete analysis of the issues. After 1976, "large-scale study of Chinese-American relations and of the friendship between the two peoples began." Now there is close attention to specific questions about the early years of contact, the open door policy, missionary activity, and many other issues. "On the whole, the work is still weak and there is not yet published material reflecting two hundred years of relations."

In particular, Jiang decries the stress on political relations. He contends that the "history of American and Chinese economic, military, and cultural relations has not been studied adequately."

Most studies written before 1966 take American aggression against China as their starting point. "Regarding other aspects of Sino-American relations, such as the friendly contact between the people of the two countries, there is a serious lack of complete, systematic analysis. At the same time, research into other areas also suffers from a shortage of concrete analysis. For example, several essays investigate American businessmen in the early period and their attempts to establish normal transactions with China. These essays agree with the traditional notion that this was 'penetration by force.' Moreover, they agree that the United States was the major enemy of China from the beginning. Additionally, there is no distinction drawn between the period of an independent U.S. policy and American entrance into the imperialist period; there is no differentiation between the newly rising power of the United States and the traditional imperialism of England and France. No distinction is made between the subjective intentions and the objective results produced by the American promotion of the open door policy; between the political tendencies of each presidential administration and different secretaries of state or ambassadors; or between the Sino-American relationship during the period of resistance to Japan and during other periods.

"Since 1976, and especially since the two countries established formal diplomatic relations in 1979, research into the history of Sino-American relations has advanced to a new level. This is demonstrated mainly in two ways: research concerning the friendship between the two peoples has increased, and concrete analysis of questions has proceeded.

"In 1979 with the normalization of relations, scholars of Sino-American relations published several articles discussing the friendship between our peoples. Huang Shaoxiang, in his essay entitled in English 'The Friendship of the Chinese and American People' (*Shijie lishi*, 1 [1979]), points out that in the early period of contact, Americans respected the ancient Chinese civilization and were friendly towards the Chinese people. In 1925 when the Chinese people rose in the May 30th anti-imperialist movement, New York and twenty-five other large cities all held demonstrations and marches declaring their support for the anti-imperialist movement. Throughout China's resistance to Japan, the American people gave their support to the Chinese, thereby making a large contribution to the Chinese revolutionary victory. The article suggests that during the Chinese resistance to Japanese aggression, U.S. officials carrying on the American mission in China gave their sympathy and support to China.

"Li Yuanliang's article, translated as 'The Friendship Between the Chinese and American People' (*Lishi jiaoxue*, 2 [1979]), introduces the famous American writers Anna Louise Strong, Edgar Snow, Agnes Smedley, and American Marine Commander Evans Carlson, and praises them for their activities in China and for their contributions to the Chinese revolution and furtherance of friendship between Americans and Chinese.

"Chen Shenglin's article entitled in English 'Chinese Understanding of and Introduction to the United States at the Time of the

Opium War' was published in two parts in *Zhongshan daxue xuebao* (1 and 2 [1980]). The first article describes systematically the beginnings of Sino-American relations, the stages of development of Chinese understanding of and introduction to the United States. . . .

"The author considers Sino-American cultural exchanges to be especially important to the creation of modern records. He analyzes the Opium War period . . . [and] demonstrates that at the time Chinese patriots were first opening their eyes to the world, the United States had a deep influence through its own struggle to establish and develop a nation. The introduction of American history and experiences of independence and rapid development was eagerly received in China. Especially influential were the history of the American struggle for independence, the search for a rich and strong country, and the establishment of a democratic system. . . . [The history of the United States was studied] not only to widen the limits of the Chinese views, but also to . . . [find ideas] to save the country and the people. Chen considers these early students of American history to be pioneers, starting China on the path to democracy through their efforts. . . .

"Zhu Jieqin's article, translated as "Chinese Work in American Development in the Nineteenth Century" (*Lishi yanjiu*, 1 [1980]), is a penetrating and comprehensive analysis of the reasons for large-scale entry of Chinese in the nineteenth century into the United States. . . . He discusses Chinese workers' participation in developing the United States, and he examines the sharp class conflicts in relationship to movements to expel Chinese from America. . . ."

Like Luo Rongqu, Jiang is struck by the controversy provoked by Wang Xi's article, entitled "A Brief Discussion of Several Questions in the History on Sino-American Relations" (*Shijie lishi*, 1 [1976]), and some of the responses. Further controversy followed publication of articles by Xiang Liling, Wu Jiajing (in English, "A Discussion of the Open Door Policy," *Fudan xuebao*, 5 [1980]), and Xiang Rong (translated as "The Open Door—A Page in the History of American Policy in China"). "An enthusiastic discussion arose surrounding issues of early Sino-American relations, the open door policy, and the spread of the gospel. In addition, the China-U.S.

Historical Research Society recently met for its annual meeting at Yantai and discussed matters relating to the open door policy and [General Joseph] Stilwell.''

The early period of Sino-American relations, 1784 to 1844, has generally "been considered a time when American trade and capital took Chinese wealth and fleeced the Chinese people.'' Jiang notes Luo Rongqu's new interpretation in which he argues "that from 1784, when the U.S. trading vessel the *Empress of China* arrived in China, to 1844 with the Treaty of Wangxia, relations between China and the United States were basically equal and friendly. Although there were many American smugglers in private trade and pirates who robbed other private ships, most transactions in this early period were carried on in the normal manner of international trade. Therefore, American trade with China could not be called the result of piratical robbery. Luo contends that in early trade relations, American businessmen basically followed Chinese regulations and limitations much better than English businessmen. Relations between Chinese and American businessmen were also relatively good. At the same time, he feels that these transactions were beneficial to China. Before the Opium War the balance of trade favored China slightly. The United States was the market for Chinese tea leaves and cotton.

"Chen Shenglin's article, which is entitled in English 'Chinese Understanding of and Introduction to the United States at the Time of the Opium War,' divides early Sino-American relations before 1844 into two levels. For the first thirty years the relationship was one of living and working together equally. From 1821 on, American businessmen looked down upon Chinese authority, and more and more each day this good relationship was injured. Chen points out that because the United States followed the English and had a hand in the opium trade, it posed as an accomplice during the Opium War and forced the Qing dynasty to sign the Treaty of Wangxia. Before the Opium War, the United States and China had friendly relations, but afterwards more and more damage was done, until finally the relationship became one of invading and being invaded.''

Wang Xi's article, "Questions on the History of Sino-American Relations,'' revived the controversy over the open door policy. Wang sees the open door as "a policy aimed at attaining, safeguarding, and enlarging American economic and political benefits in China. In executing the open door policy the United States vacillated between opposing and compromising with the other major powers, compromising more often than not. But other facts should be recognized. When this policy was finally announced in 1899, China was very near partition. Later, during various national emergencies (in 1915, 1931, and 1937) and at other times, the United States repeated this policy of respect for China's independence (including the principle of territorial sovereignty at international conferences). . . . Objectively speaking, this policy had the effect of delaying or suppressing imperialist aggression in China.

"Ding Mingnan and Zhang Zhenkun in 'Research on the History of Sino-American Relations: A Step Forward or a Step Backward?' reject Wang Xi's view. They argue that Wang Xi's list of instances when the open door policy 'suppressed or delayed' imperialist aggression in China does not fit the historical facts. They consider the open door policy to be a manifestation of great power diplomacy, the goal being to protect and enlarge American control over China and exploit the Chinese people. This is seen as a completely imperialist policy.

"Luo Rongqu . . . [contends that] the open door policy must be considered together with characteristics of national political and economic circumstances. He notes the increasing involvement of the United States in international affairs at the time when the open door policy brought American China policy to a new level—from that of following English policies to that of carrying out independent imperialism. The author feels that the open door policy was completely in accord with American needs to promote their own interests and that Americans were unable simply to ignore the subtle effects of international politics in China. He considers that in proposing the open door policy, the United States complicated European and Japanese competition in China. . . ."

A discussion of this issue developed at the American History Research Association of China's first annual meeting in 1980, which was covered in an article in *Guangming ribao* on December 2, 1980. The paper reports:

The discussion proceeded to the point of considering the American implementation of the open door policy, differentiating between the subjective intentions of the administrations and the objective fruits produced. The aim of the policy was to put the United States in the crowded line of aggressive powers. But as this was at a time when China faced the disaster of being divided, the objective effect was to suppress the division of China.

"Wang Xi also considers missionary activities in China to be a major issue in Sino-American relations. . . . After the Opium War, foreign missionary activity in China was based on the unequal treaties. The missionaries' identity and privileges were the results of extraterritoriality and most-favored-nation status. The missionaries and the unequal treaties were closely intertwined. After the Chinese people resolved to solve their problems, the missionaries sent Bibles, so of course they were not welcomed by the Chinese people. The power of the American church in China had played a role in American policy toward China. But Wang contends that at the time the missionaries were spreading the gospel in China, they also brought schools and hospitals and scientific techniques. In the early period American missionaries translated and introduced Western books on scientific techniques. Their schools provided useful information and also influenced scientific and political development.

"Ding Mingnan and Zhang Zhenkun suggest that, generally speaking, foreign missionaries in China were carrying out their class responsibility according to the interests of the capitalist class. Chen Shenglin feels that the missionaries' introduction of American and world knowledge was a valuable contribution; that both the valuable contributions and the criticism of the missionaries should be listed together."

Other issues emerging among Chinese scholars include Wang Xi's emphasis on the fact that the United States was the only imperialist country that did not occupy Chinese territory. Ding Mingnan and Zhang Zhenkun stress the sad experiences of Chinese workers in the United States, arguing that these "cannot be considered a 'friendly chapter' in our peoples' history." Xiang Liling focuses on American aid to China when Chinese resistance to Japan began.

Jiang concludes: "Research into the history of Sino-American relations is a field in a state of change in China. The goal of letting 'a hundred flowers blossom and a hundred schools of thought contend' is to lead our scholars to begin to speak freely and, regarding the many issues in the history of Sino-American relations, to try very hard to push research forward. Research into the history of Sino-American relations has already entered a new phase.''

New Insights But No New Vistas: Recent Work on Nineteenth-Century American–East Asian Relations

by MICHAEL H. HUNT

IN RECENT YEARS there has been a substantial accumulation of new work on early American–East Asian relations, much of it dealing with interaction between China and the United States. Little of it, however, could be described as innovative or pathbreaking. On balance it would be fair to conclude that as an aggregate the new literature opens up no striking new vistas, leaving the basic contours of the field unchanged. In the United States, scholars have yet to face up to the task of fulfilling the field's original commitment to overcoming ethnocentrism and a narrow preoccupation with diplomacy. Meanwhile, scholars in the People's Republic of China (PRC), whom we welcome to what should be, after all, an international research enterprise, seem to share that same preoccupation with American policy—to the neglect of cultural interaction and the Chinese perspective. Their contributions to date have done little to raise fresh questions or open up new, fruitful areas of inquiry.

These generalizations carry us toward two sobering conclusions: First, the critical judgments made in the relevant essays in May and Thomson's 1972 state-of-the-field survey still stand.[1] Economic and cultural aspects of the American–East Asian relationship still deserve more attention; and the ideal of a more cosmopolitan and balanced view (requiring more work on the Asian side) has yet to be realized. Second, if current research trends in the United States and China persist, we face the discouraging prospect of a substantial—perhaps

For the purposes of this essay East Asia is taken to mean China and Japan. Early Korean-American relations are treated below by Bruce Cumings.

even the major—research effort being devoted to mining a variety of narrow and already well-worked historical veins, with diminishing yield to show for the effort invested.

This state of affairs mirrors the often noted problems of U.S. "diplomatic history," of which American–East Asian relations is in substantial measure a subfield.[2] Much of the intellectual inertia evident in both areas might be traced back to the grip on many diplomatic historians of two broad and increasingly questionable assumptions about international relations. The first of these is that states are the predominant international actors and that, consequently, priority should be accorded to the study of foreign policy elites in relation to strategic questions and the exercise of national power. This "statist" conception of the international order helps explain the persistent interest in nineteenth-century U.S. East Asian policy and the relative neglect of nondiplomatic themes and activities. It also helps explain the recurrent and now stale debate over exactly when East Asia began to bulk large in American foreign policy and whether at any time in the nineteenth century the United States figures prominently in the calculations of the Chinese and Japanese governments. John K. Fairbank in particular has questioned—with great frequency and force— the importance to Asia of U.S. policy.[3] And yet policy studies continue to appear for the nineteenth century that accord the United States an important place in the Asian scheme of things.

A move away from diplomatic studies would appease the skeptics; it might also surprise all concerned by helping us put diplomatic developments in a larger context. We need to know more about intellectual currents among the elite and popular views in the regions intimately involved in trans-Pacific contacts. For example, the United States emerged early on as one of several models for Asians interested in Western development, while China and Japan figured no less prominently as cultural types for Americans grappling with grand conceptions of social evolution and classification. Trade expanded mental maps in New England and the mid-Atlantic states in the late eighteenth and early nineteenth centuries, while emigration changed the outlook of peoples in the American West, the Canton delta, and Hiroshima prefecture through the latter part of the nineteenth century and into the twentieth. Studies along these lines, important in their own right, should enable us in turn to set the thinking of policymakers—Chinese and Japanese as well as Americans—in better perspective.

The second impediment to fresh thinking is our tendency to assume that cultural contact and change can be understood in terms of the vocabulary of modernization. An outpouring of literature over the last decade and a half reveals widespread doubts about modernization as a concept. Modernization theory may reveal, its critics tell us, more about the policy needs and social conditions of a cold war United States than about the putative object of study, the "modernizing" third world. From an analytic point of view the theory oversimplifies, particularly by insisting on a questionable distinction between "tradition" and "modernity" (a blander version of the nineteenth-century dichotomy between "barbarism" and "civilization"). Conceptually, modernization rests on a faith that all social change is progressive, organic, linear. The main danger from the hold that modernization still exercises on the imagination of historians is that they will unconsciously place themselves in the same intellectual frame of reference as the nineteenth-century Americans they study. To the degree this happens, historians lose an important perspective on those Americans and on contemporary Asian conditions. Many of the critics of modernization have espoused a "world systems" approach as a conceptual substitute for "modernization." The attraction of the former may lie in its avoidance of any stark theoretical claims. It nonetheless involves a set of fundamental assumptions about the nature of change that some historians may feel comfortable with and others not.[4] The point is not to shift from one interpretive rut into another but rather to approach early American–East Asian relations with a more self-conscious attitude toward our intellectual baggage and a receptiveness to alternative approaches that may open new vistas.

It should come as no surprise that conventional studies of China policy and above all studies of various aspects of the open door policy still dominate the literature on the nineteenth century. In the United States, the open door policy has continued to serve as the most important point of contact between those in the mainstream of U.S. diplomatic history and those closely identified with American–East Asian relations. This interest in the open door policy has been sustained by the controversy ignited in the 1960s by "new left" historians, who used the term open door to describe a far-reaching American policy of market penetration and control ("open door imperialism"). China served for them as an early and prominent case sustaining their view of the primacy of economic considerations in U.S. foreign policy. Over the last decade a few new works have developed this economic theme in relation to China. Ernest Paolino turned his hand to a full-scale portrait of William Seward as a master strategist of informal empire, a view anticipated by Walter LaFeber's cameo of that secretary of state in his *The New Empire*. A sketch of Charles Denby by David Healy underlined the market preoccupations of that influential envoy. Kenneth Hagan laid out the evidence for viewing the navy as an instrument of commercial expansion—in China as elsewhere abroad. And James J. Lorence dealt with the American Asiatic Association, the economic interest group most actively behind the formal open door policy.[5]

In general, however, explaining nineteenth-century China policy in terms of the pursuit of the China market seems to have lost its appeal—perhaps prematurely. It is not the latter part of the century (toward which much of the new left looks) but rather the earlier decades that best support an emphasis on the economic component in U.S. policy. Though China before the 1870s was, to be sure, less prominently a part of Washington's concerns than it was to become by the 1890s, nonetheless those concerns were dominated by considerations of trade, whereas after 1870 and well into the 1890s the often conflicting considerations associated with the exclusion controversy and the problems of missionary protection intruded at the expense of market calculations. Some of the new works that support this point include Samuel Kim's and David Anderson's conventional and admiring sketches of Anson Burlingame; the more rounded picture of Burlingame and S. Wells Williams by Martin Ring; the published papers of minister J. Ross Browne edited by Lina Ferguson Browne; and James Merrill's and E. Mowbray Tate's studies of the American naval presence off the China coast.[6]

Some new works have taken issue with the new left interpretation of the open door. Gerald Eggert attempts to measure the importance of economic concerns in the mind of one forceful policymaker at a crucial juncture and concludes that in Secretary of State Richard Olney there is little to support the new left case. Gary Best reaches the same conclusion with regard to James H. Wilson, an active concession hunter. My own ''Americans in the China Market'' casts doubt on the claim of a strong link between major exporters and the government, indeed argues on the basis of several test cases that divergent strategies and goals constituted a formidable barrier to practical cooperation from the 1890s onward. George Paulsen's study of Washington's attitude toward investment in China's textile mills highlights official fear of exporting American jobs rather than a desire to promote American trade.[7]

Other recent studies touching on policy in the 1890s simply ignore the market question in U.S. policy. This is true of the reappraisals of John Hay, William W. Rockhill, and William McKinley. Indeed, Kenton Clymer's full-scale biography of McKinley's secretary of state is less concerned with China policy (treated but briefly) than with the social and political milieu out of which this ''gentleman'' diplomat emerged. Peter Stanley's sketch of Rockhill, like Clymer's work, puts aside the subject of the open door policy in favor of an examination of personality and the problems a pioneering China expert faced in government service. William R. Braisted's study of the president once derided as ''a chocolate eclair'' follows the trend established earlier by Margaret Leach and Walter LaFeber to upgrade McKinley's importance as a policymaker. Braisted praises as prudent and able McKinley's handling of the Boxer crisis.[8]

This tendency to skirt the market question is also evident in a number of topical treatments of China policy in the 1890s. Jeffrey Dorwart offered a full-scale account of the U.S. part in the Sino-Japanese War, though little new comes out of his treatment aside from his debatable proposition that the conflict marked for U.S. policy a watershed between the old era of nonentanglement and a new era of intervention in Asian affairs. George Paulsen's study of a spy case into which American diplomats in China blundered during the war shows (contrary to Dorwart) President Grover Cleveland and

Secretary of State Walter Q. Gresham becoming ever more cautious in the face of partisan Republican attacks on their "pro-China" policy. Mission policy remains inadequately surveyed, a serious oversight because incidents in China in the late 1880s and the 1890s confronted Washington with complex problems that the organized missionary movement would not allow policymakers to sidestep. The culmination of an interventionist missionary policy came in 1900 with American participation in the Allied expedition, a subject treated in my own account of the U.S. army's occupation of Peking. Robert McClellan Jr.'s survey of attitudes toward China through the 1890s and just beyond confirms the findings of Harold Isaacs' classic study.[9]

In general, this recent writing on U.S. China policy is witness to the dwindling appeal of the new left approach. That development is in part the result, no doubt, of a changing political climate in the United States. But it is also the result of the new left's insistence on too confining a model of a market-oriented policy and its excessive preoccupation with political influentials to the neglect of the actual workings of the economy to which those influentials supposedly responded. New left work has also invited attack and created confusion through loose use of the term "imperialism." Should imperialism be understood as the product of objective economic forces or of merely the perceptions on the part of the elite of an impending economic crisis? Should imperialism be understood as constituting simply a desire for or even an attempt at dominance over other peoples? Or should it be understood as the actual exercise of dominance? Without a clear and meaningful definition that could be tested against the evidence, new left historians could claim to see signs of imperialism everywhere, while skeptics could get away with denying they saw it anywhere. Imperialism thus became in this semantic tangle little more than an epithet to be hurled by those who are convinced the United States has pursued a deplorably aggressive policy or to be repelled by those who cannot bear to see the United States labelled an empire (whatever that might mean in concrete terms).[10]

An economic interpretation of U.S. policy—of diminished appeal among American historians—continues to prevail in works prepared in the PRC. Even so, a lively controversy has recently developed there over the nature of American China policy, a topic not subjected to reexamination since the flood of works in the Korean War era condemning American aggression. The stage for this historical reexamination was set by the authoritative *People's Daily* in January 1979. The same day it announced the formal restoration of diplomatic relations with the United States, it also printed an anonymous piece rehabilitating the idea of an historic Sino-American friendship. For those who had missed the point the first time, two weeks later it published another essay, this time by a Beijing University historian, Luo Rongqu, once again developing the theme of friendship.[11]

Emboldened by this invitation to reevaluate earlier Sino-American relations, historians rushed into print in the scholarly journals, and they soon found themselves in a warm debate over the significance of the open door policy. Wang Xi, an historian at Fudan University in Shanghai, set the controversy off by contending, contrary to the conventional wisdom, that the open door policy was not entirely pernicious in its effects on China. Rather, he claimed, it had on several notable occasions significantly benefitted China when the United States had moved to check or slow the advance of other, more dangerous imperialist powers. His position was subsequently endorsed not only by Wu Jiajing, also at Fudan, and Xiang (Shong) Liling at Shanghai Teacher's College, but also by Luo himself (albeit in qualified terms).[12] The reaction against this favorable reinterpretation of American policy became apparent almost at once. The most weighty of the responses from historians still wedded to the older view came from Ding Mingnan and Zhang Zhenkun, both with the Institute of Modern History in the Academy of Social Sciences in Beijing. (Ding himself had previously been closely associated with the noted historian Liu Danian in writing on Chinese foreign relations.) A paper coauthored by Ding and Zhang challenged Wang Xi's interpretation of the open door policy—most tellingly on the grounds that his version of China's foreign policy crises of 1899–1900, 1915, 1931, and 1937 was flawed. Ding and Zhang contended that the United States was in fact ineffectual on these occasions. Yet another rejoinder, by Xiang Rong, gave credit for turning back the imperialist danger to the resistance of the Chinese people. For Chinese in a period of international danger to rely on American assistance rather than on their own strength would, Xiang pointedly warned in his conclusion, be to draw the wrong lessons from the past and ignore the real nature of U.S. policy.[13]

Whether this controversy will stimulate investigations along fruitful new lines of inquiry depends fundamentally on Chinese historians breaking their dependence on the now badly dated English-language literature (including prominently the works of Tyler Dennett and A. Whitney Griswold) on which much of their work three decades ago was also based. The subsequent appearance in the United States of new left works with an interpretive theme compatible with basic historiographic assumptions in China has not gone unnoticed by some of the more discerning, so that at least now William Appleman Williams' *Tragedy of American Diplomacy* finds an occasional place in the notes. But the chief impression left by scanning the sources cited in recent Chinese work is of scholars working in libraries whose historical collections have not even begun to keep up with the explosion in American publications in the last few decades. Some Chinese scholars seem keenly aware of these deficiencies and eager to overcome them and to push on into the political, social, and economic context in which U.S. China policy took shape, while Luo Rongqu has gone a step farther in calling for the promotion of American studies in China.

A second deficiency, which has gone unnoticed by scholars in the PRC, threatens to impede the development of this new opening in the study of Sino-American relations. Much like the works of the late 1940s and early 1950s, the most recent work places almost exclusive emphasis on American policy with only brief references to the "bankrupt" policies of the "feudal" Qing dynasty. Chinese historians thus face the same challenge as their American counterparts—to see contacts with the United States as a dynamic process of interaction in which Chinese attitudes, initiatives, and responses play a crucial part.[14] Precisely because of this curiously American-centric quality of recent writings, Chinese scholars seem unaware of the extent to which their own reflections on the nature of the United States and the open door policy bear a striking family resemblance to those of early nineteenth-century Chinese policymakers and intellectuals who first began to wrestle with the problem of using the United States to enhance Chinese security.

That these related problems of understanding and dealing with the United States go back a century and more has long been evident from the *Chouban yiwu shimo* collection (made partially available in translation by Earl Swisher for the era of the opium wars). It has more recently been underlined for that same era by Fred W. Drake's account of Xu Jiyu (Hsu Chi-yü) and Jane Kate Leonard's study of Wei Yuan. Both Chinese, it becomes evident from these accounts, pursued their interest in the United States in the 1830s and 1840s with diligence and seriousness and with results that compare favorably with contemporary American studies on China. The persistence of an interest in the United States through the balance of the nineteenth century and into the twentieth becomes clear from Noriko Kamachi's picture of Huang Zunhsian (Huang Tsun-hsien); the Li Hongzhang (Li Hung-chang) material long available—and neglected—in translation in a study by Charles Leavenworth; Lee Enhan's recounting of Zhang Chidong's (Chang Chih-tung) and Sheng Xuanhuai's (Sheng Hsuan-huai) handling of the Hankow-Canton railway concession; my own study of Manchurian policy; and Linda Shin's biography of Wu Tingfang (Wu T'ing-fang).[15] A clearer sense of Chinese perceptions of the United States and their implications for policy during the nineteenth and twentieth centuries is essential if we are to confirm the view that the United States was of scant significance to Chinese policymakers, test the American assumption that Chinese have historically regarded the United States with gratitude and hope, or evaluate the current Chinese claim that Qing policy toward the United States was passive and in general, in such areas as "self-strengthening" and manipulation of the balance of power, bears no fundamental resemblance to contemporary Chinese policy dilemmas.

The effort to break away from an essentially diplomatic conception of U.S.–East Asian relations, endorsed by the essayists in the May and Thomson volume, has made some progress in the last decade, especially in the Chinese mission studies promoted by John Fairbank at Harvard. His most notable recent contribution was to arrange a conference on the topic in 1972 and publish some of the resulting papers in *The Missionary Enterprise in China and America.* That volume reveals the diversity of perspectives and approaches involved in the study of the mission field, ranging from Stuart Miller's indictment of missionary coercion to Philip West's exploration of the Chinese perspective. It also reveals, nowhere clearer than in Fairbank's own introduction, the Harvard school's emphasis on Western contributions to China's modernization. Fairbank turns away charges against missionaries as cultural imperialists and instead makes of them "spiritual reformers" who undermined the traditional order and contributed to "the regeneration of China in the decades after 1900."[16]

Other recent Harvard-originated works include Ellsworth Carlson's account of early Fuzhou (Foochow) missions. That work is notable for its evocation of the spirit of grace, pugnacity, and frustration that generally characterized mission life in China. Irwin T. Hyatt Jr.'s sketches of three Shandong missionaries of a later period provides a sensitive treatment of this same spirit. Edward Gulick's *Peter Parker and the Opening of China* deals with a fascinating figure who encompassed the major causes into which the mission movement was to channel its energy—diplomacy and good works as well as evangelism. Still other Harvard-connected studies have dealt with the cultural isolation of mission stations from the surrounding Chinese world (Sidney Forsythe), the rise of a logistical support organization in the United States (Valentin Rabe), the missionary struggle against opium (Hilary Beattie), and the development of the YMCA (Shirley Garrett).[17]

The role of missionaries as conveyors of Western ideas, one of the favorite themes of the Harvard school, has been developed in diverse contexts by Suzanne Wilson Barnett, Elizabeth Malcolm, Wang Shuhuai, Adrian Bennett, and Kwang-Ching Liu. Their work offers a useful reminder of the Anglo-American nature of much of the early mission effort in China, a point further underlined in Peter Fay's look at Protestants in Canton before the Opium War.[18]

Perhaps the most striking account on missions yet to appear is Jessie Lutz's *China and the Christian Colleges, 1850–1950.*[19] More work of the sort Lutz has produced—broadly drawn and to some extent synthetic—is needed to highlight the evolution of mission work and to permit carefully drawn comparisons with mission activity elsewhere overseas as well as in the United States itself.[20] We are far from having a clear sense of the global ramifications of U.S. mission interests, or of the nature of Anglo-American or, still more broadly, Christian proselytizing in China. The role of women in missionary activity (a subject addressed at least for the early twentieth century by Jane Hunter), the make-up of the Chinese church, and the character and influence of anti-Christian attitudes and activity (about which Lu Shiqiang continues to write) are other topics deserving of further study.[21] Ronald Robinson's stimulating observations on the crucial role of "native" collaborators in "imperial" situations are clearly applicable to more purely cultural forms of interaction, and they might with profit be applied in research on the missionaries' Chinese "helpers," who were indispensable in extending and sustaining work in the countryside.[22]

Work on other nondiplomatic aspects of the American presence in China has yielded some interesting if scattered insights. Our knowledge of the early China trade has been enhanced by Jacques Downs' research into the opium trade (his second article on the subject), James Kirker's study of the search for profitable exports to China, and Yuan Chung Teng's examination of the commercial difficulties occasioned by the Taiping rebellion.[23] Thomas Cox notes China's importance as a market for U.S. raw materials before the transcontinental railways finally made the American East Coast more accessible to West Coast producers than Shanghai and Tientsin had been. The entry of pioneering multinational firms into the China market can be followed in Robert Davies' study of Singer Sewing Machine, Sherman Cochran's work on the British-American Tobacco Company, and my own reconstruction of Standard Oil's operations. Davies' study of Singer illustrates the difficulties multinationals faced in doing business in China. But what was true for most was certainly not true for all, as the successful marketing activities of British-American Tobacco and Standard Oil make clear. G. Kurgan-van Hentenryk's investigation into Belgian finance and high policy has incidentally shed valuable light on American financial operations. His treatment of the Hankow-Canton railway concession, the most important grant secured by American developers in the late nineteenth-century scramble, shows the giants of Wall Street playing for short-term gains, unsympathetic to Washington's desire for a long-term investment strategy. The Chinese dimension of these various economic contacts is still shadowy, although Hao Yen-p'ing for an early period and Cochran for a later period have cast some welcome light.[24]

Perhaps what economic studies most need now is a clearer sense of the way in which Sino-American relations fit into a global system of trade and investment. By the early nineteenth century European technology and capital had begun to act as a great drive wheel for global change that overrode political and natural boundaries. The resulting processes of industrialization and of the commercialization of agriculture intensified through the rest of the century with important consequences for China and the United States. The United States was initially a recipient of new technology and capital from Europe, but then by the 1890s had emerged as one of the centers from which further change was transmitted. Standard Oil's ability to draw petroleum from the ground, refine it, and ship the kerosene by-product to China and Japan is one example of this transformation. The persistent though ultimately stillborn American infatuation with railway building in China and the revolution in the technology of commercial shipping are others.

Economic studies also need business records in order for us to take a new and perhaps more conclusive look at the relationship between public policy and private economic interests—and to learn more about the indigenous conditions in foreign markets that exporters and investors had to take into account and which their operations might over time affect to some degree. The emerging picture from existing studies based on business sources is one of a tangled relationship between economic interests and government policy and a pattern of accommodation to foreign conditions, at least on the part of successful market-oriented multinationals. To clarify that picture for the nineteenth century we particularly need to know more about the large merchant houses, such as Russell and Company, which occupied a dominant place in the China trade up to the time of the rise of multinationals at the turn of the century. Their relationship with constituent firms at home, operations within China, and international network of trade and credit are but dimly understood. The same problem bedevils economic relations between the United States and Japan. Trade with Japan in tea, silk, and kerosene, American investment interests there, and technology transfer remain as much a blank today as in 1972 when Robert Schwantes commented on these topics.[25]

The subject of Chinese immigration to the United States stands out as a promising area of research that has already attracted some innovative work. It is an excellent example of what is to be gained by shifting the primary focus of inquiry away from official relations. In this case, not immigration policy but the immigrants themselves—their origins and experiences, their allies and antagonists within the United States—belong at the center of inquiry. Research here should be firmly set in a broad context. The same process of global transformation that reshaped Sino-American economic relations also left a profound impact on many lives, immigrants not least of these. Philip Taylor has demonstrated how the concentration of land holdings, the ease of long-distance travel, and the reliability of rapid communications set off an intra-European migration that finally spilled overseas.[26] In short order, these same conditions affected even peoples as distant as the Chinese, as infusions of capital in Southeast Asia and the Americas created a demand for labor that attracted millions from Guangdong and Fujian from the mid-nineteenth to the early twentieth century. Among them were half a million or so Chinese who came to the United States between 1850 and 1900.

American–East Asian specialists have good reason to give this latter group of overseas Chinese a good deal of attention. The Chinese who came to the United States far outnumbered those Americans who went to China. While the latter only numbered several thousand by the late nineteenth century, at least a hundred thousand Chinese were residing in the United States. Their historical role is rich and multifaceted. They served as perhaps the most important source of American views on China and the Chinese. They contributed to American economic development and to the livelihood of relatives at home. They were the objects of social and political protest within the United States and the cause of diplomatic skirmishing that overshadowed all other issues in relations between the United States and China from the 1870s well into the 1890s. The immigrant experience clearly belongs in the mainstream of the U.S.–East Asian field. Unfortunately, specialists in the field, despite their ostensible commitment to crossing disciplinary lines, have generally hung back from involvement in this multidisciplinary research enterprise.[27]

One barrier to new work is mastery of the extensive literature in U.S. social and political history and the history of the American West, essential to exploring the sources and structure of sinophobia and its impact on policy and public life. Stuart Miller in his provocative *The Unwelcome Immigrant* penetrated that barrier and provided a useful point of departure for further study. Miller boldly argued that sinophobia was, contrary to the prevailing historical wisdom, a national and not a regional phenomenon and that sinophobia in the United States stemmed from the negative images of China that early American travelers and residents there (whom he labeled "inside dopesters") propagated at home.[28]

Jonathan Goldstein has tested Miller's generalizations on the origins of sinophobia by looking at Philadelphia's China trade contacts. He has come away with findings at odds with Miller's. So too does Gary Pennanen in his study of Ohio politics. Moses Rischin has indirectly responded to Miller by stressing California's special experience as a state awash in "a sea of strangers, sojourners, newcomers, and footloose wanderers." Support for Miller's national sinophobia thesis, on the other hand, comes out of Jack Hammersmith's examination of attitudes in West Virginia.[29] Other works that sidestep the Miller controversy yet shed important light on the popular American reaction to the Chinese include Alexander Saxton's study of labor and Ralph Mann's and Edward Lydon's closely focused studies of anti-Chinese agitation in California.[30] Drawing comparisons and, possibly, lines of reciprocal influence between White attitudes toward Chinese on the one hand and White attitudes toward Indians, Latins, and Blacks on the other might prove a fruitful foray into the nineteenth-century American psyche, as Luther Spoehr has already indicated. More work of this sort deserves to be tried.[31]

The other major barrier to new work on Chinese immigration is the exacting requirement of language and area studies skills necessary to penetrate the Chinese community in the United States and to delineate the Canton delta conditions that substantially accounted for the rise of that community. Those interested in research on the Canton delta should first consult Robert G. Lee's helpful guide to the sources and key problems. June Mei's "Socioeconomic Origins of Emigration" is notable as a provocative and ambitious survey. It attempts to fit "push" factors into the procrustean bed of "imperialist disruption of Chinese society" and in the process reveals the limits of the "imperialist" interpretation and the need for research guided by a more flexible set of questions.[32] The lives of Chinese in the United States have attracted some sociologists, but the resulting work has neglected Chinese language sources and the problems of historical change.[33] A number of notable works by Asian Americanists have begun to supply a more historical perspective; unfortunately, at present these works collectively offer little more than tantalizing glimpses of a world too often described by scholars only from the perspective of contemporary Whites.[34]

Any broadly conceived new research here clearly faces a formidable set of obstacles. To describe the Canton delta setting will require a command of local history. To trace the arrangements for travel to the United States and, once there, for employment and social security will involve social and economic history techniques of a high order. To trace changing patterns of immigration from the 1850s onward—patterns affected by altered conditions in the delta, by economic opportunities in the United States (as well as in competing labor markets abroad), and by attitudes toward Chinese in the United States—will require patient yet imaginative historical reconstruction. Strategies of survival employed by the Chinese community in the face of mounting White hostility have yet to be systematically examined. The international controversy that this immigrant community gave rise to deserves attention from the perspective of the Chinese government and its agents in the United States no less than from the better studied official American perspective.[35] In pushing research forward on these several fronts it will undoubtedly be useful to have a sense of the Chinese experience elsewhere abroad, both as a basis for comparison with the experience in the United States and as a guide to the difficult-to-document aspects of community organization in the United

States. Fortunately, there is a large literature on overseas Chinese and several first-rate works on the Chinese in Southeast Asia to serve this function.[36]

The Perry expedition and the ensuing diplomatic relations between the United States and Japan down to the turn of the century have long since ceased to entrance historians. With no generally controversial open door policy to sustain interest, quarrying of U.S. government archives for this period has come to a virtual halt.[37] Scholars interested in politics and diplomacy have long since moved on to tracing the road to Pearl Harbor and, more recently, to exploring the complexities of the postwar Occupation. Some nondiplomatic work has appeared, though in neither the quantity nor the quality to suggest that research on nineteenth-century Japanese-American relations is moving ahead with vigor or producing fertile new insights.

Perhaps the greatest vitality is to be found in the work of those attempting to reconstruct early Japanese images of the United States. Here there is heartening evidence of primary sources being exploited with good results.[38] By contrast, there is little new to report in regard to work on American perceptions of Japan in this period. This is all the more regrettable because the time is fast approaching when an accumulating body of literature should enable students of American–East Asian relations not only to delineate with precision and sweep the mutual images that sprang from cross-cultural contact but also to make comparisons among them. When we reach that stage, we may find American views of Japan the most obscure and difficult to integrate. Neil Harris' examination of the impressions left by Japanese participation at American fairs, revealing as far as it goes, illustrates the need for a broader approach.[39] American views of Japan should be juxtaposed against those the Japanese entertained toward the United States (drawn where possible from Japanese-language sources). Moreover, American attitudes toward one set of "Orientals" might be weighted against attitudes toward other "Orientals" under similar conditions. (For example, the Philadelphia fair of 1876, at which the Japanese made their debut in the United States, could profitably be treated alongside the China museums that were the rage in that same city some three decades earlier.) Finally, image studies should attempt to link early American perceptions of the Japanese to such larger issues as Miller's national racism thesis and the sources of the later hostility to Japanese immigrants.

Japanese immigration, a subject which in its broader outlines properly belongs to the twentieth century, nonetheless deserves at least brief mention as an aspect of that cultural interpenetration that occurred between Japan and the United States in the nineteenth century. Scholars have already begun to use Japanese sources to explore the immigrant experience from the inside. Particularly notable is Wakatsuki Yasuo's revealing treatment of such topics as reasons for emigration, perceptions of the United States held by emigrants, perceptions of emigrants held by other Japanese, the flow of remittances, and the social status of emigrants. Ito Kazuo's compilation of reminiscences by the first generation of Japanese in the United States, first published in Japanese in 1969, has since appeared in English. Despite the filiopietistic tone of the editorial material, these recollections bring the *issei* experience to life as no history has yet managed.[40]

An effort to understand American–East Asian relations in terms of sweeping cultural and economic abstractions should not obscure the role of individuals. Some of the literature on the nineteenth century that has appeared over the last decade has served to keep the human dimension in view and inspires the hope that biography, perhaps leavened with imaginative use of psychohistorical techniques, may yet throw valuable light on those emotional needs and costs that must have figured prominently for many who undertook a trans-Pacific journey. A diverse group of mercenaries, political advisors, and cross-cultural adventurers and intermediaries has understandably attracted the most attention. But the unconventional lives—romantic and sometimes bizarre—that they led along the coastal fringes of East Asia have to date received but conventional treatment, with little reference to the fantasies that actuated them. Those Americans who took up arms against the Taiping rebels have come under reappraisal with Richard J. Smith's account of the Ever-Victorious Army, a work which has the virtue of setting the activities of such mercenaries as

Frederick Townsend Ward and Henry Burgevine firmly in the Chinese context.[41] The career of Charles LeGendre as U.S. consul in Fuzhou, coolie trade entrepreneur, and Japanese agent in Taiwan and Korea demonstrates a fascinating versatility and a self-confident opportunism that have already generated a small academic industry.[42] Americans serving in Japan have also come under scrutiny in works more concerned with documenting contributions to "modernization" than with explaining what made these devotees of foreign service tick.[43] The story of East Asians such as Rong Hong (Yung Wing), who travelled the other way across the Pacific as the first step in a lonely voyage of cultural exploration, also belongs here.[44]

John Fairbank defined the tasks for the American–East Asian field in 1968 against the backdrop of an increasingly controversial Vietnam conflict. "We need another dimension to our self-knowledge, for we in America need watching and self-control even more than our adversaries, if only because we have greater capacities."[45] To the extent that scholars in this field have supplied this self-knowledge, it seems to have come in the form of the rediscovery of original sin. Where once accounts of American approaches to East Asia emphasized benevolence, they have become in the last decade or so more self-critical, stressing racism, paternalism, violence, and unsavory self-interest. The Vietnam trauma thus has clearly left its mark in the form of a more introspective attitude on the part of American historians.

This critical introspection is undoubtedly a welcome development but one that by itself falls far short of helping us elucidate our recent foreign policy problems. It needs to be joined to a heightened sensitivity to other cultures and to the limits of a statist, power-oriented conception of international relations. Vietnam was a blank slate that the American government determined to write on out of a sense of might and cultural superiority as well as moral rectitude. We now realize our arrogance and inhumanity, but so little have we yet come to grips with the culture and tradition of Vietnam that we still carry only the foggiest notions of the internal forces once arrayed against us. The multiple perspectives that our Vietnam experience demands are the same that our other, more current international problems require.

No less are they the ones we need to apply to our understanding of our more distant past. Yet American–East Asianists working on the nineteenth century seem disturbingly oblivious to the need to reconsider our approach to the study of international relations. Their work remains to a substantial degree mired in what Marilyn Young called in 1972 the "slough of parochialism," preoccupied with an American perspective and above all the perspective of the White males of good birth and breeding who were engaged in the policy process.[46] For American–East Asianists, as for diplomatic historians generally, the challenge for the next decade primarily involves finding broader international and comparative frameworks into which they can place their studies.

American scholars still wearing their Vietnam hair shirts are suddenly, for the first time in three decades, face to face with Chinese colleagues just emerging from their own cultural revolution trauma. The fall of the "gang of four," the start of a modernization program that calls for "seeking truth from facts," and finally a transformed relationship with the United States have combined to create a favorable environment for historical reappraisal unprecedented since liberation. There is now at least the prospect of a more variegated picture of American policy in both its conception and its consequences for China, but whether that prospect will be realized is a question as dependent on political developments and provisions for research support within the PRC as on the instincts of individual Chinese scholars.

A juxtaposition of these trends in the United States and China suggests an ironic divergence at one level. While Chinese studies move perceptibly toward a more positive estimate of U.S. policy, American studies have gone in the other direction. At another level, however, scholars of both countries face a common set of tasks. They need a better understanding of the Chinese side of the relationship, essential to recreating the dynamic of nineteenth-century relations, and they need to integrate into the better known diplomatic story the tangled skein of economic and cultural interaction that arguably constituted the bedrock of the relationship. Scholars on both sides can help each other in dealing with these tasks. Our respective national experiences and professional outlooks differ too much to expect anything as simple as a division of labor to work—with Chinese concentrating on the Chinese story, Americans on the American story, and some invisible historical hand stitching the two halves together. Each side will surely have to grope toward its own conception of the issues and the appropriate framework within which to set them. We have nonetheless much to teach and to learn from each other about the historical literature, promising source materials, and our differing national experiences and styles. The nineteenth century is a rich place to start.

NOTES

1. These deficiencies are noted in the five essays dealing with nineteenth-century American–East Asian relations by Edward Graham, John K. Fairbank, Kwang-Ching Liu, Robert Schwantes, and Marilyn Young in Ernest R. May and James C. Thomson, Jr., eds., *American–East Asian Relations: A Survey* (Cambridge: Harvard University Press, 1972).

2. The most recent general critique is Charles S. Maier, "Marking Time: The Historiography of International Relations," in Michael Kammen, ed., *The Past Before Us: Contemporary Historical Writing in the United States* (Ithaca, N.Y.: Cornell University Press, 1980).

3. Fairbank, both in his 1972 essay and in an earlier set of reflections (" 'American China Policy' to 1898: A Misconception," *Pacific Historical Review,* 39 [Nov. 1970]), singles out for criticism the tendency of some accounts of early Sino-American relations to neglect the British role. Fairbank's essential argument is that Britain as the dominant power on the China coast defined the context within which Americans functioned at least until the end of the nineteenth century. The United States had no distinct China policy because, he contends, it had no need of one as long as Britain minded the shop.

4. I have profited from reading Robert A. Nisbet, *Social Change and History: Aspects of the Western Theory of Development* (New York: Oxford University Press, 1969); Robert A. Packenham, *Liberal America and the Third World: Political Development Ideas in Foreign Aid and Social Science* (Princeton: Princeton University Press, 1973); Dean C. Tipps, "Modernization Theory and the Comparative Study of Societies: A Critical Perspective," *Comparative Studies in Society and History,* 15 (1973), esp. 204, 206–16; Aidan Foster-Carter, "From Rostow to Gunder Frank: Conflicting Paradigms in the Analysis of Underdevelopment," *World Development,* 4 (March 1976), esp. 172, 174–75; J. Samuel Valenzuela and Arturo Valenzuela, "Modernization and Dependency: Alternative Perspectives in the Study of Latin American Underdevelopment," *Comparative Politics,* 10 (July 1978); Tony Smith, "The Underdevelopment of Development Literature: The Case of Dependency Theory," *World Politics,* 31 (Jan. 1979).

5. Paolino, *The Foundations of the American Empire: William Henry Seward and U.S. Foreign Policy* (Ithaca, N.Y.: Cornell University Press, 1973); LaFeber, *The New Empire* (Ith-

aca, N.Y.: Cornell University Press, 1963); Healy, *US Expansionism: The Imperialist Urge in the 1890s* (Madison: University of Wisconsin Press, 1970); Hagan, *American Gunboat Diplomacy and the Old Navy, 1877–1889* (Westport, Conn.: Greenwood Press, 1973); Lorence, "Coordinating Business Interests and the Open Door Policy: The American Asiatic Association, 1898–1904," in Jerry Israel, ed., *Building the Organizational Society* (New York: Free Press, 1972).

6. Kim, "Burlingame and the Inauguration of the Cooperative Policy," *Modern Asian Studies,* 5 (Oct. 1971); Kim, "America's First Minister to China: Anson Burlingame and the Tsungli Yamen," *Maryland Historian,* 3 (Fall 1972); Anderson, "Anson Burlingame: American Architect of the Cooperative Policy in China, 1861–1871," *Diplomatic History,* 1 (Summer 1971); Ring, "Anson Burlingame, S. Wells Williams and China, 1861–1870" (Ph.D. diss., Tulane University, 1972); Browne, ed., *J. Ross Browne: His Letters, Journals and Writings* (Albuquerque: University of New Mexico Press, 1969); Merrill, "The Asiatic Squadron: 1835–1907," *American Neptune,* 29 (April 1969); Tate, "American Merchant and Naval Contacts with China, 1784–1850," *ibid.,* 31 (July 1971).

Several accounts of early envoys to China were overlooked in May and Thomson: P. C. Kuo, "Caleb Cushing and the Treaty of Wanghia, 1844," *Journal of Modern History,* 5 (1933); Richard E. Welch, Jr., "Caleb Cushing's Chinese Mission and the Treaty of Wanghia: A Review," *Oregon Historical Quarterly,* 58 (Dec. 1957); and Laurence Schneider, "Humphrey Marshall, Commissioner to China, 1853–1854," *Register of the Kentucky Historical Society,* 6 (April 1965). Jules Davids has facilitated research on early U.S. China policy by editing *American Diplomatic and Public Papers: The United States and China* (Wilmington, Del.: Scholarly Resources, 1973–). The two series that have appeared to date cover 1842–1860, and 1861–1893 respectively.

7. Eggert, *Richard Olney: Evolution of a Statesman* (University Park: Pennsylvania State University Press, 1974); Best, "Ideas Without Capital: James H. Wilson and East Asia, 1885–1910," *Pacific Historical Review,* 49 (Aug. 1980); Hunt, "Americans in the China Market: Economic Opportunities and Economic Nationalism, 1890s–1931," *Business History Review,* 51 (Autumn 1977); and Paulsen, "Machinery for the Mills of China: 1882–1896," *Monumenta Serica,* 27 (1968).

8. Clymer, *John Hay: The Gentleman as Diplomat* (Ann Arbor: University of Michigan Press, 1975); Stanley, "The Making of an American Sinologist: William W. Rockhill and the Open Door," *Perspectives in American History,* 11 (1977–1978); Braisted, "The Open Door and the Boxer Uprising," in Paolo E. Coletta, ed., *Threshold to Internationalism: Essays on the Foreign Policies of William McKinley* (Jericho, N.Y.: Exposition Press, 1970).

9. Dorwart, *The Pigtail War: American Involvement in the Sino-Japanese War of 1894–1895* (Amherst: University of Massachusetts Press, 1975); Paulsen, "Secretary Gresham, Senator Lodge and American Good Offices in China, 1894," *Pacific Historical Review,* 36 (May 1967); Hunt, "The Forgotten Occupation: Peking, 1900–1901," *Pacific Historical Review,* 48 (Nov. 1979); McClellan, *The Heathen Chinee: A Study of American Attitudes Toward China, 1890–1905* (Columbus: Ohio State University Press, 1970). Raymond Esthus has updated his classic "realist" survey of the early career of the open door policy. See his "The Open Door and the Integrity of China, 1899–1922: Hazy Principles for Changing Policy," in Thomas H. Etzold, ed., *Aspects of Sino-American Relations Since 1784* (New York: New Viewpoints, 1978).

10. The exchange provoked by James A. Field, Jr., "American Imperialism: The Worst Chapter in Almost Any Book," *American Historical Review,* 83 (June 1978), illustrates some of these points.

11. Both essays pointed to missionary translations, which opened an early window on the West for Chinese intellectuals, and to the contributions of Chinese workers to the development of California as manifestations of this friendship. *Renmin ribao,* Jan. 1, 1979, p. 4; and Luo, "Mantan Zhong-Mei liangguo renmin di zaoqi jiaowang" [Notes on early contact between the Chinese and American peoples], *ibid.,* Jan. 15, 1979, p. 6.

12. Wang, "Luelun Zhong-Mei guanxi shi di jige wenti" [A brief discussion of several questions on the history of Sino-American relations], *Shijie lishi,* no. 3 (1979); Wu, " 'Menhu kaifeng': Meiguo dui Hua zhengce shi yiye" [The "open door": A page in the history of U.S. policy toward China], *Fudan xuebao,* no. 5 (1980); Xiang, "Zenyang xiangqian tuijin—Zhong-Mei guanxi shi yanjiu zhong di jige wenti" [How to take a step forward—Several questions in the study of the history of Sino-American relations], *Shijie lishi,* no. 5 (1980); Luo, "Guanyu Zhong-Mei guanxi shi he Meiguo shi yanjiu zhong di yixie wenti" [Some questions concerning the history of Sino-American relations and research on American history], *Lishi yanjiu,* 3 (1980).

13. Ding and Zhang, "Zhong-Mei guanxi shi yanjiu: xiangqian tuijin, haishi xianghou datou?" [Research on the history of Sino-American relations: A step forward or a step backward?] *Jindaishi yanjiu,* no. 2 (1979); Xiang, "Lun 'menhu kaifeng' zhengce" [On the "open door" policy], *Shijie lishi,* no. 5 (1980). The old negative verdict on the open door policy had only recently been confirmed in several standard surveys of Chinese history. See *Zhongguo jindai shi* [Modern Chinese history] (Beijing: Zhonghua shuju, 1977), 287–88; and *Zhongguo shi gangyao* [Outline history of China] (Beijing: Xinhua shudian, 1979), 4:93–94.

14. The recent appearance of a perceptive and well-researched study of early Chinese views of the United States is a welcome step in the right direction. See Chen Shenglin, "Yapian zhanzheng qianhou Zhongguo ren dui Meiguo di liaojie he jieshao" [The Chinese understanding of and introduction to the United States at the time of the Opium War], *Zhongshan daxue xuebao,* nos. 1 and 2 (1980).

15. Swisher, ed. and tr., *China's Management of the American Barbarians: A Study of Sino-American Relations, 1841–1861* (1953; reprinted New York: Octagon Books, 1972); Drake, *China Charts the World: Hsu Chi-yü and His Geography of 1848* (Cambridge: East Asian Research Center, Harvard University, 1975); Leonard, "Wei Yüan and the *Hai-kuo t'u-chih:* A Geopolitical Analysis of Western Expansion in Maritime Asia" (Ph.D. diss., Cornell University, 1971); Kamachi, "American Influences on Chinese Reform Thought: Huang Tsun-hsien in California, 1882–1885," *Pacific Historical Review,* 47 (May 1978); Leavenworth, *The Loochoo Islands* (Shanghai: *North China Herald* office, 1905); Lee, "Zhong-Mei shouhui Yue-Han luquan jiaoshe" [Sino-American negotiations over the recovery of rights over the Canton-Hankow railroad], *Zhongyang yanjiu yuan jindaishi yanjiu suo jikan,* no. 1 (1969); Hunt, *Frontier Defense and the Open Door: Manchuria in Chinese-American Relations, 1895–1911* (New Haven: Yale University Press, 1973); Shin, "China in Transition: The Role of Wu T'ing-fang (1842–1922)" (Ph.D. diss., University of California at Los Angeles, 1970). A special issue of *Modern Asian Studies* (vol. 6, pt. 2 [April 1972]) is devoted to the Chinese discovery of the West. It includes essays by Drake and Leonard as well as Suzanne W. Barnett and Peter M. Mitchell.

16. Fairbank, *The Missionary Enterprise in China and America* (Cambridge: Harvard University Press, 1974), pp. 2–3 (for quoted phrases).

17. Carlson, *The Foochow Missionaries, 1847–1880* (Cambridge: East Asian Research Center, Harvard University, 1974); Hyatt, *Our Ordered Lives Confess: Three Nineteenth-Century American Missionaries in East Shantung* (Cambridge: Harvard University Press, 1976); Gulick, *Peter Parker and the Opening of China* (Cambridge: Harvard University Press, 1973); For-

sythe, *An American Missionary Community in China, 1895–1905* (Cambridge: East Asian Research Center, Harvard University, 1971); Rabe, *The Home Base of American China Missions, 1880–1920* (Cambridge: East Asian Research Center, Harvard University, 1978); Beattie, "Protestant Missions and Opium in China, 1858–1895," *Papers on China,* 22A (May 1969); and Garrett, *Social Reformers in Urban China: The Chinese Y.M.C.A., 1895–1926* (Cambridge: Harvard University Press, 1970).

18. Barnett, "Silent Evangelism: Presbyterians and the American Mission Press in China, 1807–1860," *Journal of Presbyterian History,* 49 (Winter 1971); Malcolm, *"The Chinese Repository* and Western Literature on China, 1800 to 1850," *Modern Asian Studies,* 7 (April 1973); Wang, *Wairen yu wuxu bienfa* [Foreigners and the reform movement of 1898] (Taibei: Zhongyang yanjiu yuan jindaishi yanjiu suo, 1965); Wang, "Qingji di guangxue hui" [The Christian Literature Society during the late Qing], *Zhongyang yanjiu yuan jindaishi yanjiu suo jikan,* no. 4 (May 1973); Wang, "Jidujiao jiaoyuhui ji qi chuban shiye" Christian Education Society and its publishing enterprise], *ibid.,* no. 2 (June 1971); Peter W. Fay, "The Protestant Mission and the Opium War," *Pacific Historical Review,* 40 (May 1971). Bennett and Liu's essay on missionary literature appears in Fairbank, *The Missionary Enterprise.* Adrian Bennett has also prepared research guides for two of the more influential Chinese-language mission publications: *Research Guide to the "Chiao-hui hsin-pao" ("The Church News"), 1868–1874* (San Francisco: Chinese Materials Center, 1975); and *Research Guide to the "Wan-kuo kung-pao" ("The Globe Magazine"), 1874–1883* (San Francisco: Chinese Materials Center, 1976).

19. (Ithaca, N.Y.: Cornell University Press, 1971).

20. Tantalizing ties between mission work with Indians and with Chinese were already evident in Clifton Phillips, *Protestant America and the Pagan World* (Cambridge: East Asian Research Center, Harvard University, 1969), and have since been further underlined by Bernard Sheehan, *Seeds of Extinction: Jeffersonian Philanthropy and the American Indian* (Chapel Hill: University of North Carolina Press, 1973), pt. 2. James A. Field, *America and the Mediterranean World, 1776–1882* (Princeton: Princeton University Press, 1969), as Fairbank and Liu note in the 1972 survey, offers one basis of comparison. Works by Spencer J. Palmer, *Korea and Christianity: The Problem of Identification with Tradition* (Seoul: Hollym Corp., 1967) and Sandra C. Taylor, "The Sisterhood of Salvation and the Sunrise Kingdom: Congregational Women Missionaries in Meiji Japan," *Pacific Historical Review,* 48 (Feb. 1979), offer still others.

21. Hunter, "Imperial Evangelism: American Women Missionaries in Turn-of-the-Century China" (Ph.D. diss., Yale University, 1981), might be usefully read alongside Barbara Welter, "She Hath Done What She Could: Protestant Women's Missionary Careers in Nineteenth-Century America," *American Quarterly,* 30 (Winter 1978). Since the appearance of his monograph on the reasons for opposition to Christianity, Lu Shiqiang has continued to publish on the subject. His articles include "Zhou Han jiao'an" [The anti-Christian case of Zhou Han], *Zhongyang yanjiu yuan jindaishi yanjiu suo jikan,* no. 2 (June 1971); "Chongqing jian'an" [The Chongqing antimissionary cases (of 1863 and 1883)], *ibid.,* no. 3 (Dec. 1972); and "Wan Qing Zhongguo zhishi fenzi fanjiao yanlun di fenxi" [An analysis of methods advocated by late Qing intellectuals for opposing Christianity], *ibid.,* no. 4 (May 1973).

22. Robinson, "Non-European Foundations of European Imperialism: Sketch for a Theory of Collaboration," in Wm. Roger Louis, ed., *Imperialism: The Robinson and Gallagher Controversy* (New York: New Viewpoints, 1976).

23. Downs, "Fair Game: Exploitative Role-Myths and the American Opium Trade," *Pacific Historical Review,* 41 (May 1972); Kirker, *Adventures to China: Americans in the Southern Ocean, 1792–1812* (New York: Oxford University Press, 1970); Teng, "American-China

Trade, American-Chinese Relations and the Taiping Rebellion, 1853–1858, *Journal of Asian History*, 3 (1969). J. Wade Caruthers, *American Pacific Ocean Trade: Its Impact on Foreign Policy and Continental Expansion, 1784–1860* (New York: Exposition Press, 1973); and Edward Sanderson, "Rhode Island Merchants in the China Trade," in Linda Lotridge, ed., *Federal Rhode Island: The Age of the China Trade, 1790–1820* (Providence: Rhode Island Historical Society, 1978), are both largely derivative of earlier studies.

24. Cox, "The Passage to India Revisited: Asian Trade and the Development of the Far West, 1850–1900," in John A. Carroll, ed., *Reflections of Western Historians* (Tucson: University of Arizona Press, 1969); Davies, *Peacefully Working to Conquer the World: Singer Sewing Machine in Foreign Markets, 1854–1920* (New York: Arno Press, 1976), chap. 7; Cochran, *Big Business in China: Sino-Foreign Rivalry in the Cigarette Industry, 1890–1930* (Cambridge: Harvard University Press, 1980); Hunt, "Americans in the China Market"; G. Kurgan-van Hentenryk, *Léopold II et les groupes financiers belges en Chine: La politique royale et ses prolongements (1895–1914)* (Brussels: Palais des Académies 1972); and Hao, *The Comprador in Nineteenth Century China: Bridge Between East and West* (Cambridge: Harvard University Press, 1970). Hsiao Liang-lin's *China's Foreign Trade Statistics, 1864–1949* (Cambridge: East Asian Research Center, Harvard University, 1974) is an important research aid.

25. Schwantes, "American Relations with Japan, 1853–1895; Survey and Prospect," in May and Thomson, eds., *American–East Asian Relations*, pp. 111–14.

26. Taylor, *The Distant Magnet: European Emigration to the U.S.A.* (New York: Harper and Row, 1971).

27. For help in crossing the lines, see the following recently compiled guides to the literature: Isao Fujimoto et al., comps., *Asians in America: A Selected Annotated Bibliography* (Davis: Asian American Research Project, University of California at Davis, 1971); Gladys Hansen and William Heinz, comps., *The Chinese in California: A Brief Bibliographical History* (Portland, Ore.: R. Abel, 1970); and Nancy Foon Young, *The Chinese in Hawaii: An Annotated Bibliography* (Honolulu: Social Science Research Institute, University of Hawaii, 1973).

28. Miller, *The Unwelcome Immigrant: The American Image of the Chinese, 1785–1882* (Berkeley: University of California Press, 1969); Miller, "An East Coast Perspective to Chinese Exclusion, 1852–1882," *Historian*, 33 (Feb. 1971).

29. Goldstein, *Philadelphia and the China Trade, 1682–1846: Commercial, Cultural, and Attitudinal Effects* (University Park: Pennsylvania State University Press, 1978); Pennanen, "Public Opinion and the Chinese Question, 1876–1879," *Ohio History*, 77 (1968); Rischin, "Immigration, Migration, and Minorities in California: A Reassessment," *Pacific Historical Review*, 41 (Feb. 1972); Hammersmith, "West Virginia, the 'Heathen Chinee,' and the 'California Conspiracy,' " *West Virginia History*, 34 (April 1973).

30. Saxton, *The Indispensable Enemy: Labor and the Anti-Chinese Movement in California* (Berkeley: University of California Press, 1971); Mann, "Community Change and Caucasian Attitudes Towards the Chinese: The Case of Two California Mining Towns, 1850–1870," in Milton Cantor, ed., *American Working Class Culture: Explorations in American Labor and Social History* (Westport, Conn.: Greenwood Press, 1979); Lydon, "The Anti-Chinese Movement in Santa Cruz County, California: 1859–1900," in Chinese Historical Society of America, ed., *The Life, Influence and the Role of Chinese in the United States, 1776–1960* (San Francisco: The Society, 1976). Herbert Hill's "Anti-Oriental Agitation and the Rise of Working-Class Racism," *Society*, 10 (Jan.–Feb. 1973), repeats Saxton's findings. Eleven older case studies have been reprinted in Roger Daniels, ed., *Anti-Chinese Violence in North America* (New York: Arno Press, 1978).

31. Spoehr, "Sambo and the Heathen Chinee: Californians' Racial Stereotypes in the Late 1870's," *Pacific Historical Review,* 42 (May 1973). The groundwork for such comparisons is already well laid in such works as Sheehan, *Seeds of Extinction;* Robert Berkhofer, Jr., *The White Man's Indian: Images of the American Indian from Columbus to the Present* (New York: Knopf, 1978); George Fredrickson, *The Black Image in the White Mind: The Debate on Afro-American Character and Destiny, 1817–1914* (New York: Harper and Row, 1971).

32. Lee, "The Origins of Chinese Immigration to the United States, 1848–1882," in Chinese Historical Society, ed., *The Life, Influence and the Role of Chinese in the United States;* Mei, "Socioeconomic Origins of Emigration: Guangdong to California, 1850–1882," *Modern China,* 5 (Oct. 1979).

33. Stanford M. Lyman, "Conflict and the Web of Group Affiliation in San Francisco's Chinatown, 1850–1910," *Pacific Historical Review,* 43 (Nov. 1974); Ivan Light, "From Vice District to Tourist Attraction: The Moral Career of American Chinatowns, 1880–1940," *Pacific Historical Review,* 43 (Aug. 1974). The Lyman essay was subsequently incorporated in his survey, *Chinese Americans* (New York: Random House, 1974).

34. Yuk Ow et al., eds., *Lu Mei sanyi zonghui jianshi* [A concise history of the main branch of the Sam Yup Association in the United States] (San Francisco: Sanfanshi lu Mei sanyi zonghui guan, 1975); Thomas W. Chinn et al., *A History of the Chinese in California: A Syllabus* (San Francisco: Chinese Historical Society of America, 1969); and Lucie Cheng Hirata, "Chinese Immigrant Women in Nineteenth-Century California," in Carol R. Berkin and Mary Beth Norton, eds., *Women of America: A History* (Boston: Houghton Mifflin, 1979) are among the most helpful. Wu Cheng-tsu, ed., *"Chink!"* (New York: World Publishers, 1972), is a collection of documents. William L. Tung, *The Chinese in America, 1820–1973: A Chronology and Fact Book* (Dobbs Ferry, N.Y.: Oceana Publications, 1974), includes a bit of everything, as its subtitle indicates. Other broad works of recent vintage: Frederick Hoyt and Eugene Trani, "Chinese in America: The Nineteenth Century Experience," in Etzold, ed., *Aspects of Sino-American Relations;* Philip P. Choy, "Golden Mountain of Lead: The Chinese Experience in California," *California Historical Society Quarterly,* 50 (Sept. 1971); and Kil Young Zo, "Chinese Emigration into the United States, 1850–1880" (Ph.D. diss., Columbia University, 1971).

For regional studies that tend to be more revealing of White attitudes than Chinese conditions, see Christopher Edson, *The Chinese in Eastern Oregon, 1860–1890* (San Francisco: R. D. Reed, 1974); Gary P. BeDunnah, *A History of the Chinese in Nevada, 1885–1904* (San Francisco: R & E Research Associates, 1973); Gregg Carter, "Social Demography of the Chinese in Nevada: 1870–1880," *Nevada Historical Society Quarterly,* 18 (Summer 1975); Nancy Farrar, *The Chinese in El Paso* (El Paso: Texas Western Press, 1972); Lynwood Carranaco, "The Chinese of Humboldt County, California," *Journal of the West,* 12 (Jan. 1973).

The press is treated in Liu Beiji, "Meiguo Huaqiao baoye fazhan shilie" [A sketch of the growth of the newspaper business among overseas Chinese in the United States], *Wenyi fuxing,* no. 19 (July 1, 1971); and Karl Lo and H. M. Lai, comps., *Chinese Newspapers Published in North America, 1854–1975* (Washington, D.C.: Center for Chinese Research Materials, Association of Research Libraries, 1977). Other topical treatments: Shih-shan Tsai, "Chinese Immigration through Communist Chinese Eyes: An Introduction to the Historiography," *Pacific Historical Review,* 43 (Aug. 1974); Richard Yung-deh Chu, "Chinese Secret Societies in America: A Historical Survey," *Asian Profile,* 1 (Aug. 1973); and Richard Lingenfelter, *The Hardrock Miners: A History of the Mining Labor Movement in the American West, 1863–1893* (Berkeley: University of California Press, 1974), pp. 107–27. Jo Ann Williamson has compiled a guide (especially intriguing for its leads on court records) to *Chinese Studies in Federal Records* (San Bruno, Calif.: National Archives and Records Service, General Services Administration, 1975).

35. Aspects of the diplomacy of exclusion have been treated by David Anderson, "The Diplomacy of Discrimination: Chinese Exclusion, 1876–1882," *California History*, 57 (Spring 1978); and George Paulsen, "The Gresham-Yang Treaty," *Pacific Historical Review*, 37 (Aug. 1968). For a sense of the changing policy of the Chinese government toward overseas Chinese, see Yen Ching-hwang, "Ch'ing Changing Images of the Overseas Chinese (1644–1912)," *Modern Asian Studies*, 15 (April 1981); Shih-shan Tsai, "Reaction to Exclusion: Ch'ing Attitudes toward Overseas Chinese in the United States, 1848–1906" (Ph.D. diss., University of Oregon, 1970); Robert L. Irick, "Ch'ing Policy Toward the Coolie Trade, 1847–1878" (Ph.D. diss., Harvard University, 1971); and Michael Godley, "The Late Ch'ing Courtship of the Chinese in Southeast Asia," *Journal of Asian Studies*, 34 (Feb. 1975).

36. See guides to the literature by Joseph-john Nevadomsky and Alice Li, *The Chinese in Southeast Asia: A Selected and Annotated Bibliography of Publications in Western Languages, 1960–1970*) (Berkeley: Center for South and Southeast Asia Studies, University of California at Berkeley, 1970), and by Naosaku Uchida, *The Overseas Chinese: A Bibliographical Essay Based on the Resources of the Hoover Institution* (Stanford, Calif.: Hoover Institution, 1959); the notable case studies by G. William Skinner, *Chinese Society in Thailand: An Analytical History* (Ithaca, N.Y.: Cornell University Press, 1957), and by Edgar Wickberg, *The Chinese in Philippine Life, 1850–1898* (New Haven: Yale University Press, 1965); and the up-to-date survey by Mary F. Somers Heidhues, *Southeast Asia's Chinese Minorities* (New York: Longman, 1975). Chinese in Hawaii and the Philippines deserve particularly close attention not only because they offer a comparative perspective but also because they fell under American jurisdiction (and the exclusion laws) in 1898. On the Chinese in Hawaii, see Clarence Glick, *Sojourners and Settlers: Chinese Migrants in Hawaii* (Honolulu: Hawaii Chinese History Center and University Press of Hawaii, 1980); and Tin-Yuke Char, *The Sandalwood Mountains: Readings and Stories of the Early Chinese in Hawaii* (Honolulu: University Press of Hawaii, 1975).

37. Benjamin Gilbert, "Lincoln's Far Eastern Navy," *Journal of the West*, 8 (July 1969), for example.

38. Kamei Shunsuke, "The Sacred Land of Liberty: Images of America in Nineteenth Century Japan," in Akira Iriye, ed., *Mutual Images: Essays in American-Japanese Relations* (Cambridge: Harvard University Press, 1975); Miyoshi Masao, *As We Saw Them: The First Japanese Embassy to the United States (1860)* (Berkeley: University of California Press, 1979); Richard T. Chang, "General Grant's 1879 Visit to Japan," *Monumenta Nipponica*, 24, 4 (1969). For two recent background works, see Conrad Totman, "From *Sakoku* to *Kaikoku*: The Transformation of Foreign Policy Attitudes, 1853–1868," *ibid.*, 35 (Spring 1980); and Richard T. Chang, *From Prejudice to Tolerance: A Study of the Japanese Image of the West, 1826–1864* (Tokyo: Sophia University, 1970).

39. Harris, "All the World a Melting Pot? Japan at American Fairs, 1876–1904," in Iriye, ed., *Mutual Images*.

40. Wakatsuki, "Japanese Emigration to the United States, 1866–1924: A Monograph," *Perspectives in American History*, 12 (1979); Ito, *Issei: A History of Japanese Immigrants in North America*, Shinichiro Nakamura and Jean S. Gerard, trs. (Seattle: Japanese Community Service, 1973). For a brief thematic survey, see Roger Daniels, "Japanese Immigrants on a Western Frontier: The Issei in California, 1890–1940," in Hilary Conroy and T. Scott Miyakawa, eds., *East Across the Pacific: Historical and Sociological Studies of Japanese Immigration and Assimilation* (Santa Barbara, Calif.: American Bibliographical Center-CLIO Press,

1972). Daniels has also surveyed the literature on Japanese as well as other Asians in the United States in his "American Historians and East Asian Immigrants," *Pacific Historical Review,* 43 (Nov. 1974). Aside from Isao Fujimoto et al., *Asians in America,* see specifically on the Japanese Ichioka Yuji et al., comps., *A Buried Past: An Annotated Bibliography of the Japanese-American Research Project Collection* (Berkeley: University of California Press, 1974); and Matsuda Mitsugu, *The Japanese in Hawaii: An Annotated Bibliography,* rev. ed. (Honolulu: University Press of Hawaii, 1975).

41. Smith, *Mercenaries and Mandarins: The Ever-Victorious Army in Nineteenth-Century China* (Millwood, N.Y.: KTO Press, 1978).

42. Aside from the works on LeGendre noted in May and Thomson, eds., *American-East Asian Relations* (p. 109), see Sandra Caruthers Thomson, "Filibustering to Formosa: General Charles LeGendre and the Japanese," *Pacific Historical Review,* 40 (Nov. 1971); Leonard Gordon, "Charles W. LeGendre: A Heroic Civil War Colonel Turned Adventurer in Taiwan," *Smithsonian Journal of History,* 3 (Winter 1968–1969); Gordon, "Japan's Abortive Colonial Venture in Taiwan, 1874," *Journal of Modern History,* 37 (June 1965). On other Americans with an eye on Taiwan, see George Carrington, *Foreigners in Formosa, 1841–1874* (San Francisco: Chinese Materials Center, 1977); and Thomas Cox, "Harbingers of Change: American Merchants and the Formosa Annexation Scheme," *Pacific Historical Review,* 42 (May 1973).

43. Edward Beauchamp, *An American Teacher in Early Meiji Japan* (Honolulu: University Press of Hawaii, 1976), which deals with William E. Griffis; and Hazel H. Jones, *Live Machines: Hired Foreigners and Meiji Japan* (Vancouver: University of British Columbia Press, 1980).

44. The multifaceted career of Rong Hong somehow eluded the attention of the essayists in May and Thomson, eds., *American–East Asian Relations.* The places to begin are his autobiography, *My Life in China and America* (New York: Holt, 1909); and Edmund Worthy, "Yung Wing in America," *Pacific Historical Review,* 34 (Aug. 1965). Worthy supplies references to earlier writing on Rong Hong's role in the Chinese Educational Mission to the United States.

45. Fairbank, "Assignment for the '70s," *American Historical Review,* 74 (Feb. 1969), 874.

46. Young, "The Quest for Empire," in May and Thomson, eds., *American–East Asian Relations,* p. 138.

THREE

Americanization of East Asia: Writings on Cultural Affairs Since 1900

by AKIRA IRIYE

IN SURVEYING THE literature of American–East Asian relations since 1969, nothing is more striking than the outpouring of works that go beyond conventional diplomatic history to deal with economic, intellectual, and other aspects of the phenomenon that may be subsumed under the broad category of cultural affairs. This outpouring may have reflected both the maturing of the field and the actual state of the United States' relationship with China and Japan since the late 1960s, where cultural issues—ranging from exchange programs with the People's Republic of China to "perception gaps" with Japan—have grown in importance.

In my essay in the volume edited by Ernest R. May and James C. Thomson, Jr., I suggested that one direction the study of American–East Asian relations should take was to explore the ways in which contact among peoples contributed to their transformation: "To identify changes in Chinese, Japanese, and American life as a result of their interaction, to indicate what meaning this story has had for their respective national histories, and above all to trace subtle influences which the three peoples have exerted upon the ideas and habits of one another, provide a meaningful area of historical inquiry."[1] Defining "cultural relations" in this fashion, that is, direct and indirect contact among peoples and its impact upon their collective and individual destinies, we may begin by asking how, as a result of their encounter, Asians (Chinese and Japanese in this essay) have become Americanized, and Americans Asianized (sinified or Japanized). To the extent that historians have produced works that elucidate these phenomena, we should be in a better position to explore further the meaning of such transformations and to relate them to more formal (diplomatic, military) aspects of American–Asian relations.

1900–1910

A. G. Frank has observed that Meiji Japan successfully and quickly industrialized because, unlike most other regions of the world that were exploited by Western capitalist states, Japan was "resource poor but unsatellized."[2] Its very lack of resources enabled it to escape the fate of other countries that were turned into "satellites" of metropolitan economies, causing them to remain in a state of dependence and underdevelopment. Whatever one thinks of Frank's and other writers' formulations about the "development of underdevelopment," few would dispute that during the first decade of the twentieth century Japan became "developed" and "unsatellized" by launching its industrial revolution and regaining tariff autonomy. Starting from this base line, historians have asked if industrialization created tensions in Japanese society and alienation among individuals comparable to developments in Western countries; how the political, business, and intellectual elites sought to define national objectives once the country seemed to have attained the earlier goals of "enriching the state and strengthening the armed forces"; and what impact industrialization had on Japan's external affairs.

Some of these questions have been explored in the framework of Japanese–American relations. For example, in an essay in the three-volume *Nihon to Amerika: hikaku bonka-ron,* Sumiya Mikio summarizes the development of the labor movement in late Meiji Japan and stresses the importance of America both as a provider of ideology and organizational techniques and as a haven for alienated Japanese socialists.[3] Indeed, during the first decade of the century the United States offered a free, open environment for the discussion of social issues and enabled such leading radicals as Katayama Sen and Kōtoku Shūsui to refine their ideas by discussing them with America's labor leaders and social critics, as well as with European émigrés who also found the United States a refuge from oppressive governments. But others besides socialists and radicals flocked to America at the turn of the century. As Katayama wrote in 1903, "Going to America has now become the ultimate wish of our people. All men from all classes—students, laborers, gentlemen, businessmen—have joined their voices to repeat the wish and put their brains together to study it."[4] Japanese who came to the United States, numbering 40,000 on the eve of the war with Russia, represented only one-tenth of one percent of the population at home, but, Katayama and others argued, they would be the spearhead of massive waves of emigration that would turn North America into "a new Japan."

This phenomenon has been studied from a number of angles, and in *Pacific Estrangement* I tried to put it in the context of Japanese expansion that made its appearance at the end of the nineteenth century, simultaneously with the emergence of the United States as an expansionist power. No matter how one analyzes the immigration episode, it surely must have furthered the Americanization of Japanese consciousness. Japanese were coming to view America as an extension of their world, a place to move to and to settle. They idealized American society as offering far greater opportunity and freedom than that available in their own country. Such an idealized image of the United States gave dissidents and radicals an alternative vision with which to criticize and condemn the situation at home. When, upon coming to America, they learned that it was not as they had imagined it, and that in fact Americans viewed their invasion as a threat to their ways of life, some grew extremely bitter and narrowly chauvinistic. That, too, became part of Japanese consciousness.

The emergence of the Japanese-American crisis during the decade 1900–1910 has been traced by Saeki Shōichi, Hata Ikuhiko, and others.[5] Here again, our understanding of the crisis has been enhanced by these writers' efforts to delineate the psychological aspect, for it is evident that at bottom lay the perception that Japan would be a different nation because of its encounter and involvement with America. Even when they were not concerned with specific issues such as emigration, Japanese writers in the late Meiji period showed unmistakable signs of embracing America as part of their mental universe. This, of course, had begun in 1853 when not a few Japanese noted in their diaries that the coming of American ships was about to change their country's and their own personal destinies.[6] By 1900 the Japanese had learned far more about the United States than ships, guns, and locomotives. They internalized American literary and philosophical figures, routinely turned to American graphic journals for artistic inspiration, and, most notably with Nagai Kafū, learned to appreciate Western music and theater through their exposure to them in America. How all this affected Japanese sensitivity, artistic taste, or literary imagination is a fascinating question that has not been sufficiently explored. But recent studies of late Meiji intellectual life clearly indicate that American cultural expressions were already providing part of the vocabulary for the Japanese as they sought to define what the poet Ishikawa Takuboku called "the contemporary labyrinth."[7] And Sharon Nolte's examination of the controversy between neo-Kantians and pragmatists among Japanese philosophers at this time goes a step further than generalized accounts to show that, at least for some intellectuals, America no less than Europe provided a point of reference for scholarly discourse.[8]

Chinese intellectual and artistic engagement with America in the first decade of the twentieth century seems to have been less extensive, but the United States did provide an inspiration to Ch'ing officials after the Boxer uprising when they sought to undertake legal and educational reforms. Monographs by Chang P'eng-yuan, Jerome Ch'en, and Chang Hao, while not directly addressing the issue of Chinese–American cultural interactions, nevertheless are filled with data that demonstrate the degree to which the Chinese looked to the United States for guidance in such matters as constitutionalism, provincial assemblies, public opinion, and mass education.[9] Although Michael H. Hunt's *Frontier Defense and the Open Door* belongs more to diplomatic than to cultural history, it contains valuable data regarding the ways in which Ch'ing officials perceived the roles America could play in Chinese politics and development.[10]

Reformers and radicals, too, sought inspiration and funds in America. Leo Lee has shown that the first Chinese translation of *Uncle Tom's Cabin,* published in 1901, was a political document through which the translator, Lin Shu, called on his countrymen to fight for freedom. The staging of the play by Chinese students in 1907 at a

Tokyo theater joined Chinese, Japanese, and American threads together to create a community of people sharing certain perceptions.[11]

Tens of thousands of Chinese in this period probably associated America with its exclusionist immigration policy. Ten times as many Chinese as Japanese lived in North America, and there has been a history of anti-Chinese attacks going back to the 1870s. (One exasperated Chinese official told an American diplomat in 1887, "In China not a single American has lost his life by mob violence, while in the past three years more than thirty Chinese have been murdered through mobs in the United States.") For the Chinese, probably to a greater extent than for Japanese, the United States was a land of both opportunity and violence, of fabulous riches as well as blind hatred. The sense of injustice and indignation felt not simply by Chinese in America but by merchants, students, and intellectuals at home who launched an extensive boycott in 1905 may have contributed to developing modern Chinese nationalism. As Tsai Shih-shan has argued, the Chinese concluded that the only way for them to be treated with decency abroad was to make their country strong and respected. That goal, in turn, led to reform and revolutionary activities on the grounds that the Ch'ing dynasty was hopelessly incapable of undertaking the task. The Chinese side of the immigration dispute has been documented in monographs by Chang Ts'un-wu, Edward Rhoads, Delber L. McKee, and others.[12] It is evident that if nothing else, the crisis induced Chinese to think of themselves as a national entity.

A more direct instance of China's Americanization has been splendidly described in Sherman Cochran's study of the British-American Tobacco Company.[13] Making use of Chinese as well as Western sources, Cochran traces the impact of the introduction of the Western tobacco industry upon China's economy and politics. Covering the period 1890–1930, the book shows how Chinese merchants, capitalists, and workers involved with the company learned American business methods, including advertising, and how they coped with nationalistic campaigns against the use of foreign cigarettes.

Just as Chinese and Japanese were becoming increasingly Americanized, it is possible to argue that American consciousness was being Asianized in certain respects. At the turn of the century Americans gained a sense of their nation as an Asian power: Their emergence as an imperialist nation and a world power was related to the war in the Philippines, participation in the Boxer expedition, and the growth of the Pacific fleet. Equally important was renewed interest in missionary activities in China. As shown by such works as Valentin Rabe's *The Home Base of American China Missions* and Warren I. Cohen's *The Chinese Connection,* Americans were genuinely interested in the modernizing potentialities of the Chinese and energetically promoted educational, medical, and other cultural activities in China. Although fascination with China was nothing new, these studies, as well as Hunt's careful analaysis of Manchurian railway schemes, reveal the awareness that the United States had a task to perform in China now that it had emerged as an Asian power and needed American capital, technology, and cultural input for modernization.[14]

The idea of America's special ties with China had its counterpart in the psychology of estrangement from Japan, abetted by the immigration crisis and the general sense of rivalry over China's destiny. I have traced one aspect of this phenomenon in my essay in *Mutual Images.* This volume also contains Neil Harris' examination of Japanese participation in world fairs held in the United States. Americans, he notes, were of mixed minds about Japanese exhibits. They seemed to be impressed by both Japan's modernizing skills and its traditional craftsmanship. Whether modernization fundamentally altered Japanese traditional character, and, if so, whether this was a good thing for Japan and for the world continued to intrigue Americans. Hirakawa Sukehiro's recent biography of Lafcadio Hearn makes many pertinent observations on this point.[15]

1910–1920

The second decade of the twentieth century has been extensively treated in terms of the development of Wilsonian liberal capitalist internationalism. Its domestic roots have been traced ably by such authors as Jerry Israel, Burton I. Kaufman, and Michael J. Hogan.[16] In the study of American–East Asian cultural relations, one interesting subject of inquiry would be the way in which the Wilsonian crusade opened up new horizons to Americans and drove them to educational, humanitarian, and other tasks to link the destinies of Asians and Americans closer together. Another would be the implications of the growing readiness to use military force (Wilson employed force on six separate occasions) for American thinking about overseas matters. A third might be how the rise of Bolshevism affected American attitudes toward Asia. These subjects have not been explored extensively, but some biographical sketches help initiate such inquiry. Warren Cohen's study of George Sokolsky is one example, Mordechai Rozanski's superb account of several journalists another.[17]

Changes in America had their counterpart in China and Japan. Probably the most significant development in American–East Asian relations in the decade was the emergence of what may be called "May Fourth nationalism."[18] Chinese nationalism reached a peak during the decade because it was no longer diverted to anti-Manchu conspiracies, and because it combined with an intellectual ferment among China's youth. One can read in Frederic Wakeman's *History and Will* a fascinating story of how young Chinese of the May Fourth generation avidly absorbed the work of Western thinkers from Marx to Schopenhauer and sought to free themselves from the traditional bonds of Confucianism and the family system. How China should change without destroying itself, and how to relate individual action to historical development, were, as Wakeman shows, central concerns of the country's future leaders.[19] Although such Chinese mostly turned to European philosophers for inspiration, America was not lacking in influence. Most notable was John Dewey, whose influence in Chinese education has been described by Barry Keenan in his *The Dewey Experiment in China*.[20]

Recent studies by Ernest P. Young and Madeleine Chi reveal that although Young China was eager to turn to the West for guidance and help, some Chinese were not unwilling to look to Japan.[21] Developing a theme Marius Jansen introduced in his study of Sun Yat-sen and the Japanese, Young, Chi, and others have noted that even in a decade characterized by blatant Japanese imperialism as was 1910–1920, many "Japanese connections" provided advantages to Chinese. Most of these Chinese were, as Young says, as nationalistic as their fellow countrymen who denounced Japan, but they preferred to seek national salvation in some scheme of cooperation with, not antagonism to, Japan. The relationship between American-oriented and Japanese-oriented Chinese remains mostly obscure and needs further investigation.

Japan, in the meantime, was undergoing its own transformation. Taishō democracy was inspired by many sources, but indisputably, one significant influence was American. In his contribution to *Nihon to Amerika,* Mitani Taichirō describes how Japanese came to universalize American institutions, ranging from democracy to Taylorism (*The Principles of Scientific Management* was translated into Japanese in 1911), and to argue their validity for their own country. The most significant development at this time may have been the establishment in 1918 of the Hepburn Chair of American History and Diplomacy at Tokyo Imperial University. The chair, endowed by Japanese and American contributions, was inaugurated during the war and was the first of its kind in the world. As Saitō Makoto has noted, it reflected the view among Japan's political, business, and intellectual leaders that the study of the United States was becoming imperative because of growing American influence in international politics and, even more important, in cultural affairs throughout the world.[22] "American ideas and institutions are spreading everywhere in the world," wrote Nitobe Inazō in 1919, referring to the growing influence of democracy in Japan and elsewhere. Nitobe, an American-educated internationalist, epitomized Taishō democracy's orientation toward the United States. He gave the first series of lectures for the Hepburn chair on the history of America from the colonial period to the promulgation of the Constitution. Saitō believes these were the first systematic presentations by a Japanese on early American history. In any event, from this time on Nitobe and others associated with the chair were to play leading roles in cementing intellectual ties between the two countries. Although, as Tetsuo Najita's study of Yoshino Sakuzō shows, Taishō democratic thought was also influenced by German idealism, the new climate of Japanese politics allowed intellectuals to speak more openly of America's relevance to Japanese development since all countries seemed to be emulating the United States.[23]

These ties reached a plateau during the 1920s when Japanese cultural life became more and more Americanized. As Homma Nagayo, who has done much to stress and document this theme, has argued, America's consumer culture, entertainment, and life styles had an indelible impact on Japan, especially after the earthquake of 1923. American movies were shown in even small rural communities, English words became incorporated into the Japanese language, jazz bands were organized, and American fashions so influenced life in Japan that one observer noted in 1929, "there is no part of Japan that has not been Americanized."[24]

Historians differ about the meaning of this phenomenon. It is possible to argue that because of the immigration question and rivalry in China, American–Japanese relations during the 1920s were never as friendly or compatible as one might imagine from the Americanization of Japanese life. Shumpei Okamoto's study of two leading Japanese publicists' views on Japanese–Chinese–American relations in the decade suggests the persistence of pan-Asianist thought in Japan, abetted by the felt need to respond creatively to China's militant nationalism and to America's oriental exclusion legislation.[25] To many Japanese, the nation's salvation still seemed to lie in its identity as an Asian nation, not in identifying with Western countries. Such different perspectives have, of course, also characterized diplomatic historians' interpretations of the Washington Conference system. Here it should be sufficient to note that Americanization of Japanese life went on concurrently with diplomatic confrontations in China and with the immigration dispute. Pan-Asianist sentiment, which never disappeared and in fact provided an ideological underpinning for the ultranationalistic organizations that mushroomed after the 1924 immigration crisis, never prevented Japanese from flocking to Chaplin movies or dance halls. Ikei Masaru's authoritative history of baseball in Japan recounts how the beginning of radio broadcasting instantaneously transformed the sport into a popular pastime, leading an enterprising newspaper to consider inviting Babe Ruth to Japan.[26] (Negotiations started in 1929, and the visit finally materialized in 1934.) While these developments had no direct relevance for formal diplomatic issues, they are nevertheless worth examination for, after all, changes in life styles and popular entertainment are far more durable than shifts in official policies. I have suggested one conceptual framework—peaceful expansionism—in which all these threads might be combined.[27]

China was also undergoing cultural change, but there are fewer studies of this topic. Historians have tended to focus on the development of Chinese communism or the Kuomintang-Communist rivalry in the 1920s, and few have examined American-Chinese cultural ties. Guy Alitto's *The Last Confucian,* a study of Liang Shoming, is a detailed account of a Chinese intellectual who remained outside party politics but wielded tremendous influence during the 1920s. But if he is typical, it would seem that American influence was minimal. He was more interested in using the works of Kropotkin, Bergson, Russell, and others to show that Western intellectual life was becoming orientalized (or sinified). On the other hand, Warren Cohen's study of Wellington Koo shows that at least for some Chinese, the United States provided the basic educational and intellectual point of reference.[28]

The Chinese educational scene in the 1920s was in a state of transition, from dependence on missionary schools to nationalistic control over them, and in many universities there was turmoil and debate over the extent to which Chinese secular authorities should supervise higher education. American educators such as John Leighton Stuart, president of Yenching University, were caught in the crossfire, a phenomenon chronicled by Yu-ming Shaw. Charles Lilley squarely confronts the issue of students who had returned from the United States and were beginning to make their presence conspicuous on the Chinese educational scene during the 1920s.[29] Through T. F. Tsiang, educated at Oberlin and self-consciously Americanized, Lilley examines the Americanization of Chinese learning, as well as the reaction it provoked. Particularly notable, for instance, was an incident in 1924 at Nankai University, where Tsiang taught, in which students accused American-trained professors of merely "peddling . . . the notes from the courses they had taken in the United States." This raises an extremely interesting question about the content of the courses these professors taught. We need more studies like this. It will be especially fascinating to compare the study of America in Japan with that in China during the 1920s. It may be that some of the finest Chinese minds were diverted from an intellectual concern with the United States because of domestic turmoil and, more crucial, the growing appeal of the Soviet Union.[30]

In the United States a foundation was being laid for specialized research and instruction in Asian studies. As Hugh Borton has noted recently, the American Council of Learned Societies was established in 1920, and one of its first tasks was to promote the study of East Asian culture and history.[31] Five years later the Institute of Pacific Relations was organized, followed in 1928 by the establishment of the Harvard Yenching Institute. These organizations did much to make China and Japan subjects of serious academic concern, although as late as 1929 only a handful of universities offered courses of instruction in the Chinese language, and even fewer in Japanese.

All of this probably should be put in the context of American intellectual and cultural history during the 1920s. John P. Diggins, among others, has done much to illuminate the decade's intellectual orientations.[32] His study reveals an America more urbanized, commercialized, and materialistic than ever before, but a society where stress on rationality and efficiency was giving rise to profound dismay and helplessness, which Joseph Wood Krutch termed "the modern temper" in 1929. It also seems true, however, that American culture was "more cosmopolitan than it had formerly been," as Gilman M. Ostrander has written, and that the decade saw "the democratization of the way of life that in other nations was restricted to the privileged few."[33] Such observations serve to reinforce the view that the American people in the 1920s were far more internationalist and less provincial than their alleged devotion to materialism may have indicated.

Recent studies of professional diplomats who entered the foreign service in the decade also contribute to our understanding of the cultural aspects of American-Asian relations. Robert D. Schulzinger, Gary May, Hugh De Santis, and others have chronicled the origins of professional diplomacy in the 1920s.[34] Although, as De Santis shows, most of the career foreign service officers who entered the State Department in this period represented the American establishment—Protestant, Ivy League, middle and upper class—this does not alter the fact that they did find it worthwhile to work abroad in the interest of both the United States and a Wilsonian world order which they sought to bring to reality. May's study of John Carter Vincent is valuable not only as diplomatic but also as cultural history. In many ways the young foreign service officer from Georgia, imbued with Wilsonian liberalism, typified one strand of American approaches to Asia in the 1920s. Gary Hess's ongoing study of the cultural ideas of Stanley K. Hornbeck and John V. A. MacMurray is likely to show more old-fashioned images of China and Japan. Generational differences in foreign service officers' perceptions of Asia offer a fruitful field of inquiry.

1930–1940

The study of American–East Asian relations during the 1930s has been largely confined to diplomatic and security issues. Although excellent monographs exist in these fields, historians have only begun to examine larger problems of culture and psychology. It is interesting to note, for instance, that in 1931, about the time the Mukden incident was plunging Asia into a fifteen-year war, American sociologist Robert E. Park delivered a lecture at Hangchow on "the problem of cultural differences."[35] In it he repeated old clichés about East-West differences, equating the former with tradition, immobility, and social equilibrium and the latter with action, mobility, and individualism. Whatever validity such a dichotomizing scheme may then have had, subsequent events in the 1930s would surely challenge it. Rates of economic growth would be greater in Japan than in the United States, and the proverbial quietude of Chinese society would be broken by war and revolution, in sharp contrast to a depression-plagued America where upward mobility would be drastically curtailed, if not eliminated. Nevertheless, despite these developments, generalizations about cultural differences remained and, especially in Japan, were reinforced by official doctrine. The result was that while in Park's terminology, cultural differences between America and Asia had narrowed by the end of the decade, the war between Japan and the United States gave the appearance—supported by official rhetoric—of a conflict between East and West. Japanese were taught to believe that they were leading Asia's revolt against the West, while Americans defined the war as one for the survival of Western civilization. In reality, however, Japan never ceased being Americanized, and the United States continued its economic, cultural, and psychological involvement in Asia throughout the decade.

One of the best ways to comprehend this complex phenomenon would be to turn to biographical materials. These abound, particularly in Japan, where many intellectuals who grew up in the 1930s have published memoirs, diaries, and letters. For example, Ōkōchi Kazuo's recollection of Tokyo Imperial University's economics department, Maruyama Masao's account of his first encounter with German sociology, Matsumoto Shigeru's self-portrait as a correspondent in China, and Tsuge Hideomi's testimony as an American-trained biologist who worked for Tōa Kenkyūjo (Asian Research Institute) reveal the intensity of the Western-oriented education Japanese intellectuals underwent, as well as the tensions this created between them and the increasingly totalitarian political environment.[36] What these biographies suggest is nothing as simplistic as Japan's "revolt" against the West, a theme which still predominates in historical writings. Actually, Japanese intellectuals were not alone in raising questions about bourgeois values and nineteenth-century liberalism, or in speculating about the relationship between political and economic freedom, or about the role of scholarship in public policy. These same questions were being explored by writers elsewhere, thus making the search a worldwide phenomenon in a period of profound economic dislocation and political crisis.

The same types of problems were certainly being faced by American writers. Categories of thought and methodologies utilized by Japanese and Americans were not different. In part this was due to the influence of German political science and sociology in the two countries. As H. Stuart Hughes has shown in *The Sea Change*, American social criticism and theory were transformed qualitatively by the influx of refugee intellectuals from Germany, Italy, and elsewhere, while Japanese too were receiving insights from Carl Schmitt,

Franz Neumann, and Karl Menheim.[37] Even those Japanese and
Americans whose primary intellectual milieu was not German shared
a concern with cultural definition and survival. Marxism came to be
taken seriously by widening circles of writers, internationalism tended
to be discredited in favor of nationalism (what Raymond Moley called
"intranationalism"), and fundamentalist religion challenged cosmo-
politanism.[38] In some such fashion cultural consciousness in the two
countries was coming closer, not growing apart. I have suggested in
Power and Culture that this very approximation provided the setting
for the sense of bitterness across the Pacific when war came.[39] This
subject requires far more extensive investigation.

One theme in American history during the 1930s was what Rein-
hold Niebuhr in 1932 perceptively called "the wedding of economic
and military power." As the state extended its authority to larger
spheres of private activities, and as the earlier emphasis on disarma-
ment as a way to alleviate economic ills was reversed in favor of
government spending on armament, the line separating private and
public, economic and military, became blurred. This phenomenon
belongs primarily to diplomatic and political history, but it may also
be examined comparatively by, for instance, relating it to Alan Milward's observation in *War, Economy, and Society* that warfare is
often the deliberate choice of modern societies.[40] More germane to
cultural history would be the question of the impact of militarization
upon culture. Did the depression years result in militarization of
American society, as in so many other countries? To the extent that
they did, what impact did it have on cultural affairs? Frank A. Ninkovich has suggested in *The Diplomacy of Ideas* that during the 1930s
the United States developed a cultural foreign policy as an instrument
of formal diplomacy.[41] Cultural relations were viewed as an ingredi-
ent of interstate relations, no longer just a matter for private concern.
Politicization of culture, and the use of culture as an instrument of
policy, are questions that would provide a meaningful framework for
comparative history.

Unfortunately, Chinese intellectual and cultural developments
during the 1930s have been much less thoroughly studied. Lloyd
Eastman's pioneering inquiry into China under Kuomintang rule contains an analysis of Chinese fascism, a subject which William Kirby

has also extensively examined in his dissertation.[42] The emphasis in these works, however, is on the German connection, and much less has been written about those Chinese whose outlook was more oriented toward America. John Israel's ongoing study of Chinese students and academics who gathered during the war to establish Lienta (Associated University) provides fascinating personal portraits, but we need many more.[43] It would seem that Chinese social scientists were absorbing a great deal from American sociology, anthropology, and political science. What such a process of intellectual Americanization meant, while the political leadership was under German influence and a revolutionary segment was tied to Soviet ideology, remains to be examined.

All these trends, of course, must be put in the context of the war with Japan, in which the Japanese were trying to impose their vision of pan-Asianist order. At least until 1937, hundreds of Chinese students and young academics were studying in Japan, and many more were attending Japanese-run schools in China. While they were subjected to a barrage of pan-Asianist propaganda, they also learned Western science, mathematics, and other subjects from Japanese. Japan's mission in Asia, as a writer asserted in *Chūōkōron* in October 1941, was not to repudiate Asia's Westernization, but to "Asianize the Westernization of Asia," that is, to ensure that Asians would learn from the West without becoming its slaves. If some such idea rationalized Japanese imperialism, it is clear that the cultural aspect of the Sino-Japanese War contained the two peoples' continued Westernization through mutual contact.

1940–1950

Diplomatic historians have debated the causes of the great reversal of the 1940s, from the American-Chinese partnership in war against Japan to the U.S.–Japanese alliance in a cold war confrontation with China. While some persist in simplistic geopolitical explanations, enough has been published to suggest many questions that must be explored before we can fully understand the phenomenon.

Most fundamentally, we would have to analyze the meaning of war for society and culture. How did wartime mobilization affect the cultural orientations of the three peoples? What was the impact of victory upon American and Chinese character, and how did defeat affect Japan? Were there continuities or discontinuities in the ways in which the three peoples viewed themselves and the world?

John Morton Blum, Richard Polenberg, and others have helped to elucidate wartime American social and cultural history, and Thomas Havens has done the same for Japan.[44] No comparable analysis exists for wartime China, but the essays in Paul Sih's *Nationalist China During the Sino-Japanese War* are a beginning. Predictably, these and many other writings document extremist reactions of the three peoples toward one another, a theme which is also treated in Christopher G. Thorne's massive volume, *Allies of a Kind*.[45] Given the state of war and the mutual slaughtering that went on, it is not surprising that there was intense hatred between Japanese and Americans, and between Japanese and Chinese. Antagonism across the Pacific was frequently couched in racial terms, with 13 percent of Americans insisting in 1945 on the extermination of the Japanese people, and the latter depicting Americans as brutes unendowed with human sentiments. American authorities took pains, as Sheila Johnson has noted, to point out to the public different racial and intellectual characteristics of Japanese and Chinese, so that they would not be mixed up; while Japanese appealed to Chinese to think of the two peoples as brothers fighting against greedy Americans.[46] Movies in the United States and Japan disseminated racially extremist images, as did those in occupied China. Assaults on Japanese-Americans on the West Coast of the United States were matched by the banning of English from Japanese school curricula and the burning of American dolls sent in the 1920s to Japanese children as an expression of friendship.

Yet it is far from clear if these instances of racial and cultural antagonism were more than wartime excesses and indicated fundamental changes in attitude. Actually, as both Thorne and Wm. Roger Louis have pointed out, in the United States considerable efforts were made during the war to improve the treatment of Chinese and to appeal to Asia's masses to consider America their friend and savior.[47] The United States, as officials and private individuals repeatedly asserted during the war, must stand for racial equality, if only to expose Japan's racial arrogance behind the facade of pan-Asianism. Japanese authorities, on their part, paid lip service to the same principle, reminding Asians that at the Paris peace conference in 1919 Japan had already tried to have the Western powers accept the principle of racial equality. A government spokesman noted in 1943 that America and Britain were becoming very solicitous of Asian people; if, he said, they had always been that deferential to Asians, there would never have been war.[48] The implication was that Japan was fighting for Asian equality with the West, and, therefore, that once that principle was recognized by Americans and British, the war could come to an end. This was the mirror image of the American perception, which held that war would be concluded only when the Japanese recognized the folly of ejecting the West from Asia. At the rhetorical level, in any event, the war turned out to have been fought for peaceful coexistence between Asians and Westerners, something which was acceptable to the bulk of Japanese and Americans in 1945.

On other levels, too, the war had the paradoxical result of accentuating cultural ties between Japanese and Americans. John K. Emmerson has recorded in *The Japanese Thread* his experience as an interrogator of Japanese prisoners of war in China. In a 1944 report he observed that an average prisoner "seems to lack feelings of hatred or even personal animosity" toward Americans. He had heard of American wealth, movies, and modern appliances. "The United States is more familiar to him than any other foreign country."[49] This sense, that the Japanese, despite their wartime chauvinism and racist rhetoric, never completely succeeded in eradicating American cultural influences, has been abundantly documented, and it should provide a fruitful field for further study. If, as Grant K. Goodman notes in his introduction to Leocadio de Asis' diary of wartime Japan, the character of Japanese life has remained remarkably constant from the 1940s to the present, then many aspects of the life one usually associates with postwar transformation must have been present during the war.[50]

On the American side, historians have described the changes the war brought to people's ways of life, values, and relationships. Some of the changes directly affected the Japanese in America. The last ten years have seen an outpouring of books and documentaries on the relocation of Japanese.[51] The episode is, of course, an important story in itself; but for the history of American-Japanese cultural relations it would also be necessary to study the treatment of Japanese students, tourists, artists, and others who spent part or all of the war years in the United States. Particularly informative in this respect is Murata Kiyoaki's reminiscences of his student days in wartime America.[52] Murata, who now is managing editor of the *Japan Times,* went to the United States to study on the eve of Pearl Harbor. He spent the first months of the war in an internment camp, and then moved to Chicago to study. Because it reproduces letters and personal writings recording Murata's encounter with individual Americans, the book is a source of endlessly fascinating data. On the American side, it is worth recalling that many of the postwar generation of America's Japan specialists experienced their first exposure to Japanese history and culture at special training centers in Colorado and elsewhere. All of a sudden Japanese studies, which had begun to gather momentum in the late 1930s, exploded. This would surely seem to be as important a development in the 1940s as anything else in U.S.–Japanese relations.

The Chinese, in the meantime, were also coming under further American influence. It is possible, as Barbara Tuchman states in the conclusions of *Stilwell and the American Experience in China,* that American soldiers, officials, and private citizens who went to China hardly made a difference in the way that country evolved. It would be wrong, however, to ignore the cultural interactions that did take place. Kenneth E. Shewmaker's *Americans and Chinese Communists* shows that even a limited encounter with Americans on the part of a fraction of the Chinese population seriously affected mutual understanding and perceptions. Moreover, as Ninkovich has shown and Wilma Fairbank has documented, intensive efforts were made to inculcate Chinese students and intellectuals with American social sciences and culture, and a large number of students were brought over to study in colleges and universities throughout the United States. David Arkush's work on Fei Xiaotong (Fei Hsiao-t'ung) provides one specific example of academic collaboration between scholars at the two countries. While Fei returned to China to teach, many others stayed in the United States after the war, not to see their country again for several decades. The influx of Chinese intellectuals into the United States in the 1940s needs to be examined as critically as was European emigration in the study by Hughes.[53]

In some such fashion, cultural and intellectual distances may be said to have narrowed considerably during the decade. The trend, of course, accelerated in Japan under the American occupation, where the Americanization of Japanese education, literature, music, and even religion advanced rapidly. Much of this is just beginning to be systematically analyzed, and thus far only a few historians have concerned themselves with the cultural aspect of the occupation. Even they have largely been content with documenting how occupation policy was drafted and implemented, and what reception or resistance the Japanese presented. Etō Jun's controversial essays, dealing primarily with occupation censorship of literary works, are somewhat marred by his preoccupation with today's politics concerning "postwar history," but they do serve to raise important questions about the effect of Americanization upon the Japanese mind.[54]

Americans found it much easier to affect Japanese than Chinese culture and society during the second half of the decade. Although China was to have emerged as the major U.S. partner in Asia, with close political, economic, and cultural ties, Chinese individuals and groups with strong American ties were steadily pushed from positions of influence in China's politics, business, and education. In their place marched the revolutionaries, many with far stronger ideological connections with the Soviet Union than with any other country. Some Chinese Communists had been educated in America or in missionary schools in China and would never eradicate those influences, but even they found it important to couch their ideas in Marxist, revolutionary terms. The story of the de-Americanization of Chinese life that was beginning to take place in the late 1940s, and which would continue through the 1960s, awaits extensive monographic treatment. It is also necessary to pay attention to the Americanization of Taiwan, to which some leading American-oriented intellectuals fled, most notably Hu Shi.

1950–1960

It is difficult to view the past thirty years with the kind of scholarly perspective that exists for the first fifty years of this century. As Warren Cohen's essay in this volume shows, useful beginnings have been made in the study of U.S. policy toward China during and after the Korean War. There is also a handful of monographs dealing with Chinese foreign policy during the 1950s. But most of these works deal with formal political, security, and diplomatic issues, and little has been written about the cultural aspect. This may reflect the absence of extensive cultural contact across the Pacific comparable to that during the preceding decade. In the absence of formal diplomatic relations between the United States and the People's Republic of China, no cultural exchange programs could be initiated, and the number of Americans going to China dwindled to near zero.

And yet Americans and Chinese were very much present in each other's consciousness, often in a perverted way. As Gary May says in his treatment of John Carter Vincent as a "China scapegoat," the destruction of capable China specialists in the foreign service "gives us little reason to feel nostalgic about either Harry Truman or the 1950s."[55] The China question provided a prism through which the American government and people judged one another and sought to define a domestic order free of the taint of alien influences. The sensational hearings on Alger Hiss and on the Institute of Pacific Relations, about which Allen Weinstein, John N. Thomas, and others have published useful accounts, reflected such an atmosphere.[56] China as it was (or as it appeared then) was contrasted to China as it should have been, and the difference was blamed on liberal American culture. But American liberals, too, showed little inclination to accept revolution and communism as the inevitable choice for China's transformation. Many were fascinated by the concept of modernization and development as a framework for comprehending change in non-Western societies. Taiwan, rather than mainland China, seemed to fit the concept better. This preoccupation with modernization and development has been written about by its critics, such as André Gunder Frank and Harry Magdoff, as well as by many China and Japan specialists trained in America during and after the 1960s.[57] Some of the criticism has taken the form, in part under the influence of writings like Edward W. Said's *Orientalism,* of emphasizing the politics behind scholarly activities.[58] Although Said's assertions that Orientalism never existed in the minds of the people of the Orient until Occidentals gave it to them, and that Orientalist scholarship has too often been a tool of the West to control the East, are not entirely applicable to the study of China, such views do help pinpoint one characteristic of American society during the 1950s: willingness to accept the use of military power in international affairs. Robert A. Divine has documented that throughout the decade the American people were more reluctant even than their leaders to give up nuclear bomb tests.[59] Many of the decade's writings on U.S.-Chinese relations were exercises in power-political thinking and reflected this trend. A history of the relationship between attitudes toward American power and armament on one hand and toward China on the other remains to be written.

There was more direct contact between Japanese and Americans after 1951, when the peace treaty was signed. Because the number of Japanese students arriving in the United States was limited and competition for such opportunities severe, those who studied in America in the 1950s formed an elite group who have remained influential in Japanese academia, journalism, and government. Equally significant is the America they saw. Compared with the preceding and succeeding decades, American society impressed most of them as extremely rich, politically stable, self-confident, religious, and at times even self-righteous. These were the same characteristics David M. Potter wrote about in *People of Plenty,* and which Will Herberg identified as America's "civil religion" in his *Protestant, Catholic, Jew.*[60] Whatever the validity of such generalizations, their implications undoubtedly made an indelible impact on Japanese visitors. Unfortunately, there is no systematic study of the activities and thoughts of these Japanese, even though Katō Hidetoshi's brief essay in *Mutual Images* makes an initial attempt at analysis. The same volume contains Nathan Glazer's perceptive analysis of American knowledge of and opinion about Japan in the postwar period. Not surprisingly, he notes how little Americans in general knew about the country, and how stable certain images they held of it remained.[61] One should also recall, however, that the 1950s were an extremely important period in initiating the process of transferring American technology to Japan. In view of the recent competition in such fields as automobile manufacturing, electronics, and computers, it should be illuminating to review the years right after the peace treaty when American engineers and businessmen went to Japan to help establish its first television stations, rebuild its auto industry, and organize for extensive trade drives with the rest of Asia. Few specific studies trace the roles played by Americans in this process.

1960–1970

The U.S.-Japan crisis of 1960 involving the revision of the security treaty appears to have been a landmark, not simply in the sense that, as writers have noted, it showed growing Japanese assertiveness vis-à-vis the United States, but also because it ushered in a decade of rapid economic growth and relative political stability in Japan, in contrast to domestic turmoil in America. The nature of that turmoil has been written about from every conceivable angle, but it would take future scholars with a sense of perspective to transcend instant history and give it appropriate meaning. Some bold interpretations have been attempted in such books as Daniel Bell's *The Cultural Contradictions of Capitalism,* Christopher Lasch's *Culture of Narcissism,* and Otis L. Graham's *Toward a Planned Society.*[62] These books are useful as their authors point out changes in the 1960s and thereafter in historical and comparative frameworks. It would seem that the experiences of the 1960s—assassinations, urban riots, antiwar demonstrations, civil rights and women's movements—made writers less certain about the durability of such allegedly unique American characteristics as unlimited material abundance, stable social change, and such durable values as equality of opportunity and individualism. Instead, American history came to be reinterpreted with an emphasis on violence, class conflict, and social inequities. Another popular theme was the postindustrial society: Writers suggested that aspects of the turbulent decade could be explained as a juxtaposition of segments of the society that had entered the postindustrial phase and those that had hardly experienced the industrial revolution. In these and many other ways, American self-perception began to diverge from the more confident decade of the fifties.

Such trends affected American-Asian cultural relations in a number of ways. One of the most obvious was a more critical attitude, among specialists and nonspecialists alike, toward the history of U.S.–Asian relations. Criticism ranged from revisionist writings by diplomatic historians such as Walter LaFeber, Lloyd Gardner, and Thomas McCormick, to often shrill denunciations of traditional Asian studies by the Committee of Concerned Asian Scholars. Somewhat less directly related, but of particular significance, was the willingness of American historians to examine the past in close collaboration with scholars from Asia, particularly Japan. The epoch-making Hakone symposium, the first extensive binational conference, surely stands as a monument. It was possible only because there was mutual respect on the part of American and Japanese scholars as well as shared critical sensitivity. They had come to know each other well, and they were interested in reexamining the past as scholarly colleagues, not as spokesmen for their respective governments. (Professor Hosoya Chihiro's famous paper on the Pearl Harbor decision, which he presented at the American Historical Association meeting in December 1966, was an important event in this connection.) Many participants at the Hakone conference observed, however, that no satisfactory discussion of the history of U.S.–Asian relations could be held without the participation of Chinese scholars, and without frontally discussing the nature of Japanese and American involvement in China. Unfortunately, no such trinational conference could be organized in a period characterized by little scholarly contact between Japan and China, and even less between America and China. (American scholars and students did, however, go to Taiwan for language training and research; this aspect of U.S.–Chinese cultural relations should not be ignored in any history of the 1960s.)

The domestic turmoil in the United States must have affected Asian perceptions of American society considerably, but this story has not been adequately explored. *The Pacific Rivals,* the English version of a Japanese volume written by *Asahi shimbun* correspondents after a tour of the United States in 1970, is a good source for Japanese perceptions of America at the end of the decade. Taking the 1950s through the Kennedy assassination in 1963 as a normative point of departure, they sought to describe what happened after the latter date. In contrast to later reports on America, the book is filled with observations that suggest the underlying and unchanging vigor and health of America. Indeed, even some of the leftist and radical writers were impressed with the protest movements in the United States.[63] These same developments, however, seem to have been interpreted by China's leaders—although there was no single leadership in Beijing throughout the decade—as evidence of the internal contradictions and weaknesses of American imperialism. The study of the changing responses to the United States belongs to formal diplomatic history. But one should recognize the cultural implications of the phenomenon, especially since so many American-trained scholars in China were incarcerated and forbidden to continue their work during the Cultural Revolution.

1970–1980

The 1970s saw the resumption of direct cultural contact between the People's Republic of China and the United States. Scholarly interchanges were initiated, libraries began exchanging books, and it became possible for America's China specialists, and China's America experts, to visit the countries of their respective research concerns. The enormous number of books published by Americans who went to China after 1971 attests to the real interest shown by specialists and laymen alike about the country from which they had been excluded for over twenty years. While some authors wrote of China with a sense of genuine discovery and excitement, most scholarly writings were more judicious, sober analyses. As exemplified by the title of the collection of essays edited by Ross Terrill, *The China Difference,* American observers usually noted the cultural and intellectual differences between the two peoples as something that must be recognized while they pursued exchange programs.[64] Nevertheless, such books were extremely useful reminders of the cultural dimension in U.S.–China relations. Most writings on cultural relations in the 1970s are more primary sources than scholarly sccounts, but they are nevertheless valuable additions to the literature. Essays by Lucien Pye and Frank Press are examples.[65]

Chinese scholars, in the meantime, began to rewrite the history of the United States and of the two countries' relations.[66] While PRC pamphlets reiterated the familiar theme of the rise and decline of American imperialism, they also took pains to mention, as Guo Shengming did, that "the American people are a great people with a revolutionary tradition who can be expected to make a contribution to the progress of mankind." Reinterpretations of the history of U.S.–Chinese relations, in the meantime, began to stress the two peoples' friendship. As Jiang Xiangze and others have pointed out, some of the same episodes that in the past had been represented as examples of U.S. imperialism now came to be seen as evidence of American friendship and support for China. Obviously, the process of reinterpretation has just begun, and it remains to be seen how much further it will be carried.

U.S.–Japanese cultural relations during the 1970s remained close, but there were subtle changes from the preceding decade. Japanese showed more assertiveness and initiative, as exemplified by huge grants to American institutions of higher learning and museums, and by the visits of hundreds of thousands of tourists annually to Hawaii and mainland United States. With the growing vogue for Japanese food, fashions, and consumer goods in America, it was as if the Japanization of American life had begun. "Japan Today," the nationwide "celebration of contemporary Japanese culture" in 1979, drew more Americans than ever before to performances, exhibits, and lectures presented by Japanese visitors. Books like Ezra F. Vogel's *Japan as Number One* reflected the sense that Japan had ceased to be a mere recipient of American civilization, and that it held some "lessons" for Americans.[67] The obverse of such a view, of course, was the feeling that the United States was no longer "number one" in many areas. Diminishing productivity, inflationary spirals, waste of energy resources, and other factors were blamed for the lack of self-confidence which many observers found in American society for the first time since the depression. Japanese writers, always sensitive to trends in American thinking, were quick to follow suit, so that it was not uncommon at the end of the decade to write of the crisis of American society. The *Asahi* reporters who in 1970 had found the United States on the whole vigorous and exciting despite domestic turmoil, ten years later found the situation far more grave. Many Americans they interviewed appeared to have lost hope about the future. Matsuyama Yukio, perhaps Japan's most influential journalist, warned that while in many respects—intellectual flexibility and rigor, among other things—there remained much that the Japanese must learn from Americans, the growing permissiveness in the United States should not be imitated, since it had already seriously undermined the fabric of American society.[68]

Thus in many ways the 1970s marked an important juncture in the history of U.S.–Asian cultural relations. At the very moment when Chinese and Americans were resuming their association, Japanese were discovering that the Americans who had inspired and oriented them culturally for decades were losing self-confidence and were adrift in an atmosphere of uncertainty. One was uncomfortably reminded of the 1930s, when the Japanese became convinced of the atrophy of American civilization and turned insular and chauvinistic, while at the same time engaging in a military and cultural invasion of China. In the 1970s Japan lacked the military capability to resume an aggressive foreign policy, but both the Chinese and the U.S. governments were urging it to strengthen its armed forces. Whether increased military power would once again reinforce cultural chauvinism, or whether cultural forces in the country would resist militarization of Japanese society, remained to be seen. In the meantime, Chinese and Americans were faced with similar questions of priorities. Given limited resources, both peoples had to decide how much to spend on arms and how much on education, welfare, and culture.

If, as Lewis Mumford says, culture means "man's historic birthright: man's memorable and remembered experience," it is obvious that to study cultural relations is to raise fundamental questions about the durability of human institutions, customs, ideas, and aspirations.[69] To the extent that Asia is more Americanized or Americans more conscious of Asia today than in 1900, this change marks additions to their respective historical heritages. Whether such change is more superficial than substantive, and whether it has enriched or atrophied indigenous traditions, are questions that are in themselves part of the history of cross-cultural relations. As historians, we may deal with somewhat different types of inquiry by juxtaposing cultural and more formal (diplomatic, military) relations across the Pacific. Alan Milward has suggested that modern societies have been almost continuously engaged in warfare, so that their polities and economies have been geared toward preparing for and waging war. If so, one may ask in what ways war, military preparedness, and security alliances have affected the cultural developments of, and interactions among, the United States, China, and Japan. How has a country's growing military power or loss of power influenced its culture? Conversely, what cultural forces have contributed to its militarization? What have been the subcultures that promote or discourage a society's militarization? In what ways has the state utilized culture as an instrument of power, and how have the cultural elites and the masses reacted to the augmentation of state power? Such problems would give specificity to our inquiry.

It is far from clear that cultural affinity leads to amity, or that cultural understanding produces peace. But that does not mean that efforts have not been made by individuals and groups in America and Asia to promote greater openness toward one another as a precondition for a more stable relationship. Historians of American–East Asian relations, precisely because of the drastic shifts and turns in this history, would seem to have a particular responsibility to show sensitivity toward such efforts as well as to try to understand the reasons for their frustrations and failures.

NOTES

1. Akira Iriye, "The 1920s," in May and Thomson, eds., *American–East Asian Relations: A Survey* (Cambridge: Harvard University Press, 1972), p. 242.

2. André Gunder Frank, *Latin America: Underdevelopment or Revolution: Essays on the Development of Underdevelopment and the Immediate Enemy* (New York: Monthly Review Press, 1970), p. 7.

3. Sumiya, "Nihon no shakai undō to Amerika" [Japanese social movements and the United States], in Saitō Makoto et al., eds., *Nihon to Amerika: hikaku bunka-ron* [Japan and America: comparative perspectives] (Tokyo: Nan'undō, 1973), vol. 2.

4. Akira Iriye, *Pacific Estrangement: Japanese and American Expansion, 1897–1911* (Cambridge: Harvard University Press, 1972), p. 86.

5. See *ibid.;* Saeki, "Images of the United States as a Hypothetical Enemy," in Akira Iriye, ed., *Mutual Images: Essays in American–Japanese Relations* (Cambridge: Harvard University Press, 1975); Hata, "Taiheiyo sensō to Nichi-Bei senryaku" [The Pacific war and the strategies of Japan and America], in Saito et al., eds., *Nihon to Amerika,* vol. 2.

6. See, for example, Maeda Ai, *Narushima Ryūhoku* (Tokyo: Asahi Shimbun Sha, 1976), p. 28.

7. Sumiya Mikio, *Dainihon teikoku no shiren* [Dilemmas of the Japanese empire] (Tokyo: Chūōkōron, 1966), p. 447.

8. Nolte, "Democracy and Debate in Taishō Japan: Tanaka Ōdō, 1867–1932" (Ph.D. diss., Yale University, 1979).

9. Chang P'eng-yuan, *Li-hsien-p'ai yü hsin-hai ko-ming* [The constitutionalists and the revolution of 1911] (Taibei: Taiwan Commercial Press, 1969); Ch'en, *China and the West: Society and Culture, 1815–1937* (Bloomington: University of Indiana Press, 1979); Chang Hao, *Liang Ch'i-ch'ao and Intellectual Tradition in China, 1890–1907* (Cambridge: Harvard University Press, 1971).

10. Hunt, *Frontier Defense and the Open Door: Manchuria in Chinese-American Relations, 1895–1911* (New Haven: Yale University Press, 1973).

11. Lee, "Lin Shu's Translation of Uncle Tom's Cabin" (unpublished, 1978).

12. Tsai, "Reaction to Exclusion," *Historian,* 39 (1976); Chang, *Kuang-hsü sa-i nien Chung-Mei kung-yüeh feng-ch'ao* [The Chinese-American immigration dispute of 1905] (Taibei: Institute of Modern History, Academia Sinica, 1966); Rhoads, *China's Republican Revolution: The Case of Kwangtung, 1895–1913* (Cambridge: Harvard University Press, 1975); McKee, *Chinese Exclusion versus the Open Door Policy, 1900–1906: Clashes over China Policy in the Roosevelt Era* (Detroit: Wayne State University Press, 1977). For an excellent study of American attitudes toward Chinese at the turn of the century, see Robert F. McClellan, Jr., *The Heathen Chinee: A Study of American Attitudes toward China, 1890–1905* (Columbus: Ohio State University Press, 1970).

13. Cochran, *Big Business in China: Sino-Foreign Rivalry in the Cigarette Industry, 1890–1930* (Cambridge: Harvard University Press, 1980).

14. Rabe, *The Home Base of American China Missions, 1880–1920* (Cambridge: East Asian Research Center, Harvard University, 1978); Cohen, *The Chinese Connection: Roger S. Greene, Thomas W. Lamont, George E. Sokolsky and American–East Asian Relations* (New York: Columbia University Press, 1978).

15. Iriye, "Japan as a Competitor, 1895–1917," in Iriye, ed., *Mutual Images;* Harris, "All the World a Melting Pot? Japan at American Fairs, 1976–1904," in *ibid.;* Hirakawa, *Koizumi Yakumo* (Tokyo: Shinchōsha, 1981).

16. Israel, *Progressivism and the Open Door: America and China, 1905–1921* (Pittsburgh: University of Pittsburgh Press, 1971); Kaufman, *Efficiency and Expansion: Foreign Trade Organization in the Wilson Administration, 1913–1921* (Westport, Conn.: Greenwood Press, 1974); Hogan, *Informal Entente: The Private Structure of Cooperation in Anglo-American Economic Diplomacy, 1918–1928* (Columbia: University of Missouri Press, 1977).

17. Cohen, *The Chinese Connection;* Rozanski, "The Role of American Journalists in Chinese-American Relations, 1900–1925" (Ph.D. diss., University of Pennsylvania, 1974).

18. See Hunt, "Mao Tse-tung and the Issue of Accommodation with the United States, 1948–1950," in Dorothy Borg and Waldo Heinrichs, eds., *Uncertain Years: Chinese-American Relations, 1947–1950* (New York: Columbia University Press, 1980), p. 190.

19. Wakeman, *History and Will: Philosophical Perspectives of Mao Tse-tung's Thought* (Berkeley: University of California Press, 1973).

20. Keenan, *The Dewey Experiment in China: Educational Reform and Political Power in the Early Republic* (Cambridge: Harvard University Press, 1977).

21. Young, "Chinese Leaders and Japanese Aid in the Early Republic," in Akira Iriye, ed., *The Chinese and the Japanese: Studies in Political and Cultural Interactions* (Princeton: Princeton University Press, 1980); Chi, "T'sao Ju-lin (1876–1966): His Japanese Connections," in *ibid*.

22. Saitō, "Sōsōki Amerika kenkyu no mokuteki ishiki" [The objectives of American studies in the initial phase], in Hosoya Chihiro and Saitō Makoto, eds., *Washinton taisei to Nichi-Bei kankei* [The Washington system and Japanese-American relations] (Tokyo: University of Tokyo Press, 1978).

23. Najita, "Some Reflections on Idealism in the Political Thought of Yoshino Sakuzō," in Bernard S. Silberman and Harry D. Harootunian, eds., *Japan in Crisis: Essays on Taishō Democracy* (Princeton: Princeton University Press, 1974).

24. Homma, "Nihon bunka no Amerika-ka" [Americanization of Japanese culture], in Hosoya and Saitō, eds., *Washinton taisei*.

25. Okamoto, "Nihon chishikijin no Bei-Chū kankei-kan" [U.S.-Chinese relations as seen by Japanese intellectuals], in Hosoya and Saitō, eds., *Washinton taisei*.

26. Ikei, *Hakkyū Taiheiyō o wataru* [Baseball across the Pacific] (Tokyo: Chūōkōron, 1976), pp. 104–34.

27. Iriye, "The Failure of Economic Expansion," in Silberman and Harootunian, eds., *Japan in Crisis*.

28. Alitto, *The Last Confucian: Liang Shu-ming and the Chinese Dilemma of Modernity* (Berkeley: University of California Press, 1979); Cohen, "Wellington Koo" (unpublished paper, presented at University of Chicago, 1979).

29. Shaw, "John Leighton Stuart: The Mind and Life of an American Missionary in China, 1876–1941" (Ph.D. diss., University of Chicago, 1975); Lilley, "Tsiang T'ing-fu: Between Two Worlds" (Ph.D. diss., University of Maryland, 1979).

30. See Arif Dirlik, *Revolution and History: Origins of Marxist Historiography in China* (Berkeley: University of California Press, 1978).

31. Borton, "Nihon kenkyū no kaitakusha tachi" [Pioneers of Japanese studies], in Hosoya and Saitō, eds., *Washinton taisei*.

32. Diggins, *Mussolini and Fascism: The View from America* (Princeton: Princeton University Press, 1972). See also his *Up from Communism: Conservative Odysseys in American Intellectual History* (New York: Harper & Row, 1975).

33. Ostrander, "The Revolution in Morals," in John Braeman et al., eds., *Change and Continuity in Twentieth-Century America: The 1920's* (Columbus: Ohio State University Press, 1968).

34. Schulzinger, *The Making of the Diplomatic Mind: The Training, Outlooks, and Style of United States Foreign Service Officers, 1908–1931* (Middletown: Wesleyan University Press, 1975); May, *China Scapegoat: The Diplomatic Ordeal of John Carter Vincent* (Washington, D.C.: New Republic Books, 1979); De Santis, *The Diplomacy of Silence: The American Foreign Service, the Soviet Union, and the Cold War, 1933–1947* (Chicago: University of Chicago Press, 1979).

35. Park, *Race and Culture* (Glencoe, Ill.: Free Press, 1950).

36. Ōkōchi, *Kurai tanima no jiden* [My life in the valley of darkness] (Tokyo: Chūōkō-ron, 1979); Maruyama, "Shisōshi no hōhō o mosaku shite" [In search of methodology in the history of ideas], in *Hōsei ronshū*, 77 (1978); Matsumoto, *Shanhai jidai* [Years in Shanghai] (Tokyo: Chūōkōron, 1974–1975); Tsuge, *Tōa Kenkyūjo to watakushi* [The Asian Research Institute and I] (Tokyo: Keisō shobō, 1979).

37. Hughes, *The Sea Change: The Migration of Social Thought, 1930–1965* (New York: Harper and Row, 1975).

38. For an excellent study of American fundamentalism in the 1930s, see Richard Hofstadter, *The Paranoid Style in American Politics, and Other Essays* (New York: Knopf, 1965).

39. Iriye, *Power and Culture: The Japanese-American War, 1941–1945* (Cambridge: Harvard University Press, 1981).

40. Milward, *War, Economy and Society* (Berkeley: University of California Press, 1979).

41. Ninkovich, *The Diplomacy of Ideas: U.S. Foreign Policy and Cultural Relations, 1938–1950* (New York: Cambridge University Press, 1981).

42. Eastman, *The Abortive Revolution: China Under Nationalist Rule, 1927–1937* (Cambridge: Harvard University Press, 1974); Kirby, "Foreign Models and Chinese Modernization: Germany and Republican China, 1921–1938" (Ph.D. diss., Harvard University, 1980).

43. Israel, "Southwest Associated University: Preservation as an Ultimate Value," in Paul K. T. Sih, ed., *Nationalist China During the Sino-Japanese War, 1937–1945* (Hicksville, N.Y.: Exposition Press, 1977).

44. Blum, *V was for Victory: Politics and American Culture During World War II* (New York: Harcourt, Brace, Jovanovich, 1976); Polenberg, *War and Society: The United States, 1941–1945* (Philadelphia: Lippincott, 1972); Havens, *Valley of Darkness: The Japanese People and World War Two* (New York: Norton, 1978).

45. Thorne, *Allies of a Kind: The United States, Britain, and the War Against Japan 1941–1945* (New York: Oxford University Press, 1978).

46. Johnson, *American Attitudes Towards Japan, 1941–1975* (Stanford: Stanford University Press, 1975). For Japanese propaganda toward China, see my essay, "Toward a New Cultural Order: The Hsin-min Hui," in Iriye, ed., *Chinese and Japanese*.

47. Thorne, *Allies of a Kind;* Louis, *Imperialism at Bay: The United States and the Decolonization of the British Empire, 1941–1945* (New York: Oxford University Press, 1978).

48. *Asahi shimbun,* December 9, 1943.

49. Emmerson, *The Japanese Thread: A Life in the U.S. Foreign Service* (New York: Holt, Rinehart and Winston, 1978).

50. Leocadio de Asis, *From Bataan to Tokyo: Diary of a Filipino Student in Wartime Japan, 1943–1944* (Lawrence: Center for East Asian Studies, University of Kansas, 1979).

51. Examples are Paul Dayton Bailey, *City in the Sun: The Japanese Concentration Camp at Poston, Arizona* (Los Angeles: Westernlore Press, 1971); Frank K. Chuman, *The Bamboo People: The Law and the Japanese-Americans* (Del Mar, Calif.: Publisher's Inc., 1976); Roger Daniels, *Concentration Camps USA: Japanese Americans and World War II* (New York: Holt, Rinehart and Winston, 1971); Dorothy Swaine Thomas, *The Salvage: Japanese American Evacuation and Resettlement* (Berkeley: University of California Press, 1952).

52. Murata, *Saigo no ryūgakusei* [The last foreign student] (Tokyo: Tosho Shuppansha, 1981); Ishigaki, *Saraba waga Amerika* [Good-bye, my America] (Tokyo: Sanseidō, 1972).

53. Tuchman, *Stilwell and the American Experience in China, 1911–45* (New York: Macmillan, 1970); Shewmaker, *Americans and Chinese Communists, 1927–1945: A Persuading Encounter* (Ithaca, N.Y.: Cornell University Press, 1971); Ninkovich, *Diplomacy of Ideas;*

Fairbank, *America's Cultural Experiment in China, 1942–1949* (Washington, D.C.: U.S. Government Printing Office, 1976); Arkush, *Fei Xiaotong and Sociology in Revolutionary China* (Cambridge: Harvard University Press, 1981).

54. Etō, *Wasureta koto to wasuresaserareta koto* [Things we have forgotten, and things we have been forced to forget] (Tokyo: Bungei Shunju, 1980).

55. May, *China Scapegoat,* p. 11.

56. Weinstein, *Perjury: The Hiss-Chambers Case* (New York: Knopf, 1978); Thomas, *The Institute of Pacific Relations: Asian Scholars and American Politics* (Seattle: University of Washington Press, 1974); O. Edmund Clubb, *The Witness and I* (New York: Columbia University Press, 1974).

57. Frank, *Capitalism and Underdevelopment in Latin America: Historical Studies of Chile and Brazil* (New York: Monthly Review Press, 1967); Magdoff, *The Age of Imperialism: The Economics of U.S. Foreign Policy* (New York: Monthly Review Press, 1969).

58. Said, *Orientalism* (New York: Vintage Books, 1979).

59. Divine, *Blowing on the Wind: The Nuclear Test Ban Debate, 1954–1960* (New York: Oxford University Press, 1978), pp. 108, 205.

60. Potter, *People of Plenty: Economic Abundance and the American Character* (Chicago: University of Chicago Press, 1954); Herberg, *Protestant, Catholic, Jew: An Essay in American Religious Sociology* (Garden City, N.Y.: Doubleday, 1960).

61. Katō, "America as Seen by Japanese Travellers," in Iriye, ed., *Mutual Images;* Glazer, "From Ruth Benedict to Herman Kahn: The Postwar Japanese Image in the American Mind," in *ibid.*

62. Bell, *The Cultural Contradictions of Capitalism* (New York: Basic Books, 1976); Lasch, *Culture of Narcissism: American Life in an Age of Diminishing Expectations* (New York: Norton, 1979); Graham, *Toward a Planned Society: From Roosevelt to Nixon* (New York: Oxford University Press, 1976).

63. Asahi shimbun, *The Pacific Rivals: A Japanese View of Japanese-American Relations* (New York: Weatherhill, 1972).

64. Terrill, ed., *The China Difference: A Portrait of Life Today Inside the Country of One Billion* (New York: Harper and Row, 1979).

65. Pye, "Building a Relationship on the Sands of Cultural Exchanges," in William J. Barnds, ed., *China and America: The Search for a New Relationship* (New York: New York University Press, 1977); Press, "Scholarly Exchange with the People's Republic of China— Recent Experience," in John K. Fairbank, ed., *Our China Prospects* (Philadelphia: American Philosophical Society, 1977).

66. Examples of the former are Guo Shengming, *Meiguo duli zhanzheng* [The American war for independence] (Beijing: Shangwu yinshuguan, 1973); Luo Ruihua, *Meiguo nanbei zhanzheng* [The civil war in America] (Beijing: Shangwu yinshuguan, 1973); Shi Zhan, *Meiguo jianshi* [A short history of the United States] (Beijing: Shangwu yinshuguan, 1972); and Dong Hengsun et al., eds., *Meiguo wenxue jianshi* [A short history of American literature] (Beijing: Renmin wenhua chupanshe, 1978).

67. Vogel, *Japan as Number One: Lessons for America* (Cambridge: Harvard University Press, 1979).

68. Matsuyama, *Nihon shindan* [Diagnosing Japan] (Tokyo: Asahi Shimbun Sha, 1977).

69. Mumford, *The Pentagon of Power (The Myth of the Machine,* vol. 2) (New York: Harcourt, Brace, 1964), p. 58.

FOUR

The Middle Years, 1900–1945, and the Question of a Large U.S. Policy for East Asia

by WALDO HEINRICHS

MANY YEARS AGO A. Whitney Griswold asserted that from the open door notes through the Manchurian crisis of 1931–1932 the United States repeatedly set out to gain objectives in East Asia that were beyond its vital needs and reach. It would try, fail, and try again in cycles of advance and retreat.[1] This cyclical framework proved unsatisfactory but the two poles between which policy oscillated have continued to set the terms of historical discourse on American East Asian policy. On the one hand, Griswold argued, this policy had been visionary, interventionist, and adventurous. At the other extreme, American interests seen in their true proportions called for caution, reserve, and peaceable diplomacy. Since Griswold some historians have held to the first proposition, seeing like him a prevailing tendency toward a large policy. Other works present a different picture, suggesting that policy in fact ran closer to the second proposition, a modest course based on marginal interests.

Not that the period under review is currently a battleground of contending philosophies. These middle years of 1900–1945 witnessed continuous great-power involvement in East Asian affairs by the United States, however active or passive that role was, as distinct from the sporadic attention and minor role characteristic of the nineteenth century when interests were transitory or still forming. At the same time the middle years form a separate past now, distinct from the cold war years that followed and less directly related to the present. This distancing, as well as the rush of scholars to the newly opened archives of the late forties, have left the middle years a relatively sedate period of inquiry. While not particularly contentious, the period is richly documented, providing opportunities for new approaches which have greatly enhanced the interpretive capabilities of the field as a whole.

The basic facts of American–East Asian relations in the period under review were the growing involvement of the United States with China and the growing alienation from Japan, leading to war and the conquest of Japan. Griswold's *Far Eastern Policy of the United States,* published in 1938, is still the only synthesis of American policy toward the region as a whole. Warren I. Cohen's *America's Reponse to China* is the first major restatement of American policy since Griswold.[2] Cohen's volume is far more balanced, presenting the Chinese side of relations as well. His thesis differs from Griswold's in holding that there was a fundamental and consistent strain of realism and conservatism in American policy in contrast to the sentimental rhetoric of Americans about China. American statesmen from John Hay to Franklin Roosevelt understood that American interests were marginal and acted on that assumption. The destiny of China was, at bottom, a matter of indifference to them, leading to treatment of China not as a nation in its own right but as an object to be used in warfare and diplomacy directed elsewhere. Michael Schaller's *The United States and China in the Twentieth Century,*[3] which concentrates heavily on the period since 1936, summarizes policy before that date in much the same way; his different treatment of the post-1936 period will be considered below.

The companion volume to Cohen's, Charles Neu's *Troubled Encounter: The United States and Japan,* offers the same perspective.[4] Neu sees Theodore Roosevelt's reconstruction of Japanese-American relations and the Washington Conference as solitary episodes of conservative statesmanship in a relationship plagued by misunderstanding, racism, bureaucratic confusion, and economic crisis. In the thirties the two nations seemed to drift helplessly toward war. Similarly, Akira Iriye rejects the notion of inherent expansiveness. Indeed, his *Across the Pacific,* the broadest possible treatment of American–East Asian relations, has a chapter entitled "America's Failure to Assist China."[5] For Iriye, however, the problem was less a political than a cultural one. He stresses "misunderstanding, misperception, and miscalculation" not only in America but in China and Japan as well.[6]

Clearly influenced by Griswold was George Kennan's realist critique of American foreign policy, *American Diplomacy, 1900–1950.*[7] Kennan argues that the United States cast its policy in moralistic or legalistic terms which gave the impression of a greater willingness to act than really existed. For Kennan the open door policy was a stellar example of this mischievous tendency to enlarge the American interest and of American naïveté in a world of power politics. A work in the same spirit is Paul W. Schroeder's *The Axis Alliance and Japanese-American Relations, 1941.*[8] Schroeder argues that when every security consideration militated against war in the Pacific, American moralistic concern for China finally blocked settlement with Japan. Both Kennan and Schroeder, writing in the early cold war years, may have been influenced by persistent attempts at the time to broaden commitments to Chiang Kai-shek to the detriment of America's Europe-first strategy.

Those most clearly identifiable with the large policy perspective are new left, otherwise known as radical or revisionist, historians. New left writings on the cold war have various ideological underpinnings, some Marxist, some not. Those dealing with earlier American policy are more homogeneous: most follow the economic expansion thesis laid down by William Appleman Williams in *The Tragedy of American Diplomacy,* which first appeared in 1959. Williams and those most closely identified with him—Walter LaFeber, Lloyd Gardner, and Thomas McCormick—acknowledge their debt to Fred Harvey Harrington, whose biography of the missionary-diplomat Horace N. Allen is a pioneering study of the intertwining of ideals and economic interest.[9] They also draw on Charles A. Beard with his stress on domestic and economic factors in foreign policy and his critical view of America's burgeoning role in world affairs.[10] The Williams school carried forward into the cold war the Progressive, reformist dissent from American foreign policy. It gained momentum as the high tension of the early cold war abated and a more complex confrontation engaging the Third World ensued and as McCarthyism gave way to a more questioning attitude toward foreign policy. In the wake of the

Bay of Pigs episode Williams enlarged and revised *Tragedy* and published it in paperback.[11]

The constant factor in American foreign policy, according to Williams, and the ruin of American ideals, has been the quest for unrestricted access to foreign markets, or the open door for trade. Central to that policy formulation were the Hay notes of 1899–1900. Williams and more particularly McCormick claim that these reflected an overriding American concern to increase exports as a means of disposing of surplus product.[12] The prevailing conviction of American leaders, more an ideology than a matter of precise calculation of interest, was that increasing exports would keep factories running, maintain prices and profits, and preserve the existing domestic social order. The object was the peaceful conquest and domination of the economies of the underdeveloped world, preferably in concert with advanced capitalist nations. This was imperialism without colonialism, or, as two British historians aptly described it, "informal empire."[13]

The Wisconsin critique of American foreign relations was by no means a narrow-front assault limited to the export question. Export expansion involved a multitude of activist or interventionist tactics from tariff manipulation to the fostering of banking consortia. Market domination was taken in the broadest possible sense to mean establishment abroad of American-oriented political as well as economic systems. Ultimately defense of the open door policy meant counterrevolutionary intervention. At first American leaders hoped to secure the open door policy by cooperating with Japan as it expanded in China, and when that failed by assisting China against Japanese encroachment. Finally the doomed open door policy led America to intervention against the Chinese Communists, at which point the Wisconsin critique merges with the broader current of cold war revisionism.

Positioned at this important juncture between the old and new, World War II and the cold war, market expansion and global counterrevolution, is Michael Schaller's *The U.S. Crusade in China, 1938–1945*.[14] Making good use of the wide array of sources now available, it outdates Herbert Feis's *The China Tangle* and Tang Tsou's *America's Failure in China*.[15] It is more conceptually oriented than Paul

A. Varg's *The Closing of the Door: Sino-American Relations, 1936–1946*,[16] which nevertheless contains useful material on American activities in China. Schaller argues that President Roosevelt expected China to tie down Japan during the war and to assist the United States in maintaining a stable postwar Asia. Chiang Kai-shek was the president's chosen instrument for these tasks, but he proved hopeless. Schaller contends that "by 1942, in the face of an increasingly popular and powerful Communist movement, the United States could not justifiably maintain that exclusive support for the KMT was either successful or a moral policy for China."[17] Instead of modifying his policies so as to assist the Communists, the president sought to coopt the Russians by his approval of their gains and aims in Outer Mongolia and Manchuria, and he sought to press the Yanan Communists into a compromise with the Kuomintang. This was a strategy flawed in conception and execution.

This argument has been reinforced by the work of a China specialist, James Reardon-Anderson's *Yenan and the Great Powers: The Origins of Chinese Communist Foreign Policy, 1944–1946*.[18] Reardon-Anderson sees Yanan's foreign policy defined primarily by circumstances, which were dire, rather than by ideology. In 1944 the leadership sought to establish relations with the United States to gain arms and American support in their bid for power. They failed and all American personnel were removed. Both Reardon-Anderson and Schaller maintain that there was indeed a "lost chance" in China. Both decry not the interventionism of American policy but intervention on the wrong side.

New left history was provocative and during the 1960s and early 1970s stirred lively debate and controversy. Critics contended that the Williams approach was a Procrustean bed for the historian, denying innovation and lacking all suppleness and subtlety where these qualities were vital in analyzing the immensely complex and often contradictory strains of American policy. To their way of thinking, economic gain did not have the primacy in causation attributed to it, and in any case a monocausal approach denied the relevance of important, if not more important, motivations. Policy often minimized the American role where economic interest would maximize it. They pointed out that, after all, American exports remained a small fraction of national product; American trade went to established trading partners; the China market was a dream, a myth. Economic expansionist historians responded that however small, American exports represented a bellwether factor in domestic prosperity and that policymakers clung to the myth and acted on it. In that case, critics countered, the leadership could hardly have been as rational and hardnosed about the planned American empire as new left historians had pictured them.

Lately the controversy has died down. Few new left histories have appeared recently. After a freshening in the first half of the seventies production dwindled sharply. Possibly this particular vein has been played out; the arguments have been stated and refined; a textbook has appeared.[19] Interest may have shifted to different contexts and problems. In part success explains the decline of controversy. A process of assimilation has been occurring. The mainstream of American diplomatic history has moved over to adopt important segments of new left history and a more critical attitude toward United States policies. For example, historians might disagree about the policy result but not about the broad public interest in export expansion in the years 1893–1929.

As Vietnam has faded into memory and the intellectual climate has become less heated, the lines of controversy seem less clearcut. New left histories appear diverse and often incongruent. Cold war revisionism, dealing with the immensely complex structures of the American economy after World War II, seems a far cry from the straightforward correlation of the open door idea and policy earlier in the century. Gabriel Kolko, emphasizing investment outlets and cheap raw materials, differs substantially from the export expansionists.[20] So do those like Charles S. Campbell who look for specific interest-group pressure on policy makers.[21] Some historians, such as N. Gordon Levin, Jr. and Jerry Israel, pair economic with reformist political goals, arguing that each reinforces the other.[22] Some offer no discernible economic basis for a radical critique of policy. Diversification and assimilation have removed much of the distinctiveness of new left history.

While new left history may have lost distinctiveness within American diplomatic history, it may be gaining interpretive power by moving into a new transnational framework. This is the world systems approach identified with Immanuel Wallerstein and the Fernand Braudel Center at the State University of New York at Binghamton.[23] At this level of analysis it is not the American economy but the world capitalist system that is the motive force in international affairs. Within this system the United States was a growing element before World War II and a predominant one thereafter. In the view of this school, which is heavily but not exclusively influenced by neo-Marxist writings, capitalism knows no boundaries and cannot be understood using a national unit of analysis. In the world perspective capitalism is composed of a core of advanced industrial nations and a periphery of satellite economies in Asia, Africa, and Latin America.

Peripheral economies, instead of serving intrinsic national needs, are skewed toward the needs of core capitalism. André Gunder Frank and other dependency theorists argue that this pernicious embrace by external capitalism not only hinders economic independence but develops underdevelopment.[24] The focus of dependency theory is Latin America and it is a question whether East Asian circumstances are at all comparable, but clearly Wallerstein's and related schemes provide a significant redefinition of economic imperialism.

One of the few specific applications of the world economy idea to East Asia is Frances V. Moulder's *Japan, China, and the Modern World Economy*.[25] Moulder argues that the reason why Japan developed rapidly and successfully and China did not is that the Western powers incorporated China into the world economy as a satellite but never had such pervasive influence on the more remote Japan. Japan was allowed time to react and thereby managed to industrialize and militarize on its own terms while world economy forces swept away the already weakened state system of China. Questions have been raised about the book, for example whether China and Japan were in fact at comparable levels of development before the Western intrusion.[26] The world economy scheme does not allow enough play for indigenous factors in China and Japan that differentiated their development. Nevertheless, this is a stimulating new approach. For the student of American-East Asian relations it suggests greater emphasis on the joint Western imperial impact on China than on purely American forces. And this may be beneficial, for where the American role is marginal alone, it becomes more significant in the larger scheme, especially with growing American power in the world economy.

The difficulty with history of this broad sweep is relating it to the narrowly defined subjects on which most American–East Asianists work. But the larger history can inform and illuminate the smaller, as Bruce Cumings demonstrates in his new study of Korea in the aftermath of World War II.[27] Applying the core-periphery paradigm to Japanese imperialism in Korea, he shows how under Japanese rule the structures of the ancient kingdom were uprooted and realigned toward Tokyo, and how this thoroughgoing colonialism paved the way for revolution in Korea in 1945 on the eve of the arrival of the Americans.

The new left theme of international economic cooperation during the late Wilson years and the 1920s fits readily into a world systems approach. In this view Woodrow Wilson sought a stable postwar world order run by leading capitalist nations, most prominently the United States, an order which would reintegrate defeated nations and integrate the "waste" or colonial areas into the world order. This is the interpretive framework for Brian T. George's dissertation on the open door policy in China, 1917–1928.[28] American capitalism would thrive by integration with the world economy and China would thrive, as Wilson saw it, by American participation in its modernization. The object was liberation of China from closed spheres and the means was cooperation of leading capitalist nations in the second banking consortium.

Farthest removed from the macroeconomic world system are the particular industry and firm, which have been attracting increasing attention in the past decade. Especially valuable has been Sherman Cochran's study of British-American Tobacco (BAT), which on balance reinforces the economic expansion theory.[29] Cochran shows that the China market was no myth for this cigarette manufacturing firm. It achieved a dominating position and returned fat profits to the founder, James Duke. Further, BAT's success involved imperialist exploitation; the company reinvested a declining share of profits in China; it tied its Chinese peasants to growing a less profitable tobacco leaf; it drove out most Chinese competitors by price wars; it secured favorable tax treatment from the weak Chinese government; and it profited from the low tariff of the unequal treaty system.

Clearly such activities were inimical to China, but the picture Cochran presents is not simple. Chinese competition was not eliminated completely: BAT's chief competitor survived and grew because of special advantages enjoyed by the indigenous firm. And the success of BAT was in large measure due to its ability to use Chinese distributors and adapt its marketing to Chinese circumstances. As Michael Hunt suggests, BAT gained control of the China market in cigarettes by, to a degree, surrendering to it.[30] Furthermore, BAT was not invariably able to secure official Western support. In two important instances it failed: in its bid to secure a cigarette monopoly from the Chinese government and in its advice in 1927 to put on a display of force in North China.

The case of Standard Oil is also complex, as Hunt and others have shown.[31] This American giant, through an aggressive and innovative marketing strategy, achieved a major and at times dominant position in the China market for kerosene as an illuminant. Chinese benefitted during fierce price wars between Standard and its foreign rivals but suffered in ensuing periods of market division and price collusion. Standard kerosene undercut local vegetable oils as an illuminant, but Chinese processors turned abroad and found a better market. Standard profited from low tariffs of the unequal treaty system, but as an eminently visible foreign business it encountered a variety of local taxes and regulations inspired by rising Chinese nationalism.

The American response to the Nationalist phase of the Chinese revolution cannot be understood simply through application of economic theses. Using Standard Oil as an example, David A. Wilson illustrates how the goals and tactics of business and government differed and how this difference was significant for China and the United States.[32] In the face of taxation by the Canton government in 1925–1927, Standard Oil chose to deal with the Chinese authorities for the best terms it could secure, contrary to the advice of the State Department, which was concerned to uphold the treaty order in China, partly to maximize opportunities for all American businesses. At times the American government supported Standard's protests, but generally it had little influence on the firm's operations, its competition, the Chinese government, or Chinese nationalist sentiment.

At times the government was more inclined to appeasement than was the firm; at times the opposite was the case. Rarely did both agree and cooperate effectively. One of these exceptions has been the subject of intensive and fruitful examination by Irvine H. Anderson, Jr.[33] Japanese expansion in the 1930s posed such an extensive threat to the markets and properties of the Standard-Vacuum Oil Company that it drove Stanvac into complex working arrangements with British oil companies and between them and their governments. The result in 1941 was a common front to carry out the oil embargo which precipitated war.

More studies are needed, but the successes of BAT and Standard Oil appear exceptional. The conclusion seems to be that the American business response to opportunities in China was lackadaisical. In some cases the structure of the industry militated against pursuit of the market, as Michael Hunt's brief but telling account of the rise and fall of cotton textile sales in China suggests.[34] From a high in 1905 of one-third of the cottons China imported, American sales fell to almost nothing by 1929. Just as the rise was due to the passing of the comparative advantage in production from Britain to the United States, the decline was partly due to a similar shift from America to Japan. The failure was also due, however, to the American industry's preference for its growing and protected home market. The China market thus was peripheral, an alternative in case of a slump at home, rather than a primary market to be cultivated in its own right.

New left history faces a dilemma. The twentieth-century firm eludes one's grasp in a national setting. Ostensibly American firms often lacked American character and purpose. Their influence on government policy seems negligible or unpredictable. Probably the greatest exploitation of China derived from the unequal treaty system, which the United States benefitted from but which it was not as readily identified with as Great Britain. Multinational, transnational, and world system approaches offer a better picture of the firm's operations and impact. Yet movement to a broader setting weakens the peculiarly American foundation of much new left historiography, especially of the Williams school. If the dynamo is not primarily the expansionist American capitalist system but some more diffuse and obscure entity, then this history loses political relevance and force.

On one side, historians describe constant pressure for a large policy in East Asia, for intervention, for hegemony—economic, political, or cultural. In spite of failures, the United States always resumes the quest. On the other side is a more disparate group of historians, united more in opposition to this sort of history, which they regard as simplistic, than in anything else. They reject the notion that the United States persistently and characteristically followed any particular policy. Suspicious of monocausal explanations, they argue for complexity rather than consistency and singleness of purpose. They are more eclectic in approach, interested in the effect of cultural dissimilarities, the relevance of policies directed elsewhere, the constraints of multinational settings. They seek the broadest possible array of explanatory devices, especially those developed in allied fields of the social sciences. At the same time they acknowledge the importance of the irrational, of chance, misperception, bewilderment, ignorance, and bias. Above all they have been experimental, bringing to the American–East Asian field a variety of insights and frames of analysis.

On this side, the economic thesis is by no means dismissed, but neither is it accorded principal or exclusive explanatory position. Rather it is taken as a valuable paradigm, occasionally controlling, usually significant, at times irrelevant.

Another experimental approach is bureaucratic analysis. The premise here is that the organization as such, apart from substantive issues, plays a role in shaping policy and decision. This approach is most elaborately set forth by Graham Allison's study of the Cuban missile crisis.[35] It assisted Roger Dingman in developing the national defense poli...cs scheme for *Power in the Pacific,* which deals with the origins of the Washington Conference of 1921–1922.[36] The State Department begs for extensive and intensive bureaucratic analysis. Along these lines James C. Thomson, Jr.'s, essay on the Far Eastern Division in the 1930s is suggestive.[37]

One reason bureaucratic models have not been more influential in this period is that as one moves back toward the turn of the century bureaucracy becomes smaller and simpler and therefore less deter-

minative of outcomes. Further, the method has limitations: Strong
presidents control decisions and strong presidents were in office for
half the period covered here. The bureaucratic politics approach may
illuminate the event or decision, but it has less value for longer-term
developments. The Allison bureaucratic process model seems more
relevant to the military than to the State Department. Yet it could be
the more fruitful of the two if it were taken to include, besides the
flow of work, how members relate to each other, how they go about
decisions, how they conceive of their jobs and the purpose of their
organization, in short, if it were defined as the sociology of the bureaucratic unit. This approach with prosopography might yield new
insights about the China hands of the foreign service and in particular
about the group savaged by McCarthyism, for which our data are
now very extensive.[38]

A third approach, broadly defined, is best summed up in the
world attitude, meaning how one looks at the world, not photograph-
ically, but filtered through personal experience, personality, and the
assumptions, values, and modes society provides. Illustrations abound
in Ernest R. May's *"Lessons" of the Past,* such as the unfortunate
belief of Franklin D. Roosevelt and his advisers that the aftermath of
World War II would be very much like that of World War I.[39] Elsewhere May has noted that one difference between Roosevelt and his
successor in foreign affairs was their remembered pasts, Roosevelt
reaching back to a Europe he knew firsthand before World War I and
Harry Truman beginning to think seriously about the world only in
the 1930s, the time of fascist aggression.[40] Further, insights from the
field of cognitive psychology have been applied to international relations and seem promising for such a richly documented field as this.[41]

Society filters perception too. Akira Iriye has led the way in
showing how Japanese, Chinese, and Americans have formed images
of each other that reflect their different cultures and how these have
affected their relations. Now he has gone further. Building on the
concept of "cultural system," he explores relations of cultural systems with each other and with power systems.[42] According to Iriye,
certain basic assumptions about society and its ordering spill over
from the domestic setting to the international and influence foreign
policy and interstate relations. Thus one way to examine more con-

cretely the impact of the cultural system is to view it in relation to its complementary power system, which organizes and sustains the cultural system. Such pairs can then be compared across national frontiers as well as examined in their interactions.

Iriye puts the method to work in his recent *Power and Culture: The Japanese–American War, 1941–1945,*[43] in which he describes a startling convergence of American and Japanese views about the postwar world while their armies and navies fought each other. Jerry Israel argues along these lines, though less elaborately, in *Progressivism and the Open Door,* examining the external correlates of an internal reform movement. Ways by which Americans sought to cope with the problems of scale in their domestic institutions, he believes, suggested ways of dealing with problems internationally. Thus the cooperative open door policy succeeded to the nationally competitive open door policy, somewhat after the fashion of the new and old Progressivism at home. It seems reasonable that a modernizing and industrializing America would think of internal and external problems in somewhat similar fashion, but making this sort of analogy presents obvious difficulties.

Between power and culture, the public and private sectors, and through China at crucial junctures during its long revolutionary history ran the careers of three Americans whose values and influence are examined by Warren I. Cohen in *The Chinese Connection.*[44] Such studies of opinion leaders not only show how private citizens influence foreign policy but also extend the foundations for generalizing about cultural patterns and foreign policy. In the latter connection, two essays, one by Tu Wei-ming on Chinese perceptions of America and the other by Warren Cohen on American perceptions of China, draw important insights from a broad array of sources.[45]

Biographies of diplomats are beginning to populate the field. Books have appeared recently on Paul S. Reinsch, John Carter Vincent, and Patrick J. Hurley, as well as a dissertation on E. T. Williams, two biographical essays on Stanley K. Hornbeck, and essays on Nelson T. Johnson, Joseph C. Grew, John V. MacMurray, and W. Cameron Forbes.[46] The biographical method becomes more useful to the history of American–East Asian relations as that history becomes better defined and biographers can work within an interpretive structure instead of having to create it themselves. They can ask questions with a more general bearing and try conclusions from comparable biographies. Of particular interest and value will be the mindset of the individual; the social and educational factors contributing to it; how it changed and why; the interaction of American with East Asian values; and the impact of diplomacy as a job and a profession.

The American–East Asian historian has available, in addition to the economic, bureaucratic, and cultural approaches, four well-tried international frames of reference. The first of these is the traditional bilateral framework. Developers of the American–East Asian field have been especially concerned to establish adequate language competence to ensure that bilateral studies are truly two-way streets, fully utilizing East Asian sources and history. That effort is represented most notably by the works of Akira Iriye and Michael Hunt.

Second is the multinational framework focusing on the Asian-Pacific region. Given the extraordinary language demands, it is the rare scholar who can write a full-scope international history of East Asia. Two studies by Christopher Thorne, however, set forth Western policies in East Asia as a whole, one on the Manchurian crisis, the other on World War II.[47] Roger Dingman, though eschewing the diplomatic side of the Washington Conference, establishes its multinational basis in *Power in the Pacific.* Given the requirements of such studies, it seems likely that the international setting will usually be constructed by conference volumes or by piecing together narrower studies.

The third frame of reference is the comparative study. Two deliberate efforts in this direction are the Dingman volume and Iriye's *Power and Culture.* In both cases the national settings are relatively isolated, in Dingman's by the lull between the Paris and Washington conferences and in Iriye's by war. Thus it was possible to compartmentalize the analysis and seek out distinctive features.

The fourth frame of reference is the general foreign policy of each of the national actors, especially the United States. No one needs reminding of the central importance of conceptions of world order that animated a whole generation of American statesmen from Woodrow Wilson through Franklin Roosevelt. Neither can one understand the relations of the United States and Japan in 1940–1941 without taking into account the enlarging European war.

This variety of techniques has produced a complex history. Operating without a controlling interpretation such as that of the new left, experimenters have reached rich and novel but narrow conclusions. With exceptions, such as the syntheses by Cohen and Iriye, these historians have not attempted to fill in a larger tapestry. Nevertheless, in spite of this diversity, common themes and conclusions emerge that form a surprisingly coherent picture of American East Asian policy.

What these disparate studies suggest is that, with all its rhetoric, illusion, and befuddlement, American East Asian policy tended in fact to be cautious, conservative, and founded on the view that American interests in East Asia, considered alone, were marginal. Policy in fact took the position that Griswold thought desirable. When East Asia assumed critical importance it was for larger, worldwide reasons or because of its relation to European concerns.

This tendency of historians to downplay East Asia in American policy is particularly evident in the decade of rapid change from the Sino-Japanese War to the Peace of Portsmouth. Marilyn B. Young's conclusion that American policy took a major turn toward Asia in these years remains valid.[48] Acquisition of the Philippines, participation in the Boxer force, and the open door notes established the United States as a power to be consulted on China questions. Yet, as Raymond Esthus reaffirms in an expanded version of his original essay on the open door policy, the concept was changeable and hazy.[49] Perhaps it was deliberately so. The object was to secure as much as possible of the old trading advantages without incurring undue risk. As Cohen suggests in reference to the first note, Hay and McKinley probably secured all they could hope for with six pieces of paper.[50] Thenceforth shifting usage reflected different circumstances, risks, and stakes. What accounts such as those of Esthus, Young, and Cohen show is a sharp divergence between powerful economic aspirations and minimalist, opportunistic, diplomatic operations.

Benevolence had little part to play in American policy toward China, according to Michael Hunt's article on the Boxer indemnity remission.[51] What part it did play was patronizing rather than responsive to Chinese definitions of need. Elsewhere Hunt points out that even when Americans did in fact confer benefit on China, as in the case of the American contingent occupying Peking after the Boxer revolt, they would not necessarily understand they had done so.[52] Lieutenant General Adna Chaffee left Peking, after supervising helpful interaction between his forces and the Chinese, confirmed in the opinion that threat of force was the key to dealing with Asiatics. This notion of a hardfisted but relatively narrow interest in China is the persistent theme of Cohen's *America's Response to China*.

Little of note has been added to the modern reconstruction of Theodore Roosevelt's East Asian policies, summarized by Esthus and Charles Neu in May and Thomson's *American–East Asian Relations*.[53] On China the president huffed and puffed at the boycott movement, incidents involving missionaries, and cancellation of the Canton-Hankow railroad concession, but in fact did very little. As Cohen writes, Roosevelt "found no vital American interests in China and devoted little time or attention to the country."[54]

Japan occupied more of his attention. He was aware of Japan's new-found pride and power and, with sensitivity and sophistication, worked on the emerging strains imposed on Japanese-American relations by trade rivalry in Manchuria, American weakness in defense of the Philippines, and racial tensions involving Japanese immigrants in the United States. Charles Neu's conclusion about Roosevelt's policy of seeking accommodation with Japan is a concise summary of the minimalist point of view:

[Roosevelt] was willing to see Japan's expansionist thrust absorbed on the mainland of Asia where there was little friction with the United States. It was Japan's task, not America's, to lead China along the road to modernization. . . . Immigration and racial tensions, not Japanese expansionism, endangered Japanese-American friendship, and Roosevelt subordinated the vague American stake in China to the control of those explosive issues.[55]

The Taft administration reversed the thrusts of Roosevelt's diplomacy respecting Japan and China. Taft himself, in spite of recent studies, remains an enigma, but his administration's new concern for

China and opposition to Japan marked a distinct policy shift. Most historians agree with Neu that this shift became decisive in the Wilson administration.[56] In any case the Taft years have taken on new significance.

Two major recent works deal with this policy shift, the first being Akira Iriye's *Pacific Estrangement: Japanese and American Expansion, 1897–1911*.[57] Iriye picks up Japanese-American relations in 1905, the point of divergence when active American racism and exclusion began shrivelling Japan's expectations of peaceful, private migration and economic expansion around the Pacific basin. He shows how extensively Americans feared the yellow peril and war with Japan and how exclusion contributed to Japan's formal, particularist expansion on the continent. He also describes how new American interest in China as a democracy struggling to be born added a further burden to Japanese-American relations. According to Iriye, foundation existed neither for substantial Chinese-American economic ties nor for fears of disruption of the really solid economic ties between Japan and the United States. Japanese-American estrangement was founded on illusion.

How much more meaningful those histories are that deal fully and effectively with the East Asian side has been shown repeatedly by Iriye and now by Michael Hunt's pathbreaking study of Chinese-American interaction over Manchuria.[58] Hunt tells of China's search for a distant foreign friend to assist China in resisting encroachment by Japan and Russia in the strategic Manchurian sector and of the ultimate selection of the United States for that role. He sees a latent activism in Hay's open door policy directed at guaranteeing investment as well as trade opportunity and supporting China's integrity. This strain, he says, surfaced in the Taft administration among young, ambitious State Department officials led by Secretary of State Philander Knox, a far more dominant figure than we had supposed. The key figures were Knox and his first assistant secretary F. M. Huntington Wilson, not Willard Straight, whose historic proportions Hunt whittles down with gusto. Particularly prompting the activists was a sharp drop in American exports to Manchuria, which they attributed to Japan. The Knox neutralization scheme failed, according to Hunt, because of discord in Peking and especially because of the devastating ignorance, parochialism, and maladroit diplomacy of Knox and company.

Taft policy approximated the Griswold cycle of advance and retreat. More attuned to domestic concerns than international realities, Taft's administration let missionary idealism and the urge to market expansion drive policy forward. The Roosevelt administration, sensitive to both domestic and international concerns, ignored or moderated such pressures. Historians agree that Taft's policy was venturesome, but, as Hunt shows, it was not nearly venturesome enough to affect the powers in China.

It is often useful to step back and view American–East Asian relations in comparison with British–East Asian relations. In this instance a parallel weakening of Anglo-Japanese relations occurred, which has been detailed in Ian Nish's *Alliance in Decline*.[59] The British watered down the 1911 version of their alliance with Japan in order to preclude its invocation against the United States, hoping thereby to solidify British-American relations with an arbitration treaty, which ultimately failed in the Senate. More needs to be known about the British-Japanese-American triangle in 1911 when, besides the arbitration treaty and alliance, Japan negotiated commercial treaties with Britain and the United States.[60] Was the Taft administration more reconciled to Japanese expansion on the continent when the sting had been removed from the alliance?

World War I undermined the old diplomacy in East Asia as elsewhere and rearranged the capabilities of the powers. The United States emerged in a preeminent position and under Woodrow Wilson's leadership redefined the basis of international conduct. This great departure has been well established by the work of Arno J. Mayer and N. Gordon Levin.[61] Roger Dingman deals extensively with "Wilson's design for a new world order" in *Power in the Pacific*. Despite the importance of the shift to the New Diplomacy, however, little is known about what it meant specifically for the East Asian region. It is ironic that the literature of American–East Asian relations should be lively for the relatively quiet years just before World War I and stagnant for the epochal war years.

Particularly intriguing and valuable would be a full-scale multinational analysis of the China diplomacy of the powers in World War

I and at the peace conference. Madeleine Chi's account is multiar-chival but brief, only 145 pages of text.[62] Recent studies by Don Dignan, Peter Lowe, Robert J. Gowen, and Nish clarify British pol-icy.[63] The picture on the American side is more spotty. Arthur Link's magisterial biography of Wilson has stopped short of American entry into the war. Noel Pugach offers a view of the misty mind of Wil-son's minister to China, Paul S. Reinsch.[64] Otherwise, Burton F. Beers' study of the Lansing-Ishii accord remains the only major inter-pretational departure since the first investigators in the 1930s and 1940s.[65] No one has fully examined how the problems presented by the European war affected East Asian policy in the Wilson adminis-tration. Similarly, the general and European questions at the Paris Peace Conference have not been examined in relation to East Asian–Pacific questions in terms of consistency of principle and bargaining tactics. Instead, as exemplified in the work of Roy Watson Curry, Tien-yi Li, and Russell H. Fifield, East Asian questions have been lopped off for special treatment.[66]

While America's ideological and sentimental attachment for China deepened significantly during the Taft and Wilson years, the extent to which this feeling affected policy is by no means clear. Beers indicates a surprising amount of interest in practical accom-modation with Japan, overridden by Wilson's moralistic imperatives. Generally, policy seems to lack direction. According to Donald R. Lyman, the first years of the Wilson administration witnessed ex-treme weakness in conception and implementation of American East Asian policy.[67] The British, in spite of involvement in the war, suc-cessfully resisted Group V of the Twenty-one Demands, while the American response was later and far weaker, as Esthus shows.[68] The subsequent Bryan caveat only compounded confusion, and the Lan-sing-Ishii accord was hardly a model of clarity. Preoccupation with neutrality and lack of leverage weakened American diplomacy. Even so, Britain was far more deeply engaged in Europe and still managed to hold its own with Japan. The image of American policy is one of retreat and progressive abandonment of the open door policy.

The weakness of American diplomacy might be investigated by organizational analysis. In this context it is apparent that Wilson's work habits, his distrust of subordinates, the poor quality of officials he was able to attract into the State Department and ambassadorships, their lack of experience, and the woefully weak work force and quaint routines of the State Department all made it difficult to manage an adequate diplomacy.

After the United States entered the war Wilson emerged as a far more effective diplomat, his East Asian policy reflecting a powerful global vision. However, the exigencies of interallied cooperation, the task of establishing a world organization, and problems of peacemaking imposed severe limitations on American efforts to promote a modern, democratic China. General agreement exists on the importance of the cooperative approach to China by leading capitalist nations, a point emphasized by revisionists. Warren Cohen's study of Thomas Lamont shows, however, that while the State Department might throw forward the flag for investment in China, business preferred to give the appearance of picking it up rather than actually doing so.[69] Business activity rarely coincided with business rhetoric or with government policy.

The twenties were a forward decade in American foreign relations, not a retreat. It was preeminently a decade of business expansion overseas, but it was also a decade of cultural expansion. No war or international crisis intervened to test these endeavors against national means and other priorities. Historians have differentiated the thrusts of cultural and economic expansion in the decade as they have those of government and business. The American response to the emerging Chinese Nationalist revolution is a case in point. Warren Cohen shows that Roger Greene and the missionary-philanthropic community he represented strongly influenced Secretary of State Frank B. Kellogg and American China policy in the wake of the Taku Incident of 1926.[70] The aspirations for China of these Americans contradicted the expressed wishes of the business community in China and the policy of upholding the treaty order. Idealism here was not merely a rhetorical cloak for self-interest. Historians taking an eclectic approach argue that while the economic variable predominated in the 1920s it was not exclusive. The making of policy was ultimately a political process. Tactics, personalities, hopes mattered.

One of the principal organizing concepts for American–East Asian relations in the interwar years has been Akira Iriye's Washington Conference framework set forth in *After Imperialism.*[71] This has been a useful way of viewing regional relations in the period, but, as Iriye says, the framework never became more than that. The tenuous foundations of this new order are apparent in Dingman's sophisticated analysis of the arms limitation side of the Washington Conference.[72] Dingman sees three separate political universes—London, Tokyo, and Washington—bringing about the conference. He shows that the common denominators were far less important than the national factors. Looking ahead to Iriye's most recent book, *Power and Culture,* this diversity raises the question of how much of a common fund of experiences or ideas of the 1920s Americans and Japanese could have drawn on as their thinking about peace seemed to converge during the latter part of World War II.

A great gap existed between the community of nations Wilson hoped to create and such international consolidation as occurred. Some people were undoubtedly building toward Wilson's vision, while others, like the Henry Cabot Lodge pictured by William C. Widenor, were building in more conventional ways.[73] Even America's economic role, one author has said, was played "haltingly and irresponsibly."[74]

The key role of the world economic crisis that began in 1929 in shaping the diplomacy of the 1930s has been generally accepted. Osamu Ishii in his dissertation on the cotton textile industry argues that discrimination by the West against Japanese textiles reinforced Japan's move toward imperial isolation.[75] On the other hand, the American silver purchase act, which was designed to assist the American mining industry, incidentally worsened American economic opportunity in China.[76] The role of economic autarky and competition in the intensified international political rivalry of these years needs further exploration.

The Manchurian crisis of 1931–1932, a major factor in unravelling the international political arrangements of the interwar period, now has a full-scale international history. Christopher Thorne's *The Limits of Foreign Policy* spills out on a vast canvas: London, Washington, Geneva, Paris, Tokyo, China. It contains innumerable subplots and excursions, as well as telling descriptions: Hornbeck appears "fairly spewing forth memoranda"; Simon "sway[s] to the other man's breeze.'' Aside from these touches, Thorne comments on the confusions of Washington and London, their deep-seated reluctance to take action, their similarities as well as differences, and the problem of acting on normative principles in a time of systemic power change. His judgment is that Stimson was wrong and the pragmatic British approach was on the whole wiser. Manchuria, he argues, should not be taken as a starting point on the road to Pearl Harbor, nor proof of the League's failure and an invitation thereby to aggressors in Europe. Thorne's judgment on American policy seems severe but it is not likely that anyone will soon leap to the defense of Henry Stimson.

The effect of Thorne's work is to isolate the crisis from the great events following later in the decade and to marginalize it. Seen this way Stimson's activity seems less significant than the inactivity of the West. The transition to Franklin Roosevelt's policy of noncondonation but nonprovocation, so indisputably set forth by Dorothy Borg, seems less abrupt.[77]

In 1969 Japanese and American historians met in conference at Lake Kawaguchi, Japan to combine their knowledge and insights about the origins of the Pacific War. Parallel papers on key bureaucracies and opinion groups produced a composite of great complexity. In place of the prevailing wartime and postwar assumption of a monolithic Japan making a calculated, step-by-step bid for empire, the conference revealed opportunism, division, and chaotic decision-making. Seeing Japan as highly volatile and reactive meant scrutinizing more closely American policy, hitherto regarded as righteous and defensive, and finding inflexibility, parochialism, and miscalculation. The published results of the conference, *Pearl Harbor as History,* edited by Dorothy Borg and Shumpei Okamoto, inaugurated a new stage of interpretation of the conflict, one distributing responsibility for the conflict more equally and emphasizing Japanese-American interaction.

While the Pacific War has moved from the passion and rhetoric surrounding the conflict into perspective as history, a fresh synthesis on its causes remains to be written. This lack is evident in the only major recent work on American policy in the period, Robert Dallek's *Franklin D. Roosevelt and American Foreign Policy, 1932–1945.*[78]

The book is a painstaking, balanced reexamination of Roosevelt's policies in the light of the wide range of sources now available, but it contains few new departures in interpretation. Iriye, reviewing the book, finds the familiar portrait of a *Realpolitiker,* despite Dallek's characterization of the president as an idealist and internationalist.[79]

Precisely when American policy moved from the passivity depicted by Dorothy Borg into active opposition to Japan is important not only for the origins of the war but for the long-term evolution of American East Asian policy as well. Clearly, America was heavily involved in Asia during the cold war. As suggested, some historians argue it pursued a large policy throughout the twentieth century, while the work of others permits the conclusion that policy up to this point at least was essentially cautious and modest. The turn against Japan, then, can be taken as a watershed.

John MacVicker Haight, Jr., sees Roosevelt taking his first step in the new direction in 1937.[80] He believes that in the Quarantine Speech the president had in mind strong action against Japan, but that he later backed down in the face of criticism. The prevailing interpretation has been that of Dorothy Borg, who contends that the president had no clear idea of what action he might take.[81] Dallek agrees, noting that public approval of the speech arose from the belief that the president had some peaceful means of isolating or overcoming aggressors. When it became apparent that Roosevelt had no new idea, enthusiasm waned.[82]

More persuasive has been Michael Schaller's choice of a turning point. In *U.S. Crusade in China* he argues that the American tung oil loan to China in 1938 was a point of departure for a policy of containment of Japan pivoting on China, which in turn set the stage for the containment of Russia at the end of the war. Bradford Lee in his study of British policy in these years takes the same view of the importance of the move: It was America's "first significant intervention in the Asian conflict," though it fell short of the joint loan the British hoped for.[83] In the most extensive study of the tung oil loan, Frederick C. Adams calls it "the first material pressure which the United States government took in its attempt to restrain the post-1937 Japanese expansion and thereby safeguard American interests in China."[84]

This raises a further important issue, namely, whether China, either as market or simply as foe of Japan, was more important than Japan's advance into Southeast Asia in 1940–1941 as a cause of war. Schaller ties the two together. He contends that in 1938 Roosevelt officials developed a "primitive domino theory" holding that loss of China would "undermine the entire Western position right across Southeast Asia and the Pacific." The southward advance confirmed these predictions, and since Japan's ambitions appeared limitless, compromise over China seemed "both immoral and unrealistic."[85]

An alternative view places greater weight on the impact of European developments, in particular German victory in the West in the spring of 1940. This catastrophe precipitated Japan's southward advance, the Axis alliance, and American economic warfare against Japan. American policy toward Japan, in this view, was thereafter less affected by East Asian circumstances than by Roosevelt's grand strategy in forming and sustaining a coalition to defeat Hitler and his allies. Thus it was the coupling of East Asian and world politics in 1940 that finally produced a fundamental American commitment in East Asia.[86]

The extent of misguided diplomacy and policy during the final confrontation remains unclear. R. J. C. Butow's *The John Doe Associates: Backdoor Diplomacy for Peace 1941,*[87] deals exhaustively with the bizarre diplomatic venture of Father Drought and his partners. Their amateur effort so muddied the already murky waters, says Butow, that whatever chance that existed for agreement was destroyed. Dallek dismisses the John Doe Associates with a sentence.[88] More likely to hinder diplomacy were the machinations of regular bureaucrats. Irvine Anderson and Jonathan Utley have both examined the role of the export and monetary control administrators (such as Dean Acheson) during July–August 1941 in tying up all oil shipments to Japan, against the president's intention of only a reduction. Anderson finds "an unguided bureaucracy biased at the working level against liberality to Japan."[89] Nevertheless, the president soon accepted the de facto embargo. The question remains, what if anything guided the president, not the bureaucrats.

Great progress has recently been made in filling the need for studies of British diplomacy in East Asia to match and compare with the American experience. Particularly bountiful has been the decade before Pearl Harbor, with studies by Malcolm D. Kennedy, Bradford Lee, Wm. Roger Louis, Ann Trotter, and Peter Lowe.[90] The reasons for British weakness in the thirties are well known. What is surprising is the extent to which Britain was prepared to adopt a strong policy in defense of its interest in China. The policies of the two governments were more symmetrical than has been assumed, and this parallelism makes the failure of cooperation all the more puzzling.

The interpretation of American China policy during the war depends greatly on one's perspective. In a bilateral framework it does indeed appear, as Schaller argues, that the United States tied itself willy-nilly to Kuomintang fortunes. In the perspective of global strategy, however, as Dallek views it, American involvement remained at a minimum, no greater than necessary to meet the larger requirements of the war. Roosevelt, says Dallek, was eager to keep the Japanese fighting in China and to "avoid the blow to Allied morale from a Chinese collapse." He also appreciated "the extraordinary grip China held on American opinion." The people saw China as "untainted by communism or imperialism, a victim rather than a practitioner of power politics . . . a natural democratic ally." The president did what he could to boost Chinese morale, "feeding illusions about her status and emphasizing long-term gains." He believed it was impossible to impose American habits on China. Intervention might "precipitate political collapse, force China out of the war, and destroy plans for Japan's defeat." He hoped to win China's goodwill, expecting that ultimately China would indeed be a great power, say twenty-five to fifty years in the future.[91]

When Roosevelt gave in to Chiang on the issue of Stilwell's command of Chinese forces, "he essentially gave in on pushing the Chinese into effective action." Fresh assurances from Stalin and transPacific gains made China less important from the military point of view. Finally, Roosevelt chose to work through the Russians, seeking to persuade Moscow to urge a coalition government on Yanan. He rejected Ambassador Hurley's proposals for a meeting with Chiang and Mao because there was no evidence that it would produce an agreement.[92]

Piecing the Dallek interpretation together in this fashion suggests

that Roosevelt placed greater emphasis on winning the war and securing American public commitment to the war and an internation-
ist peace than on any long-range value China might have for the
United States. This conclusion is consistent with a string of others
stretching back through the era delimited by the two Roosevelts. Together they suggest a minimalist hypothesis respecting American East
Asian policy which, if confirmed, would add coherence to the middle
period and perhaps further distinguish it from the cold war years that
followed.

NOTES

1. Griswold, *The Far Eastern Policy of the United States* (1938; reissued, New Haven:
Yale University Press, 1962). See also Dorothy Borg, comp., *Historians and American Far
Eastern Policy* (New York: East Asian Institute, Columbia University, 1966). My essay deals
broadly with the political and economic historiography of American–East Asian relations in the
1900–1945 period, but it does so primarily through works published since 1970. For earlier
scholarship, see the relevant essays in Ernest R. May and James C. Thomson, Jr., eds., *American–East Asian Relations: A Survey* (Cambridge: Harvard University Press, 1972).

2. *America's Response to China: An Interpretive History of Sino-American Relations,* 2d
ed. (New York: Wiley, 1980).

3. (New York: Oxford University Press, 1979).

4. (New York: Wiley, 1975).

5. *Across the Pacific: An Inner History of American–East Asian Relations* (New York:
Harcourt, Brace, World, 1967).

6. *Ibid.*, p. xvi.

7. (Chicago: University of Chicago Press, 1951).

8. (Ithaca: Cornell University Press, 1958).

9. Harrington, *God, Mammon and the Japanese: Dr. Horace N. Allen and Korean-American Relations, 1884–1905* (Madison: University of Wisconsin Press, 1944).

10. Beard, *The Idea of the National Interest* (New York: Macmillan, 1934).

11. (New York: Dell, 1962).

12. Thomas J. McCormick, *China Market: America's Quest for Informal Empire, 1893–
1901* (Chicago: Quadrangle, 1967).

13. Ronald Robinson and John Gallagher, *Africa and the Victorians* (Garden City, N.Y.:
Doubleday, 1968), p. 8; Gallagher and Robinson, "The Imperialism of Free Trade," *Economic
History Review,* 2nd ser., 6 (1953).

14. (New York: Columbia University Press, 1979).

15. Feis, *The China Tangle: The American Effort in China from Pearl Harbor to the
Marshall Mission* (Princeton: Princeton University Press, 1953); Tsou, *America's Failure in
China, 1941–1950* (Chicago: University of Chicago Press, 1963).

16. (East Lansing: Michigan State University Press, 1973).

17. Schaller, *U.S. Crusade*, p. 304.

18. (New York: Columbia University Press, 1980).

19. Lloyd C. Gardner, Walter F. LaFeber, and Thomas J. McCormick, *Creation of the American Empire* (New York: Rand McNally, 1973).

20. *The Roots of American Foreign Policy* (Boston: Beacon Press, 1969).

21. *Special Business Interests and the Open Door Policy* (New Haven: Yale University Press, 1951).

22. Levin, *Woodrow Wilson and World Politics* (New York: Oxford University Press, 1968); Israel, *Progressivism and the Open Door: America and China, 1905–1921* (Pittsburgh: University of Pittsburgh Press, 1971).

23. Wallerstein, *The Modern World System* (London: Academic Press, 1974); Walter Goldfrank, ed., *The World System of Capitalism: Past and Present* (Beverly Hills, Calif.: Sage Publications, 1979); Terence K. Hopkins and Immanuel Wallerstein, *Processes of the World System* (Beverly Hills, Calif.: Sage Publications, 1980). See also Paul Baran, *The Political Economy of Growth* (New York: Monthly Review Press, 1957). An example of the multinational and comparative framework is Perry Anderson, *Lineages of the Absolutist State* (London: Humanities Press, 1974).

24. Frank, *Latin America: Underdevelopment or Revolution* (New York: Monthly Review Press, 1969); James D. Cockcroft, A. G. Frank, and Dale L. Johnson, *Dependence and Underdevelopment: Latin America's Political Economy* (Garden City, N.Y.: Anchor, 1972).

25. (Cambridge: Cambridge University Press, 1977).

26. Carl Riskin, "East Asia and the World Economy," *Bulletin of Concerned Asian Scholars*, 10 (July–Sept. 1978).

27. *The Origins of the Korean War: Liberation and the Emergence of Separate Regimes, 1945–1947* (Princeton: Princeton University Press, 1981).

28. "The Open Door and the Rise of Chinese Nationalism: American Policy and China, 1917–1928" (Ph.D. diss., University of New Mexico, 1977).

29. *Big Business in China: Sino-Foreign Rivalry in the Cigarette Industry, 1890–1930* (Cambridge: Harvard University Press, 1980).

30. "Americans in the China Market: Economic Opportunities and Economic Nationalism, 1890s–1931," *Business History Review*, 51 (Autumn 1977), 295.

31. *Ibid.*, 281–84, 291–98.

32. "Principles and Profits: Standard Oil Responds to Chinese Nationalism, 1925–1927," *Pacific Historical Review*, 41 (Nov. 1977).

33. *The Standard-Vacuum Oil Company and the United States East Asian Policy, 1933–1941* (Princeton: Princeton University Press, 1975).

34. Hunt, "Americans in the China Market," 285–89.

35. *The Essence of Decision* (Boston: Little, Brown, 1971).

36. *Power in the Pacific: The Origins of Naval Arms Limitation, 1914–1922* (Chicago: University of Chicago Press, 1976).

37. "The Role of the Department of State," in Dorothy Borg and Shumpei Okamoto, eds., *Pearl Harbor as History: Japanese-American Relations, 1931–41* (New York: Columbia University Press, 1973), pp. 81–106.

38. E. J. Kahn, Jr., *The China Hands: America's Foreign Service Officers and What Befell Them* (New York: Viking, 1971); Joseph W. Esherick, ed., *Lost Chance in China: The World War II Despatches of John S. Service* (New York: Vintage, 1975); John S. Service, *The Amerasia Papers: Some Problems in the History of U.S.–China Relations* (Berkeley: University of California Press, 1971); Anthony Kubeck, *The Amerasia Papers: A Clue to the Catastrophe*

of China, U.S. Senate Committee on the Judiciary, 91st Cong., 1st Sess. (2 vols.; Washington, D.C.: U.S. Government Printing Office, 1979); John Paton Davies, Jr., *Dragon by the Tail* (New York: Norton, 1972); John K. Emmerson, *The Japanese Thread: A Life in the Foreign Service* (New York: Holt, Rinehart & Winston, 1978); Gary May, *China Scapegoat: The Diplomatic Ordeal of John Carter Vincent* (Washington, D.C.: New Republic, 1979); Kenneth E. Shewmaker, *Americans and Chinese Communists, 1927–1945* (Ithaca: Cornell University Press, 1971); O. Edmund Clubb, *The Witness and I* (New York: Columbia University Press, 1974).

39. *"Lessons" of the Past: The Use and Misuse of History in American Foreign Policy* (New York: Oxford University Press, 1973).

40. Dorothy Borg and Waldo Heinrichs, eds., *Uncertain Years: Chinese-American Relations, 1947–1950* (New York: Columbia University Press, 1980), p. 6.

41. Joseph De Rivera, *The Psychological Dimension of Foreign Policy* (Columbus: Ohio State University Press, 1968); Irving L. Janis, *Victims of Groupthink* (Boston: Houghton Mifflin, 1972); Robert Jervis, *Perception and Misperception in International Politics* (Princeton: Princeton University Press, 1976); John Steinbrunner, *The Cybernetic Theory of Decision* (Princeton: Princeton University Press, 1974).

42. "Culture and Power: International Relations as Cultural Relations," *Diplomatic History,* 3 (Spring 1979).

43. (Cambridge: Harvard University Press, 1981).

44. *The Chinese Connection: Roger S. Greene, Thomas W. Lamont, and George E. Sokolsky and American-East Asian Relations* (New York: Columbia University Press, 1978).

45. Both in Michel Oksenberg and Robert Oxnam, eds., *Dragon and Eagle: United States-China Relations, Past and Future* (New York: Basic Books, 1978), pp. 54–106.

46. Noel H. Pugach, *Paul S. Reinsch: Open Door Diplomat in Action* (Millwood, N.Y.: KTO Press, 1979); May, *China Scapegoat;* Russell D. Buhite, *Patrick J. Hurley and American Foreign Policy* (Ithaca: Cornell University Press, 1973); Dmitri Lazo, "An Enduring Encounter: E. T. Williams, China, and the United States" (Ph.D. diss., University of Illinois, 1978); Richard Dean Burns and Edward M. Bennett, eds., *Diplomats in Crisis: United States-Chinese-Japanese Relations, 1919–1941* (Santa Barbara, Calif.: ABC-Clio Press, 1974); Russell D. Buhite, "The Open Door in Perspective: Stanley K. Hornbeck and American Far Eastern Policy," in Frank J. Merli and Theodore Wilson, eds., *Makers of American Diplomacy: From Theodore Roosevelt to Henry Kissinger* (New York: Scribners, 1974).

47. *The Limits of Foreign Policy: The West, the League, and the Far Eastern Crisis of 1931–1933* (London: Hamish Hamilton, 1972) and *Allies of a Kind: The United States, Britain, and the War Against Japan, 1941–1945* (New York: Oxford University Press, 1978).

48. *The Rhetoric of Empire: American China Policy, 1895–1901* (Cambridge: Harvard University Press, 1968).

49. "The Open Door and Integrity of China, 1899–1922: Hazy Principles for Changing Policy," in Thomas H. Etzold, ed., *Aspects of Sino-American Relations Since 1784* (New York: New Viewpoints Press, 1978).

50. Cohen, *America's Response to China,* p. 52.

51. "The American Remission of the Boxer Indemnity: A Reappraisal," *Journal of Asian Studies,* 31 (May 1972); Richard H. Werking, "The Boxer Indemnity and the Hunt Thesis," *Diplomatic History,* 2 (Winter 1978).

52. "The Forgotten Occupation: Peking, 1900–1901," *Pacific Historical Review,* 48 (Nov. 1979).

53. Esthus, "1901–1906," and Neu, "1906–1913," in May and Thomson, eds., *American-East Asian Relations.*

54. Cohen, *America's Response to China*, p. 67.

55. Neu, "1906–1913," in May and Thomson, eds., *American–East Asian Relations,* pp. 157–58.

56. *Ibid.,* p. 172; Walter V. and Marie V. Scholes, *The Foreign Policy of the Taft Administration* (Columbia: University of Missouri Press, 1970); Ralph Eldin Minger, *William Howard Taft and United States Foreign Policy: The Apprenticeship Years, 1900–1908* (Urbana: University of Illinois Press, 1975).

57. (Cambridge: Harvard University Press, 1972).

58. Hunt, *Frontier Defense and the Open Door: Manchuria in Chinese-American Relations, 1895–1911* (New Haven: Yale University Press, 1973).

59. *Alliance in Decline: A Study of Anglo-Japanese Relations* (London: Athlone Press, 1972).

60. Nish, "Policies Toward Britain," and Akira Iriye, "Policies Toward the United States," in James W. Morley, ed., *Japan's Foreign Policy, 1868–1941: A Research Guide* (New York: Columbia University Press, 1974), pp. 202–205, 421–27.

61. Mayer, *The Political Origins of the New Diplomacy, 1917–1918* (New Haven: Yale University Press, 1959); Levin, *Woodrow Wilson and World Politics.*

62. *China Diplomacy, 1914–1918* (Cambridge: Harvard University Press, 1970).

63. Dignan, "New Perspectives on British Far Eastern Policy, 1913–1919," *University of Queensland Papers* (Jan. 1969); Lowe, *Great Britain and Japan, 1911–1915* (New York: Macmillan, 1969); Gowen, "Great Britain and the Twenty-one Demands: Cooperation versus Effacement," *Journal of Modern History,* 63 (March 1971); Clarence B. Davis, "Limits of Effacement: Britain and the Problem of American Cooperation and Competition on China, 1915–1917," *Pacific Historical Review,* 48 (Feb. 1979); Nish, *Alliance in Decline.*

64. Pugach, *Paul S. Reinsch.*

65. *Vain Endeavor: Robert Lansing's Attempts to End the American-Japanese Rivalry* (Durham, N.C.: Duke University Press, 1962).

66. Curry, *Woodrow Wilson and Far Eastern Policy, 1913–1921* (New York: Bookman Associates, 1957); Li, *Woodrow Wilson's China Policy, 1913–1917* (New York: Twayne, 1952); Fifield, *Woodrow Wilson and the Far East, The Diplomacy of the Shantung Question* (New York: Crowell, 1952).

67. "The United States and Japan, 1913–1921" (Ph.D. diss., University of North Carolina, 1976).

68. "The Open Door and the Integrity of China."

69. *The Chinese Connection,* ch. 2. On Wilson at Paris and East Asia, a recent account is David F. Trask, "Sino-Japanese-American Relations During the Paris Peace Conference of 1919," in Etzold, ed., *Aspects of Sino-American Relations.*

70. *The Chinese Connection,* ch. 5. See also Linda Papageorge, "The United States Diplomats' Response to Rising Chinese Nationalism" (Ph.D. diss., Michigan State University, 1978).

71. *After Imperialism: The Search for a New Order in the Far East, 1921–1931* (Cambridge: Harvard University Press, 1965).

72. *Power in the Pacific.*

73. Widenor, *Henry Cabot Lodge and the Search for an American Foreign Policy* (Berkeley: University of California Press, 1980).

74. Fred L. Block, *The Origins of International Economic Disorder: A Study of the United States International Monetary Policy from World War II to the Present* (Berkeley: University of California Press, 1977), p. 18. See also Joan Hoff Wilson, *American Business & Foreign Policy* (Boston: Beacon Press, 1971).

75. "Cotton Textile Diplomacy: Japan, Great Britain, and the United States, 1930–1936" (Ph.D. diss., Rutgers University, 1977).

76. Arthur F. Sewall, "Pittman and the Quest for the China Market," *Pacific Historical Review*, 44 (Aug. 1975).

77. Borg, *The United States and the Far Eastern Crisis of 1933–1938; From the Manchurian Incident Through the Initial Stage of the Undeclared Sino-Japanese War* (Cambridge: Harvard University Press, 1964).

78. (New York: Oxford University Press, 1979).

79. Akira Iriye, "The Making of a *Realpolitiker,*" *Reviews in American History,* 8 (March 1980).

80. "Franklin D. Roosevelt and a Naval Quarantine of Japan," *Pacific Historical Review,* 40 (May 1971).

81. "Notes on Roosevelt's 'Quarantine Speech,' " *Political Science Quarterly,* 72 (Sept. 1957), and *U.S. and the Far Eastern Crisis,* ch. 13.

82. *Roosevelt,* p. 151.

83. *Britain and the Sino-Japanese War, 1937–1939: A Study in the Dilemmas of British Decline* (Stanford: Stanford University Press, 1973), p. 163.

84. "The Road to Pearl Harbor: A Reexamination of American Far Eastern Policy, July, 1937–December, 1938," *Journal of American History,* 58 (June 1971). See also Adams, *Economic Diplomacy: The Export-Import Bank and American Foreign Policy, 1934–1939* (Columbia: University of Missouri Press, 1976).

85. *U.S. Crusade in China,* pp. 28, 63.

86. Iriye, *Across the Pacific,* p. 201. See also my tape cassette, "The Coming of the Pacific War," in the Michael Glazier series, "Voices of Diplomatic History" (Wilmington, Del., 1980); Jonathan Garrick Utley, "The Department of State, 1937–1941: A Study of the Ideas Behind Its Diplomacy" (Ph.D. diss., University of Illinois, 1970).

87. (Stanford: Stanford University Press, 1974).

88. *Roosevelt,* p. 271.

89. Anderson, *Standard-Vacuum Oil,* p. 178; Utley, "Upstairs, Downstairs at Foggy Bottom: Oil Exports and Japan, 1940–1941," *Prologue: The Journal of the National Archives,* 8 (Spring 1976).

90. Kennedy, *The Estrangement of Great Britain and Japan* (Berkeley: University of California Press, 1969); Lee, *Britain and the Sino-Japanese War;* Louis, *British Strategy in the Far East, 1919–1939* (Oxford: Oxford University Press, 1971); Trotter, *Britain and East Asia, 1933–1937* (Cambridge: Cambridge University Press, 1975); Lowe, *Great Britain and the Origins of the Pacific War; A Study in British Policy in East Asia, 1937–1941* (Oxford: Oxford University Press, 1977). See also Roberta A. Dayer, *Bankers and Diplomats in China, 1917–1925; The Anglo-American Relationship* (London: F. Cass, 1981); Deborah Nutter Miner, "United States Policy Toward Japan, 1941: The Assumption that Southeast Asia Was Vital to the British War Effort" (Ph.D. diss., Columbia University, 1976).

91. Dallek, *Roosevelt,* pp. 328, 329, 388, 389, 390, 391, 490.

92. *Ibid.,* pp. 498–501.

FIVE

Military and Naval Affairs
Since 1900

by ERNEST R. MAY

LOOKING OVER THE last decade's scholarship concerning military and naval aspects of American–East Asian relations, I am struck first of all by the high proportion devoted to very recent events. When pre-1970 work was surveyed at the Cuernavaca conference in early 1970, writings on the then most recent quarter century (1945–1970) seemed comparatively sparse. Work of the 1970–1980 decade seems by contrast to have concentrated on the immediate past, especially on the 1960s.

I am struck secondly by the extent to which the 1970s saw the interwar years, World War II, and the period of Harry Truman's presidency become history as distinct from current affairs. Scholarship shifted from discussion of guilt and innocence to more dispassionate exploration of why events turned out as they did.

Third and most striking of all is the very fact that a survey of writings of the 1970s requires a separate essay on those concerned with military and naval affairs. When the Cuernavaca survey was planned, there did not seem enough such writing to deserve a separate essay. That one seems needed now is testimony to the comparative prominence that military dimensions of the past acquired during the 1970s.

The first characteristic noted—the degree of emphasis on the very recent past—is traceable in part to emotions stirred by the war in Vietnam. Those emotions could have generated only polemics, however, had it not been for the accompanying, partially coincidental success of assaults on some of the barriers to serious research on nearly contemporaneous events. Respect for executive privilege eroded. Information supposed to be kept secret leaked into the press or received unauthorized disclosure elsewhere. Daniel Ellsberg's release in 1971 of the so-called Pentagon Papers, a Defense Department compilation of chronologies and documents concerning the Vietnam War, was the most celebrated case. With the events that led to President Nixon's 1974 abdication, leaks became torrents. Congressional committees probed where they had not probed before, as, for example, into activities of intelligence agencies.[1] The Freedom of Information Act and new executive orders meanwhile facilitated access to thousands of documents that would otherwise have been long kept from public view.

The extent of change between 1970 and 1980 can be illustrated by reference to two books. At the very beginning of the decade a volume by William R. Braisted, Jr., appeared, concerning the United States Navy in the period 1897–1922.[2] In the preface, Braisted writes that his manuscript had been ready for publication in 1966. It did not appear until 1971 because the Office of Naval Intelligence objected to his identifying naval attachés by name or citing their dispatches. The names had, of course, been printed in innumerable diplomatic registers. The danger that a source or an intelligence-gathering method could be compromised by citation in 1966 of a pre-1922 document was, to say the least, slight. Yet Braisted's book only appeared after he agreed to use code-names for attachés and to cite "attaché reports" with no other identifying data.

The contrast in circumstances a decade later is evidenced by William Shawcross's *Sideshow: Kissinger, Nixon, and the Destruction of Cambodia*.[3] Writing of events only eight to ten years in the past, Shawcross could cite previously secret documents pried loose from all parts of the executive branch. He quotes or refers to once top-secret cables exchanged between Washington and the American embassies in Saigon and Pnomh Penh, messages to and from the Joint Chiefs of Staff and military commands in the Pacific and East and Southeast Asia, memoranda sent to the White House from the State and Defense departments and the Central Intelligence Agency, and records of National Security Council subcommittees and of the National Security Council itself. He exhibits little restraint in discussing and naming even clandestine agents of the United States.

To be sure, the availability of evidence concerning very recent events has resulted more often than not merely in polemical works with quotations and footnotes. Some books dealing with the 1960s and 1970s, however, can in varying degrees be classified as scholarship, and their number is larger by an order of magnitude than was the number of scholarly works on the 1950s and 1960s existing at the beginning of the 1970s. Without implying that all omitted titles are mere tracts, I would single out Warren I. Cohen's study of Dean Rusk as secretary of state; general analyses of the Vietnam War by Leslie Gelb and Richard K. Betts, Guenther Lewy, and especially George C. Herring; monographs on diplomatic aspects of the war by Gareth Porter and Allan E. Goodman; and works by Peter Braestrup, Alexander Kendrick, and Herbert Y. Schandler on some of its domestic effects.[4] Cohen's *Dean Rusk* and Herring's *America's Longest War* are *tours de force*. No work on Thomas Jefferson as secretary of state achieves evenhandedness and scholarly detachment comparable to Cohen's on Rusk. No study of the U.S.–Mexican War of the 1840s exhibits fairness and judiciousness comparable to that of Herring on the war in Vietnam.

Work of the 1970s concerning the very recent past deals chiefly with the 1960s and with Vietnam. The 1950s receive very little attention. Writing in 1981 a brief synthetic description of the Eisenhower administration's foreign policies, Robert A. Divine has had to depend largely on memoirs.[5] Monographic literature on the period of Eisenhower's presidency remains almost as skimpy as at the beginning of the 1970s.

The same is true for aspects of American–East Asian relations in the 1960s not related to the war in Vietnam. Practically the only secondary works of enduring interest to historians are Martin E. Weinstein's *Japan's Postwar Defense Policy, 1947–1968* and I. M. Destler's collection of interview-based case studies, *Managing an Alliance*.[6] The latter reconstructs the 1960 negotiations over revision of the security treaty, the arrangements in 1969 for restoration of Japanese control over Okinawa, and the controversies over textile imports at the beginning of the 1970s.

Coverage of very recent history is thus uneven. Nonetheless, it remains noteworthy that the decade 1970–1980 produced so much scholarly work on events so freshly in the headlines.

Still more noteworthy is the second phenomenon mentioned in my prologue—the altered character of writing concerned with the less immediate past, particularly the twenty years or so separating the Manchurian crisis and the Korean conflict. At the Cuernavaca conference Waldo Heinrichs labelled the period 1931–1937 "a hazy interval in world history." Discussing the subsequent four years, culminating in the Pacific War, Louis Morton dealt chiefly with controversy as to whether the Japanese attack on Pearl Harbor had been wittingly provoked by the Roosevelt administration. Though from two quite different perspectives, Jim Peck and Robert Dallek concerned themselves with the question of whether, or to what extent, U.S. policy was to blame for the fact that World War II and its aftermath produced a new China and a long period of American-Chinese hostility. (Their essays were printed just before the Nixon administration's "opening to China.")

In Heinrichs' essay, to be sure, there are clear indications of the turn being taken by historical writing on the early 1930s. He mentions books of the mid- and late 1960s that are not entirely in the stream of earlier controversial literature. Among them are studies by Sadako N. Ogata and James B. Crowley which, in contrast to most previous English-language works on Japanese policy-making, avoid the approach and tone of a war crimes prosecution. Heinrichs also refers to Dorothy Borg's meticulous dissection of U.S. policy-making and, having seen drafts of papers presented at a binational conference held at Lake Kawaguchi, Japan, in 1969, notes what was to be the most important single work of the 1970s, the collection of essays edited by Dorothy Borg and Shumpei Okamoto as *Pearl Harbor as History: Japanese-American Relations, 1931–1941.*[7]

Among the more noteworthy essays in *Pearl Harbor as History* are those by Heinrichs himself on the role of the United States Navy in American-Japanese relations, by Russell F. Weigley on the corresponding role of the War Department and the army, and by Asada Sadao on "The Japanese Navy and the United States."

Heinrichs clinically dissects an American naval officer corps confronted with practical dilemmas and internally divided. One dilemma existed because of the Philippines. The army had more or less steadily maintained that the Philippines could not be defended in the event of war with Japan. As a result, no workable joint plan for operations in the western Pacific had ever been devised. Moreover, in 1934 Congress provided for eventual independence for the islands, thus putting even more in doubt whether the navy should lay plans for fighting in Philippine waters. Yet, as Heinrichs observes, the navy needed a western Pacific mission because it was that mission that underpinned both its building program and its planned force posture. The second, superseding dilemma made its appearance as a result of the outbreak of World War II and the fall of France, for the prospect of Nazi Germany's taking over the French fleet—and possibly the Royal Navy as well—entailed the possibility of an unfavorable balance of naval power in the Atlantic even if the western Pacific were to be abandoned.

Internal differences within the navy concerned operational platforms and administrative structures, pitting pilots and submariners against "black shoe" battleship advocates and, at the same time, seagoing officers against managers in the old-line bureaus. Naval officers also differed over the extent, if any, to which the United States and Britain shared common interests. Just after World War I the services had been torn by dispute between champions of Anglo-American cooperation and proponents of the view that the United States should prepare to fight any foe—including the United Kingdom and the British Commonwealth. By 1940–1941 this had translated itself into the new strategic dilemma, one school holding that the navy should accept the long-held army view and adopt for the Pacific a strategy of holding only the line from Alaska to Hawaii to Panama, a second school contending that the far Pacific was the proper theater for major naval operations, almost regardless of conditions in the Atlantic.

The Japanese Navy, as Asada portrays it, suffered similar splits. It was not the conservative, antiwar force that testimony at the Tokyo war crimes trials had made it out to be. Many officers, to be sure, perceived the relative weakness of Japan as compared with the United States. In one way or another, however, they found a way of rationalizing optimism about the outcome of a conflict. After June 1941 they were presented with dilemmas rising out of the German attack on the Soviet Union. As Asada makes plain, a number of key naval officers reacted by becoming *more* committed to the proposition that the United States was enemy number one and that the Japanese-American struggle could not long be postponed. In part, they were animated by concern lest a campaign against the Soviet Union divert resources from the navy to the army. Meanwhile, like naval officers in the United States, they fought among themselves over the comparative merits of aircraft carriers, submarines, and battleships and of varieties of staff and command arrangements.

Neither Heinrichs nor Asada argues even by implication that there might have been more happy outcomes if the naval staffs had behaved differently. Their quest is to understand these officers in their own terms.

The same detachment characterizes Stephen Pelz's *Race to Pearl Harbor,* which deals with both the American and Japanese navies in the early and mid-1930s. It also characterizes two works by the prodigiously energetic British scholar, Christopher Thorne, *The Limits of Foreign Policy* and *Allies of a Kind.*[8] The first deals only incidentally with the military services. *Allies of a Kind,* on the other hand, is the most comprehensive and richly documented of all studies describing and analyzing the interplay of policy, strategy, and military and naval operations in the Pacific War.

Though Thorne's book draws upon and synthesizes the rich literature previously produced by American, British, and Japanese official historians, it is much more than a summation of that literature. In the first place, it reviews American-British differences over strategy and over the future of the Pacific and East Asia without noticeable partiality for either. Secondly, Thorne brings more clearly into view than has any other scholar the extent to which both American and British thinking about Asia was colored by the assumption of white Anglo-Saxon cultural and intellectual superiority. Thirdly, in the most striking departure from the official canon, *Allies of a Kind* is not an explanation and celebration of an American-British victory. Thorne suggests that, on the contrary, the end of the Pacific War should probably be seen overall as a triumph of the Asian nationalism for which Japan had battled. Amplifying this interpretation of the outcome of the Pacific War is Wm. Roger Louis's remarkably full, careful, and objective account of the crisis of Western colonialism, *Imperialism at Bay*.[9]

A third work setting the Pacific War in a new light is Akira Iriye's *Power and Culture: The Japanese-American War, 1941– 1945*.[10] Saying relatively little about the clashes of navies and armies, Iriye focuses instead on debates concerning war aims and postwar prospects. He brings to light evidence that the spectrum of opinion in Japan was not wholly unlike that in the United States. Many Japanese, inside as well as outside the Tōjō government, viewed the war as serving interests much broader than those of the Japanese state. Some pan-Asianists, writes Iriye, "stressed themes such as regional cooperation, harmony, selflessness, and the subordination of the individal to the community" (p. 5). Opposing them were, among others, exponents of precepts resembling Woodrow Wilson's and champions of a restoration of the Washington system. In the autumn of 1943, Iriye reports, the Japanese government issued a five-point statement of war aims responding to and modelled on the Atlantic Charter. He points out many similarities between debates in Tokyo and concurrent debates in Washington, where concern about postwar security and the postwar economic order also jostled against aspirations for some type of ideal world order.

Though not yet with the sweep and authoritativeness exemplified in the Thorne, Lewis, and Iriye books on World War II, recent writings on "the China tangle" and the background of the American-Chinese war in Korea also suggest new perspectives. In *Uncertain Years: Chinese-American Relations, 1947–1950*, edited by Dorothy Borg and Waldo Heinrichs, Steven M. Goldstein observes that historians of the 1960s challenged "the McCarthyite charge that the State Department 'lost' China because of a strong sympathy with the Chinese Communists with the equally simplistic assertion that the State Department 'lost' China because of its blind hostility to them."[11]

During the 1970s, most writing on wartime and postwar Chinese-American relations fell into one or the other of these interpretive veins. In captivating prose, Barbara Tuchman depicts General Joseph W. Stilwell as having recognized that Chiang and the Kuomintang were corrupt and doomed, that the future of China lay with the Communists, and that the right course for the United States was to court Mao. In a 1972 *Foreign Affairs* article, Tuchman argues that as late as 1949, Mao was receptive to taking some type of Titoist position, aligned with neither the Soviet Union nor the United States, but, she says, Washington rejected his overtures.[12]

Though remaining more or less within the same interpretive framework, some scholarly writing of the 1970s brings to light complexities in the wartime and postwar relationship between the United States and China.[13] *The U.S. Crusade in China, 1938–45* by Michael Schaller exhibits sympathy similar to Tuchman's with the policy attributed to Stilwell. It shows, however, that a variety of opinion existed among Americans in China and that many American military and naval officers in China were partisans of Chiang or others in the Kuomintang and actively opposed any cooperation with the Communists. In *Dilemma in China: America's Policy Debate, 1945,* Kenneth S. Chern assembles evidence of further crosscurrents in Washington, where some officials of the War and Navy departments espoused support of Chiang while others opposed, taking the ground that conflict with the Chinese Communists could lead to conflict with the Russians and thus complicate efforts to stabilize Europe. Though evidencing some regret about the fact, Schaller and Chern make it plain that there was very little favor within American officialdom for even exploring accommodation with the Communists.

Work of the 1970s illuminating the Chinese side of the relationship makes possible a shift toward a new set of questions. One book describes the hitherto ignored activities of Chinese who collaborated with the Japanese. Several analyze internal developments among the Communist Chinese.[14] Laying particular stress on strain between Mao and his generals are James Reardon-Anderson's tightly focused *Yenan and the Great Powers* and the more broad and compendious *The Chinese High Command,* by William Whitson and Chen-hsia Huang.[15]

Indicative of progress beyond the "lost China" vs. "lost opportunity" debate is the whole set of essays in *Uncertain Years.* In one, Nancy Bernkopf Tucker depicts the disarray of the Chinese Nationalists, with various factions working at cross-purposes when trying to capitalize on sympathy in the United States. They had actual and potential allies in the press, in Congress, and especially in the Pentagon, but they were unable to concert a strategy for pulling these allies together. Michael Hunt and Steven Goldstein make it clear that Mao, whether one construes him as more a pragmatist or more an ideologue, had precious little maneuvering room and probably never during the 1940s entertained the notion of pursuing any policy other than one of leaning toward the Soviets.

With regard to the American side of the postwar American-Chinese relationship, the best scholarship of the 1970s turns to the questions of when, how, and why Asia became a theater of the cold war. In two exploratory essays, John L. Gaddis argues that the Korean conflict marked the turning point.[16] Previously, the American government had sought to have in Asia a sharp boundary between the communist and noncommunist spheres. This was the policy advertised in Secretary of State Acheson's famous Press Club speech of January 1950, defining a defense perimeter that excluded Taiwan and all of continental Asia.

Other scholars—most notably, Akira Iriye and William Whitney Stueck, Jr.—see American policy as in a process of change well before June 1950.[17] In Iriye's view, NSC 48/2, a National Security Council paper adopted in December 1949, evidenced the Truman administration's turn to the position that Asia had become a decisive area of competition with the Soviets. Stueck, making use of newly released documents, argues that well before Acheson's Press Club speech, the administration had in fact decided that it could not and would not allow communists to gain control of South Korea, Taiwan, or any part of Southeast Asia. He attributes the change simply to the increasing Manichaeanism manifested contemporaneously in drafts of NSC 68.[18] Iriye, while not discounting the transitory mood of the period, suggests that the United States, from the time of becoming a Pacific power, had been torn between a Chinese and a Japanese orientation. Postwar events forced the choice of Japan as ally. Meanwhile, the success of containment in Europe inspired concern that the Soviets would seek offsetting gains elsewhere, probably in Asia. Thus, Iriye outlines an explanation of American policy largely in terms of the international system within which the United States was the most powerful actor.

The next decade or two ought to see scholarly work on the period 1945–1960 develop much as has work on the 1930s. Research not only in Japan, Taiwan, and Hong Kong but also in Korea, mainland China, and parts of Southeast Asia should yield more and more evidence about Asian perceptions, actions, and policies.[19] Meanwhile, research in records in the United States and Western Europe should permit more detailed mapping of the American side, comparable to that effected for the 1930s by Borg and by contributors to *Pearl Harbor as History*.

There are, however, at least two problems more severe for scholars working on the postwar era than for those studying earlier periods. The first is the central role of the Soviet Union coupled with the extraordinary difficulty of being certain about what was going on within the Soviet government or even what that government was doing. There are almost no certainly authentic documentary sources concerning Soviet foreign policy for any date after the exile of Trotsky. What was going on in Moscow has to be pieced together by methods akin to an archaeologist's from occasional pieces of partisan testimony and from things displayed in public. And much of what was done by Soviet agents comes to light only when one such agent defects or when foreign counterintelligence agencies are lucky. James Reardon-Anderson's convincting reconstruction of debates in Yanan in 1945 could not have been written without the aid of a memoir, published in Bombay in 1974, by Pyotr P. Vladimorov, who was an almost unknown and unnoticed Soviet agent in China in 1943–1945.[20] For most periods and events, scholars will have no comparable sources. They will have to resort to guesswork.

The second problem is a partial counterpart on the Western side. For the 1930s, the sources concerning American policy are abundant but comparatively neatly compartmentalized and, for practical purposes, entirely accessible. Even the MAGIC intercepts have now been published.[21] For the war years, the archives are fuller and more diverse. Historians have to master the filing systems not only of preexisting organizations but of wartime creations such as the Joint Chiefs of Staff and the Office of Strategic Services. Still, a patient and energetic researcher can have some hope of locating and using whatever significant records survive.

For periods or events after the onset of the cold war, historians are not likely at any time in the foreseeable future to have access to all the relevant American records. Part of the problem is the sheer volume of archival material. Given the engagement of planning staffs in the Executive Office, various parts of the State Department, the Defense Department, the Joint Chiefs, each service, the specified commands, the Pacific command, NATO, etc., together with the fact that the whole complex budget process was involved, significant archival data concerning the Eisenhower administration's Indochina policy between 1953 and 1956 (from the war that did not happen to the Diem-Ho election contest that did not take place) probably exceed in volume the entire body of significant archival material concerning American–East Asian relations for the interwar years, 1919–1941.

Another part of the problem is the inaccessibility of some material potentially crucial for interpretation. Of course, there are unrecorded telephone conversations and such, but there have always been unrecorded conversations. The great increase in numbers of stenographers, the mushrooming of staffs, and the advent of the electric typewriter and the tape recorder probably ensure that historians will see more evidence for the 1950s and 1960s than for the 1930s or earlier concerning informal transactions within governments. But what they are likely not to see are pieces of written evidence guarded by special security arrangements—reports from the clandestine services, communications and signal intercepts, reconnaissance photographs, and the like. Answering the traditional question—who knew what when?—will be far more difficult for historians working on the postwar era.

This observation brings me back to the third point made at the outset—the fact that so much writing of the decade of the 1970s has focused on military and naval affairs. The reason is not hard to divine. Trailing slowly behind scholars in disciplines with less time-consuming research methodologies, historians have reacted to the greatly increased prominence of the military establishment in the American government. They have been curious about the background of this development. In some cases, curiosity among Americans has extended to military establishments elsewhere.

As a rule, the implicit question underlying this research has concerned internal developments within the United States or other nations, not interaction between nations or peoples. That question can, however, be posed in comparative form, for one might argue that in the course of the twentieth century the United States and Japan have exchanged attributes. At the outset of the century *the* embodiment of bourgeois antimilitarism, the United States became by the 1960s a prodigiously militarized nation with many—though by no means all— the traits that Harold D. Lasswell ascribed to a "garrison state."[22] Japan meanwhile had an exactly opposite history. Previously a warrior society, it was by the late twentieth century the least militarized of all major powers. The outpouring during the last decade of literature on American military history and, to a lesser extent, on Japanese military history fosters musing on the questions of how and why these changes occurred.

To begin with, a recent body of writing describes the internal evolution of the American armed services through World War II. It depicts with some clarity the genesis and growth of an American navalism not markedly different from navalism elsewhere or from the militarism most conspicuously evident in Imperial Germany and in Japan of the 1930s. Peter Karsten has examined its origins within the consciously professional naval officer corps of the late nineteenth century. Braisted, in the work delayed by ONI clearance requirements, traces efforts by naval officers to influence national policy during the Progressive era. In *Admirals, Generals, and American Foreign Policy, 1898–1914,* Richard Challener deals with the same topic in a wider framework, and Paolo Coletta's biography of Admiral Bradley A. Fiske highlights one of their leaders. Thomas H. Buckley and Roger Dingman have written of the navalists' setbacks in the era of the Washington conference. In his contribution to *Pearl Harbor as History,* Heinrichs describes their recovery of ground as a result of crises of the 1920s. With less specific focus on the Pacific, other scholars have amplified this story and gone on to tell of how the navy made preparations to prevent the new postwar era from being like the last.[23]

What one sees more or less consistently portrayed is a group of senior naval officers who take a dark view of human nature and especially of humans aggregated as nations. These men see international relationships as almost entirely functions of actual or potential

coercive power. They are skeptical about the possibility of cooperative action or mutual concessions except under the lash of fear. Aware
that the majority of civilians share the premises of Locke and Mill
rather than those of Machiavelli and Hobbes, these officers are conscious of being much in a minority. They share a conviction, however, that the civil majority is deluded, and they know as a matter of
fact that if civilians act upon falsely optimistic assumptions, the nation will be helpless when those assumptions are proved false. For
naval forces cannot be conjured up in a sudden emergency; they have
to be planned and ordered years in advance. Faith and knowledge
combine thus to provide these navalists with moral justification for
manipulative behavior—for exaggerating present danger or urgency
in order to bring about preparedness for danger to come.

Even in the most sympathetic of the works mentioned, these
naval officers appear ineffectual. They are ignored or snubbed. Challener (p. 51) quotes a pre-World War I memorandum protesting that
civilian authorities will not disclose to the military establishment
enough information about foreign policies to permit intelligent com-
mentary. And this document dated from 1908 when the "realist,"
Theodore Roosevelt, was president and was unsuccessfully battling
Congress for a large dreadnought construction program. Though Wilson committed himself to "a navy second to none," he never exhibited much trust in his professional naval advisers. In developing the
Washington treaties, Harding and Hughes not only rejected the navy's recommendations but took some pains to keep it in the dark
about their plans. The State Department refused any formal consul-
tation about foreign affairs until 1938, when war in Europe was only
a year away. Not until approximately that time did Franklin Roosevelt, as president, exhibit much interest in professional naval opinion.
Thus, the American naval officer corps reached World War II clas-
sically militarist in disposition but, in general, isolated and without
influence.

For the American army, the picture is quite different. Recent
writings on the army's history before and through World War II describe an institution very much at home in Lockean, laissez-faire,
liberal America. Contradicting legend, Graham A. Cosmas' *Army for
Empire: The United States in the Spanish-American War* portrays the

turn-of-the-century army as, in general, an efficient professional organization.[24] He shows its uniformed leaders bickering with one another and with their civilian superiors. He does not, however, show them to be distinctive in either belief or opinion. With particular reference to Asia, John M. Gates' *Schoolbooks and Kraps: The United States Army in the Philippines, 1898–1902* forcefully underlines this point.[25] Influenced by then-current questions about America's "pacification" efforts in Vietnam, Gates sought to explain the army's comparative success against its Filipino opponents. He argues that "pacification" in the Philippines proceeded in two stages. The first phase involved undertakings in public education and disease control which won over people in settled areas. Faced with this success, the nationalist leader, Aguinaldo, turned to guerrilla tactics and terrorism. The second phase in the American effort involved matching responses—counterintelligence, countersubversion, and counterterror—combined with continued pursuit of the previous policy. Of crucial importance to eventual American victory, argues Gates, was the reelection of William McKinley and the inference drawn therefrom by both American soldiers and Filipinos that the public at home wholeheartedly supported the effort abroad.

Gates portrays the American army as an agent of American progressivism. General Arthur MacArthur insisted that even his most harsh measures were consistent with "the imperishable ideas of Americanism" (p. 199). Hailing surrender of the last guerrillas, President Theodore Roosevelt said that, with "surprisingly few individual exceptions," the army's conduct had been "characterized by humanity and kindness." To the Filipinos it had brought "individual liberty, protection of personal rights, civil order, public instruction, and religious freedom" (p. 265). Though the tone and approach are quite different, Gates' findings are not inconsistent with those in David F. Healy's *The United States in Cuba, 1898–1902: Generals, Politicians, and the Search for Policy,* where the army is characterized as an instrument of "open door imperialism."[26] In neither case is it easy to distinguish the military from the civilian nation as a whole.

This condition appears to have persisted into the 1930s and beyond. Writing of the U.S. Army in *Pearl Harbor as History,* Weigley takes it to task not for being militaristic but for being "apolitical." In fact, he concludes his essay by criticizing army leadership for not seeking a larger role in policy. "The U.S. army contributed to the tragedy of the war," he writes, "not through the bellicose militarism of which popular opinion is so quick to accuse the professional soldier, but through failing to perform consistently its proper duty to acquaint the civil government with the military dimensions of national policy" (p. 188).

Bearing out Weigley's thesis are two major biographies of army leaders, one by D. Clayton James on Douglas MacArthur and one by Forrest Pogue on George C. Marshall.[27] James' study supports Weigley's assertion that the militaristically inclined MacArthur was an isolated figure with only a small coterie sharing his opinions. Marshall, on the other hand, appears to have been the ideal-type of an army general officer and, at the same time, someone entirely in sympathy with the civilian ethos. Two quotations illustrate the point. In the first, Marshall replies to Pogue's question about whether the professional military ought to have a voice in policy. Though speaking in 1957, after he himself had served as a special ambassador and as secretary of state and secretary of defense, Marshall said that, in general, he thought otherwise:

I do not think the military authorities should make any political decisions unless they are instructed accordingly, because the effects are too wide-reaching, there are too many influences involved, and it is quite a question of how much of this would be familiar to the military participants. Also, it must be remembered the military responsibility in operations is very, very large, and it has with it a terrible measure of casualties. I know I was very careful to send Mr. Roosevelt every few days a statement of our casualties. . . . I tried to keep before him all of the time the casualty results because you get hardened to these things and you have to be very careful to keep them always in the forefront of your mind.[28]

The second quotation is from Pogue's interview with John H. Hilldring, whom Marshall during World War II placed in charge of preparing forces for the postwar military governing of Germany and Japan. According to Hilldring, Marshall said to him:

I'm turning over to you a sacred trust and I want you to bear that in mind every day and every hour. . . . We have a great asset and that is that our people, our countrymen, do not distrust us and do not fear us. . . . We are completely devoted, we are a member of a priest-hood really, the sole purpose of which is to defend the republic. We concentrate our time and attention on that subject. That doesn't mean that we don't understand other things, but it simply means that we devote our time and attention exclusively to this. And I don't want you to do anything, and I don't want you to permit the enormous corps of military governors you are in the process of training and that you are going to dispatch all over the world, to damage this high regard in which the professional soldiers in the Army are held by our people. . . .[29]

There could hardly be a sharper contrast than that between a Marshall and a prototypical militarist.

After World War II conditions changed. In the first place, there was now an air force concerned, like the navy, about the lead time required for preparedness. Secondly, memories of Pearl Harbor and Hiroshima, together with the development of a hostile relationship with the Soviet Union, elevated the intensity of this concern not only among professional sailors and airmen but among a much larger public.

Like writings on postwar American foreign relations in general, writings on American–East Asian relations indicate the very large increase in the influence of the military establishment as compared with the prewar era. Gaddis' two essays on China policy illustrate the point. The first, published in 1977, draws primarily on State Department documents, for the relevant *Foreign Relations* volumes had recently appeared. The second, issued in 1980, draws upon a large body of source material opened via the Freedom of Information Act and related executive orders. It shows the Joint Chiefs, the services, and elements of the Far East Command as major actors in the development of policy. Partly because of the origin of the Pentagon Papers but partly also reflective of reality, the history of American–Southeast Asian relations in the 1960s has thus far been reconstructed chiefly in terms of interplay among the White House, the military establishment, and paramilitary components of the Central Intelligence Agency.

In the postwar United States, the military, of course, has not intervened in politics as did the Japanese military in the 1930s. At the end of the 1940s and again in the mid- and late 1950s, periods when presidents were putting fiscal considerations far ahead of preparedness, some military leaders did seek to build congressional and public coalitions that would frustrate their commander-in-chief. The B-36/supercarrier controversy and allegations of a ''bomber gap'' and a ''missile gap'' were among the results. And army officers were as active as any others. Generals Matthew Ridgway, Maxwell Taylor, and James Gavin actively and publicly campaigned to overturn decisions by President Eisenhower on army force levels.[30] Such activity was, however, a far cry from the plotting that occurred among Japanese soldiers in prewar years. Nonetheless, the American military establishment as a whole obviously became significantly more militaristic and more influential after World War II.

It is even more obvious that Japan's postwar military establishment is pronouncedly different from that of the prewar era. It has commanded a much smaller share of Japanese resources and has been much less conspicuous in Japanese public life. The standard explanation begins with the occupation and strong American encouragement of demilitarization, including provisions in the Japanese constitution placing limits on the Self-Defense Force. It then attributes to Japanese public opinion a profound and continuing antimilitarist bent and to Japanese political leaders pragmatic recognition that the United States was prepared to defend Japan and that Japanese resources could therefore be invested more profitably in economic development.[31] Weinstein's historical survey adds only the point that Japanese political leaders saw more reason to be concerned about internal security than about external attack and designed the Self-Defense Forces accordingly.

Other historical literature of the 1970s enriches the explanation. Dingman's study of the origins of the Washington system, Pelz's *Race to Pearl Harbor,* and Asada's essay in *Pearl Harbor as History* establish almost beyond doubt that the Japanese Navy was as thoroughly militaristic as the army. These writings make it clear that almost no Japanese senior officer, whatever his service, was free of some responsibility for Japan's engagement in World War II.

In *Power and Culture,* Iriye underlines the point that the Japanese armed services assumed full responsibility for the conduct of the war. Even with General Tōjō as prime minister, the army's supreme command guarded its independence of any political control. As a result, the military clearly bore blame for the reverse of 1944–1945 and such calamities as the fire bombing of Tokyo and the devastation of Hiroshima and Nagasaki. The only action that was an exception was the actual surrender, effected by the emperor in spite of strong opposition from the officer corps. Histories of Japan before and during the war thus point to one reason why opposition to militarism became so vigorous in subsequent Japanese life.

By mirror effect, the writings on Japan suggest hypotheses explaining the contrary trend in the United States. The conspicuous role given the chiefs of staff by FDR meant that they, together with field commanders such as Eisenhower, MacArthur, and Nimitz, issued from the war with primary credit for the victory. The depression and the New Deal had previously undermined public confidence in one of the traditional national leadership groups, the business and financial elite. A general cultural trend had simultaneously eroded the influence of the clergy. There was a vacuum waiting to be filled, and, in the anxious period following the war, the military fitted the opening better than did any other group.

All this is, of course, speculation. Historical writing of the past decade has called attention to the fact that, in both the United States and Japan, the roles of military and naval establishments have undergone transformations. Items high on the agenda for historians writing in the next decade must be, first, further exploration of the effects of these changes and, second, efforts to explain why the changes occurred.

NOTES

1. Especially 94th Congress, 2nd session, U.S. Senate, Select Committee to Study Governmental Operations with Respect to Intelligence Activities, *Final Report* (April 23, 1976). Book 4 provides a detailed administrative history of the CIA from 1946 to 1975.

2. *The U.S. Navy in the Pacific, 1897–1922* (Austin: University of Texas Press, 1958–1971), 2 vols.

3. (New York: Simon and Schuster, 1979).

4. Cohen, *Dean Rusk* (Totowa, N.J.: Cooper Square Publishers, 1980); Gelb, with Betts, *The Irony of Vietnam: The System Worked* (Washington, D.C.: Brookings, 1979); Lewy, *America in Vietnam* (New York: Oxford University Press, 1978); Herring, *America's Longest War: The United States and Vietnam, 1950–1975* (New York: John Wiley and Sons, 1979); Porter, *A Peace Denied: The United States, Vietnam, and the Paris Agreement* (Bloomington: Indiana University Press, 1975); Goodman, *The Lost Peace: America's Search for a Negotiated Settlement of the Vietnam War* (Stanford: Stanford University Press, 1978); Braestrup, *Big Story: How the American Press and Television Reported and Interpreted the Crises of Tet 1968 in Vietnam and Washington,* 2 vols. (Boulder, Colo.: Westview Press, 1977); Kendrick, *The Wound Within: America in the Vietnam Years, 1945–1974* (Boston: Little, Brown, 1974); Schandler, *The Unmaking of a President: Lyndon Johnson and Vietnam* (Princeton: Princeton University Press, 1977). Wallace J. Thies, *When Governments Collide: Coercion and Diplomacy in the Vietnam Conflict, 1964–1968* (Berkeley: University of California Press, 1980) is also comparatively clinical, as is James Clay Thompson's analysis of the U.S. bombing campaign: *Rolling Thunder: Understanding Policy and Program Failure* (Chapel Hill: University of North Carolina Press, 1979).

5. *Eisenhower and the Cold War* (New York: Oxford University Press, 1981).

6. Weinstein, *Japan's Postwar Defense Policy, 1947–1968* (New York: Columbia University Press, 1971); Destler et al., *Managing an Alliance: The Politics of U.S.-Japanese Relations* (Washington, D.C.: The Brookings Institution, 1976). One might add J. H. Kalicki's *The Pattern of Sino-American Crises: Political Military Interactions in the 1950s* (New York: Cambridge University Press, 1975), though it is designed more as a contribution to social scientists' debates than as historical reconstruction.

7. Ogata, *Defiance in Manchuria: The Making of Japanese Foreign Policy, 1931–1932* (Berkeley: University of California Press, 1964); Crowley, *Japan's Quest for Autonomy: National Security and Foreign Policy, 1930–1938* (Princeton: Princeton University Press, 1966); Borg, *The United States and the Far Eastern Crisis of 1933–1938: From the Manchurian Incident through the Initial Stage of the Undeclared Sino-Japanese War* (Cambridge: Harvard University Press, 1964); Borg and Okamoto, eds., *Pearl Harbor as History: Japanese-American Relations, 1931–1941* (New York: Columbia University Press, 1973).

8. Pelz, *Race to Pearl Harbor: The Failure of the Second London Naval Conference and the Onset of World War II* (Cambridge: Harvard University Press, 1974); Thorne, *The Limits of Foreign Policy: The West, the League, and the Far Eastern Crisis of 1931–1933* (New York: G. P. Putnam's Sons, 1972); Thorne, *Allies of a Kind: The United States, Britain, and the War Against Japan* (New York: Oxford University Press, 1978). Indicative of the level of Thorne's approach is the fact that he cites the numerous operational histories of the war far fewer times than he cites E. L. Woodward, *British Foreign Policy in the Second World War*, 5 vols. (London: H.M.S.O., 1970–1976) and Norman Gibbs et al., *Grand Strategy*, 6 vols. (London: H.M.S.O., 1956–1976), from the British official histories, and Maurice Matloff and Edwin L. Snell, *Strategic Planning for Coalition Warfare, 1941–1942* (Washington, D.C.: Office of the Chief of Military History, 1953), Maurice Matloff, *Strategic Planning for Coalition Warfare, 1943–1944* (Washington, D.C.: Office of the Chief of Military History, 1959), and Louis Morton, *Strategy and Command: The First Two Years* (Washington, D.C.: Office of the Chief of Military History, 1962), from the American official histories.

9. (New York: Oxford University Press, 1977).

10. (Cambridge: Harvard University Press, 1981).

11. Goldstein, ''Chinese Communist Policy Toward the United States: Opportunities and

Constraints, 1944–1950,'' in Borg and Heinrichs, eds., *Uncertain Years: Chinese-American Relations, 1947–1950* (New York: Columbia University Press, 1980), p. 235.

12. Tuchman, *Stilwell and the American Experience in China, 1911–1945* (New York: Macmillan, 1971); Tuchman, "If Mao Had Come to Washington: An Essay in Alternatives," *Foreign Affairs*, 51 (Oct. 1972). Complementing Tuchman's book is Russell Buhite, *Patrick J. Hurley and American Relations with China* (Ithaca, N.Y.: Cornell University Press, 1973). Defending Chiang and attacking Stilwell is Chin-tung Liang, *General Stilwell in China, 1942–1944: The Full Story* (New York: St. John's University Press, 1972).

13. Schaller, *The U.S. Crusade in China, 1938–45* (New York: Columbia University Press, 1979); Chern, *Dilemma in China: America's Policy Debate, 1945* (Hamden, Conn.: Archon, 1980). Schaller has also written a more general study, *The United States and China in the Twentieth Century* (New York: Oxford University Press, 1979).

14. John H. Boyle, *China and Japan at War, 1937–1945: The Politics of Collaboration* (Stanford: Stanford University Press, 1972) deals with the collaborators. Among noteworthy recent works on Communist China are Jonathan R. Adelman, *The Revolutionary Armies: The Historical Development of the Soviet and the Chinese People's Liberation Armies* (Westport, Conn.: Greenwood, 1980); Jacques Guillermaz, *A History of the Chinese Communist Party* (New York: Random House, 1974); James P. Harrison, *The Long March to Power: A History of the Chinese Communist Party, 1921–1972* (New York: Praeger, 1972); Suzanne Pepper, *Civil War in China: The Political Struggle, 1945–1949* (Berkeley: University of California Press, 1978); and Richard C. Thornton, *China: The Struggle for Power, 1917–1972* (Bloomington: University of Indiana Press, 1973).

15. Reardon-Anderson, *Yenan and the Great Powers: The Origins of Chinese Communist Foreign Policy 1944–1946* (New York: Columbia University Press, 1980); Whitson and Huang, *The Chinese High Command: A History of Communist Military Politics, 1927–1971* (New York: Praeger, 1973).

16. "Korea in American Politics, Strategy, and Diplomacy, 1945–1950," in Yonosuke Nagai and Akira Iriye, eds., *The Origins of the Cold War in Asia* (New York: Columbia University Press, 1977), pp. 277–98, and "The Strategic Perspective: The Rise and Fall of the 'Defensive Perimeter' Concept, 1947–1951," in Borg and Heinrichs, eds., *Uncertain Years*, pp. 61–118.

17. Iriye's views are developed in *Origins of the Cold War*, pp. 378–407 and 429–36; his separate book, *The Cold War in Asia* (Englewood Cliffs, N.J.: Prentice-Hall, 1974); and his "The United States in Chinese Foreign Policy," in William J. Barnds, ed., *China and America: The Search for a New Relationship* (New York: New York University Press, 1977), pp. 11–52. Stueck's book is *The Road to Confrontation: American Policy Toward China and Korea, 1947–1950* (Chapel Hill: University of North Carolina Press, 1981).

18. See Samuel F. Wells, Jr., "Sounding the Tocsin: NSC 68 and the Soviet Threat," *International Security*, 4 (Fall 1979).

19. Robert R. Simmons, *The Strained Alliance: Peking, Pyongyang, and the Politics of the Korean Civil War* (New York: The Free Press, 1975) offers one construction of fragments on the Asian side of the Korean conflict; Okonogi Masao offers another in "The Domestic Roots of the Korean War," in Nagai and Iriye, eds., *Origins of the Cold War*, pp. 299–320. Bruce Cumings is producing a more extensive study.

20. Vladimirov, *The Special Region of China, 1943–1945* (Bombay: Allied Press, 1974).

21. U.S. Department of Defense, *The "Magic" Background of Pearl Harbor*, 8 vols. (Washington, D.C.: U.S. Government Printing Office, 1977–1978). The printed intercepts

commence in February 1941; earlier intercepts, going back to 1938, are on microfilm (Washington, D.C.: University Publications of America, 1979).

22. Lasswell, *National Security and Individual Freedom* (New York: Columbia University Press, 1950), pp. 23–49. See Samuel P. Huntington, *The Soldier and the State* (Cambridge: Harvard University Press, 1957), pp. 346–50.

23. See Karsten, *The Naval Aristocracy: The Golden Age of Modern Navalism* (New York: The Free Press, 1972); Challener, *Admirals, Generals, and American Foreign Policy, 1898–1941* (Princeton: Princeton University Press, 1973); Ronald Spector, *The Professors of War: The Naval War College and the Development of the Naval Profession* (Washington, D.C.: U. S. Government Printing Office, 1977); Spector, *Admiral of the New Empire: The Life and Career of George Dewey* (Baton Rouge: Louisiana State University Press, 1974); Coletta, *Admiral Bradley A. Fiske and the American Navy* (Lawrence: University of Kansas Press, 1979); Buckley, *The United States and the Washington Conference, 1921–1922* (Knoxville: University of Tennessee Press, 1970); Dingman, *Power in the Pacific: The Origins of Naval Arms Limitation, 1914–1922* (Chicago: University of Chicago Press, 1976); Robert G. Albion, *Makers of Naval Policy, 1789–1947* (Annapolis: Naval Institute Press, 1980); Kenneth J. Hagan, ed., *In Peace and War: Interpretations of American Naval History* (Westport, Conn.: Greenwood Press, 1977); and Coletta, *The United States Navy and Defense Unification, 1947–1953* (Newark: University of Delaware Press, 1981).

24. (Columbia: University of Missouri Press, 1971).

25. (Urbana: University of Illinois Press, 1971).

26. (Madison: University of Wisconsin Press, 1963).

27. James, *The Years of MacArthur,* 2 vols. (Boston: Houghton Mifflin, 1970–   ); Pogue, *George C. Marshall,* 3 vols. (New York: Viking, 1963–   ).

28. Pogue, *George C. Marshall,* vol. 3, p. 316.

29. *Ibid.,* pp. 458–59.

30. See particularly Samuel P. Huntington, *The Common Defense* (New York: Columbia University Press, 1961); Edward A. Kolodziej, *The Uncommon Defense and Congress, 1945–1963* (Columbus: Ohio State University Press, 1966); and Adam Yarmolinsky, *The Military Establishment: Its Impacts on American Society* (New York: Harper and Row, 1971).

31. See James E. Auer, *The Postwar Rearmament of Japanese Maritime Forces 1945–1971* (New York: Praeger, 1973) and John K. Emmerson and Leonard A. Humphreys, *Will Japan Rearm? A Study in Attitudes* (Stanford: Stanford University Press, 1973); Herbert P. Bix, ''Japan: The Roots of Militarism,'' in Mark Selden, ed., *Remaking Asia: Essays on the American Use of Power* (New York: Pantheon, 1974), pp. 305–61, and Harold Hakwon Sunoo, *Japanese Militarism, Past and Present* (Chicago: Nelson-Hall, 1975) argue that the condition is transitory or illusory or both.

SIX

The United States and China Since 1945

by WARREN I. COHEN

IT IS THE wont of diplomatic historians to hover over the archives and to dive into each newly opened mass of documents. Our work, therefore, tends to concentrate in that span of time, thirty or so years ago, to which the combined machinations of archivists, foreign service officers, and budget-cutters have failed to deny us access. In the last decade most of the documentary evidence for the Truman era has become available and—as the pages of *Diplomatic History* make abundantly clear—this is the era on which the most work is being done. The study of Chinese-American relations since 1945 fits comfortably into this pattern.

Historians are also studying the foreign relations of the United States during the years of the Eisenhower presidency. Not least have they probed the mind and rhetoric of John Foster Dulles. Little, however, has been written about policy toward China. Nonetheless, important insights are emerging. The Kennedy and Johnson presidencies have received considerable scholarly attention and an unusually large amount of documentary material has become available early, thanks to Daniel Ellsberg and his friends, and to the Freedom of Information Act. Vietnam has been the focus of most attention, but the outline of policy toward China is becoming clear. For the 1950s and 1960s, historians have learned to use such government procedures as mandatory review and freedom of information to obtain documentary evidence without waiting for new issues in the *Foreign Relations* series or the opening of large blocs of material. They have also found oral history interviews of great value. Not even an antihistorical management of government archives can dampen the present-mindedness of diplomatic historians.

But a line must be drawn somewhere. For the Nixon, Ford, and Carter years—the decade of the 1970s—we have but a few trickles of documentary evidence, and a torrent of Kissinger. This is an era too early to discuss except perhaps as a guide to those who will take up the torch for us in 1990.

When Tsou Tang published *America's Failure in China, 1941– 1950,*[1] documentary evidence, other than the *White Paper,* was not available. Oral histories were scarce and of little value. Memoirs of key participants—Dean Acheson and George Kennan, for example— had not yet appeared. When Tsou wrote, the key historical event was Chinese intervention in Korea, presumably proving Chinese Communist enmity toward the United States and the threat China posed to American interests in East Asia. He wrote as a Chinese who did not share Marshall, Acheson, and Kennan's perception of the relative unimportance of China. He wrote as an anticommunist Chinese whose family was also alienated from Chiang Kai-shek and the dominant faction within the Kuomintang. China was worth saving from both the communists and Chiang Kai-shek.

Tsou was critical of foreign service officers, specifically John S. Service and John Paton Davies, for believing that the Chinese Communists could be weaned away from Moscow, for believing CCP professions of friendship for the United States. He assumed that while communist parties might differ in their internal policies, in international affairs their attitudes would be the same. Tsou was critical of the United States for its unwillingness to use force to achieve its ends in China: "Any policy based upon a refusal to intervene militarily in the Chinese civil war would have been doomed to failure."[2] Aware of Chiang's deficiencies, the deficiencies of the Kuomintang government, Tsou was persuaded that the United States could have obtained the necessary reforms and created a viable noncommunist regime.

By the late 1960s neither Tsou's diagnosis nor his prescription was acceptable. The Sino-Soviet split had existed for a decade. American scholars, appalled by events in Vietnam, rejected notions of monolithic communism and disparaged the idea that the United States could use its power to reform corrupt and repressive regimes and prop them up as barriers to native communist forces. As American power proved bankrupt in Vietnam, the idea that it might have worked in China was manifestly absurd. A new generation of historians, rather than condemning Service and Davies for naivety, praised them for their foresight and brooded about the "lost chance" to have befriended the Chinese Communists in the Truman era. Whereas the killing of Americans by Chinese Communists during the Korean War had provoked charges of treason against these and other foreign service officers critical of Chiang, the war in Vietnam begged a reversal of that judgment. Indeed, some argued, had Truman and his advisors listened to Service and Davies, the conflicts in Korea and Vietnam might have been avoided or so limited as to have saved scores of thousands of American lives and the lives of millions of Asians. The Korean War had produced a political climate conducive to one set of assumptions and questions. The Vietnam War resulted in a very different climate in the 1970s.

Other developments in the 1970s underscored the trend toward assuming that opportunities for American cooperation with the Chinese Communists had been cast aside in the 1940s. The Kissinger and Nixon trips to the People's Republic, resulting in the Shanghai Communique and photographs of friendly contacts between American and Chinese leaders, suggested a resumption of the warmth that had existed in Yanan in 1945. Hadn't Mao Zedong and Zhou Enlai wanted to come to Washington in 1945? Hadn't Chinese leaders always wanted that American connection? Hadn't Zhou always had his hand extended toward friendship with the United States? Rapprochement healed the wounds of Korea, led to questions about old assumptions, and took even Tsou Tang to the streets of Beijing.

In addition to the "lessons" of Vietnam and rapprochement, writing in the 1970s was affected by access to an enormous amount of new documentary evidence. The files of the Department of State and the papers of key participants became available. An unusual source, the papers of V. K. Wellington Koo, ambassador of the Republic of China to the United States, 1946–1954, was opened to scholars—providing rare insight into the behavior of his government. The floodgates had been raised.

Much of the writing about the Truman administration's relations

with China focused on the "lost chance" issue. Many analysts argued in considerable detail about the substance of Truman's policy
toward China and the reasons for it, particularly the role of the "China
Lobby." Others have offered more impressionistic accounts of Chinese
Communist policy toward the United States.

The story begins with the resignation of Ambassador Patrick J.
Hurley in November 1945, which forced Truman and his advisors to
consider the consequences of civil war in China. They viewed the
situation in that country as linked to the adversary relationship developing between the United States and the Soviet Union. Soviet troops
were lodged in Manchuria and Stalin's desire for North China was
assumed. In addition, one contender in the Chinese struggle was a
communist party, presumably linked to Moscow. The unstable situation in China in a context of increasing Soviet-American tension,
highlighted by the flash of Hurley's resignation, resulted in the appointment of George Marshall, one of the most prestigious men in
America, to lead a mission to China.

Martin J. Sherwin has argued that Truman merely continued a
policy toward China designed by Roosevelt to contain communism.
Indeed, Sherwin argues that the containment policy for which Kennan and the Truman administration are generally credited or blamed
began in China with Roosevelt's determination to create a stable anti-
Soviet government under Chiang Kai-shek. Although there is widespread agreement that many Americans, including Roosevelt, assumed a postwar competition for power between the United States
and the Soviet Union—as Sherwin demonstrates in *A World
Destroyed*[3]—few would agree that China was central to Roosevelt's
plans for coping with Stalin's fears and ambitions. The evidence,
including Roosevelt's attitude toward Chiang and his arrangement with
Stalin at Yalta, will not stand the strain. An attractive alternative is
posed by Akira Iriye's stress on the Yalta agreement as a plan for
world order including a division of spheres in East Asia. Roosevelt
accepted Soviet demands on Manchuria and Outer Mongolia, allow-
ing the Russians to reestablish themselves as the dominant power in
Northeast Asia. In return, the Soviet Union conceded American hegemony in the Pacific and over Japan. The two countries would cooperate to maintain an equilibrium between them in China—which

would be friendly to both. Similarly, John Gittings argues that the United States simultaneously rejected Chinese Communist overtures—such as Mao's request for an invitation to Washington—while soliciting and obtaining Soviet cooperation in China. Neither Iriye nor others who question the Sherwin approach have any illusions about American altruism toward China. Most would accept the argument of Gabriel and Joyce Kolko that the United States wanted a China strong and independent, and susceptible to American influence.[4]

The question of Roosevelt's legacy to Truman neatly reveals the change in climate. No longer is Roosevelt defended against charges that he sold out to the communists. In the 1970s he was more likely to be accused of starting the cold war—with the defense quite happily pointing to Roosevelt's quest for partnership with the Soviet Union. Least likely was the charge that he neglected American interests.

When Truman became president, a wide range of problems took precedence over China. Nonetheless, American intervention on behalf of Chiang's government began immediately at the end of the war, as American forces facilitated Kuomintang control of strategic points in China. Hurley's resignation forced attention to these activities, Soviet activities in Manchuria, and the looming civil war in China. Kenneth S. Chern has demonstrated how the administration, in its zeal to silence Hurley, prevented a careful airing of policy toward China.[5] Instead, Marshall left for China in December 1945 to determine how American interests could be served best—starting with the assumption that a civil war, which would allow the Soviets to consolidate their hold on Manchuria and perhaps expand into North China, was to be avoided.

As the archives opened, the Kolkos' claim that Marshall was sent to China by a government committed to Chiang Kai-shek and that he sought to mediate a conflict in which he favored the Kuomintang against the Communists was sustained. Iriye suggests that the United States was extending its influence into China proper, beyond limits understood by the Yalta signatories, and finds Marshall "subtly redefining the Yalta framework" to accommodate this American thrust. Steven I. Levine's important study of the Marshall Mission provides a new focus.[6] He argues that although mediation failed, Marshall's primary purpose was to contain the Soviet Union, and he was therefore successful. Levine contends that Marshall was sent because Truman and his advisors feared Soviet intentions in China, especially in Manchuria. When Marshall ascertained that the Soviets were not actively engaged in the civil war in China, that they were withdrawing their forces from Manchuria, the importance of mediation declined. As the containment strategy evolved in Washington, there seemed no need to apply it to China. China was of no danger to anyone, "a backwater of marginal geopolitical importance."

Clearly, by the 1970s historians were less hesitant to call attention to U.S. efforts to extend its influence and to protect its interests even when these required intervention in the internal affairs of another state. Levine stresses lack of impartiality as a major reason for Marshall's failure to avert civil war in China. Arguments about the extent of Soviet involvement in that struggle gave way to arguments about the extent of and reasons for American interference.

The United States continued to support the Kuomintang government after Marshall left China and despite Marshall's contempt for that regime. Tsou and an earlier generation of analysts were likely to ask why American aid was limited and inadequate. In the 1970s historians were asking why there had been any aid at all. Why had the United States persisted in wasting aid on a government in whose survival it had little faith? And as the United States extricated itself from the war in Vietnam, Ernest R. May asked how the United States had succeeded in staying out of China.[7]

Scholars are agreed that the United States did not want the Chinese Communists to win the civil war, but there is also general acceptance of the idea that the limits of American power precluded open-ended support of Chiang when China ranked low among American priorities. The Kuomintang regime was not deemed vital to American security. But Russell Buhite argues that officials in Washington had developed a new category of interests between "vital" and "peripheral"—"major" interests—and that China was one of them. Not important enough for unlimited support, China was too important to abandon. Total withdrawal was unacceptable. William Whitney Stueck's work stresses a concern for "credibility" in American policy toward both China and Korea from 1947 to 1950. This idea is shared by John Feaver, who focuses more sharply on aid to the Kuomintang in 1947 and 1948. Both Stueck and Feaver find in the Department of State a great concern for assuring European nations that the United States would not shirk the use of its power, as in the interwar period. There would be no "retreat to isolationism." The world had to expect the United States to act, to aid its friends and punish its enemies. What happened in China was less important than the lessons other nations would draw from American action there. To young scholars weaned on Dean Rusk's explanation for American action in Southeast Asia, the perceived need to demonstrate credibility was striking.[8]

May, Buhite, and John Lewis Gaddis all note that the Pentagon was more disposed to act in Chiang's behalf than was the Department of State.[9] May draws striking parallels between military analyses of the Chinese and Vietnamese revolutions and of military assurances of success based on small-scale intervention. He also notes that outside the Office of Far Eastern Affairs, opinion in the State Department resembled that of the military. Marshall was preoccupied in 1947 with European affairs, the military and the Wedemeyer Mission pressed for aid to the Kuomintang, Chiang's friends stirred up Congress and the media, and "piecemeal decisions set an apparent trend toward all-out aid to the Nationalists." May demonstrates that Americans in the field were just as optimistic in China in the 1940s as in Vietnam in the 1960s. But in a taut eight-page analysis he explains the difference, and why American troops stayed out of the Chinese civil war. By examining why the disaster in Vietnam occurred, May offers insight into what happened—or did not happen—in 1947 and 1948.

A turning point came in November 1948 when Marshall and his advisors recognized that a Chinese Communist victory was impending. The Soviet Union clearly had played a minor role in the war. Tito's split with Stalin earlier in the year allowed for doubt that all communists would be the pliant tools of the Kremlin. Perhaps China could be prevented from becoming "an adjunct of Soviet power." It was time to separate the United States from a doomed Kuomintang regime, and to attempt to divide Soviet from Chinese communists, while seeking an accommodation with the latter.

Nonetheless, aid to Kuomintang China continued in 1949. Par-

ticipants have explained prolonged support for the forces of Chiang
Kai-shek as a necessary response to pressures from Congress and the
public, generally attributed to the machinations of the "China lobby."
Historians have been responsive to this argument, as witnessed by
the subtitle of Lewis McCarroll Purifoy's book, *Harry Truman's China
Policy: McCarthyism and the Diplomacy of Hysteria, 1947–1951.*
Ross Y. Koen, in his classic *China Lobby in American Politics,* readily available only in 1974, sees his subject as responsible for decisions to aid China in 1947 and 1948, as well as later. On the other
hand, the Kolkos and Walter LaFeber have denied that the Truman
administration's policy was forced on it by Congress, the public, or
any lobby. They insist that Truman and his advisors followed their
own counsel.[10]

For the period 1947–1948 there can no longer be any doubt that
the Kolkos and LaFeber are correct. Levine and Stueck demonstrate
clearly that Truman and both his civilian and military advisors saw
the Chinese Communists as an extension of Soviet power and were
determined to block their expansion to the maximum extent possible
with limited resources. Although Chiang was not widely esteemed in
Washington and although most of Truman's advisors gave higher
priority to Europe, the administration aided Kuomintang China because, as Buhite suggests, China was also important—and they hoped
to deny it to the communists. The China lobby was of negligible
importance.

For 1949 and 1950 the picture is a little cloudier. The Kolkos'
argument that by the spring of 1949 no one of importance in Washington believed that elimination of the Chinese Communists was possible or worth the effort would not likely be challenged by any scholar.
But the Kolkos perceive no interest on the part of the Truman administration in accommodation with the People's Republic. That part of
their argument can no longer be taken seriously. Writers across a
broad ideological spectrum, including Harold Hinton, Franx Schurmann, and myself, have found ample evidence that the Department
of State, despite what Hinton calls "articulate Republican opposition," was preparing for recognition of the People's Republic of
China.[11] In my essay "Acheson, His Advisers, and China, 1949–
1950," I conclude that Acheson ignored the advice of his subordi-

nates, the pressures of the Pentagon, antiadministration forces in Congress, and the efforts of the China lobby, to pursue a policy of salutary neglect on the Asian mainland. He was contemptuous of Chiang, disdainful of public opinion, and angered by lobbying efforts. Why, then, did the United States not come to terms with Mao's government?

I argue that fear of public and congressional opinion did obstruct Acheson's efforts to reach an accommodation with Beijing. Nancy Bernkopf Tucker provides the most valuable analysis of interest group activities.[12] Acheson may have been confident of his ability to ignore Congress and the public, but President Truman was not. On several critical occasions, Truman overruled Acheson and prevented steps that might have led to early normalization of Chinese-American relations. Both Hinton and Schurmann, however, stress Chinese actions as responsible for Acheson's failure. Hinton, generally a harsh critic of the Chinese Communists, contends that "calculated mistreatment of American diplomatic and consular personnel then remaining in China" ended State Department consideration of recognition.[13] Schurmann, generally more critical of the United States, contends that Mao's visit to Moscow and the resulting alliance undermined Acheson. But Schurmann argues that Mao yielded to Stalin's demands because he took American machinations in Taiwan more seriously than he did contrary signals from Washington. Robert G. Sutter also sees Acheson working for rapprochement with the Chinese Communists but finds no interest among the latter in improving relations with the United States in 1949.[14]

One result of much of the work of the 1970s is reduction of the importance of the China lobby as an influence on policy from 1947 to 1950. Most analysts—with the notable exception of Purifoy—have found American policymakers moved by their own perception of what was happening in China, its significance for the United States, and their rationally conceived estimates of what could and should be done. But there were clearly restraints that prevented Acheson from acting exactly as he wished, when he wished. Bureaucratic rivalry, most obviously with the Pentagon, was one such restraint. Another, which needs more careful attention, was the political advice the president was getting from the White House staff. There is little evidence of the kind of power struggle between the secretary of state and the palace guard that has become common of late, but we do know that Clark Clifford and others were able to overrule Marshall on policy toward Palestine. Why did Truman, generally so responsive to Acheson, back away from some of his recommendations on China? Were pro-Chiang lobbyists, unable to reach the secretary of state, as successful with the White House staff as they were with the secretary of defense?

Questions about American policy toward Taiwan (Formosa) seem to have been resolved insofar as 1949 is concerned, but Buhite has posed an interesting question relative to the decision to intervene again in 1950, at the outset of the Korean War. Documentary evidence available in the 1970s indicates without doubt that there was widespread agreement in the American government about the strategic value of the island. John Gaddis has noted that the Department of State wanted to deny the island to the Kuomintang as well as to the Communists. Kennan at one point suggested using American troops to throw Chiang out and seize the island for the United States—as Teddy Roosevelt might have done! I have found Acheson interested in the Taiwan independence movement, willing to work with it covertly if there was a chance of success. When he realized Chiang's friends were entrenched, however, he prepared to abandon the island. He feared American involvement on the island would deflect Chinese attention from Soviet involvement in Manchuria, Mongolia, and Xinjiang. In any event, Chiang would inevitably muck up Taiwan as he had the mainland, and there was little point in volunteering for that albatross.

Despite greater interest in Taiwan on the part of the Pentagon—and General Douglas MacArthur in Tokyo—the National Security Council decided early in December 1949 that the United States would not use force to defend the island. The Central Intelligence Agency estimated that the Communists would invade in the summer of 1950 and that the island would fall to them by December. Acheson was prepared to move on, but, as Gaddis Smith and John Gaddis show, Secretary of Defense Louis Johnson and MacArthur were able to reopen the issue and never gave up, despite Truman's continued support for Acheson's position.[15] Buhite explains that as the Communists approached victory on the mainland, Taiwan became a "major interest" in the minds of military leaders and key members of Acheson's staff. John Gaddis argues that "at no point during 1949 and 1950 was Washington prepared to acquiesce in control of the island by forces hostile to the United States *and* capable of taking military action against other links to the offshore island chain."[16] The United States could tolerate Chinese Communist control of the island, provided there was no Soviet pressure.

All through the spring of 1950, after the signing of the Sino-Soviet pact, Dean Rusk and John Foster Dulles urged Acheson to reconsider policy toward Taiwan, but without apparent success. Buhite argues that the fact that Acheson had not recommended a commitment to Taiwan derived more from bureaucratic inertia than from a different assessment of the situation. An overt policy change would require some sort of a shock: "Korea was more the occasion for U.S. intervention in Taiwan than the reason for it."[17] I found Acheson leaving the door open to a policy change *if* an independent Taiwan emerged that might appear as a showcase of democracy, but adamantly opposed to an attempt to rescue Chiang. Although the Sino-Soviet pact had been a serious setback for his policy, Acheson was still thinking in terms of accommodation with the People's Republic, eager to have the civil war—and Chiang—out of the way. Nonetheless, the possibility remains that pressure for a new policy conditioned Acheson's response when the Korean War started. Others would argue that Truman and Acheson had been compromised by the outbreak of war in Korea and were reacting to protect themselves against Chiang's friends. Allen Whiting suggests that Acheson was trapped by bureaucratic compromise; that he had been willing to grant Chiang's friends and the Pentagon words about the importance of Taiwan (in which he did not believe) so long as he could prevent a commitment to the island.[18] When the war came he was confronted by his own words and forced to concede that the island had to be denied to hostile forces.

Much of the recent discussion of policy in 1949–1950 leans implicitly on Graham Allison's models of analysis, focusing on policy as the result of bureaucratic politics.[19] Tensions are perceived between the Pentagon and the Department of State, within the department and the Pentagon. Policies are formulated that may or may not relate directly to the problem, but which suffice to gain support of the disparate elements that must be won over before anything can be done. Judging by the results, Rube Goldberg rather than George Kennan is the model policy planner. Unquestionably, awareness of bureaucratic politics enables the analyst to solve otherwise unanswerable puzzles and allows for infinitely more sophisticated explanations. No one would argue, however, that the Allison models obviate the need to study traditional concerns, such as the role of public opinion, ideology, or special interests.

To the evidence that Acheson and his colleagues resisted the importuning of the China lobby, Nancy Tucker adds useful explanation.[20] Examining the efforts of Chiang's government to win support in the United States, she finds it plagued by factionalism that inspired contempt among Americans. If the Kuomintang could not unite even in the face of pending disaster, how could it be worthy of aid? As Koen and I show, the China lobby was not a monolithic force, but rather a hodgepodge of individuals and groups with little in common except opposition to American policy.[21] Tucker demonstrates that not even those elements presumably representing the Chinese government could be harnessed for a common effort. So much for the China lobby.

Analysis of the Chinese Communist side is hampered by the absence of equivalent documentation. Nonetheless, there is a wealth of information available for the 1940s. Mao's writings, CCP newspapers and periodicals, and documents captured by the Kuomintang during the civil war provide at least as much material as that available to Kremlinologists. Scholars who have worked with these materials agree on the basic outline of Chinese Communist attitudes toward the United States. Mao and his colleagues seemed friendly, interested in ties with the United States during World War II. They became increasingly less friendly in the postwar years, choosing to side with the Soviet Union against the United States in the cold war, allying with the Soviet Union early in 1950, and attacking American forces in Korea later that year.

Tsou Tang argued that Americans were naive to see CCP professions of friendship as anything but tactical. Mao and his followers were communists and there was never any question but that they would support the Soviet Union in international affairs. In the late 1960s I argued that Stalin's betrayal of the CCP in 1945 created an "open historical situation" in which CCP mistrust of the Soviet Union provided a possible opportunity for the United States to bid for friendship with the Chinese Communists.[22] It seemed clear that the bid was never made, and Mao was left no choice but to take whatever terms Stalin was willing to offer.

In the 1970s the evidence was richer and the arguments more sophisticated. There was even awareness of possible disagreements among CCP leaders. But the lines of division have remained the same. Was there an opportunity for early rapprochement between the United States and the Chinese Communists? Were the Chinese ideologically committed to the Soviet Union or were they responsive to American actions? A reconciliation of the two positions does seem imminent, however.

John Gittings and Michael H. Hunt have made the best cases for a pragmatic Mao, flexible in his policies, determined to exploit contradictions between the Soviet Union and the United States for the benefit of China. Gittings readily concedes that the Chinese Communists entered World War II with an ideological commitment to the Soviet Union and suspicion of the United States. He concedes that Mao's warmth toward the United States during the war was largely tactical. Mao's foreign policy, like that of all national leaders, consisted of tactics designed to serve the interests of his country. But experience with Americans did modify CCP attitudes, as did disappointments in Soviet behavior, some of which dated back to the 1920s. Mao and other Chinese leaders were not blind ideologues. They responded to the reality of American and Soviet actions. When Mao's request for an invitation to Washington was denied, when Hurley promised all aid to the Kuomintang, when the United States intervened in the Chinese civil war to help Chiang, it was all too clear that CCP overtures to the United States had been rejected. As Whitting has said, Mao had reason to fear Stalin, but he also had reason to hate American imperialism. Gittings suspects that there was opposition to Mao's occasional overtures to the United States, but he concludes that most Chinese hoped for less than complete alignment with the Soviet Union.[23]

Hunt focuses more sharply on Mao and concludes that he was less interested in an American connection than was Zhou Enlai but was willing to suspend ideological judgments and respond rationally to the situation. While Hunt concedes that the People's Republic would inevitably align with the Soviet Union, he sees the real issue as the one Zhou posed for Marshall: how far the PRC leaned toward the Soviet Union depended on the United States. Hunt also makes good use of the work of Nancy Tucker and Warren Tozer, who demonstrate respectively that the Communists were strikingly tolerant of American missionaries and businessmen in China.[24]

The best argument for the overriding effect of ideology on Chinese Communist attitudes toward the United States and the Soviet Union are presented by Okabe Tatsumi and Steven M. Goldstein.[25] Okabe concludes that ideological attachment to the Soviet Union overwhelmed any consideration of economic and political advantages that might accrue from turning to the United States. The Chinese Communists viewed the Soviet Union as qualitatively different from other nations. Nothing the United States did could have changed that situation. Apparently the Soviet Union had not yet done enough to undermine that ideological attachment.

Goldstein's argument is more complex. He does not deny the possibility of early rapprochement, but stresses the ideological restraints on both sides. In the context of the cold war, of capitalist America versus communist Soviet Union, Mao—like other communists—saw his place at Stalin's side. Goldstein nonetheless concedes that the CCP gave up on the United States for good reason, given American aid to the Kuomintang regime. Focusing more on the possibility of rapprochement in 1949 and 1950, he argues that the CCP had stressed anti-Americanism in its propaganda campaign, and that it was difficult to reverse course so quickly. Noting the work of James Reardon-Anderson,[26] Goldstein argues that rank-and-file communists were more hostile to the United States than were party leaders. There were, therefore, too many restraints on the leadership for easy overtures toward the Americans.

Buhite, Levine, and Donald Zagoria also carefully examine the idea of a lost chance in China.[27] All three focus on 1949 and rely more than others on perceptions of Soviet policy. Buhite argues emphatically against the idea that the United States might have weaned China away from alliance with the Soviet Union. His principal argument is that the People's Republic could not respond to the United States because of Soviet pressures. He contends that Moscow was fearful of Titoism and willing to use its leverage in Manchuria and its proponents within the CCP leadership to keep the People's Republic distant from the United States. More so than Hunt, Buhite takes the Zhou-Keon demarche seriously, but claims Zhou retreated under Soviet pressure. In this context, the Chinese could not have obtained American aid without incurring Stalin's wrath.

Zagoria perceives similar Soviet pressures on the People's Republic, but he insists that Mao was looking for an escape from Stalin's embrace, a counterweight to exclusive dependence on the Soviet Union, that Mao and Zhou wanted diplomatic and economic relations with the United States, and that the United States did not oblige. Zagoria also shares Buhite's sense that domestic political reasons—public pressures—explain at least in part the failure of the United States to respond.

Levine, however, offers an interesting synthesis that suggests how little really divides those who argue both sides of the "lost chance" debate. He contends that Mao and his comrades were communists who, despite some dissatisfaction with Stalin's policy, were by no means so alienated as to be able to conceive of allying with the United States against the Soviet Union in the cold war. They had hoped to work with both the United States and the Soviet Union in the continuation of the Grand Alliance envisaged at Yalta. Once that hope was shattered and the cold war took its place, the Chinese Communists aligned with and received important aid from the Soviet Union. They would have liked formal contact and trade with the United States as well. Chinese alliance with the Soviet Union was not an act of desperation, but the only alternative given an apparently hostile United States.

If one defines rapprochement in 1949 or 1950 in terms of diplomatic relations between Beijing and Washington and the development of a modest trade in nonstrategic items, the arguments are readily reconciled. None of the writers is contending that Sino-Soviet tensions were anything like those that developed after 1959, or that a Chinese-American alliance against the Soviet Union was possible in 1949 or 1950. No one is contending that the Chinese were such fanatic ideologues that they were uninterested in contacts with the West. China could not be weaned from the Soviet Union, but relations with China like those enjoyed with the Soviet Union—or Germany in the 1930s—were certainly feasible. On the other hand, such relations were not easily obtained because of Soviet apprehensions and pressures, ideological considerations, and internal political difficulties in both Washington and Beijing. In short, intense hostility that mounted after Korea was not inevitable, but the complex international situation—and the complex domestic situation in both countries—required leaders in both to move slowly and carefully. With the coming of war in Korea, time ran out on them.

What is different in the analysis that emerged in the 1970s is awareness that both Chinese and American leaders were interested in and groping uneasily toward accommodation. More sophisticated understanding of Chinese communism, based largely on Chinese revelations in the 1960s and 1970s, points toward recognition of policy differences among Chinese leaders, as well as the nature of the Sino-Soviet link. Greater understanding of the bureaucratic process, as well as more insight into the minds of key leaders, permits us to read between the lines of stated American policy. Better tools and more evidence suggest a consensus on the "lost chance" question that is likely to endure.

The Chinese side, both Kuomintang and Communist, still requires more detail. Documentation for the Kuomintang is available in the Koo collection, which contains everything but Chiang's innermost thoughts, and some insight into those as well. The Chinese Oral History Project at Columbia contains material of great value. It is not inconceivable that in the next decade we will obtain more evidence from the archives of the People's Republic as we commence our cooperation with scholars from that country. Discussions of an oral history project already have begun in Beijing. On the American side, the last frontier is the White House and the search for an explanation for those occasions when Harry Truman overruled Dean Acheson.

When we turn to the Eisenhower administration, the problems are markedly different, as we wait for Divine Providence—or those who presume to speak in its name—to provide us with the documents. We are still trying to determine what the policy of Eisenhower and Dulles toward China was, trying to separate rhetoric from reality. But we know enough now to sketch the main outlines of the Eisenhower era.

One obvious starting point is a reminder that the idea that Eisenhower and Dulles reversed American policy toward Taibei and Beijing is a partisan myth. For all the hostility Acheson and Truman undoubtedly felt toward Chiang Kai-shek, they were responsible for the reintervention of the United States into the Chinese civil war during the first year of the war in Korea. They were the ones who decided to shield Taiwan from a communist invasion, to step up aid to the Kuomintang regime and to cooperate with it in covert operations against the People's Republic. It was their assistant secretary of state who referred to Mao's China as a "Slavic Manchukuo." The branding of China as an aggressor by the United Nations was engineered by the Truman administration. In brief, the Eisenhower administration inherited a policy of increasing support for Chiang's regime in the context of war with the People's Republic.[28]

Once the background and context are recalled, it is no longer necessary to find the devils that drove John Foster Dulles. Dulles' belief that Asia deserved more attention had been shared by Rusk and many, if not most, of Acheson's advisors before the Korean War. Acheson had accepted it, however reluctantly, in 1951. More attention did not mean, however, primary attention. Dulles, like Rusk, was a universalist, but he did not doubt the primacy of European affairs. Eisenhower's focus remained Europe throughout his life. According to Robert A. Divine, he was "ill at ease dealing with Asia."[29] War in Asia, however, required even the most Euro-centered of American leaders to divert their attention across the Pacific.

Between Eisenhower's election in November 1952 and his inauguration, Chiang tried to commit Eisenhower and Dulles to more active support of his cause, including a willingness to provide whatever was necessary to permit a successful counterattack on the mainland. Eisenhower was noncommital, of course. Dulles was quite specific: The United States was not interested in going to war. The Eisenhower administration sought a peaceful settlement with the Soviet bloc. Dulles mistrusted Chiang and did not attempt to disguise that fact from Chiang's foreign minister or ambassador. Indeed, he kept Taibei at arm's length for two years before agreeing to a mutual defense treaty—and even then imposed terms that infuriated the Kuomintang leader. One biographer, Michael Guhin, argues that Dulles was aiming not at the destruction of the Chinese Communist regime, but rather at separating it from the Soviet Union. Similarly, Robert Donovan contends that Eisenhower's goal was to divide the People's Republic and the Soviets. This goal and Dulles' tactic of labeling Mao's followers as tools of the Kremlin were clearly carry-overs from the policies of the Truman administration. Eisenhower's thoughts are more difficult to discern, but Chiang's friends could see little change in policy between that of Truman and that of Eisenhower.[30]

And yet in his State of the Union message in February 1953, Eisenhower "unleashed" Chiang Kai-shek to attack the mainland. Dulles and especially his assistant secretary for Far Eastern affairs, Walter Robertson, frequently called for the collapse of the communist regime. What was policy, what was rhetoric, and why?

Eisenhower's announcement that the Seventh Fleet would no longer protect the Chinese Communists from Kuomintang attacks is generally recognized as part of administration strategy for ending the war in Korea. Donovan argues that Eisenhower did not want an invasion of the mainland, but rather was threatening the PRC should it persist in Korea. Neither Dulles' sympathetic sister Eleanor[31] nor his unsympathetic cousin Foster Rhea would disagree. Chiang's government had not been consulted before the announcement and his representatives were not happy with the explanations they received.

A disheartened Ambassador Karl Lott Rankin in Taibei was forced to tell Chiang to rein in his expectations, to take no offensive action without consulting the senior American military officer present. Worried about how Chiang might respond, the administration delayed delivery of the first jets to his air force until assurances were received. As J. H. Kalicki notes, the administration had to tell Taibei's representatives to hold back because it was not prepared to support concretely an attack on the mainland. The Chinese were told that if their raids against the People's Republic brought an attack on Taiwan, the United States would provide air and sea cover, but no troops. Offshore islands in Kuomintang hands were not included in the protective umbrella. Ambassador Koo noted in his diary on March 13, 1954: "Practically no one in the U.S. government favors an attack on the mainland for the purpose of recovering it to our control. . . ." Moreover, Dulles was insisting that Kuomintang troops in Burma be withdrawn to Taiwan. Acheson had also spoken of the problems caused by these troops, but Koo found Dulles much more insistent. And finally, Chiang's people were told not to expect increased aid in 1953—the new Congress was economy-minded, seeking retrenchment.[32]

Schurmann suggests that the Eisenhower administration's unleashing of Chiang came in the form of intensified covert warfare against the Chinese Communists. There seems no doubt that this was true, but Foster Rhea Dulles notes that covert operations had begun in the Truman era. He contends that "unleashing" did not increase Kuomintang military capability. Quantitative information on the numbers and size of raids is not yet available, and it is not clear whether the raids after January 1953 were more worthy of being labelled "massive" than those before.

The matter of rhetoric is less easily resolved. Foster Rhea Dulles insists that John Foster was not surrendering to the China bloc, "for he basically shared its ideas." He contends that the secretary and Robertson thought alike and were convinced that Mao was a Soviet puppet. He finds in John Foster Dulles a "sense of almost personal resentment" against the Chinese Communists for destroying what he had perceived to be enduring ties of friendship between prerevolutionary China and the United States. Guhin, on the other hand, stresses domestic political pressures. Public hostility to the People's Republic after Chinese had killed thousands of Americans in Korea precluded recognition or any other steps toward accommodation. Stanley D. Bachrack demonstrates the greatly expanded base of the so-called China lobby in the early 1950s. Important liberals had signed on with the Committee of One Million, including Paul Douglas, Hubert Humphrey, Jacob Javits, and Eugene McCarthy. Resolutions hostile to the

People's Republic were passed in the Senate by unanimous votes. The year 1953 was still the era of Joe McCarthy, and many of his friends and attitudes survived his censure in 1954. Fred Greenstein, in a persuasive analysis of Eisenhower's style of leadership, contends that Dulles was "assigned the 'get tough' side of foreign policy enunciation, thus placating the fervently anticommunist wing of the Republican Party."[33]

There is no doubt that hostility toward the Chinese Communists was widespread and intense in the early 1950s. The question that remains is whether these public attitudes or congressional attitudes or lobbying activities forced Eisenhower and Dulles to do anything other than that dictated by their own ideology or predilections. In terms of policy, the answer is almost certainly "no." In terms of public education, the answer may be different—and of consequence. If, by pandering to attitudes associated with the China lobby, the Eisenhower administration's public pronouncements and behavior—such as Dulles' refusal to accept Zhou's hand at Geneva—provided confusing signals to the Chinese government, the existing potential for easing tensions was squandered. To the extent that fear of American intentions forced Chinese dependence on the Soviet Union, Dulles' threats were counterproductive. Still, while all might agree that Dulles' rhetoric did no good, the harm it did is not easily documented or measured.

Once the Korean War ceased to be an issue between China and the United States, questions emerged about China's role in Indochina. Few scholars doubt that Chinese aid to the Viet Minh was important. Fewer still would argue that the Chinese were ever the driving force behind the Viet Minh. Foster Rhea Dulles claims, however, that Eisenhower thought they were, and it seems clear that the administration was fearful of large-scale Chinese intervention in late 1953 and early 1954. Guhin, Richard Goold-Adams,[34] and Kalicki, among others, agree that massive retaliation was designed to deter the Chinese—a deliberate hint of irrationality calculated to worry Mao and his advisors. The Chinese, of course, had other, excellent reasons for staying home. The Korean War had been costly for them and they were eager to concentrate their limited means on the reconstruction of their country. Nonetheless, apprehension about the

American response very likely reinforced the disinclination to inter-vene—a disinclination further strengthened by the success of the forces the Chinese supported.

Kalicki offers an important observation about the American de-cision not to intervene in Indochina in 1954. He notes that ultimately, ideological anticommunism did not determine the American re-sponse. The desire to contain, even roll back communism, was abun-dantly present in Washington, but it was not allowed to override practical considerations, such as a possible Chinese response, as in Korea, or the absence of British and congressional support. The es-timate of China's action was rational rather than ideological. The surprise with which this revelation strikes Kalicki indicates the extent of Dulles' success at persuading the world of the irrationality of his East Asian policy.

After the Eisenhower administration acquiesced in what some critics called a "Far East Munich"—the Geneva Accords of 1954—Dulles moved quickly to shore up the Free World's position. Ever since NATO had been conceived, the idea of a Pacific treaty organi-zation had been bandied about. The Truman administration had not been much tempted, but it did agree to a bilateral arrangement with the Philippines and the ANZUS pact in 1951 as a way of soothing friends uneasy about Washington's plans for Japan. In March 1953 Chiang's ambassador raised the possibility of a mutual defense pact between Taibei and Washington. Dulles said then—and his aides re-peated for many months afterward—that it was a good idea in prin-ciple, but there were *so* many problems: it was very difficult to have such a treaty with a country in the midst of civil war. Soon Chiang learned that Dulles planned to create a Southeast Asia Treaty Orga-nization (SEATO), from which his government would be excluded. Chiang was furious, his friends were furious, but, as Roderick MacFarquhar suggests, there was to be no Washington-Taibei pact until Mao, Zhou and the People's Liberation Army inadvertently came to Chiang's rescue.[35]

In August 1954 Zhou spoke sharply of a Washington-Taibei plot to attack the People's Republic. Several weeks later, with Dulles in Manila to sign the SEATO pact, mainland batteries began the heavy bombardment of the Kuomintang-held island of Chinmen (Quemoy),

a few miles from the coast. Thus began the first crisis over the offshore islands. There is widespread agreement that the People's Republic was responding to a reasonably perceived threat. SEATO was
designed, indisputably, as an anti-Chinese alliance. American military aid to Taiwan had increased in 1954 and Chiang had apparently
strengthened his garrisons on the islands and stepped up raids. Hinton
suggests that the Kuomintang islands also interfered with Beijing's
efforts to expand its trade in Southeast Asia, but, no less than Gittings or Edward Friedman[36] or Schurmann, he insists that the shell-
ing of Chinmen was not evidence of CCP aggressiveness. He finds
Communist troop dispositions at the outset of the crisis to be defensive. Others, such as Kalicki, MacFarquhar, and Robert Sutter, stress
PRC dissatisfaction with SEATO and fear that the United States was
preparing to incorporate Taiwan into its alliance system. Interest-
ingly, only Foster Rhea Dulles, the Americanist, for all his criticism
of Washington's actions, argues that the People's Republic was seeking to test America's will in the area.

Several scholars focus on the offshore islands as the place where
Beijing could press the United States most effectively—the area in
which American imperialism seemed most vulnerable. In the absence
of diplomatic relations, unable to discuss fears and grievances, the
People's Republic acted as the British had in Canton in 1839—it
resorted to use of force to gain attention and bring about negotiations.
Gittings suggests that Zhou sought to reduce tension in the strait by
temporarily raising it. Kalicki suspects that Beijing underestimated
Chiang's willingness to defend the islands.

Ambassador Rankin has confirmed scholarly speculation on the
fears of Eisenhower and Dulles that Chiang would try to draw the
United States into war. One of the kinder things Foster Rhea Dulles
says about his cousin is that John Foster was no more willing than
Acheson to let Chiang dictate American policy. As Schurmann has
suggested, there were forces in Washington, especially in the U.S.
Navy, that were eager to seize the opportunity to "roll back" the
communists in East Asia. Another group Schurmann labels "containment liberals," aimed at a "two Chinas" solution to the problem.
What becomes strikingly clear in recent works and in recently obtained evidence is that Dulles and Eisenhower, perhaps even Walter

Robertson, become "containment liberals" by that definition. Very likely the label will have to go. In brief, the behavior of the Eisenhower administration throughout the crisis leaves no doubt that it sought to end the Chinese civil war on the basis of what Dulles told Chiang's ambassador was the reality that there were two Chinas.[37]

The crisis heightened in the late fall and winter of 1954 as the People's Republic tested the treaty. The Tachens were blockaded and attacks on them grew heavier. The PLA seized the small island of Yijiangshan. The American Joint Chiefs urged Eisenhower to defend the Tachens but he refused. As Robert Donovan explains, the president was determined to avoid war over the offshore islands. He agreed, however, on the need for an explicit warning to Beijing about Taiwan—thus the Formosa Resolution in January 1955.

While Robertson tried to convince Chiang's people that Dulles was their best friend, Chiang raged over being forced to abandon the Tachens and public statements by Dulles and Eisenhower indicating that the United States was not committed to defending any of the offshore islands. Koo recorded his leader's suspicion that even the Formosa Resolution was part of an Anglo-American plot to bring about two Chinas and that the Americans, using Dag Hammarskjold, had reached a secret agreement with Zhou Enlai to trade the Tachens for Americans held by the Communists.[38] Chiang was not far from the mark. Kalicki reveals that in February 1955 Dulles told Anthony Eden that the United States would withdraw its support for Chinmen and Matsu if the People's Republic would agree to a ceasefire in the strait. Also in February Dulles, arguing with Koo and George Yeh, insisted that there were two Chinas—just as there were two Germanys, two Koreas, two Vietnams.[39] He suggested that Chiang emulate Adenauer's patience. In March Dulles went to the lion's den. In Taibei he told Chiang that the United States saw the conflict between Taiwan and the People's Republic as an international war, not a civil war. The United States supported UN efforts to obtain a ceasefire, and it wanted Chiang to stop his internal propaganda campaign for a return to the mainland. Moreover, he refused to commit the United States to veto a place for Beijing in the UN.[40]

Both Schurmann and Friedman contend that Beijing recognized American restraint. Schurmann suggests that American acquiescence in the seizure of the Tachens and the forcing of Chiang's withdrawal indicated that the United States was less threatening than had been assumed. Similarly, Friedman portrays Zhou's invitation to talks, issued at Bandung in April 1955, as an outcome of this new perception of the United States as less irrational than feared. Kalicki's argument is a little more complex. The United States, he contends, had signalled not only its restraint on the offshore islands but also its willingness to risk general war in Asia in defense of Taiwan. Kalicki, Hinton, and others argue that keeping the remaining offshore islands in Kuomintang hands was deemed useful by all Chinese eager to avoid a two Chinas solution. There was, therefore, no point in continuing the crisis.

In April Zhou offered to talk. Two days later Robertson and Admiral Radford were sent to Taibei in an unsuccessful effort to get Chiang to evacuate Chinmen and Matsu. Before the month was out, Eisenhower publicly declared the United States would never launch a first strike against the People's Republic. The stage was set for negotiation between the People's Republic and the United States. The United States hoped for an accommodation on the basis of two Chinas.

The standard work on the ambassadorial talks between the United States and China remains Kenneth Young's *Negotiating with the Chinese Communists*.[41] Little substantive information has been added to Young's record. His analysis of the meetings, especially during the Eisenhower years, has been widely revised. In brief, Young contends that the United States was consistently forthcoming, but the Chinese refused to negotiate. Differences over Taiwan proved irreconcilable. And yet Young himself provides ample evidence for other interpretations. He notes that the administration agreed to meet with the Chinese under pressure from Democratic leaders in the Senate, from Great Britain, and from India, and in part to avoid a multinational conference on the strait crisis as urged by Moscow. He refers to Dulles' skillful parrying of Zhou's initiatives. He contends that Zhou ceased to be interested in negotiating in 1958. He found the talks useful for the United States, but he wondered what use they might be for China. In other hands, Young's discussion could and, of course, does result in the image of a reluctant Dulles, forced to negotiate, yielding as little as possible in contrast with a patient Zhou Enlai, striving for almost three years to find a solution short of surrender.

Foster Rhea Dulles stresses the cold, conditional response of Dulles to Zhou's initiative. He finds Eisenhower much more eager for talks, blames Dulles for the deadlock that emerged by January 1956, and condemns him for his refusal to meet with Zhou. He contends that Dulles was implacably opposed to recognition of the People's Republic and backed away from any action that might lead in that direction.

Specialists on China appear to be unanimous in arguing that Zhou had stressed the peaceful liberation of Taiwan, even the distant liberation of Taiwan—everything short of a categorical renunciation of sovereignty over the island. Hinton, certainly skeptical of Chinese Communist purposes, accepts as genuine their effort to liberate Taiwan peacefully through agreement with the Kuomintang until the antirightist campaign began in 1957. Kalicki recognizes the antirightist campaign as the death knell for Zhou's flexible approach to the United States, but he is critical of American rigidity, of Dulles' refusal to take Zhou's initiatives seriously.

Why was Dulles so unresponsive? MacFarquhar contends that he perceived Chinese overtures as a trick—an explanation consistent with Young's discussion. Sutter, like Foster Rhea Dulles, argues that the United States was not interested in accommodation. Dulles was interested solely in stability in the strait and was playing games toward that end. Gittings implies that the United States was contemptuous of a weak China and would not respond until forced to. Schurmann's analysis, stressing Dulles' purpose in the talks as containment directed toward the goal of two Chinas, is perhaps most persuasive and is consistent with the core of most other interpretations of the 1970s. As Sutter contends, Dulles wanted stability in East Asia, and acceptance by Taibei and Beijing of the two Chinas formula appeared to be the key. He was not interested in de jure recognition of the People's Republic or trade with it, conceivably because of his intense hatred of communism and hopes spurred by the Hundred Flowers campaign in 1957, or perhaps because, as Foster Rhea Dulles notes, both Democratic and Republican platforms in 1956 opposed recognition, and trade was hardly important enough to justify trouble with William Knowland and Walter Judd.

By mid-1957 the talks seemed pointless. The antirightist campaign in China had hemmed Zhou in. The American decision to install on Taiwan Matador missiles capable of carrying tactical nuclear weapons had poisoned the atmosphere. Dulles attacked the Beijing government in the harshest terms he had ever used, insisting communism was merely a passing phase in China. Finally, completing Kalicki's list of reasons for the end to Zhou's initiative, came the Soviet launching of Sputnik, which convinced Mao that a shift had occurred in the world balance of power, that the East wind would prevail over the West. If the Chinese could not yet command respect for their own power, Gittings suggests, Mao assumed Soviet power would now suffice to force the United States to meet China on equal terms. At the end of the year the talks halted, as the American representative was transferred to another post and the United States indicated no interest in resuming them.

Although the United States made some conciliatory gestures toward China in the early months of 1958, it resisted the Chinese demand for a resumption of ambassadorial talks. In late August the PLA began bombarding Chinmen and the second strait crisis was underway. Tsou Tang argued as early as 1959 that the crisis had been provoked by Chiang—with at least the tacit consent of Radford, Robertson, and other friends—to involve the United States in war with the People's Republic.[42] Other writers in the 1960s and 1970s, while varying in their endorsement of conspiratorial overtones, have described a situation in which the People's Republic had reason to be uneasy. Many refer to the placement of Matador missiles on Taiwan in May 1957. Writing in 1966, Hinton reported a large increase in American aid to Taiwan in 1957 and major buildups of Kuomintang forces on Chinmen and Matsu. The Taibei regime was acquiring the capability to attack in force and was very likely interested in exploiting the unrest on the mainland. F. R. Dulles and Schurmann provide variations on the same theme, with the latter pointing to a Dulles speech in June 1958 as a signal to Beijing of a new hardening of the American attitude.

Once again, Kalicki's analysis is the most complex and persuasive. He sees American inflexibility in 1955, 1956, and 1957 as important in understanding the Chinese reaction. The expansion of military aid to Taiwan and the placement of Matador missiles on the island led to an emergency meeting of the CCP Central Committee's Military Committee that same month. Out of that meeting came a decision to liberate Taiwan, and shortly thereafter the antirightist campaign began. The United States, by its actions and inaction, forced Beijing off on a new tack. Kalicki explicitly minimizes Taibei's role in the crisis. Instead, he contends that the People's Republic was testing both the United States and the Soviet Union. Like Chiang, Mao was angered by the willingness of his superpower patron to accept the status quo, a de facto two Chinas. In the context of *Sputnik* and the missile gap, Mao decided to see how the United States would respond to a probe—and what kind of support he would get from Moscow. Implicit in this analysis is the possibility that Beijing was indeed after Taiwan, as Eisenhower and Dulles assumed, and not the offshore islands. Indeed, Whiting had suggested in 1960 that Mao was deliberately trying to link Taiwan to Chinmen to frustrate the two Chinas policy.

Had Taiwan not been a target in August 1958, Kalicki contends, the United States still had to defend Chinmen. Once Chiang had concentrated his best troops and most advanced equipment on the islands, Eisenhower and Dulles could not contend that their defense was irrelevant to the security of Taiwan. Chiang had trapped them. Guhin's Dulles understood that the United States was being tested. Its credibility was at stake. It would have to display a willingness to defend the offshore islands and, as Dulles told Eisenhower, once the United States intervened, it could not abandon the effort—even if it meant general war in Asia.

Eisenhower, according to F. R. Dulles, remained apprehensive of Chiang. He was also quickly aware of the overwhelming opposition of the American public to risking a war over Chinmen and Matsu—and it was an election year. These public pressures are stressed in particular by Charles C. Alexander in his explanation of American restraint in the crisis[43] and may have helped the president resist pressures from the military to attack China, as noted by Schurmann and Kalicki. Instead, the United States took the happy middle ground between surrender and offensive action: It facilitated Kuomintang defense of the offshore islands and warned that it might fight if necessary—a contingency precluded by the success of Chiang's air force in using "sidewinder" missiles to maintain control of the air over the strait.

Hinton and Kalicki state what appears to be the consensus on the Soviet response to the crisis. It came late, after the crisis had passed, and fooled none of the participants. Both men agree that obvious Soviet hesitance assured that American actions and threats would constitute a credible deterrent.

The People's Republic, humiliated by Chiang's air force, was forced to back out of the crisis in the presence of an American threat and the absence of Soviet support. Hinton offers the only consolation. Despite its tactical defeats, Beijing had taken effective preemptive action against Chiang's buildup on the islands. Mao had sent the Americans a message that was understood in Washington. When talks were renewed, the United States clearly attempted to defuse the offshore islands. Implicit in the arguments that the crisis of 1958 resulted in part from Chinese frustration over American disinterest in resuming ambassadorial-level talks is a second Chinese accomplishment. Now the Americans were eager to talk.

In the discussions that followed the crisis of 1958, Dulles made his last effort to realize his two Chinas policy. He declared publicly that Chiang's concentration of forces on Chinmen and Matsu was foolish and that the Kuomintang could not recover the mainland by itself. Moreover, he declared the United States was not committed to aiding Chiang in recovering China, even if there were an uprising on the mainland; thus he stressed the defensive nature of the alliance. Privately he reiterated the idea that Chiang was attempting to draw the United States into war. In October he flew to Taibei and pressed Chiang to accept two Chinas. Chiang was unmoved, yet he was left no choice but to declare publicly that his return to the mainland would be by peaceful means, not by force. If the People's Republic would accept a two Chinas policy, Dulles would persist in efforts to have Chinmen and Matsu abandoned to the PLA. Beijing, of course, was as outraged as Taibei. MacFarquhar and John Wilson Lewis are among those who demonstrate the unhappiness of both Mao and Chiang with

Dulles' effort.[44] Lewis explicitly refers to their collusion in exaggerating the importance of the offshore islands, but he carries the argument a bit far by contending that neither Taibei nor Beijing intended to change the status quo in the strait—merely to involve the United States and to demonstrate the civil war nature of their conflict. To John Foster Dulles, it was clear that both Chinese capitals were in collusion in their abuse of him. If Mao did not want Chinmen and Matsu, there was not much point in baiting Chiang and his American friends on the point.

Kalicki concludes that Republicans wanted two Chinas just as Democrats did, but they were unwilling to abandon the offshore islands. How unwilling remains to be seen. It is clear that Dulles was content to dictate that the islands were not to be used for offensive purposes. They became Taiwan's shield rather than its advance bases.

Hinton, Zagoria, and David Mozingo, among others, are persuaded that Nikita Khrushchev also wanted two Chinas, and so informed Mao in October 1959.[45] Mao, as is well known, was infuriated by his ally's indifference to China's vital interests, whether it be Taiwan or the Sino-Indian border. MacFarquhar and Mozingo stress Mao's opposition to detente, and Mozingo and Hinton are not far apart in explaining why. Like Schurmann, Hinton points to Chinese apprehension about American activities in the late 1950s. Mozingo provides a veritable catalogue of reasons for China's inability to share Khrushchev's perception of the United States as a status quo power. By 1959 the United States had nuclear-armed forces operating from bases in Korea, Japan, and Okinawa. Chiang's forces had been trained and equipped with advanced weapons and were conducting raids on China's coast. The Taiwan economy, underwritten by the United States, was booming, and Matador missiles sprouted on the island's coast. SEATO had been created and the United States was building another bastion of anticommunist strength in southern Vietnam, as well as running covert operations in Laos. As India and China moved toward collision, the United States poured millions into the Indian economy—and may indeed have been behind the Tibetan rebellion. To Beijing, Khrushchev's advice may well have seemed bizarre as well as offensive.

The principal new insights into the 1950s come from China specialists and primarily from political scientists. Historians, especially those who focus on the American side, are still waiting for documents. Those who study the People's Republic of China do not often see much more than what is available at the time of an event. Political scientists are accustomed to working with current affairs, and those who study China, like those who study the Soviet Union, are adept at reading between the lines of government newspapers and magazines. Much of what they have told us in the 1970s is based on information available in the 1960s, indeed more often than not in the 1940s. Their evidence seems overwhelming on two points: first, that Eisenhower and Dulles pursued a two Chinas policy only marginally different from that of their predecessors (Doak Barnett takes sharp exception to this view, stressing Dulles' consistent refusal to concede the legitimacy of the People's Republic), and, second, that the Chinese were genuinely willing to compromise on the Taiwan question to achieve an accommodation between 1955 and 1957. Why were so many analysts blind to this evidence earlier?

There are two probable reasons for the misreading of Eisenhower and Dulles' policy toward China. One is that scholars delight in comparing and contrasting, and they are prone to contrast the work of Democratic and Republican, liberal and conservative administrations. Dulles' rhetoric and Eisenhower's studied bumbling also invited partisan attacks—of which the Townsend Hoopes volume is one of the more reasonable.[46] Radical historians, more likely to stress continuity in American policy, seemed convinced that neither the Truman nor the Eisenhower administration could have pursued a policy designed to do anything but destroy Communist China. The first group ignored the continuity of policy, for better or worse. The second group saw only the worst. The other reason for misreading policy in the 1950s has been the focus on Dulles. To portray a man with his career as a simpleton is merely silly; to make him one-dimensional reveals little. His mind must be understood—and the interplay of his mind with that of the president who employed him—but it is not enough to grasp his Weltanschauung as a means of interpreting his *rhetoric*. The actions of the United States government and the interplay of those actions with those of other governments must be understood as well. Moreover, it has become increasingly evident that Eisenhower and not Dulles was in command. In sum, there have been too many attempts to explain policy by biographers whose research and outlook are too narrow for the study of international politics.

The failure to recognize Chinese flexibility in the mid-1950s derives from an American image of the Chinese as dangerous, irrational, and aggressive. There were writers who told us otherwise, but they won few converts in the 1950s and 1960s. Not new evidence but the experiences of the 1970s, especially the work of Zhou Enlai and Richard Nixon in 1971, have led us to perceive the Chinese more favorably—just as the experiences of the 1960s taught us to be less trusting of positions taken by our own government. An obvious caveat remains: The sincerity of Zhou in 1971 and the lies of American leaders in the 1960s are not proof that the Chinese were and the American negotiators were not sincere in the 1950s.

Historians will wait a long time—apparently until the next century—before they are allowed to see most of the State Department record of the 1960s. Political scientists who study China have not waited, however, and a few historians have tried their hands.

The idea of contrasting conservative and liberal administrations, Republican and Democratic, obviously affects the study of the Kennedy and Johnson years as well as that of the 1950s. Most scholars looked first for differences between Kennedy's policy toward China and that of his predecessor. They are agreed that Chester Bowles, Adlai Stevenson, and perhaps a few others wanted a new policy, but the "new policy" turns out to be the old two Chinas policy, explicitly stated—a position that by the late 1950s the entire foreign policy establishment appears to have shared. Why was the policy not implemented? James C. Thomson blames Secretary of State Dean Rusk and his department, especially the inertia of his doctrinaire Division of Far Eastern Affairs.[47] Foster Rhea Dulles and I are persuaded that Kennedy was unwilling to contemplate a change, at least in his first administration. I go further than Dulles in arguing that Rusk was responsive to, indeed supportive of the initiatives of Bowles and Stevenson, but was impeded by the president's hostility toward the People's Republic. I suggest that Thomson and other participants were

misled by what Kennedy told them and were unaware of secret commitments he had made to Chiang. Some of the confusion is based on
Thomson's mistaken belief that Hilsman slipped his famous Commonwealth speech of December 1963 past an unwitting Rusk. Rusk
had in fact cleared the idea, was fully informed, and had supported
the policy implied for years. The Hilsman initiative was possible only
after Kennedy's death.

Why did Kennedy refuse to initiate a new policy toward China?
Arthur Schlesinger, Jr.,[48] and Dulles note his fear of public opinion
and congressional opposition—the kind of trouble the China lobby
could stir. Certainly men like Rusk, who had been close to the fire
in the Truman era, might fear a resurgence of McCarthyism. And the
president, conscious of the narrowness of his electoral victory, did
indicate that he would be willing to try something in his second term,
when, presumably, he was safe from retribution. But there is little in
Kennedy's attitude toward the People's Republic or the policies he
secretly pursued to suggest that he was interested in changing course,
in seeking accommodation with Beijing.

The Kennedy administration's policy toward Taiwan proves to
have been very similar to that of its predecessor. In 1962, when
Chiang massed forces for an apparent attack on the mainland and,
Hilsman tells us,[49] there was support for the idea in the CIA, Rusk
ridiculed the idea. Kennedy gave the People's Republic his assurance
that the United States would not support or condone an attack. On
the other hand, as Schurmann notes, covert warfare against China
was intensified during the Kennedy years. I find evidence that Kennedy had offered Chiang assistance for covert operations and promised to use the veto if Beijing were voted into the United Nations.

Ambassador Young, Schurmann, and I have found Kennedy ob-
sessed by fear of a nuclear China. Schurmann cites Joseph Alsop to
the effect that Kennedy was so troubled that he ordered exploration
of the idea of collaboration with the Soviet Union in preemptive action against China's nuclear program. Schurmann contends that Kennedy was more concerned about China than about his war in Vietnam. On the other hand, Schurmann concludes, curiously enough,
that the Chinese recognized American restraint and were not fearful.

My findings certainly suggest that they should have been apprehensive, that Kennedy and Rusk, at least, were convinced that China needed to be taught a lesson before it would be ready for detente.

Obviously, it is too early for confident judgments on the Kennedy years. More recent interpretations are less sympathetic to Kennedy, in part because of new evidence, in part because we are more distant from the assassination, less given to hagiography. In general, we are less dependent on participants, who gave honest accounts but were not as well-informed as they believed themselves to be. The best lesson learned from the histories of the Kennedy years is to be wary of accounts by participants—to view them like the blind men describing the elephant in the old Indian fable.

Lyndon Johnson's policy toward China has been all but lost in the shadow of his war in Vietnam. By all accounts, the president was more conciliatory toward the Chinese than was his predecessor—although there can be little doubt that some of his gestures were designed to disarm critics of his decisions on Vietnam. Young reports that the Johnson administration used the Warsaw talks to assure the Chinese the United States would not attack China or try to crush the Hanoi regime. Both Johnson and Rusk, responsive to Whiting's analysis of what had gone wrong in Korea, sent frequent signals to the Chinese. Apprehensive about another clash with the PLA, they indicated their desire for friendlier relations with the People's Republic.

The issues that emerge in the literature of the 1970s are relatively minor. When did the administration reach a tacit modus vivendi with Beijing? What was Rusk's role in all this? I find that in April 1964 Rusk went to Taibei to assure Chiang that Johnson would honor Kennedy's commitment to veto a place for Beijing in the United Nations and to support covert operations against the mainland. Later that year a Chinese offer to negotiate an agreement promising not to be the first to use nuclear weapons was rejected. Friendly signals to Mao and Zhou obviously came later.

Morton Halperin,[50] Hinton, MacFarquhar, Schurmann, Tsou, and I find indications that sometime between November 1965 and mid-1966, Washington and Beijing were reasonably satisfied with each other's assurances. The United States ceased to fear massive Chinese intervention and the People's Republic ceased to view American activities in Vietnam as a threat to its security. It may not be possible to date this point more precisely.

The differences on Rusk are more pronounced. Foster Rhea Dulles, who relies heavily on Thomson, stresses Rusk's continued intransigence. Schurmann, while finding Johnson flexible, reports that Rusk was prepared to risk war with China. My work, of necessity more detailed on Rusk, concludes that he was haunted by fear of a clash with China, very mindful of the mistakes of 1950—and certainly opposed to policies that risked war. He continued, however, to view China as expansionist and revolutionary, a threat to the kind of world order he envisaged. The Chinese had to be taught a lesson so that they would abide by accepted norms of international behavior, as found in the UN Charter. But he did learn and he did become more flexible, responsive to Whiting and the Barnetts, Doak and Robert.

Analysts of Chinese policy are agreed that Beijing had decided against a major intervention in Vietnam in late 1965 and had ceased to fear a U.S. attack by mid-1966. MacFarquhar notes earlier fears aroused by Kennedy's loose talk about preemptive nuclear strikes, and Mozingo stresses the long series of American provocations that antedated Kennedy's inauguration. During the Kennedy years, the Chinese responded to American pressure—and Soviet disinclination to combat that pressure—by endorsing wars of national liberation. Mozingo and Peter Van Ness[51] leave no doubt that desire to embarrass the United States was an important element in Beijing's decision about which movements to support. Van Ness explains that if the United States was aiding a regime, the Chinese were inevitably on the other side. The more likely the revolution was to succeed and the more involved the United States was on the losing side, the greater the visibility of the Chinese role. Careful, national calculation of China's interests was evident.

The only other question that emerges is whether the Cultural Revolution was a response to American threats, or to the absence of American threats. The answer appears to be both. Gittings argues the traditional "China's response to the West" theme: Mao turned China inward to prepare to meet outside pressures. Tsou contends that it was primarily Mao's timing that was related to external affairs. Mao perceived a need for reordering, but acted only after he had American assurances. Only then was he willing to disrupt the national unity he would have needed for war. Schurmann concludes that a sense of danger from without led to preparations for the Cultural Revolution, as evident in mid-1965, but he agrees that its launching came only after the danger had passed. More evidence from China has become available in the last year, and perhaps scholars will be able to resolve this issue to their satisfaction in the very near future.

The work of the last decade has made better use of Chinese sources and revealed a better understanding of the process by which the Chinese and especially the American government decided policy. Analysts have been more sophisticated in their penetration of rhetoric, more aware that policymakers must speak to a variety of audiences. Methodologically, political scientists rather than anthropologists, demographers, psychologists, or sociologists have proved most helpful.

If the issues of the 1940s, 1950s, and 1960s cannot yet be treated as dispassionately as those of the Peloponnesian War, there is nonetheless less disposition to use that past for some ideological or partisan goal. Rapprochement with the People's Republic in the 1970s ended the need to use the history of past relations to legitimize new initiatives or justify old policy. The interpretations of the 1970s give more credence to the "lost chance" idea, although they conceive of the missed relationship in increasingly less idyllic terms. In general, the Chinese get more sympathetic treatment, as does the Eisenhower administration. Kennedy fares less well, and the underlying continuity of the American quest for a two Chinas policy from 1951 through at least the 1960s is apparent. Public opinion, most notably the power of the China lobby, seems of less consequence than it did to earlier defenders of Truman and Acheson, Eisenhower and Dulles, Kennedy, Johnson, and Rusk. Lastly, there is no sense of the emergence or contention of new schools of thought on Chinese-American relations in the postwar era. The postrevisionism of the 1970s has brought us close to a new consensus history, much to the left of the 1950s consensus—and much more skeptical about the American government.

For the future, I see no imminent conceptual breakthroughs. The age of computers is upon us, but I am hard-pressed to think of any problems in the study of Chinese-American relations that will be solved by more sophisticated counting. Anthropology and sociology help a little, as we attempt to understand the effects of cross-cultural contacts. An enormous amount of work along the lines suggested by Akira Iriye can be done in China as well as in the United States.

Perhaps our greatest progress in the last decade is indicated by the increased number of scholars able to understand Chinese as well as American culture and society. Conceivably, the more sympathetic analysis of Chinese policies derives from this increased understanding, as much as from anything else. In the end, however, a few men and an occasional woman, such as Jiang Qing, make policy, and we will continue to study their personalities and thought, their interactions, and the influences on them, wishing that psychological insights were more easily obtained.

Peter Van Ness argues persuasively, nonetheless, that a new conceptual approach is both necessary and possible. In particular, he calls for concepts that will link aggregate domestic social change to foreign policy. How does the breakdown of cohesion in a society— as in the United States in the late 1960s—affect foreign policy? How will the crisis of disbelief in China today or the new line, the new strategy for achieving socialist development, affect foreign policy? Others, such as Charles Maier, demand a systemic analysis comparable to the work of Immanuel Wallerstein and his followers.[52] A host of American scholars continue to explore the impact of ''corporate liberalism'' on external affairs. As diplomatic historians rush to bring their field to the cutting edge of the discipline, some will undoubtedly ask what the ''Annales'' school has to offer students of Chinese-American relations.

I have one, more modest, hope for a breakthrough in the next decade or two. The usefulness of the Koo collection underscores the great value of material from the Chinese side. Perhaps before long, some of us will gain access to Chinese archival material for the postwar period. More likely, our Chinese colleagues, free at last to explore forbidden subjects, will find some answers for us.

NOTES

1. (Chicago: University of Chicago Press, 1963).

2. Tsou, *America's Failure in China,* p. 218.

3. (New York: Knopf, 1975).

4. See Waldo Heinrichs, "Roosevelt and Truman: The Presidential Perspective," in Dorothy Borg and Waldo Heinrichs, eds., *Uncertain Years: Chinese-American Relations, 1947–1950* (New York: Columbia University Press, 1980), pp. 3–12; Iriye, *The Cold War in Asia: A Historical Introduction* (Englewood Cliffs, N.J.: Prentice Hall, 1974); Gittings, *The World and China, 1922–1972* (New York: Harper & Row, 1974); Kolko, *The Limits of Power: The World and United States Foreign Policy, 1945–1954* (New York: Harper & Row, 1972).

5. Chern, *Dilemma in China: America's Policy Debate, 1945* (Hamden, Conn.: Archon Books, 1980).

6. Levine, "A New Look at American Mediation in the Chinese Civil War: The Marshall Mission and Manchuria," *Diplomatic History,* 3 (1979).

7. May, *The Truman Administration and China, 1945–1949* (Philadelphia: Lippincott, 1975).

8. Buhite, " 'Major Interests': American Policy Toward China, Taiwan, and Korea, 1945–1950," *Pacific Historical Review,* 47 (1978); Stueck, *The Road to Confrontation: American Policy Toward China and Korea, 1947–1950* (Chapel Hill: University of North Carolina Press, 1981); Feaver, "The China Aid Bill of 1948: Limited Assistance as a Cold War Strategy," *Diplomatic History,* 5 (1981).

9. Gaddis, "The Strategic Perspective: The Rise and Fall of the 'Defensive Perimeter' Concept, 1947–1951," in Borg and Heinrichs, eds., *Uncertain Years,* pp. 61–118.

10. Purifoy, *Harry Truman's China Policy* (New York: New Viewpoints, 1976); Koen, *China Lobby in American Politics* (New York: Harper & Row, 1974); Kolko and Kolko, *Limits of Power;* LaFeber, "American Policy-Makers, Public Opinion, and the Outbreak of the Cold War, 1945–1950," in Yonosuke Nagai and Akira Iriye, eds., *The Origins of the Cold War in Asia* (New York: Columbia University Press, 1977).

11. Hinton, *China's Turbulent Quest* (Bloomington: Indiana University Press, 1972); Schurmann, *The Logic of World Power* (New York: Pantheon Books, 1974); Cohen, "Acheson, His Advisers, and China, 1949–1950," in Borg and Heinrichs, eds., *Uncertain Years,* pp. 13–52.

12. Tucker, *Patterns in the Dust: Chinese-American Relations and the Recognition Controversy* (New York: Columbia University Press, 1983).

13. Hinton, *China's Turbulent Quest,* pp. 264–65.

14. Sutter, *China Watch: Toward Sino-American Reconciliation* (Baltimore: Johns Hopkins University Press, 1978).

15. Smith, *Dean Acheson* (New York: Cooper's Square, 1972).

16. Gaddis, "Defensive Perimeter Concept," p. 93.

17. Buhite, "Major Interests."

18. Whiting, quoted by Heinrichs, in Borg and Heinrichs, eds., *Uncertain Years,* p. 125.

19. Allison, "Conceptual Models and the Cuban Missile Crisis," *American Political Science Review,* 63 (1969).

20. Tucker, "Nationalist China's Decline and Its Impact on Sino-American Relations, 1949–1950," in Borg and Heinrichs, eds., *Uncertain Years,* pp. 131–71.

21. Cohen, "The China Lobby," in Alex DeConde, ed., *Dictionary of the History of American Foreign Policy* (New York: Charles Scribner's Sons, 1979).

22. Cohen, "The Development of Chinese Communist Policy Toward the United States, 1934–1945," *Orbis,* 12 (1967).

23. Gittings, *The World and China;* Hunt, "Mao Tse-tung and the Issue of Accommodation with the United States, 1948–1950," in Borg and Heinrichs, eds., *Uncertain Years,* pp. 185–233; Whiting, "Mao, China, and the Cold War," in Nagai and Iriye, eds., *Origins of the Cold War,* pp. 252–76.

24. Tucker, "An Unlikely Peace: American Missionaries and the Chinese Communists," *Pacific Historical Review,* 45 (1976); Tozer, "Last Bridge to China: The Shanghai Power Company, the Truman Administration, and the Chinese Communists," *Diplomatic History,* 1 (1977).

25. Okabe, "The Cold War in China," in Nagai and Iriye, eds., *Origins of the Cold War,* pp. 224–51; Goldstein, "Chinese Communist Policy Toward the United States: Opportunities and Constraints, 1944–1950," in Borg and Heinrichs, eds., *Uncertain Years,* pp. 235–78.

26. *Yenan and the Great Powers: The Origins of Chinese Communist Foreign Policy, 1944–1946* (New York: Columbia University Press, 1980).

27. Buhite, "Missed Opportunities? American Policy and the Chinese Communists, 1949," *Mid-America,* 61 (1979); Levine, "Notes on Soviet Policy in China and Chinese Communist Perceptions, 1945–1950," in Borg and Heinrichs, eds., *Uncertain Years,* pp. 293–303; Zagoria, "Choice in the Postwar World (2): Containment and China," in Charles Gati, ed., *Caging the Bear: Containment and the Cold War* (New York: Bobbs, Merrill, 1974), pp. 109–27.

28. O. Edmund Clubb, "Formosa and the Offshore Islands in American Policy, 1950–1955," *Political Science Quarterly,* 74 (1959); Foster Rhea Dulles, *American Policy Toward Communist China: The Historical Record, 1949–1969* (New York: Crowell, 1972); Warren I. Cohen, *Dean Rusk* (Totowa, N.J.: Cooper's Square, 1980).

29. Divine, *Eisenhower and the Cold War* (New York: Oxford University Press, 1981).

30. Notes of conversation between Dulles, George Yeh, and Koo, 19 November 1952, Summary of conversation between Yeh and Eisenhower, 2 January 1953, Telephone conversation with Yeh, January 2, 1953, Box 197; Memorandum of conversation with Judd, July 16, 1954, Box 191, Koo Papers; Walter Judd interview, Columbia Oral History Collection; Guhin, *John Foster Dulles* (New York: Columbia University Press, 1972); Donovan, *Eisenhower: The Inside Story* (New York: Harper & Row, 1956).

31. Eleanor Lansing Dulles, *John Foster Dulles: The Last Year* (New York: Harcourt, Brace & World, 1963).

32. Rankin, *China Assignment* (Seattle: University of Washington Press, 1964); Kalicki, *The Pattern of Sino-American Crises: Political-Military Interactions in the 1950s* (London: Cambridge University Press, 1975); Diary entry, March 17, 1953, Box 219, Notes of conversation with Dulles, March 19, 1953, Box 168, Memorandum of conversation with Rankin, June 5, 1953, Box 187, Koo Papers.

33. Dulles, *American Policy*, pp. 133–34; Guhin, *John Foster Dulles;* Bachrack, *The Committee of One Million: "China Lobby" Politics, 1953–1971* (New York: Columbia University Press, 1976); Greenstein, "Eisenhower as an Activist President," *Political Science Quarterly*, 44 (1979–80).

34. Goold-Adams, *Time of Power: A Reappraisal of John Foster Dulles* (London: Weidenfeld & Nicholson, 1962).

35. Memorandum of conversation with Dulles, March 19, 1953, Box 187, Koo Papers; MacFarquhar, *Sino-American Relations, 1949–1971* (Newton Abbot, G.B.: David & Charles, 1972).

36. Friedman, "Peking and Washington: Is Taiwan the Obstacle?" in Bruce Douglass and Ross Terrill, eds., *China and Ourselves* (Boston: Beacon, 1970).

37. Memorandum of meeting between Yeh, Koo, and Dulles, February 10, 1955, Box 195, Koo Papers.

38. Diary entry for January 22, 1955, Box 220, Koo Papers.

39. Memorandum of meeting between Yeh, Koo, and Dulles, Box 195, Koo Papers.

40. Record of conversation between Chiang and Dulles, March 3, 1955, Box 168, Koo Papers.

41. *Negotiating with the Chinese Communists: The United States Experience, 1953–1967* (New York: McGraw-Hill, 1968).

42. Tsou, "The Quemoy Imbroglio: Chiang Kai-shek and the United States," *Western Political Quarterly*, 12 (1959).

43. *Holding the Line: The Eisenhower Era, 1952–1961* (Bloomington: Indiana University Press, 1975).

44. Lewis, "Quemoy and American China Policy," *Asian Survey*, 2 (1962).

45. Mozingo, "The Maoist Imprint on Chinese Foreign Policy," in Frank Armbruster et al., eds., *China Briefing* (Chicago: University of Chicago Press, 1968).

46. *The Devil and John Foster Dulles* (Boston: Little, Brown, 1973).

47. "On the Making of U.S. China Policy, 1961–1969: A Study in Bureaucratic Politics," *China Quarterly*, 50 (1972).

48. *A Thousand Days: John F. Kennedy in the White House* (Boston: Houghton-Mifflin, 1965).

49. *To Move a Nation* (Garden City, N.Y.: Doubleday, 1967).

50. "Chinese Attitudes Toward Nuclear Weapons," in Ping-ti Ho and Tsou Tang, eds., *China in Crisis* (Chicago: University of Chicago Press, 1968), 2.

51. Van Ness, *Revolution and Chinese Foreign Policy* (Berkeley: University of California Press, 1970).

52. "Marking Time: The Historiography of International Relations," in Michael Kammen, ed., *The Past Before Us: Contemporary Historical Writing in the United States* (Ithaca: Cornell University Press, 1980), pp. 355–87.

SEVEN

Entangling Illusions—
Japanese and American Views
of the Occupation

by CAROL GLUCK

CONSIDERATIONS OF JAPANESE-AMERICAN relations in the twentieth century seem drawn almost inescapably to the Second World War. For the prewar years this has meant recounting the events of several decades to explain their culmination in Pearl Harbor, while the postwar period is often treated as if the relationship between the two countries had been created wholly new in the aftermath of the war. Just as surely as one era ended in hostility in 1941, so it is thought that a new age of alliance began in 1945. The Pacific war bisects the century, appearing in both Japanese and American sources as an epochal break between the past and the present. The illusion of a new beginning after the war, which originated in the immediate postwar months, still underlies much of what is written on U.S.–Japanese relations since 1945. After nearly forty years, conceptions of America and Japan remain suspended in a seemingly perpetual "postwar" phase.

Of the several reasons for this, there are two that particularly affect the increasing number of works of history devoted to the period. The first is that contemporary Japan itself is partly a product of Japanese-American relations. The postwar occupation intruded the United States into the middle of one of the most critical periods in the history of modern Japan. And there it remained, one country entangled in another's national history. This has not been the case in Germany, where postwar historiography treats the allied occupation as an ever-receding episode in West Germany's domestic past, and discussion of U.S.–German relations has long since returned to the conventional categories of international diplomacy. The scholar studies one or—if he is ambitious—both sides of a binational issue, but at least the histories of the two countries are reassuringly distinct.

In Japan the situation is different. Because so much of the structure of postwar Japan took shape, as the Japanese say, "under the occupation," the occupation period is considered fundamental to interpretations of contemporary Japanese history. Far from receding, interest in it is growing, burgeoning almost, as historians on both sides of the Pacific reconstruct the origins of postwar Japan. Immediately as they do they confront the United States and the question of the role it played during those important years. Even if the subject is not directly concerned with foreign relations, American ideas, institutions, and ideology are at issue—not because they were all-determining, but because they were inextricably enmeshed in the process by which the Japanese reestablished themselves after the war. This U.S. invasion of domestic Japanese history, which complicates postwar historiography to an unusual extent, also influences policy analyses of Japanese-American relations in the present. This is because the basic framework of alliance—whether in its political, economic, or military aspects—was established during the occupation period when the United States dominated Japan's decisions about its relations with the world. The close but lopsided relationship between the two countries since the occupation is well reflected in the writings of each about the other. Japanese contemporary discourse betrays nearly obsessive concern with the United States, while the fraction of American comment devoted to Japan tends to take the postwar alliance rather casually for granted.

The second factor, then, that affects historical contemplation of Japanese-American relations as they emerged after the war is their persistent contemporaneity. Because the "postwar" past remains part of the present, the useful present-mindedness that impels historians to pose questions of some relevance to their own age still overlaps with the more immediate involvement characteristic of writings on nearly contemporary events. Although there is no sure way to calibrate the gradations by which an event "becomes history," the occupation seems now to be in just that process of transition. For a variety of familiar reasons—the passage of time, the opening of documents, the first crossing of the great divide of 1945 that had arbitrarily separated history from social science in American scholarship on Japan—historians in the 1970s turned to the occupation with an energy the results of which have swelled the literature in both countries. But it was not only the new material and the allure of an as yet untilled patch of the past that drew this amount of scholarly attention. In each country it was the present as much as the past that brought the occupation to center stage. In Japan, where the seventies saw both a new sense of national self-esteem and a new wave of social self-criticism, writers reevaluating the shape and direction of postwar society returned to its beginnings during the occupation. In the United States, where the Vietnam war had provoked deep questioning of America's role in the postwar world, scholars reexamined the occupation of Japan as an early instance of U.S. foreign policy at work in Asia. In both cases, though of course more dramatically in Japan, the ongoing reappraisal of the occupation is an issue of contemporary controversy and importance.

These general characteristics may help explain why the occupation threatens for the moment to usurp the entire subject of postwar Japanese-American relations, at least as far as works of history are concerned. While political scientists, economists, security analysts, and futurologists comment in ever expanding volume on other contemporary issues between Japan and the United States, historians are absorbed in the occupation period. For, like the road to the Pacific war, it appears strewn with interpretive possibilities. And like the "lost China/lost chance" questions in the study of Chinese-American relations, the occupation is likely to require time and considerable debate before it slips definitively into the past.

THE HISTORY OF THE HISTORY OF THE OCCUPATION

Japan and the United States are entangled not only in their postwar history but also in their historiography. Views of the occupation have not evolved in altogether separate or parallel phases on either side of the Pacific. There is instead a geometry in which Japanese and Amer-

ican versions intersect with one another at some points and then veer
off into different planes at others. In the years since the war one can
already identify three such instances in occupation historiography: first,
the apparent convergence of Japanese and American visions of the
occupation in the earliest postwar months of late 1945 and early 1946;
second, the widely divergent renderings that gained authority in each
country in the fifties and sixties; and third, the interacting, and sometimes collaborative, reinterpretations produced by younger Japanese
and American scholars since the beginning of the seventies.

What the occupiers and the occupied shared in the autumn of
1945 was the fervent belief that Japan should—and could—be remade. For the Japanese it was an article of faith that the end of the
war must mean a new beginning and a full break with the past. The
voluminous collections of contemporary responses are filled with this
conviction, and narrative histories to this day often contain the envi-
ably precise statement that the present began at noon on August 15,
1945.[1] The Americans who arrived soon thereafter also felt that Japan's future was at hand. The confidence in their victor's mission
that characterized MacArthur's pronouncements was shared, if less
apocalyptically, by many members of the occupation in the early
months. They felt that they had come to aid in the elimination of the
old order and attend the birth of a "new Japan." These views abound
in the once standard source of occupation history, *The Political Reorientation of Japan,* which was a report (and sometimes holy writ)
recording the first three years of the occupation as seen by the Government Section of the Supreme Commander for the Allied Powers.[2]
Both Japanese and American sources reveal that, in the initial tumult
of the postwar scene, the goals of the former enemies could also
seem to sound alike. Occupation officers stated their plans to "de-
mocratize" and spoke of revolutionary change, while Japanese newspapers and magazines called for the completion of the "democratic
revolution." That everyone, progressive and conservative, Japanese
and American, used the same word—democracy—but understood it
differently, set the stage for mutual disillusion in the time to come.
Any apparent convergence between the views of MacArthur and the
Japanese left, for example, was soon proved false. But neither the
Japanese nor the Americans wholly abandoned their earliest illusion

that in the wake of a terrible war Japan could somehow begin again. Together, but for different reasons, they had conjured a kind of creation myth for postwar Japan, which would greatly affect subsequent views of the occupation.

When reflective studies began to appear in the years after the occupation ended, it was clear that the effect had been rather spectacularly different in the two countries. Most of the American writers on the subject had had some connection with Japan, before the war, during the occupation, or in the military language schools from whose ranks the field of Japanese studies sprang practically whole in the 1950s.[3] For this reason the Pacific part of World War II was central to their experience. In general they regarded the occupation as a success, for the reforms seemed at least to have abolished the odious militarism and fascism that had brought Japan to war. Moreover, their assessment of Japan of the sixties as reliably democratic served to reaffirm their view that the "massive experiment in 'planned' or 'directed' political change" had indeed succeeded.[4] In examining what was often called the legacy of the occupation, they therefore stressed the early political and social reforms and evaluated their relative effectiveness. They described the role of the United States as catalytic and treated the occupation primarily as a phase in domestic Japanese development, with little attention to its relation to American foreign policy. Although they judged the record as far from perfect, on balance they regarded the collaboration between the Japanese and the Americans as a creditable achievement in institutional change.

At the same time most of their Japanese counterparts, profoundly affected by their own wartime experience and their own postwar hopes, were describing the occupation as a failure and a betrayal. In the wake of the war that desecrated their lives and their country's modern history, Japanese intellectuals had envisaged deep and radical change. But the democratic revolution had not materialized, and Americans, once viewed as liberators, seemed instead to have acted in their own cold war interests to halt the democratic process before it could establish itself. The betrayal of the progressive promise of the early reforms became the dominant theme of the occupation in Japanese historical scholarship, which remained as before the war preponderantly Marxist in approach and anti-establishment in politics.[5] The question these historians asked of the occupation was not one of legacy but of continuity, and their attention was ineluctably drawn to those aspects of postwar Japan that seemed *not* to have changed since prewar times. Focusing on the latter part of the occupation when the early reforms were partly compromised or undone, they emphasized the resurgence of conservative politics, the renewed suppression of the left, and the resurrection of prewar economic and financial structures. In most of these developments, the United States and its foreign policy were assigned a central, often virulently negative role. By the sixties, when Americans were judging Japanese democracy a moderate success, many Japanese intellectuals saw it imperiled by an unreconstructed bureaucracy and apparently endless one-party rule. They regarded this as evidence that Japan was at best only tenuously democratic, which in turn confirmed their view of the occupation as a revolution that had failed.

For both the Japanese and American scholars, this was history written close to the bone. It was their own experience, their ideals, their illusions that had been either violated or fulfilled in the course of the occupation. Thus both produced what Herbert Butterfield would have called "heroic narratives," whose dramatic structure and sometimes fervent tone reflected the writers' engagement in the events.[6] Granted the discrepancy in political stance between the predominantly leftist Japanese historians and the predominantly liberal Americans, the divergent outcome of the two narratives is not surprising. Yet the gap between the two accounts opened as wide, and in the Japanese case as bitterly, as it did for more reasons than that of ideological difference. Had Japanese intellectuals and American occupationaires not invoked a new beginning and even imagined a community of purpose in those early postwar months, they might have told a tale less stark when the occupation was over. Instead the creation myth appeared with two dramatic, but different, endings. Out of the void of war, in American scholarship, came contemporary Japanese democracy; out of the wartime chaos, in the Japanese view, came a promise of change that ended as a misbegotten apocalypse. And although neither the Japanese nor American version was an officially decreed orthodoxy in the sense of being without significant opposition, both remained the most familiar, accepted, and authoritative retelling of occupied Japan in the scholarship of their respective countries.

Indeed, if the entangled illusions of a new Japan from 1945 and 1946 constitute the first phase of occupation historiography, and the separate heroic narratives of the fifties and sixties the second, then the third stage can fairly be said to have begun in the seventies when Japanese and American scholars undertook the exacting task of complicating the received narratives. Some assaulted the larger framework, though most chipped away at some sections, while refining others. The opening of the American documents, in particular the vast archives of the Tokyo occupation authorities, unleashed an onslaught of historians from both countries. Binational collaboration, long severed by the gap between the two heroic versions, became increasingly common. Japanese and Americans often worked away at the same mountainous mass of U.S. material, because in Japan—where sunshine laws refer to building heights and not to information—authorities are far charier of their archives than many scholars find acceptable. And until some change occurs in this policy, it is likely that occupation history, however binational in origin, will remain somewhat one-sided in documentary fact.[7] Still, scholarly progress has been substantial. Major bibliographies and general historiographical essays have appeared in both languages.[8] Initial attempts at cataloging sources are underway, as is a rash of interviewing to produce an oral history while it is still possible to do so.[9] Detailed monographic and what the Japanese call "empirical" (as distinguished from "ideological") studies have contributed to broadening the substantive range of occupation history.[10] Of the younger generation of scholars asking questions provoked by their own postwar—not wartime—experience, Takemae Eiji in Japan and John Dower in the United States have led the way in their own work and encouraged others to the subject.[11]

For Takemae and other Japanese writers, the impetus to occupation study lay in their sense of Japan at "a turning point where the politics and economics evolved over the quarter century since the war had reached an impasse."[12] What kind of democracy was Japan practicing and where did it come from; what economic priorities might supersede the quantitative growth pursued successfully since the latter part of the occupation, but with increasing domestic and international repercussions; what version of postwar history should be conveyed to even younger generations accused of forgetting its genesis in war and occupation (if more than half the poulation can be said to have forgotten what they themselves had never known)? In the wake of the more recent Nixon and oil shocks, writers reconsidered the original "occupation shock," which Takemae defined not as the reforms themselves, but as the trauma of "being touched by the spirit of American democracy which underlay those reforms."[13]

These concerns, thoroughly domestic in origin, again turned the attention of scholars toward America, but with a different aim and a finer brush than before. Instead of a broad schematic portrayal of U.S. imperialism, recent works have examined the American documents in painstaking, sometimes microscopic detail to decipher the "intentions" behind individual policies. Then they have proceeded to the Japanese "response" and implementation of the policy in question. Most often this has meant tracing specific policies—labor, land reform, the emperor system, rearmament[14]—through the process of decision-making by individuals—MacArthur, Truman, Kennan[15]—without attempting to pronounce a final judgment. Not that the younger scholars dispute the general shape of the received narrative; they just seem less interested in retelling it. Most have preferred to seek the concrete, the empirical, and "through research into labor policy [for example] to make clear the substance of occupation policy from the viewpoint of the mechanism of policy-making and the special characteristics of the policy context."[16] Commonplace as this may sound to American historians and political scientists (some of whom have provided theoretical models for this work), in Japanese studies of the occupation this methodological hugging of the ground for data while avoiding the aerial picture signified something of a departure. And it was a departure that occurred at the same time in the late sixties and early seventies that the younger American scholars were moving along quite different lines.

Propelled by the evolution (or devolution) of U.S. Asian policy during the Vietnam era, Dower and others reviewed the relationship between "Occupied Japan and the American Lake," which the ear-

lier narrative had portrayed as a largely "benevolent" one.[17] Now
the question became not what the well-intentioned United States had
done for Japan in political and social reform, but what the United
States had, for its own ideological and security interests, done *to*
Japan in the way of economic and military involvement. Conjoined
with this revisionism was a call for larger structural explanations,
both of global capitalism and of its Japanese instance. This would
supply an antidote to what Dower called the Western "scholarship of
scatter," which diffused the real nature of the occupation by treating
specific people, policies, and decisions as if they possessed no ultimate relationship either with one another or with the larger imperatives of American policy.[18] In practice this has meant studying the
occupation in the context of cold war foreign relations on the one
hand, and on the other, attending to such economic issues as labor
and economic recovery in order to locate the interaction between existing Japanese structures and the overall design of U.S. interests.[19]
It has also meant, particularly in Dower's masterfully documented
work, greater attention to the Japanese side of things, with the result
that the Japanese have become active agents instead of passive re-
spondents in the processes of occupation.

At first glance it may seem as if American revisionists had em-
braced the critical view of the occupation that had long been standard
in Japanese scholarship, while some Japanese scholars, without necessarily revising their criticism of the United States, had muted it in
favor of the kind of descriptive social science associated with the
earlier work of American writers. It is true that signs of a reciprocal
realignment were conspicuous in footnotes in both languages. Where
for years in Japanese citations the most congenial source for what
America should have attempted in postwar Japan was Owen Lattimore, now Joyce and Gabriel Kolko were quoted to explain how
U.S. economic and security interests blocked the radical change that
both Lattimore and the Japanese intellectuals had advocated.[20]
Younger American writers, for their part, were able to consult postwar Japanese historians without dismissing their premises as unac-
ceptably Marxian, while some of their Japanese colleagues came to
rely as much on theories of bureaucratic politics as on Lenin and

evinced greater interest in the intricacies of Washington opinion than in the operation of global capitalism.[21] Yet it is not quite so simple as it sounds.

Most Japanese historians of Japanese history remain today what they have been since the late 1920s, conceptual islands of tutored Marxist and post-Marxist thought in a thoroughly bourgeois social sea. Nor is pro-Americanism their general fashion. The heroic narrative of the occupation continues to appear in updated, authoritative versions, and the new work shares many of its assumptions.[22] But a greater diversity of viewpoints now exists, a product partly of the historians themselves, partly of Japanese Americanists and diplomatic historians, as well as of political scientists with specialties in international relations, many of whom have spent time at U.S. universities. Without becoming old America hands, they often share with their colleagues in Japanese history a fair skepticism about U.S. policy, even as they employ methodologies generated by, and draw conclusions congruent with, postwar American scholarship.[23] Popular works and journalistic coverage have added yet another element of diversity to occupation history, whether in the media debates among intellectuals over the nature of "the postwar" or in best-selling volumes where MacArthur, the "blue-eyed shogun," sometimes appears as a kind of folk hero, a role the General might well have cherished, but not one for which the Japanese scholarly world ever thought him suitable.[24]

In the United States, too, diversity and synergism among viewpoints have enriched the study of the occupation. Japan specialists in the seventies were joined by American diplomatic historians. Together they created so insistent a literature on the occupation as an aspect of U.S. foreign policy that Ray A. Moore found it necessary in 1980 to remind *both* Japanese and American scholars that the occupation must also be considered a part of the history of Japan.[25] Otherwise U.S. dominance over Japan during the occupation might be further perpetuated in a historiography now critical but still preoccupied with the American point of view. American political scientists have also reexamined the subject, a number of them in a binational project chaired by Robert Ward and Sakamoto Yoshikazu, whose own bibliographies had earlier laid the basis for much of the new work.[26]

And the witness of occupation participants, once unleavened, began to mingle with the inquiries of younger scholars, until the proceedings of the MacArthur Memorial symposia on the occupation, begun in 1975, expanded from slim mementos into hulking tomes, laced with provocative discussion between those who were there and those whose documents gave them a different perspective.[27] Mingling, of course, is not melding, and the Western scholarship like the Japanese betrays wide and not always temperate divergence of opinion.[28]

More interesting perhaps is the convergence, by virtue of which similar reinterpretations of the heroic narratives have appeared on both sides of the Pacific, but for different reasons. Indeed Japanese and American scholars on the occupation now often appear to have reached the same interpretive point at the same time. This appearance, however, is deceiving, since the political and historiographical context in each country remains a separate, national matter. The two heroic narratives are still essential referents, and the similar adjustments in them that have occurred in both countries are not the result, plain and simple, of revisionism. Heroic narratives in any case are seldom wholly wrong, only larger than life. Recent research has scaled the narratives down, and complicated but not demolished them. In the complications, though, the occupation has assumed a slightly altered historical shape.

THE SHRINKING OF SCAP

MacArthur, for example, has shrunk. Not in size or bombast perhaps, but in importance within policy-making, the General's role has been reduced. It could not, it is true, be anywhere as diminished as it was in Japanese Marxist accounts of the early fifties, where in an authoritative historical dictionary, MacArthur received six and a half lines to Joseph McCarthy's twenty-seven and thirteen for Edward Alexander MacDowell.[29] This political demythologizing aside, strict materialist accounts of postwar Japanese capitalism seldom spared space for individuals. In general, however, the Supreme Commander for the Allied Powers, or SCAP, had figured as an absolute historical presence, negative in most scholarly accounts, positive in the popular mind.[30] In the United States he had not loomed all that small either, the result of both his own efforts and those of admiring colleagues.

The recent diminution has not occurred as a result of reevaluation of MacArthur himself, who has yet to undergo the kind of detailed revision that is bringing his old rival Eisenhower back into scholarly fashion. He has in fact been little treated. Except for his evangelical attempt to Christianize Japan, his proposal for an early peace treaty, and the conundrum that besets a sector of Japanese scholarship—who was responsible for Article Nine, the Constitution's renunciation-of-war clause?—MacArthur during the occupation of Japan remains much as he was in older memoirs and biographies.[31] What has happened instead is the shrinking of SCAP in relation to other loci of authority. As the processes of policy-making have become clearer, Washington, the occupation bureaucracy, and the Japanese government have come to assume larger roles in the accounts of the complex business of determining and implementing specific occupation policies.

The importance of Washington is stressed in two instances: first, the wartime planning that preceded and conceived the occupation, and second, the political role later played by the U.S. government in redirecting occupation policy. While hardly new to the literature, wartime planning has attracted renewed attention, especially in Japan, where close examination of the presurrender planning documents contradicted the prevalent Japanese view that "Washington determined basic policy in a broad and general way while SCAP decided the concrete policies." Many of the concrete policies, it turned out, had also originated in Washington.[32] Understandably drawn to "the particulars by which their own fate was being decided without their having anything to do with it,"[33] Japanese writers have focused on the drafting of the Potsdam Declaration, the meaning of unconditional surrender as the Americans intended it (unconditionally conditional, most scholars agree, which was how the Japanese at the time understood it), the question of direct versus indirect occupation, and the fundamental issue to which each of these relate—the fate and future of the emperor system, including the question of war responsibility.[34] SWNCC (State-War-Navy Coordinating Committee) documents fascinate, as does the image of Hugh Borton quietly penning the emperor into posterity while others preoccupied with Germany or China or U.S. public opinion envisaged more radical transformations.[35] The preoccupation with Germany worked both ways: Germany remained (as it had been since the thirties) the source from which by analogy Japan was conceived, often mistakenly; and it also remained the overshadowing concern, leaving the small Japan crew to make their plans unimpeded by the principal government figures whose interests lay elsewhere, at least for the moment. When they did at last turn to Japan in 1944 and 1945, the cast of wartime planners grew suddenly larger, and in the light of recent research it becomes even more surprising that the early plans of the Japan specialists survived to the extent that they did.

Although opposition to the Japan group's proposals from the China hands and other State Department officials who favored a harsher approach to postwar Japan is often emphasized, the process of wartime planning proved more complicated than accounts confined to the conflicts of opinion within the State Department can adequately suggest.[36] More bureaucratic actors were involved, notably the Treasury and War departments, interdepartmental committees and special commissions from the still spreading acronymic canopy of war-related policy-making, and military planners and civilian consultants recruited in advisory positions. More ideological factors were introduced, as moderates, reformers, liberals, anticommunists, Roosevelt-like internationalists, and free-enterprise capitalists put their thoughts on Japan to paper. Part of what is consistently referred to as the inconsistency, contradiction, irony, and ambivalence of U.S. occupation policy toward Japan is the result of exactly that—inconsistency, contradiction, irony, and ambivalence among those who made the policy.

In the case of plans for the Japanese economy, Marlene Mayo's studies have shown the bureaucratic conflicts, jurisdictional squabbles, and plain differences of opinion that were responsible for the sometimes tortured evolution of U.S. policy. Early proposals by State Department Japan experts had argued only that "a viable Japanese economy is to be considered a first prerequisite of lasting peace in the Pacific." Treasury and Foreign Economic Administration officials held their own less generous views, often taking Germany for their model. State Department economists inserted the reformist call for "the development of democratic organizations in labor, industry, and agriculture . . . and a wider distribution of ownership, management, and control of the Japanese economic system."[37] And finally, military planners in the War Department oversaw the inclusion of the express provisions for *zaibatsu* dissolution, the economic purge, and general economic democratization. These were introduced into the basic planning document (SWNCC 150), but only in mid-August 1945.[38] Whether their motives were theoretical or vengeful, concerned with security or the world economy, these planners represented very different visions of postwar Japan, often within the same directive. And all of this was *before* there was a SCAP and his bureaucracy with visions of their own.

Such scholarly enthusiasm for the bureaucratic anatomy of Washington sometimes runs to extremes. In the flush of the discovery that SCAP "exhibited virtually no autonomy" in 1945 and 1946, one Japanese writer suggested that items such as the Constitution and Article Nine, which were not plainly enumerated in the presurrender plans, were present at least by "indirection."[39] At other times the policy-making emphasis begins to paint a *pointilliste* picture of bureaucrats thinking and writing in little pockets, "unaware" of larger matters like Soviet relations or presidential elections that were "unrelated" to their work. U.S. public opinion, and its severe views of how the defeated enemy should be treated, is scarcely mentioned. Also, the concentration on bureaucratic paper fosters a kind of document blindness that makes the policy seem the clear reality and renders everything but what is written invisible. In this light the occupation may be summarized in numerical shorthand—from SWNCC 150 to NSC 13/2 to NSC 48/4[40]—which surely suggests for Washington a closer control over history than it in fact ever had. Similarly, the relentless pursuit of the intentions, motivations, and images that guided American planners has apparent limits, both in individual instances and in general. An equal emphasis on implementation seems more and more essential.

The U.S. government's role in making and remaking occupation policy in the cold war context has long been a staple in the literature.

During these same years, roughly from 1948, Washington also figured as a political actor in the increasingly triangular relations between the United States, SCAP, and the Japanese government. To
the tug of war between the U.S. government and MacArthur and the
chafing between occupation and official Japanese perspectives was
added a third element, as the Japanese government short-circuited
Tokyo channels and began to communicate with Washington directly.
American criticism of MacArthur, coupled with the appearance in
Tokyo of such emissaries as Dodge and Dulles, enabled Yoshida and
his conservatives to use these politics to their own purposes. Japanese
economic thinkers who favored a deficit financing, inflationary policy
were no happier with Dodge's disinflation than they had been with
SCAP's version of price controls, but now the government could better express its concerns. This it did in the form of an economic mission to Washington in May 1950, which presented Dodge not only
with Japanese opinion on fiscal matters but also with a secret proposal offering U.S. bases in Japan in exchange for an early peace
treaty. On that occasion the Yoshida government's offer played on
American anticommunism with the familiar specter of possible internal unrest if a treaty were long delayed.[41] When Yoshida met with
Dulles in June 1950, he stood staunchly against rearmament, called
MacArthur in to support him (possibly by way of apology for having
gone behind SCAP's back to Washington the previous month, suggests one scholar),[42] and left Dulles feeling like Alice in Wonderland.[43] When Dulles visited again in 1951, Yoshida was arguing
against a too rapid rearmament, taking issue with a statement by
MacArthur on Japan's self-defense, and belittling the communist threat
both internally and abroad. What storybook character Dulles felt like
at that point is unrecorded, but Yoshida was also playing domestic
politics, *his* favorite game, and using both Washington and Mac
Arthur to help him.[44]

　　Recent work has also revealed that in nearly every instance where
triangular politics was practiced, its channels were opened by a small
group of Americans who are now known as the "Japan lobby."[45] Its
formal organization was established in 1948 as the American Council
on Japan; its informal organ was *Newsweek* magazine, which campaigned against the occupation's left-wing "crackpots" and "radi-

cal" economic reforms from early 1947 on. Its central figures were *Newsweek* journalists Compton Pakenham and Harry Kern, who cultivated high-level contacts in Tokyo and Washington; the business lawyer James Kauffman, whose 1947 report both blasted and leaked FEC 230, the economic deconcentration bill, to its most likely opponents in the U.S. and Japanese bureaucracies;[46] Eugene Dooman from the old Japan crowd at State, finally able to retaliate against the economic reformers whose more radical views had prevailed over his conservative ones during the last stages of wartime planning; and from the former State Department elite, Joseph Grew and William Castle as honorary cochairmen. This group, and particularly the ubiquitous Harry Kern, was involved in many of the dealings that surrounded the reversals in economic policy, the reconstitution of the Japanese corporate structure and its revived relations with American business, and the anticommunist blueprint for Japan in Asia. When a "nongovernmental source" provided a confidential document, or a dinner was arranged for Dulles to meet influential conservative Japanese, or an intermediary brought Undersecretary of the Army Draper together with General Eichelberger, who was then hired as an army consultant on Japan under Tracy Voorhees—it was Harry Kern each time.[47] The small but well-connected Japan lobby was another link in the chain of influence that—in this case quite purposefully—contributed to the shrinking of SCAP's power in the later years of the occupation.

Accounts of conflict and diversity within the occupation bureaucracy are having something of the same effect on the image of MacArthur as master policymaker. The impression of the visionary general, his loyal Bataan Boys, the civilian New Dealers, and their conservative military counterparts is giving way to a less autocratic, more bureaucratic rendition of SCAP's operations in Tokyo. Even as new participants' accounts either repeat the heroic narrative according to Government Section, as Justin Williams does, or confirm its categories of liberal, reformist, and conservative, as Alfred Oppler has, these same memoirs also shed light on the less than systematic process by which occupation decisions were taken and implemented.[48]

In the archive of occupation materials the grand tapestry from MacArthur's speeches and the public record begins to unravel into a more credible tangle of administrative infighting between sections and subsections over questions of policy, jurisdiction, and budgetary support for particular pet projects. Because of the interest in economic issues, General Marquat's Economic and Scientific Section (ESS) appears prominently, adding another perspective to the familiar division between the civilian (and liberal) Government Section (GS) headed by General Whitney and the military (and conservative) Intelligence Section of General Willoughby (G-2). ESS positions sometimes conflicted with the thinking of Government Section, compared to which in 1946 the economic planners appeared conservative on *zaibatsu* dissolution. Sometimes the conflict was with G-2, to which periodically before 1948 and increasingly thereafter ESS appeared "communistic" in labor and fiscal matters. (Indeed ESS was ultimately purged.) And sometimes ESS members just wrangled among themselves over such issues as the most appropriate and continuously elusive solution to Japan's plaguing inflation.[49]

In addition to the discord and uncoordination within and between sections, the occupation bureaucracy suffered continued onslaught from outside in the form of the missions dispatched from Washington to pronounce "expert" opinion on one subject or another. Confronted with the recommendations of these financial, legal, or educational specialists, the occupation civilians, many of whom had been equally innocent of knowledge of Japan when they started, now felt both seasoned and proprietary. Sojourners like Draper and Dodge (who themselves disagreed on the methods for achieving economic self-sufficiency) swept into Tokyo in the late forties thinking of many things—the Soviet Union, U.S. business, China, the German occupation, European recovery—but, in the eyes of SCAP's economists, few of their thoughts related to Japan.[50] Just as with wartime planning, there were so many cooks at work on the broth that it was no wonder it tasted peculiar. Still, scholars persist in uncovering "basic conflicts" in occupation policy such as the one between "the ostensible goal of economic democratization—implying the establishment of free markets—and the regime of comprehensive international controls which, in practice, the occupation imposed upon

Japan.''[51] In fact, some favored free trade, others controls, while still others favored only U.S. imports (against which Japan in turn used these same restrictions once the occupation was over).

The change in occupation personnel over time also contributed to the confusion. As people left for home, or were driven out for political reasons, the Tokyo bureaucracy waned from within, and the administration of policy reflected this. Following one issue, as Takemae has done for labor policy, reveals an array of what he calls "inputs," both from within GHQ and from outside.[52] These different sources help to explain how "the same" occupation both promoted unions and halted the general strike, presided over both the 1945 Trade Union Law, which strengthened labor, and its 1949 revision, which weakened it, and at first permitted, but in 1950 purged, communist leadership in the unions. It was not, in the course of years, "the same" occupation at all.

The question of who made occupation policy is persuasively answered in the plural. In Takemae's informal survey of occupationaires who had been involved in labor issues, 60 percent said that SCAP and his bureaucracy made nearly all labor policy, while only 30 percent gave Washington the credit or the blame. In more specific chronological terms, Washington (SWNCC and State) ranked first before 1948, then the GHQ Labor Division, then MacArthur, and then the Allied Far Eastern Commission (FEC), predictably at the bottom. After 1948, MacArthur placed first, GHQ Labor next, Washington third, and still last, the FEC.[53] In recent works it is not the alternation between MacArthur and Washington that has attracted attention, but the persistence in second place of the middle-level occupation bureaucracy in Tokyo, which like most middle-level bureaucracies did a great deal of the work. This is true also of the Constitution, for which the members of Government Section—allegedly on the assumption that they were producing a model, not the actual text of another country's first law—churned out a draft in little more than a week. Neither MacArthur's "three principles" nor the program outlined by Washington in SWNCC 228 accounted for the detailed content and ambitious scope of many of the articles. The subcommittees assigned to the different chapters had gathered their wits, their experience, and the constitutions of the United States, Estonia, and elsewhere, and proceeded to compose a constitution.[54] Beate Sirota, a young woman charged with the subject of social and economic rights, prepared a comprehensive set of social measures that originally included a provision for the care of nursing mothers—which was struck—and one decreeing that marriage be based on mutual consent and maintained through mutual cooperation of husband and wife—which became Article Twenty-Four of the Japanese Constitution.[55] Enough of the original wording remained unchanged that to the Japanese the language of their own Constitution "reeks of butter," which means that it is outlandishly Western.[56] Since the provenance of the Constitution is a vital political issue in Japan, people take an active interest in the reminiscences of Charles Kades and the precise details of how the subcommittees of Government Section produced the "MacArthur Constitution."[57]

THE JAPANESE PERSPECTIVE

The interest in bureaucratic process, whether in Washington or the Tokyo GHQ, may have helped shrink MacArthur's part in the story, but it has only magnified the role of the United States. This is unfortunate, since one of the salient features of the occupation of Japan was its indirect character, which meant that the Japanese government, unlike its German counterpart, continued to function. From the beginning, the Americans, in both Washington and Tokyo, worked through the existing administrative machinery, making the Japanese side of this bureaucratic tripod indispensable to an understanding of the occupation. Also indispensable, if there is life—and history— outside the bureaucracy, is the experience of the rest of the Japanese. True, the sources remain weighted in favor of the United States, but there is enough and increasingly more material for Japan, some of it available in English.[58] In the last few years scholars have begun to bring the Japanese into the discussion as a more dynamic force than was suggested by the earlier epithets "responsive," in the U.S. heroic narrative, or "resistant," in the Japanese version. Japan, often characterized in Japanese writing as the passive object of the occupation whose active subject was the American GHQ, now finally appears as a significant actor in its own right.[59]

On the top government level Yoshida Shigeru, whose "one man" presence was a symbolic match for MacArthur's during the occupation period, has received more direct attention than the General has in recent work. The last years of this "prewar 'old liberal' and postwar old guard, conservative doyen of the 'new Japan' " were so closely intertwined with the fate of postwar Japanese domestic and foreign policy that Dower's biography of Yoshida becomes an account of the whole postwar experience as seen by those who prevailed in the scramble to reconstitute Japanese political life after the defeat and "under the occupation."[60] In the early postwar months Yoshida and his group, who shared a common anticommunist vocabulary with SCAP, were aghast at such measures as the legalization of the Communist Party, encouragement of labor, economic deconcentration, and dispossession of the prewar landlords. When he could, Yoshida intervened in the factionalism between those he called the "Reds" in Government Section and the "realists" in G-2, and also opened direct channels to MacArthur.[61] Later when U.S. policy changed more to conservative liking on many matters, there remained other issues, such as the Dodge Plan, the peace treaty, and relations with China, on which the Yoshida group disagreed with the Americans and made their disagreement known. In both periods the Japanese government lost on some points and won on others, although seldom because of positions taken by either SCAP or Yoshida alone, or even by both of them together. For Yoshida, like MacArthur, was a symbol in need of shrinking, and scholars have performed this service by focusing on other actors in what was an extraordinarily complex political scene, as the bureaucracy, the parties, and the opposition attempted to reestablish themselves in an environment brimming with promise and hostility at the same time.

New materials will doubtless prompt more biographies of major government figures,[62] and efforts, most of them Japanese, to analyze the role of top- and middle-level bureaucrats have already appeared. As one of the few areas of Japanese life not slated for fundamental structural reform, the bureaucracy survived the occupation—minus a

Home Ministry here, and a few prewar personnel there—relatively unscathed, perhaps, as some writers suggest, even stronger than before.[63] How the early democratizing fervor missed a target of this size is itself a question. It is probably relevant that the original American diagnosis of prewar Japanese history had pronounced the militarists and ultranationalists—not the section chiefs—to be the source of the imperial affliction. Moreover, administrators of an indirect occupation could ill afford to dispense with their only channels of implementation and, even more important in the chaotic early days, their only source of specialized knowledge on the finer points of Japanese government. Being themselves disposed to stay in business, the Japanese bureaucrats were able to exploit their usefulness to their American counterparts as part of their effort to maintain themselves and their bureaus in functioning perpetuity.[64]

The question then becomes how they carried out their functions during the period of reform. In Amakawa Akira's treatments of the "response of the bureaucracy," he points out instances of Japanese initiative in proposing policy before the occupation had organized itself to demand that such policy be proposed. In October 1945, the Agriculture and Forestry Ministry drafted the first land reform bill, partly for progressive, partly for anticommunist reasons, but without guidance from SCAP. Similarly, the Home Ministry produced the revision of the lower house election law that passed the Diet in December without initial American involvement.[65] Other early initiatives such as those related to the police, local government, and notably the Constitution, fared less well because they contradicted or failed to satisfy the dictates of U.S. policy. Once the occupation was better established, the influence of the central bureaucracy was felt in such ways as its preference for legal rather than constitutional provisions and for centralization over decentralization.[66] This general interest in initiatives and independent (*jishuteki*) action is as important to the Japanese literature as the concern with contradictions is to the American analysis of U.S. occupation policy. For the question of whether postwar Japan is a product of reforms wholly "imposed" and in no way "spontaneous" is central to the Japanese people's critique of and support for the system under which they live. Amakawa's search for autonomous action even among those least likely to exhibit it—the immediate postwar, and hence prewar, bureaucracy—pointedly demonstrates the importance of the issue.

These attributes of spontaneity and independence more commonly appear in Japanese descriptions of political life outside the government. Despite the terrible economic conditions that compounded the uncertainty of the first postwar years, Japan had come alive in the autumn of 1945 with political activity, the intensity of which has rarely been apparent in Western works, while Japanese accounts have occasionally exaggerated it. The story American scholars usually presented as a series of occupation reforms—land, labor, constitution—Japanese historians told as the epic rising of opposition movements that flourished only to be suppressed. Now U.S. scholarship includes at least a glimpse of some of the other political participants in the exciting days when the democratic revolution seemed at hand and popular activism reached a peak. Most of this work is still done by the Japanese, however, and the student of the occupation confined to English is likely to arrive at 1947 never having heard of the democratic front or, worse, unaware of the political and intellectual ferment that electrified the emergence of postwar Japan and made phrases like "new life" and "bloodless revolution" appear to be practicable goals.[67]

One turns then to Japanese scholarship for studies of the reconstitution of the parties, with particular though not exclusive emphasis on the Communist and Socialist parties,[68] and for analyses of the democratic front and the nationwide political activity in the spring of 1946. One writer compares this movement and its failure to the Popular Rights Movement of the 1870s. He argues that just as the Meiji government's promise of a parliament in 1881 preempted the main goal of that democratic effort, the GHQ-government Constitution rent the preliminary unity of the Communist and Socialist parties by providing for *both* popular sovereignty *and* the continuation of the imperial institution. The insistence of part of the Communist leadership on the abolition of the emperor system, a position first stated in 1932, proved to be out of line not only with SCAP's views but also with those of other groups on the left.[69] In the general election of April 1946, one of the most agitated times since the end of the war, the

Communists failed to receive mass support, while many of the Socialists, who were elected in numbers, effectively removed themselves from the popular front by becoming "insiders" of a sort.[70] Workers, meanwhile, had embarked on "production control," taking over enterprises and managing them themselves, in an effort to improve the catastrophic economic situation.[71] Popular agitation demanding rice for a starving population culminated in the mass demonstrations of "Food May Day," 1946, to which both MacArthur and the Yoshida government responded with (in the words of SCAP) a "Warning against Mob Disorder or Violence." These raw denunciations of popular activism, plus SCAP's halting of the general strike in February 1947, are traditionally blamed for having destroyed the successful formation of labor's united front. But now scholars also point to the divisiveness among labor and party leaders and to such disruptive internal arguments as the strategic debate over whether to concentrate on the general strike or to promote production control in more industries and locations.[72]

These changes in recent Japanese treatments of the political and economic popular front partly reflect a difference of tone. One writer has suggested that scholars are more critical of the Communist party, less emphatic about how close Japan was to a genuine democratic revolution, and more likely to treat GHQ as a concrete factor in a nexus of power relations rather than as sheer authority, abstract and absolute.[73] The main point, however, is the political dynamism in the midst of which so many major issues—the emperor and the constitution, the election and the much delayed change of cabinets, economic crisis and the limits of protest—were all resolved in the spring of 1946.[74] In this light the plans of SWNCC begin to seem a long and remote way away.

In Japan, as in the United States, other less conspicuous activity also affected the operations of the occupation. Nongovernmental groups lobbied for their own concerns: former military men in favor of rearmament; educators, religious leaders, and social reformers for their respective causes; and Japanese businessmen on behalf of their interests, often in cooperation with the Japan lobby.[75] The way these Japanese groups related to the American occupation bureaucracy is not always clear, partly because the relationship has been more often speculated about than studied. One American suggested that the successful implementation of an occupation policy depended on the existence of a Japanese clientele for that policy. Another said that the successes—and he listed only the relief and rehabilitation program, land reform, and control of American "carpetbaggers"—occurred in areas that "did not require the cooperation of many Japanese." Yet another phrased it in terms of the failures, which resulted from the resistance and preeminence of the old guard in the Japanese political and financial worlds.[76] In Japanese scholarship both successes and failures have traditionally been described as the result of force, since SCAP wielded an authority against which no Japanese could prevail. But because the Japanese knew they could not, the appearance of cooperation was oftentimes deceiving. Manipulation of the occupation bureaucracy by the Japanese is now thought to have occurred more often than the conventional view suggested.[77]

If this analysis remains at a fairly primitive level, it is because for all the studies on policy-making in Washington or Tokyo, for all the recent attention to the different actors, bureaucratic or otherwise, for all the monographs on the "intentions" and "models" behind specific reforms, the great lacuna remains the process of implementation. One hungers to know what *happened* to all that policy when it reached the provinces, where the occupation's local organization, the military government or civil affairs teams, rendered "informal nonmandatory advice and assistance" to the local Japanese bureaucracy, which generally consisted of the same civil servants with the same civil (or uncivil) habits they had had before the war.[78]

Occasionally a scholar pursues a policy in local miniature, with tantalizing results. When nongovernmental "information committees" were established in the localities at the "suggestion" of occupation prefectural teams, the purpose was to disseminate occupation policy. Since GHQ had outlawed the prewar hamlet and block associations for having been the social building blocks of totalitarian control, local Japanese authorities complied with the occupation's suggestion—and then appointed the same members and assigned the same functions to the new information committees that the traditional local organizations had earlier performed. And out of these associations developed the present public relations organs of local administration.[79] In other cases, of which education may be the best documented, the Japanese forwarded reform proposals that had been simmering since the twenties, often employing the same vocabulary of democracy and individualism that the occupation did. This was especially true of the group of teachers weaned on progressive educational theory during the Taishō period, who despite being caught by the inspecting American soldiers in the remnants of military uniform ("Is he a militarist?" "No, he has no other clothes; he is not a militarist.") were eager to pursue educational reform. In Yamagata prefecture some pet projects of occupation education officers—the exotic "homeroom system" for example—were well received; others, such as the five-day school week (which Japan does not have to this day) and the appointment of women principals (by 1978 the prefecture could list only ten), required substantial pressure.[80] The push and pull that accompanied the establishment of the new education system, followed by what is often called the "period of reflection" during which some but hardly all of the reforms were undone, appears highlighted in this kind of local material.[81] Since there is no shortage of documents, both American and Japanese, it remains for occupation scholars to depart from examining the policy-making process and strike out into the real social world.

The same must be said of the effort to assess the situation and state of mind of the Japanese people during the occupation years. Scholars in Japan have begun to assemble documents and conduct interviews that provide the elements of which postwar social history could be made.[82] Because of the importance of the war, much of the published material centers on popular reactions to the surrender and defeat. The general resignation in the face of surrender derived in part from the fight-to-the-last propaganda of the wartime government, which had relentlessly insisted that defeat was unacceptable. When it came, argues one scholar, it was only natural that the people felt that the surrender was unconditional and submission to American policy inevitable.[83] Some of the widespread chagrin expressed over the provision that the authority of the emperor would be subject to SCAP was also provoked by the Japanese government, this time in its end-of-the-war litany of assurances that the *kokutai* would be preserved even in defeat. But provincial police reports also reveal that a number of Japanese were able to contemplate changes in the imperial institution with remarkable equanimity. Some thought U.S. policy predictably severe; others commented on its unexpected leniency. One poll of prescient local opinion, dated October 3, 1945, suggested that the unanticipated moderation in occupation policy was a response to the "delicate" relations between the United States and the Soviet Union, and if the occupation were to go on for too long, Japan might become an anti-Soviet military base subordinate to the United States. Initial reactions to the occupation troops followed a similar pattern: the fear and loathing instilled in the homefront population by wartime propaganda were soon transformed into a widely favorable reception, not because American military behavior was exemplary but because the Japanese were relieved to find the government's prophecies of brutishness untrue.[84] In each of these cases, the noteworthy point is that it was less the occupation than the wartime experience and the Japanese government to which the people were responding.

Japanese criticism of the military, the bureaucrats, and the *zaibatsu* erupted even as the early occupation policy was unfolding and wartime censorship was still in force. Farm families who had struggled "for the sake of victory" to meet their rice quotas with the labor of women and old men now resented the local authorities who still called for quotas in defeat and often commandeered scarce goods for their own use. Polls reported that the dissolution of the *zaibatsu* and removal of the militarists and ultranationalists were considered "natural," and indeed "essential" if Japan was to be reconstructed.[85] While the government called for "the hundred million to repent together" in the fall of 1945, many Japanese reflexively knew in the midst of their privation who they thought the repenters should be: the familiar triad of prewar social and political power—the military, the bureaucrats, and big business. Moreover, they felt that they needed "great statesmen like those of the Meiji Restoration" in order to become a democracy "as the Meiji Emperor had wished."[86] Some argued that once the military clique was swept away, Japan could return to its true political system, which was democratic; others saw the Allied forces as the sole hope for establishing democracy where none before existed. Even from such a meager sampling, two points are clear: one, that the Japanese possessed their own ideas for the future; and two, that these ideas were diverse, not easily character-ized or labeled. Progressive phrases like "the will of the people" coexisted in a single utterance with conservative touchstones like the Meiji emperor, and the very people who believed in fundamental change were often the slowest to respond to specific occupation re-forms. Japanese society, wartorn as it was, remained a far more com-plex phenomenon than has generally appeared in the literature.

In popular recollections of the immediate postwar period, the occupation is often referred to as a "natural disaster," a typhoon or an earthquake, which had to be lived through but would, like all catastrophes of nature, eventually pass away.[87] The same was said of the war and of the atomic bomb. Japanese intellectuals have criticized this attitude as passive and apolitical, in the sense that the people exchanged one authority, the imperial government, for another, the Supreme Commander, without exercising their autonomy in either case. This ingrained submissiveness is contrasted with the aggressive popular movements, which seemed to herald a new age in Japanese po-litical consciousness. When present-day commentators hark back to the first five years after the war as "the golden age of postwar de-mocracy . . . . The best period, when there were possibilities,"[88] they are obviously not thinking of the hardships that predominate in the popular memory of those years, but of the political potential that they feel was lost as the conservative structures of authority were reestablished. From the same contemporary vantage point writers lo-cate the origins of Japanese consumer culture and GNP-ism in those desperate days when the people turned the wartime slogan on its head and placed self ahead of state, drawing inward, away from public politics to the privatized life.[89] The occupation's economic recovery policy after 1947 is described as having reinforced these reactions, thus setting the stage for Japan's high-growth economy and for con-servative political dominance through the sixties and beyond. These arguments, long a part of contemporary political discourse, can now be refurbished with the materials of social history. The sense here, too, is that the popular political canvas during the occupation was broader and not clearly as black and white as the terms "submissive" and "apolitical" suggest.

Another neglected aspect of occupation studies is the cultural contact between Americans and Japanese which occurred sometimes because of—and sometimes despite—the best efforts of the authorities. The direct contact between occupation personnel and Japanese civilians is described in nearly all the local reports, though perhaps nowhere as poignantly as in the short story, "The American School."[90] But it is the larger, less direct experience that, while more difficult to pinpoint, is probably the more important. Takemae's account of what it meant to him as a child to listen to the occupation-sponsored English language instruction on the radio suggests that the program *"Kamu kamu Eigo"* (Come, come English) involved him and many others in a kind of grassroots democratic movement of greater significance than many of the formal institutional reforms.[91] In general, the occupation years became the second period of the "Americanization" of Japanese society in the twentieth century. The first had occurred in the 1920s when jazz, Valentino, and other aspects of *mōdan raifu* (modern life) convulsed urban youth and were identified, not fondly, as part of the phenomenon of *Amerikani-zumu*.[92] The war interrupted this surge of popular culture, which then resumed during the occupation but not necessarily because of it. Although it is an exaggeration to speak of a comparable Japanization of the United States during the occupation period, it is nonetheless true that Americans experienced a kind of cultural contact with Japan, the later history of which is now apparent as Japanese management and *sushi* take their revenge on Coca Cola.[93] In any case, it seems clear that no full account of the interaction between occupation policies and personnel and the Japanese can continue to omit the Japanese perspective or to summarize it in inert or monochromatic fashion.

Now that the Japanese people and the Japanese government, as well as Washington and the occupation bureaucracy, are each assuming a larger place in the dynamics of occupation history, where does the new scholarship leave MacArthur, once the overshadowing presence in both countries' heroic narratives? Oddly enough, it leaves him very much as he appeared during the early occupation, a figure whose single most important attribute was his vast and imposing authority—and the confidence with which he wielded it. This image would have been familiar in Washington, where it often angered people, and well known also to the occupation bureaucracy, to whom MacArthur played the field commander, deploying his troops. Once he assigned them the task of abolishing state Shinto or drafting a constitution according to general directions, they were left to fight the battle until they heard from headquarters again. Members of the occupation were able to use SCAP's authority to gain their own bureaucratic ends; some felt supported while others felt thwarted by it. Few, however, doubted his power, least of all MacArthur himself, who was a past master at occupying center stage. His position was amply conveyed to the Japanese, both through dramatic public relations like the photograph of the general towering over the emperor (which when the Japanese Home Ministry censored its publication prompted SCAP's two early directives insisting on freedom of the press) and through closed-door intimidation of the sort practiced in the meetings at which the Japanese government "agreed" to accept the GHQ draft of the Constitution.[94] Although numbers of Japanese and some Americans as well were sensitive to the irony of so oratorically democratic an occupation employing such undemocratic compulsion, the aura of authority emanating from GHQ squelched much of this consideration. "I'll tell MacArthur on you," Japanese children taunted,[95] and the same threat often existed unspoken in relations within the occupation bureaucracy and with the Japanese government.

This early projection of magisterial authority fostered a conflated image of MacArthur the Supreme Commander and MacArthur the supreme policymaker, to the point that in both heroic narratives, SCAP sometimes appeared responsible for any and all measures that took place under his command. It is this statesmanlike omnicompetence that has shrunk in the recent studies of policy-making, leaving MacArthur's role more credible for its being brought closer to size. Separated from his authority, which retains a grand scale, his influence on policy seems to have been the greatest in the areas he felt most strongly about. For these, MacArthur's own statements of the period remain a fair guide. Reading them one begins to know what *sounds* like him, what concerns, cosmic or trivial, fit into his theological visions of transplanted middle-American democracy. As part of the "spiritual revolution," for example, he took ideology very seriously, whether the abolition of prewar myths of the state or the inculcation of postwar values through democratic education and the Christianizing distribution of Bibles. Although the origins of Article Nine remain obscure, the idea of a constitutional renunciation of war sounds a good deal more like vintage MacArthur than like Prime Minister Shidehara or anyone else one finds mentioned.[96]

If MacArthur's vision was internally coherent, his statements easily lent themselves to misinterpretation. When he proposed such distinctive notions as Christianity or the emancipation of women, his meaning was clear enough. But when he seemed to be saying what others were saying about democracy or social change, the resemblance was often misleading. The heroic narrative in Japan, for example, has always stressed what are known in Japanese as "the five great reforms," referring to MacArthur's statement of October 11, 1945. In it he enjoined the Japanese government to correct "the traditional social order under which the Japanese people for centuries have been subjugated," and remarked that this effort would "unquestionably involve a liberalization of the Constitution." Five points followed: "The emancipation of women; the encouragement of the unionization of labor; the opening of schools to more liberal education; the abolishment of systems which through secret inquisition and abuse have held the people in constant fear; the democratization of Japanese economic institutions to the end that monopolistic industrial controls be revised." The statement concluded with the call for prompt action in housing, feeding, and clothing the population to prevent "major social catastrophe."[97] This was authentic MacArthur, but where the five points echo other sources, as in the need for unionizing and democratizing Japanese economic institutions, the wellsprings of his interest were often very different from those of others who held the same views. Japanese socialists and communists also opposed the *zaibatsu,* but not because they represented what MacArthur called "a form of socialism in private hands." Japanese labor leaders conceived of unions as political movements engaged in activities more far-reaching than MacArthur's idea of safeguarding the working man from exploitation and preventing child labor practices.[98] When MacArthur's subsequent actions belied this apparent convergence of intent, he is portrayed as having betrayed his own principles of reform. In fact, he had never quite meant what others had thought him to mean.

Now that the complex crosscurrents of policy-making are receiving more attention, the Supreme Commander is no longer so closely identified with occupation policy as a whole. This should make it possible to reexamine MacArthur as a prime specimen of what Japanese scholars have recently stressed as the "peculiarly American" notion of democracy that was visited upon Japan during the occupation.[99] Shrunk to mortal size, SCAP may prove a subject of renewed and fruitful interest.

THE QUEST FOR THE REVERSE COURSE

As with the actors in the occupation narrative, so with the plot—scholarship is eroding the heroic contours, drip by documentary drip, exposing layers of complexity where once things seemed smooth or simple. In the case of the actors, this has meant stressing the diverse motivations and bureaucratic mechanisms of those engaged in the making of policy and its execution. In the case of the plot, it has meant refining the reasons why the occupation turned out as it did. And because the original narratives disagreed on the outcome—the Japanese version of the occupation ending in at best "splendid failure," the American in at least "surprising success"[100]—the debates on the larger course of occupation history have generated more contention than have the analytic minutiae of bureaucratic politics. Indeed, the recent controversy over the "reverse course" stands as evidence of the historical and historiographical entanglement of Japan and America in the postwar period, and also as a cautionary example of the perils of binational scholarship.

At the 1980 Amherst conference on the occupation, Japanese scholars were startled to hear a young American named Peter Frost argue what has since been called in Japanese "the theory of the non-existence of the reverse course." This contradicted the "long-estab-

lished point of common knowledge'' among Japanese historians that
the early policies of democratization and demilitarization were halted
around 1948 and replaced with the priorities of economic recovery
and rearmament in the context of the cold war.[101] What the Americans at Amherst were loosely calling the ''reverse course'' Japanese
have long studied, most often of late employing the term ''change of
policy'' (*seisaku tenkan*), but never considering that such a change,
or reversal, had not taken place. In the Japanese heroic narrative,
1947–1948 signified the beginning of the counterrevolution—''Japan's Thermidor''—that reversed the progressive trends of the immediate postwar months and betrayed the promise of the democratic
revolution.[102] More recent scholarship, whether progressive, conservative, or ''empirical,'' has continued the inquiry into the reasons
and mechanisms behind this change in U.S. policy, which for the
Japanese has always represented the occupation at its most paradoxical. How to explain an occupation that liberated the communists then
purged them, purged the prewar leaders then liberated them, encouraged labor then stopped its strikes, undertook economic deconcentration then disavowed it, disarmed Japan constitutionally then promoted rearmament in the euphemistic name of self-defense? For
Japanese who held such great hope for the initial reforms of the occupation, the subsequent reversals remain at the very center of historical inquiry.

   No reverse course had figured in the American narrative, only a
''second phase'' in which there was a ''shift of emphasis'' from the
political to the economic and a gradual return of authority to the
Japanese. The occupation had therefore proceeded, or dwindled, rather
smoothly to its conclusion. No twists of plot or policy had sabotaged
Japan's progress toward democracy. For this reason occupation members like Justin Williams were themselves chagrined at the Amherst
conference to hear anyone still defending the concept of a reverse
course, that ''idée fixe,'' as Williams wrote in his memoirs, ''of
sympathizers with radical socialism in Japan, the 'emancipation
movement' in China, and the Labor governments of Australia and
Britain''[103]—and, he might have added, of many of the younger
American historians of the occupation, who also disagreed with the
paper that launched the debate. For a considerable portion of recent

U.S. scholarship has devoted itself to examining the sources and consequences of the policy changes that took place in 1947 and 1948, and the term "reverse course" now appears more frequently in English than in Japanese. But whatever words are used, U.S. revisionists have joined Japanese scholars in their insistence on the reversals of policy by a United States impelled by its economic, strategic, and overwhelmingly anticommunist interest to undercut the premises of its own reforms. For the Japanese this has meant scholarly ramification within the accepted interpretive framework, for the Americans, a critique of the received narrative for having minimized the impact of cold war geopolitics in favor of some variant of the "American Altruism Abroad School of postwar Japanese history."[104] The change in occupation policy, which has always drawn Japanese attention because of its connection to the fate of democracy in postwar Japan, has recently attracted American interest as a revealing instance of postwar U.S. foreign policy. The subject of the scholarship is the same, but the impetus is different, suggesting in part the complicated politics that underlay the arguments at Amherst. Before probing this point, however, it is useful to trace the recent scholarly accomplishments in pursuit of the reverse course that have appeared on both sides of the Pacific.

Once again the focus is U.S. policy, as Japanese and American scholars have explored the newly available documents to locate the reversals more precisely, both in political time and bureaucratic place. In Japanese writing the date of the occupation's change of policy has always varied, depending on the emphasis of the research. There is a chronology of social suppression which usually begins with the prohibition of the general strike in February 1947, but sometimes as early as SCAP's blunt response to the Food May Day demonstrations of 1946. It continues with restrictive labor legislation, such as the laws passed between 1948 and 1950 denying public employees the right to strike, and concludes with the "red purge" of 1949–1950, which affected public and private sectors alike. SCAP and G-2, acting to prevent the "communization" of Japan from within, have figured prominently in descriptions of this series of departures from earlier policy.[105] The main cold war chronology, on the other hand, follows U.S. anti-Soviet policy as it was articulated in Washington.

The account begins conventionally with the Truman doctrine in March 1947 and moves the cold war to the Japanese context with Secretary of the Army Kenneth Royall's speech in January 1948, in which he argued that economic reconstruction would enable Japan to "serve as a deterrent against any other totalitarian war threats" that might arise in the Far East. The policy that would make Japan a bulwark against communism in East Asia is next described as fully articulated in NSC 13/2, the National Security Council document of October 1948. Then, against the background of the Chinese revolution and the Korean War, this chronology of American cold war policy culminates with the economic recovery programs and Japan's rearmament as a U.S. ally. The U.S. military and the National Security Council receive top billing in the cast of characters responsible for these changes that affected Japan so profoundly.[106] A third and interrelated chronology pertains more directly to economic policy and sometimes begins with Dean Acheson's "Workshop of Asia" speech of May 1947. More often the shift from political reform to economic recovery is dated from the reports of the Strike and Draper/Johnston missions of February and April 1948. The first recommended decreased reparations removals from Japanese industry; the second urged curtailment of the deconcentration programs and other measures inimical to economic recovery. These recommendations were followed by the nine-point economic stabilization program of fall 1948 and its implementation in the "Dodge line" disinflation of 1949, often described as "the peak of the policy change."[107] The economic rehabilitation sought by these measures did not materialize, however, until the "special procurements boom" conferred on Japan by U.S. military purchases during the Korean War. Japanese discussions of economic policy give particular prominence to the special missions from Washington and to the role of American business. Draper, Johnston, Dodge, and the Japan lobby's Kauffman (whose report of September 1947 denouncing SCAP's economic policies as socialistic helped to scuttle the deconcentration program) are considered instrumental in reversing Japan's economic course, not only for anticommunist and anti-Soviet reasons but also in the global interests of U.S. capitalism.[108]

As these interlocking chronologies demonstrate, the occupation's "change of policy" has never been portrayed as a simple reversal of the sweeping reforms of 1945–1946, but as a series of measures that overturned or undermined elements of these reforms in the cause of anticommunism as the Americans perceived it. Recent scholarship has further complicated this portrayal by tracing the origin of the policy changes in detail, often identifying earlier antecedents, a greater diversity of motivations, and a larger number of participants in the evolution of any given policy.

In the case of labor, for example, Hayakawa Seiichirō and Takemae Eiji have pursued the origins of two legislative reversals of earlier reforms that had encouraged unions—the amended National Public Service Law of December 1948, which deprived government employees of the right to strike, and the revised Trade Union Law of 1949, which enhanced the power of management at the expense of the unions.[109] There is no doubt in either case that GHQ was supporting the reversal of legislation it had originally sponsored. It is also clear that in 1948 the reduction of Communist party influence in the unions was a vociferously expressed concern of the occupation authorities. This was true not only of such well-known examples as MacArthur's letter to Prime Minister Ashida recommending that state employees be deprived of the right to strike, but also of the routine reports of local military government teams examined by Takemae. Aghast to find that principals, too, were members of a teachers' union "controlled by a political party," one team cautioned that Japanese management was a "weak sister" even in the public school system.[110] Yet the emphasis in this recent work is less on the anticommunist motivations than on the bureaucratic prehistory of the legislative revisions, particularly the twists and turns of policy within the Labor Division of ESS. Almost as soon as the two original laws were enacted, they were on the way to revision, primarily because of inadequacies measured by the standards of traditional U.S. labor practices. Both Hayakawa and Takemae thus ruefully conclude that what scuttled the labor reforms was the peculiarly American conception of unionism, since it excluded not only the communists but most other vestiges of political activism. Outside the bureaucracy, Howard Schonberger describes similar efforts on the part of U.S. labor leaders to direct their Japanese counterparts along this same, congenially American path.[111] The fact that Japanese conservative leaders felt precisely the same way without any Anglo-American coaching ensured the success of these changes in labor policy.[112]

The crests and troughs of the cold war chronology of the reverse course have also settled into a more sedate line of changes, which shows Japan policy running nearly parallel to the general course of U.S. anti-Soviet thinking. Just as with other origins of the cold war, Western revisionists trace the assumption of a noncommunist, pro-American Japan to the security planning of the wartime and immediate postwar years.[113] The question then becomes: when did this assumption surface in occupation policy toward Japan? Again the answer is: earlier than had conventionally been assumed. The Kolkos argue that initial postsurrender directives from Washington had been at best ambivalent about reform, and Dower notes a change in MacArthur's image of Japan as early as his February 1946 proposal to terminate reparations for the sake of economic recovery.[114] According to Igarashi Takeshi, the overt intrusion of Washington's cold war policy into occupied Japan was prompted by MacArthur's proposal for an early peace treaty in March 1947, because it introduced the subject of Japan's future into the active agenda of the State Department. George Kennan and his Policy Planning Staff then took over the systematic formulation of Japan's role in the global containment of communism.[115] Kennan has received considerable attention in recent Japanese scholarship, in part because his views culminated in the central cold war statement of NSC 13/2, but also because his propensity for the written word left so large a documentary mark in the archives. Kennan's concern with Japan is another of what Hata Ikuhiko calls the "secondary indicators" of the change in U.S. policy, attention to which has broken the dramatic swerve of the reverse course into smaller and smaller increments of redirection.[116]

Since the shift from reform to reconstruction was the central issue in the change in occupation policy, the chronology of economic policy-making has also undergone meticulous adjustment. In addition to cold war considerations per se, historians have examined other aspects of the effort to set Japan back on its economic feet. Because of the economic crisis they faced daily in Japan, SCAP and some members of the occupation bureaucracy pressed for recovery well before Acheson invoked the workshop of Asia. MacArthur was therefore receptive to Washington's recommendation for decreasing reparations removals, but neither he nor the staff of ESS economists was prepared to agree to scrap the program for the dissolution of the *zaibatsu*.[117] Indeed, during the congressional debates over FEC-230, the economic deconcentration bill, MacArthur publicly stated that there would be a "blood bath and revolutionary violence" if the traditional pyramid of Japanese economic power were not torn down and redistributed.[118] In Schonberger's view, this controversy of early 1948 marked a major turning point in the reverse economic course. While there is no doubt that MacArthur's concern about communization from within was genuine, Schonberger argues that Undersecretary of the Army William Draper, who worked so forcefully for recovery and against deconcentration, "was emphatically not motivated in his Japan policies by ideological or strategic fears of the Soviet Union." Rather the "Wall Street General" had his eyes on business, for which the reconstitution of the Japanese financial community was essential, and he used anti-Soviet arguments primarily to obtain congressional funding for the economic recovery program.[119] Draper, like Kennan, is another figure whose contributing role in the evolution of U.S. policy helps to explain the larger outcome.

In similar fashion other sources for the change in economic policy have been located in Japan—in the long-standing conservative antagonism to the dissolution of the *zaibatsu,* which now found allies in Washington, the U.S. business community, and the Japan lobby. In the United States the financial burden of the occupation to the taxpayer had become an issue, though few writers mention the corresponding burden imposed on Japan by the "termination of war" expenditures that helped support the occupation.[120] Contributing to the confusion over economic policy was the diminution of the power of the occupation bureaucracy in Tokyo, as global issues once again took precedence in Washington's reconsideration of Japan policy. Indeed the latter part of the occupation, like the last stages of wartime planning, saw Japan once again the analogue of Germany, at least as far as the anti-Soviet arguments for economic reconstruction were concerned. When it came to the possibility of a Marshall Plan for Asia, however, the Japanese learned the limits of U.S. policy-making by analogy.[121] And in what way fiscal solutions doled out by such emissaries from Washington as Dodge and Shoup affected Japan's economic recovery is still a matter of debate. One scholar has moderated the Dodge disinflation of 1949-1950 into a "growth recession," though the general consensus still suggests that without the Korean War and its special procurements, the sum total of the occupation's efforts to revive Japan's economy would have remained well on the debit side.[122]

The sum total of new Japanese-American writing on the reverse course is surprisingly in balance. The two scholarly communities agree in general that the origins of the change in U.S. policy, like the origins of the cold war, consisted of a continuum of turning points that began earlier and proceeded with greater complexity than either of the two heroic narratives had allowed. But does the view that there were so many small reversals from so early in the occupation mean that there was no policy change at all? Of course not, and Frost, who chooses to emphasize continuities in American anticommunism and speak of a shifting of gears rather than a reversal of course, does not fundamentally disagree with Japanese scholars such as Takemae, who also stresses the distinctively American nature of occupation policy and chronicles roughly the same shifts in gear. What, then, caused the controversy over the existence of a reverse course?

This question can only be answered in the intellectual context of postwar Japan, where the reverse course has been both a historiographical and a political term since the early fifties. In its earliest appearance it referred not specifically to the changes in U.S. policy but to developments within Japan, including the reappearance of purged figures on the public scene and the gradual reemergence of prewar economic and political structures.[123] A series published on the feature page of a popular newspaper after the signing of the San Francisco Treaty in autumn 1951 was entitled "Reverse Course," and in twenty-five installments the United States was scarcely mentioned. Rather it was the "bureaucratic stench of the old days," "once again the age of Mitsui and Mitsubishi," the political scandals, the demise of the local police system and the specter of a reconstituted Home Ministry, the organization control ordinance, the revival of martial music—all of which were signs of continuity with the prewar period that was to have ended when the present began again after the war.[124]

But instead in 1951 the conservative government was calling for the "correction of excesses" perpetuated by the occupation and redefining the word "reforms" to mean the undoing of the original democratizing measures.[125] In the ensuing decades progressive Japanese intellectuals have continued their protest against any and all revivals of prewar political, social, and economic practices. Not unlike McCarthyism in the United States, the reverse course is part of the political experience of a generation, and its importance cannot lightly be denied. As one Japanese scholar wrote after attending the Amherst conference:

Whose reverse course was it to begin with? It was the reverse course of the Japanese people who hoped for peace and democracy. And just as it was not a reverse course for American government or business, nor was it a reverse course for the Japanese military, the conservative party, or the *zaibatsu*. Any discussion of the reverse course that excludes this viewpoint is dangerous.[126]

Similarly, the "reverse course" of the younger American historians who use the term is part of the critical revisionism of liberal views of postwar U.S. foreign policy. These scholars are equally unsympathetic to attempts like that of Frost to explain away or minimize the change in American policy, since to them any benign assessment of the "second phase" of the occupation is an ideological justification of U.S. dominance over Japan in the context of the cold war.

The controversy over the reverse course in the end may reveal more about historiography than about history. Japanese and American scholars have now come to largely similar renderings of the sequence of policy changes over the course of the occupation. They collaborate and often use the same terms, of which the "reverse course" is a prime example. But if in sharing the historiographical tasks they neglect to develop an acute sense of their respective national contexts, this interaction can engender misunderstandings of the sort that have occurred since the earliest postwar days. Disentangling—and respecting—the separate perspectives is one charge to future historians of the postwar relationship.

ENLARGING THE JAPANESE-AMERICAN PERSPECTIVE

Another charge, which scholars have begun to meet, is to broaden the perspective of what was officially an Allied occupation beyond the confines of narrowly Japanese-American relations. In Japan recent attention to other allies is part of the effort to retrieve occupation history from wholly American dominance. Studies relating to the Soviet Union, China, Australia, and England have appeared, though nothing linking them in the grand multi-archival manner of a Christopher Thorne.[127] Other evidence of what the Japanese term the attempt to "relativize" the occupation is the frequent call for comparative work. Although the Allied occupation of Germany is the most obvious and indeed the most considered case, suggestions have been made to seek material further afield in the Moors, Rome, or even Sparta.[128] Closer to home, several Japanese authors make passing and sometimes bitter references to the similarity between Japan during the occupation and prewar Manchuria under Japanese rule, although no study comparing the two has yet appeared.[129]

A different kind of comparison, and one with contemporary political relevance in Japan, is the occupation of Okinawa, which has attracted increasing scholarly interest and some controversy. Unlike the Japanese mainland, the Ryūkyū islands were administered by the U.S. military in a direct occupation that was transmuted in 1950 to a U.S. civil adminstration. By virtue of the ingenious concept of "residual sovereignty" incorporated into the San Francisco Treaty, Okinawa remained under U.S. control until it was returned to Japan in 1972. The strategic importance of these offshore islands had been continuously asserted by U.S. military planners from the closing years of the Pacific war throughout the cold war phases of anti-Soviet defense. For this reason the occupation of Okinawa from first to last possessed a character more overtly revealing of U.S. security interests than the sometimes obfuscatingly indirect mainland example. For Japanese scholars this occupation also raises another layer of questions concerning Japanese dominance of the indigenous Okinawan culture, which U.S. authorities sought to strengthen in the early postwar years as part of their effort to eliminate the baneful remnants of the Japanese central government. And now of course the Americans have been replaced by Tokyo, once again in a dominant role. An additional example of an internal Japanese comparison is Shindo Ei-ichi's work on the "divided territories," by which he means the direct American occupation of Okinawa and the separate Soviet occupation of the Southern Kuriles, the latter, as Japanese conservative groups periodically advertise, being "still occupied." Shindo's point, however, is that the Japanese government, and even the emperor, were involved in 1947-1948 in the decision to continue the U.S. military presence in Okinawa. His argument, which generated considerable comment in Japan, stresses the importance of this support in Kennan's early formulation of the concept of the defense perimeter.[130]

Studies of Okinawa, though they offer the salutary advantages of comparison, cannot escape from a concentration on American policy toward Japan and its territories. For that purpose the occupation has to be not only relativized but globalized, and the emerging monographic literature in both countries has moved expansively in this direction. The focus remains on the United States, but instead of treating its Japan policy as if it existed in a vacuum, the lens has been widened to include other concerns and other parts of the world that affected—and in some cases determined—the shape U.S. Japan policy would take.[131]

In a natural extension of perspective, Japan policy is frequently viewed within the context of U.S. policy toward Asia. Tracing the earlier strands of what by 1950 was a full-blown military, political, and economic strategy to contain communism in Asia as in Europe, scholars have concentrated on the attempts to link Japan and Southeast Asia in what Michael Schaller calls "the Great Crescent," William Borden terms an integrated regional economy, and the Japanese once knew as the greater East Asia co-prosperity sphere.[132] For it was becoming apparent even in 1947 that the economic recovery of Japan would depend to no small degree on its ability to locate suitable trading partners. There were obvious limits to direct economic assistance on the part of the United States, and Japan lacked the hard currency with which to pay for American goods in bilateral trade. As an NSC document of late 1949 tersely stated, Japan must secure its food and raw materials "from the [southern] Asiatic area, in which its natural markets lie, rather than from the United States, in which its export market is small.'' This was all the more true "in view of the desirability of avoiding preponderant dependence on Chinese sources.''[133]

Although the possibility of Sino-Japanese trade remained a debated issue until after the Korean War, Southeast Asia was increasingly emphasized both in Washington and Tokyo as the most suitable area for revived Japanese trade.[134] At the same time, the linking of the former European colonies to noncommunist Japan would serve the interests of keeping Southeast Asia noncommunist as well. Hence from 1947 to 1955 the United States experimented with several versions of "coordinated aid," subsidizing Japanese exports to Southeast Asia to promote trade within the proposed regional bloc. This economic offensive, which Japanese historians have generally designated U.S. imperialism, is now incisively chronicled by Borden, who rechristens it "multilateral neocolonialism." He then shows how this economic program was replaced by military aid in the form of the special procurements that did so much for the Japanese economy during the Korean War and beyond. He also suggests that here, as with Draper's Japan recovery program, the main concern of the more astute policymakers was global economic crisis, although the communist threat was often more persuasive to Congress and the American public.[135] Even if the two are not clearly separable, this kind of analysis helps to sophisticate the more monolithic accounts of the cold war.

Similar effect may be expected from new work on the Korean War and the signing of the peace treaty.[136] Both events figured prominently in the Japanese heroic narrative, which portrayed them as the culmination of reestablished Japanese conservatism and of U.S. cold war policy. The results were rearmament, a separate peace, and, by virtue of the Security Treaty, "subordinate independence" to the United States.[137] Without disputing the outcome of what the Japanese call the San Francisco treaty system, recent studies shatter the ultimately consistent logic of U.S. Asian policy into shards of conflicting and ambiguous antecedents. In his preliminary investigations into the security aspects of the peace settlement, Roger Dingman traces the uneven evolution of U.S. thinking about the strategic value of postwar Japan. In the years immediately following the war, naval planners had not moved beyond Guam in their arguments for a base in the Western Pacific, and State Department drafts of a peace treaty in 1947 were still primarily concerned with Japan's *dis*armament. Gradually in 1948 and 1949 Japan's importance for U.S. security was emphasized by military and diplomatic officials as well as by the American press. Even as China was "lost" and before the Korean War dramatized the military point, the necessity of a bilateral security settlement had become a tenet of American policy. But Dingman argues that it was a tenet whose precise formulation was mired in the rivalries of personal and bureaucratic politics. Army, navy, and air force planners defined their respective operational needs in Japan differently. The Joint Chiefs disagreed with the State Department on Japanese rearmament, which the Pentagon supported, and on the timing of the treaty, which the Pentagon wished to have postponed while the diplomats at State (and the Japanese) pressed for its initiation. MacArthur moved from insisting on guaranteed neutrality and the adequacy of Okinawa for U.S. military operations to accepting the characterization of all of Japan as a base in the struggle against the Soviet Union. And Dulles, suggests Dingman, went to Tokyo in 1951 with a little something for everyone (and Republicans in particular), so that U.S. bases, rearmament, and the right of intervention in case of communist subversion eventually found their way into the terms of the U.S.–Japan Security Treaty.[138]

The Japanese, in the meantime, pursued their own zigzag course toward a treaty, although independence, not security, was their guiding motive, and U.S. dominance of the peace-making process their constant constraint. In the course of the occupation, Japanese officials considered five different versions of a treaty, from the early efforts in 1946 and 1947 to counteract what was then expected to be a punitive peace to the ticklish final concessions on aspects of rearmament and U.S. criminal jurisdiction over American personnel.[139] In both the Japanese and American instances, domestic politics and international considerations outside the narrow corridor of U.S.–Japanese relations impinged on the peace-making efforts.[140] As the documents become available for the early fifties, it should be possible to reexamine the Korean War and its impact on Japan and, even more important, to trace the complicated crosscurrents in the international sphere and waves of domestic protest in Japan that attended the preparations for the San Francisco peace conference. Here again, the global context of these events—including developments in Europe, China, and Australasia, as well as in the Soviet Union—will be indispensable. Western scholars outside the United States are already doing a good deal to expand the insistently bilateral focus of occupation studies. Discussions of British or Australian perspectives revealingly describe the parts played by these nations. They also serve to correct some of the entrenched defects of vision affecting Japanese and American eyes that have been locked for too long in too blinkered a trans–Pacific gaze.[141]

The situation is similar in studies of the cold war, which Akira Iriye and others have discussed in a global perspective.[142] Often, however, the cold war simply transfers to Japan in relation to the reverse course and ends up being treated in a narrowly Japanese-American compass. Perhaps this is the result of the work of Japanese historians and American Japan specialists who sometimes tend to see the world the way MacArthur did, and as Herblock once portrayed him: sitting in front of a cubic globe with Asia occupying its entire visible face. Next to him, in front of a spherical earth with Russia in the center and Europe and China at its two extremes, sits George Marshall, who chides MacArthur gently, "We've been using more of a roundish one."[143] And so indeed was the United States throughout the period of wartime planning and the occupation. As Kennan, whose globe more resembled Marshall's, said in 1948, "Any world balance of power means first and foremost a balance on the Eurasian land mass. That balance is unthinkable as long as Germany and Japan remain power vacuums."[144] But even Kennan was more concerned with Japan than most U.S. policymakers, whose own global center was as squarely located in Europe (hovered over by the Soviet Union) as MacArthur's was in Asia. An early historian, Herbert Feis, made this point quite clear, but much of the scholarship since his time has lifted postwar Japanese-American relations out of the world in which they occurred.[145]

Recent efforts to return the occupation to its context, usually by diplomatic historians and specialists in international relations, have only begun to remedy the situation. Borden's work is one example, since he begins with global economic disequilibrium, the worldwide dollar gap caused by the disproportionate economic strength of the United States after the war, and shows how European recovery was the prime issue of the day.[146] A similar kind of analysis that compared the changes in U.S. policy toward Germany with Japan's "reverse course" would go far toward demystifying the nature of the shift, as would more accounts like those of Schonberger, who at least reveals that the Draper who advocated Japan's economic recovery was the same man who had previously served as chief economic adviser to General Clay in Germany.[147] And what of the congressmen who had not served in either place, but knew Europe far better, at least by reputation, than they did Japan? Indeed one of the most striking aspects of U.S. policymaking and opinion during the occupation years is the persistent *lack* of interest in Japan in high political places. If one were to view the American scene without antennae especially tuned to the subject of Japanese affairs, both heroic narratives might disintegrate, since there would not likely be enough material to carry so consistent a story line. Instead of a plot, U.S. policy toward Japan would become a series of sometimes disconcertingly disconnected episodes.

The same, of course, is true of Japan, which in 1945 was not a vacuum waiting to be occupied. The emphasis on the occupation as an American-Japanese encounter, while natural enough in one sense, is seriously limiting in another. The Japanese economic historians, who have developed sophisticated Marxian analyses of the evolution of capitalism from the prewar period, often stress the need to examine the long-term structural continuities as much as the discontinuities introduced by the postwar reforms.[148] Yet in matters apart from economics, America figures prominently even in their accounts. Also, the reaction of non-Marxist Japanese writers to the Marxist efforts to deemphasize the American role in internal reform has only exacerbated the question. Sodei Rinjirō, for example, who criticized the structural interpretation for diminishing the presence of the occupation forces to the point that the postwar reforms seem to have happened all by themselves, attempted to correct this distortion with a new biography of MacArthur.[149] This kind of debate, combined with the vast storehouse of American documents, has continued the tendency to overdraw the part of the United States in the larger picture.

Beginnings, however, are being made in treating the occupation period as a phase of Japanese history in which Americans were involved, but not necessarily in a dominant historical role. The increasing allusions to earlier Japanese origins of the postwar reforms suggest that an understanding of Japanese conceptions of land or educational reform may be a truer guide to the historical outcome of these measures than perpetual parsing of the American views expressed in occupation documents. In short, both versions of the occupation would benefit from an effort to correct the tunnel vision that results from too restricted a view of Japanese-American relations.

BEYOND THE HEROIC NARRATIVE

For all the scholarly achievements of this latest phase in occupation historiography, both Japanese and American views seem still to be in transition. This impression derives in part from the mosaic of monographic studies that have not yet been recreated in a new account of the occupation as a whole, although Dower is now working on just such a project.[150] Yet there are more important reasons for the sense that what has *not* happened in history writing may be as revealing in this instance as what has.

In Japan the constraints of the present are readily apparent in scholarship on the occupation, which in so many respects remains a contemporary political issue. Any consideration of postwar Japanese democracy returns inevitably to the period in which its institutional structure was established. And when the question is as politically volatile as the proposal for constitutional revision to make rearmament possible, even small changes in scholarly inflection can have significant consequences. After seven years of deliberation, in 1964, the official Commission on the Constitution determined in its majority representation that the Constitution had been enacted under duress from GHQ/SCAP, and not on the basis of what the Potsdam Declaration had described as ''the freely expressed will of the Japanese people.'' A minority concluded that ''it cannot necessarily be said that the present Constitution was not enacted on the basis of the free will of the people.''[151] This circumspect double negative concealed one of the major political debates of postwar Japan. Progressive intellectuals who had once protested the imposition of the MacArthur Constitution found themselves supporting it against conservatives who wanted it rewritten.[152] In the years since the occupation, scholars who were opposed, heart and soul, to the security alliance with the United States have nonetheless defended the reforms carried out by the Americans in the early postwar months. The sharp counterattack on Etō Jun's accusations that U.S. actions in this period were both illegal and unjust is but the latest instance of progressive scholars rising to the defense of the origins of postwar Japan, even though they themselves have serious questions about the imposed nature of the same reforms.[153]

Even more profoundly influential than matters of present politics is the obstacle of the past. For the Japanese the beginning of the occupation was the end of the war, and the war remains the abiding point of reference for conceptions of the postwar period. Since the earliest postwar days, most Japanese intellectuals have endorsed what Dower calls the ''root'' theory of modern Japanese history. Rather than dismissing the thirties as a ''historic stumble'' the way Yoshida did, they insisted that unless the very fundaments of the prewar emperor system were abolished, Japan could not be remade.[154] And because they had once thought this possible, they remained acutely sensitive to the reemergence of prewar elements in postwar society and politics.

This sensitivity has now passed to younger generations who did not themselves experience the war. Nor did they need to, since the sense of the war had so deeply colored postwar thinking.[155] Aroused by the conservative trends within Japan in the seventies they, too, rose to the defense of the postwar reforms. Etō and others were accused of ''denying the postwar,'' and historians who considered the years from the 1920s through the 1950s as a single period were criticized as reactionary because they asserted a positive continuity—rather than negative survivals—between the pre- and the postwar eras. These scholars, it was said, were attempting to ''relativize'' the significance of the postwar reforms and hence to deny the very origins of contemporary Japanese democracy.[156]

In American scholarship on postwar Japan, the experience of course is different. The subject itself is historically peripheral, though as an instance of postwar U.S. foreign policy the occupation was by no means unrepresentative. Although the initial views of the occupation had been forged in the crucible of World War II, the cold war proved more influential in the writings of the seventies. By focusing on the period from 1947 to 1951, after the change in occupation policy had occurred, the new work departed substantially from previous U.S. renderings of the experience. But on the question of the postwar reforms, the Americans, too, retain something of the early notion of what the occupation should, and could, have done. When Dower writes that the occupation "simultaneously represented a great epoch of reform and one of history's impressive holding operations,"[157] there is a sense both of idealism and of idealism betrayed. Indeed the illusion of a new Japan, once briefly shared by Japanese and Americans in 1945, has survived to inform the scholarship of the present. However much writers in either country disagree with one another on the outcome of the occupation, most remain heir to the original vision that in postwar Japan history offered a true and truly rare opportunity for radical change.

Some day as this vision fades, the two heroic narratives will subside into workaday historical accounts. Although much may be lost when this happens, certain aspects of the current portrayal might benefit from amendment sooner rather than later. There is first of all the need to reconnect the twentieth century and join pre- and postwar Japan together, not to celebrate or reject one or the other, but to view the occupation across a longer span of time. 1941 and 1945 are epochal dates to be sure, but history also moves in larger as well as in smaller steps. It is time, too, to transcend the categories of the heroic narrative and pose questions of our own. Until now scholars have accepted the organization dictated to them, usually by the occupation, and the tyranny of the bureaucratic document has held sway. But the fate of the *zaibatsu,* for example, is only one indicator of economic change, and the encounter between mid-twentieth-century American and Japanese society cannot be exhausted by a laundry list of legal or institutional reforms. Indeed, the subject cannot be illuminated very well at all if it remains imprisoned within a strictly Japanese-American context. The scholar might best abjure particularistic explanations that affix the adjective "Japanese" or "American" to areas of political, social, and economic life which in fact characterize much of the postwar industrial world. The historian who ventured to assess the middle part of the twentieth century as "a single half-century effort by reform-minded and conservative elites to exploit postwar circumstances for a successful restructuring of the hierarchies they dominated" was writing about Europe, but how familiar and accurate his portrayal sounds to the student of modern Japan.[158] For many of the developments of the period, neither the American occupation nor the Japanese experience, nor even the two together, can be assigned full historical credit or blame.

As Japanese and American scholars continue to step back from their common past, the occupation will become history and the postwar period in Japanese-American relations may finally come to a close.

NOTES

(Unless otherwise specified, all Japanese works are published in Tokyo. Japanese names are given in the Japanese order, surname first.)

1. For contemporary responses to the end of the war, see, e.g., Awaya Kentarō, *Shiryō Nihon gendaishi*, vols. 2 and 3, *Haisen chokugo no seiji to shakai*, vols. 1 and 2 (Ōtsuki shoten, 1980–81), pp. 461–71; Hidaka Rokurō, ed., *Sengo shisō no shuppatsu, Sengo Nihon shisō taikei*, vol. 1 (Chikuma shobō, 1968); Ishida Takeshi, "Sengo kaikaku to soshiki oyobi shōchō," in *Sengo kaikaku*, ed. Tōkyō daigaku shakai kagaku kenkyūjo, vol. 1 (Tōkyō daigaku shuppankai, 1974), pp. 202–18. For the beginnings of contemporary history, Fujiwara Akira, "Gendaishi josetsu," *Iwanami kōza Nihon rekishi*, vol. 22, *Gendai* 1 (Iwanami shoten, 1977), pp. 1–25; Tōkyō rekishi kagaku kenkyūkai gendaishi bukai, ed., *Nihon gendaishi no shuppatsu: sengo minshushugi no keisei* (Aoki shoten, 1978), p. iii. There is also a large genre, much of it popular, of works that relate to "August 15," ranging from Pacific War Research Society, ed., *Japan's Longest Day* (Kōdansha, 1963) to Yasuda Takeshi and Fukushima Jūrō, eds., *Shōwa nijūnen hachigatsu jūgonichi* (Shin jinbutsu ōraisha, 1973).

2. *Political Reorientation of Japan*, vol. 1 (report), and vol. 2 (documents) (Washington, D.C.: U.S. Government Printing Office, Report of Government Section, 1950).

3. On the role of the military language schools in the development of Japanese studies in the United States, see Herbert Passin, *Beirikugun Nihongo gakkō: Nihon to no deai* (TBS Britannica, 1981; English translation forthcoming from Kōdansha International, 1982). For early

impressions of members of this generation, see Otis Cary, ed., *War-Wasted Asia: Letters, 1945–46* (Tokyo and New York: Kodansha, 1975).

4. Robert E. Ward, "Reflections on the Allied Occupation and Planned Political Change in Japan," in Robert E. Ward, ed., *Political Development in Modern Japan* (Princeton: Princeton University Press, 1968), p. 477; also, Herbert Passin, "Occupation Reforms as Experiments in Guided Social Change," *The Legacy of the Occupation—Japan* (New York: Occasional Papers of the East Asian Institute, Columbia University, 1968); Ward, "The Legacy of Occupation," in Herbert Passin, ed., *The United States and Japan* (Englewood Cliffs, N.J.: Prentice-Hall, 1966), pp. 29–56; Edwin O. Reischauer, *The United States and Japan*, 3d rev. ed. (Cambridge: Harvard University Press, 1965); Grant K. Goodman, ed., *The American Occupation of Japan: A Retrospective View* (Lawrence: Center for East Asian Studies, University of Kansas, 1968); Kazuo Kawai, *Japan's American Interlude* (Chicago: University of Chicago Press, 1960); and, in the seventies from the same perspective, Robert A. Scalapino, "The American Occupation of Japan: Perspectives after Three Decades," *Annals of the American Academy of Political and Social Science*, 428 (Nov. 1976), 104–13. For an example of dissenting views, see T. A. Bisson, *Prospects for Democracy in Japan* (New York: Macmillan, 1949), and *Zaibatsu Dissolution in Japan* (Berkeley: University of California Press, 1954).

5. From the immediate postoccupation years, Inoue Kiyoshi et al., *Gendai Nihon no rekishi*, 2 vols. (Aoki shoten, 1952–1953); Hori Masanori, ed., *Nihon shihonshugi kōza: sengo Nihon no seiji to keizai*, 10 vols. and supp. (Iwanami shoten, 1953–1955), the first postwar analysis of one of the main schools of Japanese Marxian historiography (*kōza-ha*); Nihon kyōsantō chōsa iinkai, ed., *Senryōka Nihon no bunseki: Amerika wa Nihon o dō shihai shite iru ka* (San'ichi shobō, 1953), the Japan Communist Party's version of the occupation; Nihon seiji gakkai, ed., *Sengo Nihon no seiji katei* (Iwanami shoten, 1953), essays from the general progressive viewpoint of those years; for an early attempt to reveal the scars (*hankon*) left by the occupation by portraying it as it was, see "Senryō to Nihon," *Shisō*, no. 348 (June 1953). Representative surveys from the sixties include Rekishigaku kenkyūkai, ed., *Sengo Nihonshi*, 5 vols. (Aoki shoten, 1961–1962); Shinobu Seizaburō, *Sengo Nihon seiji shi, 1945–1952*, 4 vols. (Keisō shobō, 1965–1967), and Tsuji Kiyoaki, *Shiryō sengo nijūnenshi* (Nihon hyōronsha, 1966), vol. 1, *Seiji*, pp. 1–188. For a general historiographical review, see Fujiwara Akira and Yoshii Ken'ichi, "Gendai no seiji keizai," *Iwanami kōza Nihon rekishi*, 26 (1972), 347–68; and the extensive bibliographic essay by Hatano Sumio, in *Shūsen shiroku*, vol. 6, Gaimushō, ed. (Hokuyōsha, 1978).

6. The "heroic" stage of historiography is described by Herbert Butterfield as the earliest rendering of a contemporary subject, which naturally dramatizes the right and wrong of the matter because of the writer's involvement with one side or another. *History and Human Relations* (London: Collins, 1951), pp. 10–17.

7. The SCAP materials are in the National Records Center of the National Archives in Suitland, Maryland, and soon microfilms of the more than 10,000 feet of records will be available at the National Diet Library in Tokyo. See the Diet Library publication, Kumata Atsumi, "Beikoku kokuritsu kōmonjokan shozō no Nihon senryō kankei monjo ni tsuite," *Kokuritsu kokkai toshokan geppō*, 193 (April 1977), 2–20. For the scholarly controversy in Japan surrounding the return of materials confiscated by the U.S. during the occupation, see "Amerika ni okeru ōshū bunsho to shiryō no kōkai ni tsuite," *Rekishigaku kenkyū*, 388 (Sept. 1972), 25–34. For the joint U.S.-Japanese scholarly appeal to the Japanese government to make postwar documents available, see "Nichibei kenkyūsha ni yoru kōmonjo no kōkai yōsei," *Rekishigaku kenkyū*, 487 (Dec. 1980), 55–56. For examples of the popular reaction in Japan to the initial release in 1976 of Japanese Foreign Ministry papers on the occupation, see *Asahi*

shinbun, May 31, June 1–6, July 23, 1976; Kojima Noboru, "Nihon senryō," *Bungei shunjū,* August, Oct.–Nov. 1976. In English, "The Occupation of Japan," *Mainichi Daily News,* May 31–Oct. 4, 1976. The relevant volumes of the *Foreign Relations of the United States* were also published during the seventies: *1946,* vol. 8, *The Far East* (1971); *1947,* vol. 6, *The Far East* (1972); *1948,* vol. 6, *The Far East and Australasia* (1974); *1949,* vol. 7, *The Far East and Australasia,* part 2 (1976); *1950,* vol. 6, *East Asia and the Pacific* (1976); *1951,* vol. 6, *Asia and the Pacific* (1977).

8. BIBLIOGRAPHIES: in English, Robert E. Ward and Frank Joseph Shulman, eds., *The Allied Occupation of Japan, 1945–1952: An Annotated Bibliography of Western-Language Materials* (Chicago: American Library Association, 1974), which includes materials published through 1972. For more recent works, see Shulman's exhaustive continuation of this work, *Bibliography on the Allied Occupation of Japan: A Bibliography of Western-Language Publications from the Years 1970–1980* (Ann Arbor: Michigan Papers in Japanese Studies, Center for Japanese Studies, University of Michigan, forthcoming). Also John W. Dower, "Occupied Japan: A Working Bibliography," *Bulletin of Concerned Asian Scholars,* 6, 1 (Jan.–Mar. 1974), 16–21. In Japanese, Nihon gakujutsu shinkōkai (Sakamoto Yoshikazu et al.), eds., *Nihon senryō bunken mokuroku* (Nihon gakujutsu shinkōkai, 1972); Ōkurashō sengo zaiseishi shitsu, ed., *Sengo Nihon keizai bunken mokuroku: shūsen kara kōwa made* (Ōkurashō, 1973); Senryōshi kenkyūkai, ed., *Chihō ni okeru senryōshi kankei bunken mokuroku* (Nihon gakujutsu shinkōkai, 1976). HISTORIOGRAPHICAL ESSAYS: John W. Dower, "Occupied Japan as History and Occupation History as Politics," *Journal of Asian Studies,* 34, 2 (Feb. 1975), 485–504; Ray A. Moore, "Reflections on the Occupation of Japan," *Journal of Asian Studies,* 38, 4 (Aug. 1979), 721–34; Amakawa Akira, " 'Nihon senryō' kenkyū no tenbō," *Kokka gakkai zasshi,* 88, 4–5 (May 1975), 367–86; Takemae Eiji, "Senryō kenkyū no genjō to kadai," *Senryō sengoshi: tainichi kanri seisaku no zen'yō* (Sōshisa, 1980); and Iokibe Makoto, "The Occupation Period," in Sadao Asada, ed., *Post World War II Japanese Research in Diplomatic History and International Politics: A Basic Bibliography and Critical Essays* (forthcoming, in English). The Japanese original of this bibliography, though shorter on occupation sources than its English counterpart, is valuable for postwar international relations as a whole. Nihon kokusai seiji gakkai, ed., *Sengo Nihon no kokusai seiji gaku* (Yūhikaku, 1979). For a reference work on Japanese diplomatic history, Nihon gaikōshi jiten hensan iinkai, ed., *Nihon gaikōshi jiten* (Gaimushō gaikō shiryōkan, 1978).

9. The main SCAP records—and their microfilms—remain uncataloged. On the University of Maryland collection from the SCAP censorship files, see Frank Joseph Shulman, "The Gordon W. Prange Collection: Published and Unpublished Materials from the Allied Occupation of Japan," in Lawrence H. Redford, ed., *The Occupation of Japan: Economic Policy and Reform* (Norfolk, Va.: The MacArthur Memorial, 1980), pp. 375–82. Two of the many Japanese works that began to record oral history in the early seventies are the popular *Makkāsā no Nihon,* Shūkan shinchō, ed. (Shinchōsha, 1970), and the first collaborative collection edited by Shisō no kagaku kenkyūkai, *Kyōdō kenkyū: Nihon senryō* (Tokuma shoten, 1972). Takemae Eiji has published several of the interviews he conducted for his own research: "The U.S. Occupation Policies for Japan: An Interview with Theodore Cohen by Eiji Takemae" (in English), *Tōkyō toritsu daigaku hōgakkai zasshi,* 14, 1 (Sept. 1973), 1–39; Takemae and Gail M. Nomura, "Sōhyō and U.S. Occupation Labor Policy: An Interview with Valery Burati," *Tōkyō keidai gakkaishi,* 97/98 (1976), 253–94; and Takemae, "Memoire on Postwar Educational Reform in Japan: An Interview with Prof. Mark Taylor Orr by Eiji Takemae," *Tōkyō keidai gakkaishi,* 115 (March 1980), 125–30.

10. On the Japanese distinction between empirical and ideological (or Marxist), see Na-

gahara Keiji, "Sengo Nihon shigaku no tenkai to shochōryū," *Iwanami kōza Nihon rekishi,* vol. 24, *Bekkan* 1 (Iwanami shoten, 1977), pp. 27–32.

11. See Takemae's major monograph on American labor policy, *Amerika tainichi rōdō seisaku no kenkyū* (Nihon hyōronsha, 1970); also, "Senryō seisaku keisei ni kansuru jakkan no kōshō," *Rekishigaku kenkyū,* 386 (July 1972), 48–56. In both of these he called for detailed empirical (*jisshōteki*) studies, of the sort he has helped foster in an occupation research group established in 1972 and based at his university, Tokyo keizai daigaku. See its newsletter, *Senryōshi kenkyūkai nyūsu.* Other works by Takemae include, on U.S. wartime planning, "Tainichi senryō seisaku no keisei to hatten," *Iwanami kōza Nihon rekishi,* vol. 22, *Gendai* 1, pp. 27–80, and a recent collection of his articles, *Senryō sengoshi* (Sōshisha, 1980). In English, essays on labor reform in Moore, and on reformist parties and mass movements in Ward and Sakamoto; see notes 25 and 26 below.

The scholars who have concentrated on the occupation in recent years include Amakawa Akira, Hata Ikuhiko, Iokibe Makoto, Koseki Shōichi, Igarashi Takeshi, Sodei Rinjirō, Awaya Kentarō, and Yamagiwa Akira. For their works, see below.

For Dower's work, see "The Eye of the Beholder: Background Notes on the U.S.-Japan Military Relationship," *Bulletin of Concerned Asian Scholars,* 2, 1 (Oct. 1969), 15–31; "Occupied Japan and the American Lake, 1945–1950," in Edward Friedman and Mark Selden, eds., *America's Asia: Dissenting Essays on Asian-American Relations* (New York: Pantheon, 1971), pp. 146–206; "The Superdomino in Postwar Asia: Japan In and Out of *The Pentagon Papers,*" in Noam Chomsky and Howard Zinn, eds., *The Senator Gravel Edition of The Pentagon Papers,* vol. 5 (Boston: Beacon Press, 1972), pp. 101–42; "Occupied Japan as History"; and his biography of Yoshida, *Empire and Aftermath: Yoshida Shigeru and the Japanese Experience, 1878–1954* (Cambridge: Harvard University Press, 1979), especially pp. 273–470. Forthcoming is a comprehensive account of the occupation from both U.S. and Japanese sources, *Occupied Japan, 1945–1952* (New York: Pantheon Press).

Among American scholars who have extensively studied the occupation are Herbert Bix, Howard Schonberger, Ray Moore, and Marlene Mayo. For their works, see below.

12. Takemae, *Senryō sengoshi,* p. 392. Also, in the preface to the eight-volume work on the occupation produced by the Tokyo University Institute of Social Sciences: "Since the latter part of the sixties, a quarter-century after the war, there has been an unsettling (*dōyō*), both institutionally and ideologically, of various aspects of the framework established by the 'postwar reforms'. . . . Scientific elucidation of the significance and limits of the 'postwar reforms' is now a matter of some urgency." Tōkyō daigaku shakai kagaku kenkyūjo, ed., *Sengo kaikaku,* vol. 1 (Tōkyō daigaku shuppankai, 1974), p. i.

13. Takemae, *Senryō sengoshi,* p. 12.

14. E.g., on labor, Takemae, *Amerika tainichi rōdō seisaku no kenkyū,* and *Senryō sengoshi;* also Tōkyō daigaku shakai kagaku kenkyūjo, ed., *Sengo kaikaku,* vol. 5, *Rōdō kaikaku* (1974). On land reform, Iwamoto Noriaki, "Nochi kaikaku," in *Taikei Nihon gendaishi,* vol. 5, *Senryō to sengo kaikaku,* Kanda Fuhito, ed. (Nihon hyōronsha, 1979), pp. 187–227; Iwamoto, "Senryōgun no tainichi nōgyō seisaku," in Nakamura Takafusa, ed., *Senryōki Nihon no keizai to seiji* (Tōkyō daigaku shuppankai, 1979), pp. 177–202; Ōwada Keiki, *Hishi Nihon no nōchi kaikaku: ichi nōsei tantōsha no kaiso* (Nihon keizai shinbun, 1981). On economic policy, Hata Ikuhiko's large and detailed work (which covers other aspects as well), Ōkurashō zaiseishi shitsu, ed., *Shōwa zaiseishi: shūsen kara kōwa made,* vol. 3, *Amerika no tainichi senryō seisaku* (Tōkyō keizai shinpōsha, 1976). For an article by Hata in English, see "Japan Under the Occupation," *Japan Interpreter,* 10, 3–4 (Winter 1976), 360–79. On antimonopoly policy,

Miwa Ryōichi, *Shōwa zaiseishi,* vol. 2, *Dokusen kinshi* (1981). On the emperor system, Takemae, "Shōchō tennōsei e no kiseki," *Senryō sengoshi,* pp. 60–98; Takeda Kiyoko, *Tennōkan no sōkoku, 1945-nen zengo* (Iwanami shoten, 1978). For a brief excerpt in English, Kiyoko Takeda Chō, "The Dual Image of the Japanese Tennō: Conflicting Ideas about the Remoulding of the Tennōsei at the End of the War," in *Proceedings of the British Association for Japanese Studies,* vol. 1, part 1, *History and International Relations,* Peter Lowe, ed. (Sheffield: Centre of Japanese Studies, University of Sheffield, 1976), pp. 110–30; Koseki Shōichi, "Shōchō tennōsei no seiritsu katei," *Hōritsu jihō,* 52, 7 (July 1980), 92–98; 8 (Aug. 1980), 95–101; 10 (Oct. 1980), 78–83; 11 (Nov. 1980), 81–87. On rearmament, Hata Ikuhiko, *Shiroku Nihon saigunbi* (Bungei shunjū, 1976); Koseki Shōichi, "Reisen seisaku ni okeru Nihon saigunbi no kihonteki seikaku," in Rekishi kagaku kenkyūkai, ed., *Sekaishi ni okeru chiiku to minshū— 1979 nendo rekishigaku kenkyūkai taikai hōkoku* (Aoki shoten, 1979). On the police system, Takemae Eiji, "Sengo keisatsu no seiritsu katei," *Chūō kōron* (May 1975), pp. 190–202; Yoshikawa Jun, "Keisatsu kaikaku—minsei kyoku (GS) kōan ka (PSD/CIS) no tairitsu o chūshin ni," *Hōgaku seminā zōkan, Gendai no keisatsu* (Oct. 1980); Miura Yōichi, "Senryōka keisatsu kaikaku no ichi danmen: 1947-nen 9-gatsu 16-nichi Makkāsā shokan no seiritsu katei," *Rekishigaku kenkyū,* 498 (Nov. 1981), 35–51.

15. For recent examples of this methodology, see the essays in Nakamura Takafusa, *Senryōki Nihon no keizai to seiji* (Tōkyō daigaku shuppankai, 1979): economic policy (Nakamura Takafusa), cold war and the change in occupation policy (Igarashi Takeshi), George Kennan and the change in occupation policy (Igarashi Takeshi), political parties (Itō Takashi), local government (Amakawa Akira), land reform (Iwamoto Sumiaki), deconcentration (Uekusa Masu and Miwa Ryōichi), women (Yoda Seiichi), labor law (Takemae Eiji), censorship policy (Fukushima Jūrō), German occupation policy (Tezuka Kazuaki).

16. Takemae, *Amerika tainichi rōdō seisaku no kenkyū,* p. 1. An example of the earlier structural analysis infused with new empirical content is the eight-volume Tokyo University series, *Sengo kaikaku,* whose largely monographic essays are arranged in the following volumes: vol. 1, topics and perspectives; vol. 2, international environment; vol. 3, political process; vol. 4, legal reform; vol. 5, labor reform; vol. 6, land reform; vol. 7, economic reform; vol. 8, the Japanese economy after the reforms. (Tōkyō daigaku shuppankai, 1974–75.)

17. Dower, "Occupied Japan and the American Lake," pp. 146–48, and "Occupied Japan as History," pp. 486–87.

18. Dower, "Occupied Japan as History," pp. 491–92.

19. In addition to Dower's work (note 11), see Herbert P. Bix, "The Security Treaty System and the Japanese Military-Industrial Complex," *Bulletin of Concerned Asian Scholars,* 2, 2 (Jan. 1970), 30–53; "Japan: The Roots of Militarism," in Mark Selden, ed., *Remaking Asia: Essays on the American Uses of Power* (New York: Pantheon Books, 1974), pp. 305–61; "Regional Integration: Japan and South Korea in America's Asian Policy," in Frank Baldwin, ed., *Without Parallel: The American-Korean Relationship since 1945* (New York: Pantheon Books, 1974), pp. 179–233. Howard B. Schonberger, "Zaibatsu Dissolution and the American Restoration of Japan," *Bulletin of Concerned Asian Scholars,* 5, 2 (Sept. 1973), 15–31; "The Japan Lobby in American Diplomacy, 1947–52," *Pacific Historical Review,* 46, 3 (Aug. 1977), 327–59; "American Labor's Cold War in Occupied Japan," *Diplomatic History,* 3, 3 (Summer 1979), 249–72; "General William Draper, the 80th Congress, and the Origins of Japan's 'Reverse Course,' " in Ray A. Moore, ed., *Japan Under American Rule, 1945–52* (forthcoming). Michael Schaller and James Elston, "Securing the Great Crescent: The Dodge Line and Containment in Southeast Asia," also in the Moore volume; Joe B. Moore, *Produc-*

tion Control and the Postwar Crisis of Japanese Capitalism, 1945–46 (Madison: University of Wisconsin Press, forthcoming); William Borden, *The Pacific Alliance: The U.S. and Japanese Trade Recovery, 1947–54* (Madison: University of Wisconsin Press, forthcoming).

20. Owen Lattimore, *Solution in Asia* (Boston: Little, Brown, 1945). Gabriel Kolko, *The Politics of War: The World and United States Foreign Policy, 1943–1945* (New York: Random House, 1968). More often cited is Joyce and Gabriel Kolko, *The Limits of Power: The World and United States Foreign Policy, 1945–1954* (New York: Harper and Row, 1972), which deals with the occupation, pp. 300–25, 510–33. A sign of the long half-life of the early references from the heroic narrative is a 1981 essay that commends dissenting Western scholarship and mentions Lattimore, Bisson, Roth, and Norman, but none of the more recent revisionists. (Nakamura Masanori, "Gyakkōsu to senryō kenkyū," *Sekai* [June 1981], pp. 19–22.)

21. E.g., cited by Americans are such standard postwar works as Tōyama Shigeki, Imai Seiichi, and Fujiwara Akira, *Shōwashi*, rev. ed. (Iwanami shoten, 1959) and Fujii Shōichi and Ōe Shinobu, *Sengo Nihon no rekishi*, 2 vols. (Aoki shoten, 1970). Cited by Japanese are Allison, Keohane and Nye, Jervis, and Rosenau; see Nihon kokusai seiji gakkai, ed., *Sengo Nihon no kokusai seiji gaku* (Yūhikaku, 1979), pp. 223–32.

22. See Rekishigaku kenkyūkai, ed., *Taiheiyō sensōshi*, vol. 6, *Sanfuranshisuko kōwa, 1945–1952* (Aoki shoten, 1973); *Iwanami kōza Nihon rekishi*, vols. 22 and 23, *Gendai* 1 and 2 (Iwanami shoten, 1977); *Taikei Nihon gendaishi*, vol. 5, *Senryō to sengo kaikaku*, Kanda Fuhito, ed. (Nihon hyōronsha, 1979); Fujiwara Akira, *Senryō to minshū undō*, vol. 10, *Nihon minshū no rekishi* (Sanseido, 1975); Tōkyō rekishi kagaku kenkyūkai gendaishi bukai, ed., *Nihon gendaishi no shuppatsu: sengo minshushugi no keisei* (Aoki shoten, 1978). In addition to this narrative history, members of the same group have published a series of monographic essays on the "revolutionary period of postwar democracy," which they define as beginning with the defeat in August 1945 and ending with the fall of the Ashida cabinet in October 1948. Their work, which was begun in 1970, has appeared primarily in the journal *Rekishi hyōron;* for references, see below.

23. A selection of this work is available in translation in the inaugural issue of *The Japanese Journal of American Studies*, no. 1, *United States Policy Toward Asia, 1945–1950* (The Japanese Association for American Studies, 1981), which contains essays on unconditional surrender (Iokibe Makoto), MacArthur's early peace proposal (Igarashi Takeshi), American policy and the peace treaty (Hosoya Chihiro), the Truman administration and Indochina (Miyasato Seigen), the Korean War (Nagai Yōnosuke), and a review of recent literature (Asada Sadao). For an earlier general history of the occupation along these lines, see Kosaka Masataka, *100 Million Japanese: The Postwar Experience* (Kōdansha, 1972). For earlier work by Japanese Americanists, see Aruga Tadashi, "Amerika no tainichi seisaku to sengo no kokusei seiji," and Yasuba Yasuaki, "Amerika tainichi keizai gaikō seisaku: 1945–65 nen," in Takagi Yasaka, ed., *Nichibei kankei no kenkyū*, vol. 1 (Tōkyō daigaku shuppankai, 1968), pp. 105–316.

24. Central to these debates which began in 1978 are Shimizu Ikutarō ("Sengo o utagau," *Chūō kōron* [June 1978]), and Etō Jun (*Mō hitotsu no sengoshi* [Kōdansha, 1978]; *Wasureta koto to wasuresaserareta koto* [Bungei shunju, 1979]; *Shūsen shiroku, bekkan, shūsen o toinaosu: shinpojiumu* [Hokuyōsha, 1980]). Their views (e.g., in *Shokun* [July through Oct. 1980]) and the views of their opponents appeared in the weekly and monthly magazines for over two years. For a popular but documented biography of MacArthur, Sodei Rinjirō, *Makkāsā no nisennichi* (Chūō kōronsha, 1974). Other works for the general reader include *Dokyumento Shōwashi*, vol. 5, *Haisen zengo*, Imai Seiichi, ed., and vol. 6, *Senryō jidai*, Sagara

Ryōsuke, ed. (Heibonsha, 1975); Takemae Eiji, Amakawa Akira, Sodei Rinjirō and Hata Iku-hiko, *Nihon senryō hishi*, 2 vols. (Chūō kōronsha, 1977). For an earlier media series in English translation, see Asahi shinbun, ed., *Pacific Rivals: A Japanese View of Japanese-American Relations* (Asahi shinbunsha, 1971), pp. 109–209. NHK broadcast a year-long television series on the occupation in 1977–1978. In the more popular presentations, MacArthur remains a hero, which is how most Japanese outside the scholarly world still see him. See *Nihon senryō hishi*, vol. 1, pp. 16–17.

25. Comments at the International Conference on the Occupation of Japan, Amherst, Mass., Aug. 1980. Selected papers from this binational conference were published in Japanese as *Tennō ga Baiburu o yonda hi* (Kōdansha, 1982); the English manuscript is tentatively titled *Japan under American Rule, 1945–52*. Both are edited by Moore. The essays include MacArthur's religious policy (Ray Moore), labor and politics (Joe Moore), labor reform (Takemae Eiji), women and labor (Gail Nomura), educational reform (Harry Wray), censorship (Etō Jun), Kennan and the change in occupation policy (Igarashi Takeshi), "reverse course" (Peter Frost), the divided territories (Shindō Eiichi), family system and social reform (Yoda Seiichi), U.S. occupation policy and Southeast Asia (William Borden, Michael Schaller, and James Elston), and women and social roles (Donald Roden). For a summary of some of the papers, see Ray A. Moore, "The Occupation of Japan as History: Some Recent Research," *Monumenta Nipponica*, 36, 3 (Autumn 1981), 317–28. For Japanese reaction to the conference, which was considerable, see Koseki Shōichi, "Senryōshi kenkyū no genjō to kadai," *Rekishigaku kenkyū*, 489 (Feb. 1981), 55–58; Shindō Eiichi, "Hoshuka no naka no sengoshizō," *Asahi shinbun* (Sept. 12, 1980); Sodei Rinjirō, "Senryō kenkyū no rekishigaku to seiji," *Mainichi shinbun* (Sept. 16, 1980); Nakamura Masanori, " 'Gyakkōsu' to senryō kenkyū," *Sekai* (June 1981), pp. 19–22.

26. Robert E. Ward and Sakamoto Yoshikazu, *Democracy and Planned Political Change: The Case of the Allied Occupation of Japan, 1945–1952*. The manuscript, based on a conference held in 1978, includes papers on presurrender planning (Ward), international aspects (Sakamoto), constitutional reform (Theodore McNelly), legal reform (Tanaka Hideo), SCAP policy and the Diet (Hans Baerwald), bureaucratic reform (T. J. Pempel), conservative parties (Uchida Kenzō), reformist parties and mass movements (Takemae Eiji), the financial world (Otake Hideo), civil code (Kurt Steiner), local government reform (Amakawa Akira), women's rights (Susan Pharr), Okinawa (Ota Masahide), and broadcasting reform (Uchikawa Yoshimi).

27. *The Occupation of Japan: The Proceedings of a Seminar on the Occupation of Japan and its Legacy to the Postwar World* (Norfolk, Va.: MacArthur Memorial, 1976); Lawrence H. Redford, ed., *The Occupation of Japan: Impact of Legal Reform* (1977); Redford, ed., *The Occupation of Japan: Economic Policy and Reform* (1980); Thomas W. Burkman, ed., *The Occupation of Japan: Educational and Social Reform* (1981). The fifth symposium, held in October 1982, was entitled *The Occupation of Japan: The International Context*.

28. For an example of the heroic narrative in a recent general account, see John Curtis Perry, *Beneath the Eagle's Wings: Americans in Occupied Japan* (New York: Dodd, Mead, 1980).

29. *Daijinmei jiten*, vol. 8 (Heibonsha, 1954), pp. 816–18. The MacArthur entry reads in full: "American military man. Commander-in-Chief of American forces in the Philippines at the outbreak of war in 1941. In 1942, after the fall of Manila, escaped to Australia. As Commander-in-Chief of the Allied forces in the Southwest Pacific, directed the war against Japan. In 1945 was present at the signing of the surrender aboard the *Missouri* and afterwards served as Supreme Commander of the Allied Forces in Japan, but in 1951 was dismissed because of the Korean War. In 1952 became president of the Remington Rand Corporation."

30. The abbreviation SCAP, though frequently extended in U.S. writings to include the occupation bureaucracy, is here used literally as MacArthur's title. Japanese writers refer not to SCAP but to GHQ as the general term for the occupation authorities.

31. On religious policy: Laurence S. Wittner, "MacArthur and the Missionaries: God and Man in Occupied Japan," *Pacific Historical Review*, 40, 1 (Feb. 1971), 77–98; Ray A. Moore, "Soldier of God: MacArthur's Attempt to Christianize Japan," in Moore, ed., *Japan under American Rule*. See also William P. Woodard, *The Allied Occupation of Japan 1945–1952 and Japanese Religions* (Leiden: E. J. Brill, 1972), pp. 210–26, 241–49; Ashizu et al., "Shūkyō to senryō," in *Kyōdō kenkyū Nihon senryōgun: sono hikari to kage*, ed. Shisō no kagaku kenkyūkai (Tokuma shoten, 1978), vol. 2, pp. 9–91. On the early peace proposal, Igarashi Takeshi, "Tainichi kōwa no teishō to hankyōkan no isō," *Kokusai mondai* (July 1976); Igarashi, "Tainichi kōwa no teishō to tainichi senryō seisaku no tenkan," *Shisō*, 628 (Oct. 1976), 1–42. For the English translation, see note 23. On Article Nine, Hata, *Shiroku Nihon saigunbi*, pp. 47–77; Tanaka Hideo, *Kenpō seitei katei oboegaki* (Yūhikaku, 1979), pp. 90–111; in English, Theodore McNelly, "The Origins of Article Nine," *Hōritsu jihō*, 51, 6 (May 1979), 260–56. Volume 3 of D. Clayton James' *The Years of MacArthur*, which will cover from 1946, will be published by Houghton Mifflin in 1983. William Manchester's popular biography, *American Caesar* (Boston: Little, Brown, 1978), is not in treatment either new or, in its Japan sections, tolerable. In Japanese, Sodei Rinjirō, *Makkāsā no nisennichi* (Chūō kōronsha, 1974).

32. Takemae, "Senryō seisaku keisei ni kansuru jakkan no kōshō," p. 48.

33. Iokibe, "The Occupation Period," in Asada, ed., *Post World War II Japanese Research*.

34. See Iokibe, "Beikoku ni okeru tainichi senryō seisaku no keisei katei—sono kikōteki sokumen to senryōgun kōsei no mondai," *Kokusaihō gaikō zasshi*, 74, 3, 4 (Oct., Dec. 1975); "Beikoku ni okeru tainichi sengo seisaku no genkei: tennōsei no mondai o chūshin ni," *Seikei ronsō*, 25, 6 (Feb. 1976); "'Mujōken kōfuku' to Potsudamu sengen," *Kokusaihō gaikō zasshi*, 79, 5 (Dec. 1980), 29–72; and "Kairo to Nihon no ryōdo," *Hiroshima hōgaku*, 4, 3–4 (1981). Forthcoming is his monograph on wartime planning, *Beikoku no taiNichi senryō seisaku*, from which an English excerpt appears in *The Japanese Journal of American Studies* (see note 23). Koseki Shōichi, "Shōchō tennōsei no seiritsu katei," *Hōritsu jihō* (see note 14); Amakawa Akira, "Sengo seiji kaikaku no zentei: Amerika ni okeru tainichi senryō no junbi katei," in Taniuchi Yuzuru et al., eds., *Gendai gyōsei to kanryōsei*, vol. 2 (Tōkyō daigaku shuppankai, 1974), pp. 131–99; Amakawa, "Nihon senryō seisaku," in *Sōgō kenkyū Amerika*, 7 vols. (Kenkyūsha, 1976–1977); Awaya and Ara, "Nihon haisen to kyūshihai taisei no kaitai," in Rekishigaku kenkūkai,ed. *Sekai ni okeru chiiku to minshū*, (Aoki shoten, 1979); Takemae, "Shōchō tennōsei e no kiseki," *Senryō sengoshi*, pp. 60–98; Takemae, "Tainichi senryō seisaku no keisei to hatten," *Iwanami kōza Nihon rekishi, Gendai* 1, pp. 27–80. Also, substantial portions of Takemae's *Amerika tainichi rōdō seisaku no kenkyū* and of Hata's *Shōwa zaiseishi*, vol. 3, are devoted to wartime planning. On the so-called "unconditional surrender controversy" initiated by Etō Jun, see *Shūsen shiroku: bekkan*, *Shūsen o toinaosu*, pp. 112–35, and Awaya Kentarō, *Shiryō Nihon gendaishi*, vols. 2 and 3, *Haisen chokugo no seiji to shakai*, vols. 1 and 2 (Otsuki shoten, 1980–81), pp. 461–71. On war responsibility, see Ōnuma Yasuaki, *Sensō sekininron josetsu* (Tōkyō daigaku shuppankai, 1975); Awaya Kentarō, "Senso sekininron," in *Taikei Nihon gendaishi*, vol. 5, *Senryō to sengo kaikaku*, Kanda, ed., pp. 37–93.

35. State-War-Navy Coordinating Committee, established in December 1944 to consider

postwar policies for Austria, Germany, Japan, and Korea. The documents produced by this committee are drawn on heavily in the Japanese works mentioned above.

36. Marlene Mayo's forthcoming monograph, "Redesigning Japan—American Wartime Planning for Postwar Occupation and Control, 1942–1945," will treat these issues in detail. See also Ward, "Presurrender Planning for the Allied Occupation of Japan," in Ward and Sakamoto, eds., *Democracy and Planned Political Change.* Hugh Borton's often-cited essay, *American Presurrender Planning for Postwar Japan* (New York: Occasional Papers of the East Asian Institute, Columbia University, 1967), will be supplemented by his memoirs, now in progress, of which chapters 8–11 cover presurrender planning.

37. Marlene J. Mayo, "American Economic Planning for Occupied Japan: The Issue of *Zaibatsu* Dissolution," in Redford, ed., *The Occupation of Japan: Economic Policy and Reform*, pp. 209, 221.

38. *Ibid., pp.* 210–28.

39. Nakamura Takafusa, "SCAP to Nihon—senryōki no keizai seisaku keisei," in Nakamura, ed., *Senryōki Nihon no keizai to seiji*, pp. 5–9; "Senryō to kaikaku," in Nakamura and Itō, eds., *Kindai Nihon kenkyū nyūmon* (Tōkyō daigaku shuppankai, 1977), pp. 107–108.

40. Hata Ikuhiko, in Redford, ed., *The Occupation of Japan: Economic Policy and Reform*, p. 318.

41. Nakamura, "SCAP to Nihon," in Nakamura, *Senryōki Nihon no keizai*, pp. 17–19; see also Hata, *Shōwa zaiseishi*, chs. 4, 5, *passim.* On Yoshida, see Dower, *Empire and Aftermath*, pp. 374–76, 422–24.

42. Hata, *Shiroku Nihon saigunbi*, p. 132.

43. For Yoshida, see Dower, *Empire and Aftermath*, p. 383; "Alice In Wonderland" from William J. Sebald, with Russell Brines, *With MacArthur in Japan: A Personal History of the Occupation* (New York: Norton, 1965), p. 257.

44. Dower, *Empire and Aftermath*, pp. 390–95. For another view of the politics involved, Koseki, "Senryōshi kenkyū no genjō to kadai," p. 58.

45. The term is used by Howard Schonberger, "The Japan Lobby in American Diplomacy, 1947–52," *Pacific Historical Review*, 46, 3 (Aug. 1977), 327–59. For the "Nihon robii," Hata, *Shiroku Nihon saigunbi*, pp. 79–82; also, John G. Roberts, "The 'Japan Crowd' and the Zaibatsu Restoration," *The Japan Interpreter*, 12, 3–4 (Summer 1979), 384–415.

46. On the Kauffman report, Hata, *Shōwa zaiseishi*, vol. 3, pp. 300–306; Schonberger, "Zaibatsu Dissolution and the American Restoration of Japan," *Bulletin of Concerned Asian Scholars*, 5, 2 (Sept. 1973), 21–25.

47. "Nongovernmental source" of copy of FEC 230 to Senator Knowland, December 1947, Eleanor M. Hadley, *Antitrust in Japan* (Princeton: Princeton University Press, 1970), p. 137; dinner for Dulles, June 22, 1950, Watanabe Takeshi, *Senryōki no Nihon zaisei oboegaki* (Nihon keizai shinbunsha, 1966), pp. 290–97; on Eichelberger, Schonberger, "The Japan Lobby," pp. 343–44. Evidence that Kern's business contacts continued through the years was his exposure in 1979 as a "consultant" in the Grumman aircraft bribery scandal, which generated great controversy and also made Kern's occupation activities an issue in the Japanese press.

48. After canonical profiles of GS officials, Williams proceeds to SCAP-Diet relations, with which he was particularly concerned, then returns to the canon to deny the reverse course and conclude with "MacArthur: Statesman." Justin Williams, Sr., *Japan's Political Revolution under MacArthur: A Participant's Account* (Athens: University of Georgia Press, 1979); Williams' papers are now available in the East Asia Collection, McKeldin Library, University of

Maryland. Oppler presents the legal aspect of constitutional and institutional reform and also the German background for his own liberal "missionary zeal." Alfred C. Oppler, *Legal Reform in Occupied Japan: A Participant Looks Back* (Princeton: Princeton University Press, 1976).

49. Schonberger, "Zaibatsu Dissolution," pp. 18–19. Martin Bronfenbrenner, "Inflation Theories of the SCAP Period," *History of Political Economy*, 7, 2 (Summer 1975), 137–55. A prominent economist, Bronfenbrenner was in the Internal Revenue Division, ESS, 1949–1950, where he was suspected of being "subversive," but he managed despite his experience to write with admirable clarity about the SCAP bureaucracy. Also see his "The American Occupation of Japan: Economic Retrospect," in Goodman, ed., *The American Occupation of Japan*, pp. 11–25. Takemae, *Amerika tainichi rōdō seisaku no kenkyū*, pp. 142–280. Theodore Cohen, former chief of Labor Division, is currently writing his memoirs, tentatively titled *The Third Turn: MacArthur, the Americans, and the Rebirth of Japan;* for some comments, see Cohen, "Labor Democratization in Japan: The First Years," in Redford, ed., *The Occupation of Japan: Economic Policy and Reform*, pp. 162–73 and *passim;* also, Cohen interview with Takemae (see note 9).

50. See Schonberger, "General William Draper," in Moore, ed., *Japan Under American Rule, 1945–52;* Orville J. McDiarmid, "The Dodge and Young Missions," and Schonberger, "The Dodge Mission and American Diplomacy, 1945–1950," in Redford, ed., *The Occupation of Japan: Economic Policy and Reform*, pp. 59–83; Hata, *Shōwa zaiseishi*, pp. 391–99, 409–32.

51. Leon Hollerman, "International Economic Controls in Occupied Japan," *Journal of Asian Studies*, 38, 4 (Aug. 1979), 719.

52. Takemae, *Amerika tainichi rōdō seisaku no kenkyū*, pp. 357–62.

53. *Ibid.*, p. 366.

54. For the three principles (sometimes known as the "MacArthur notes") and the SCAP version of the drafting, *Political Reorientation of Japan*, vol. 1, pp. 82–118; SWNCC 228, "Reform of the Japanese Governmental System" is reprinted in Theodore McNelly, ed., *Sources in Modern East Asian History and Politics* (New York: Appleton-Century-Crofts, 1967), pp. 117–86. On the drafting process, Takayanagi Kenzō, Ohtomo Ichirō, and Tanaka Hideo, eds., *Nihonkoku kenpō seitei no katei* (Yūhikaku, 1972) contains the Milo E. Rowell papers in English with Japanese translations (vol. 1, pp. 78–320) and a narrative account (vol. 2, pp. 41–54, and part II, *passim*); also, Tanaka Hideo, *Kenpō seitei katei oboegaki*, pp. 61–89. On both the planning and the drafting, Dale Hellegers, *We, the Japanese People* (forthcoming). For remarks by Hellegers and Theodore McNelly on the subject, *The Occupation of Japan: The Proceedings of a Seminar on the Occupation of Japan and its Legacy to the Postwar World*, pp. 2–29.

55. Susan Pharr, "A Radical U.S. Experiment: Women's Rights Laws and the Occupation of Japan," in Redford, ed., *The Occupation of Japan: Impact of Legal Reforms*, pp. 125–46. For occupation policy toward women and the family, see Yoda Seiichi, "Senryō seisaku ni okeru fujin kaihō," in Nakamura, ed., *Senryōki Nihon no keizai to seiji*, pp. 267–300, and Yoda, "Sengo kazoku seido kaikaku to shin kazokukan no seiritsu," *Sengo kaikaku*, vol. 1, pp. 271–317.

56. Tanaka, *Kenpō seitei katei oboegaki*, p. 88.

57. Letters from and interviews with Kades appear as scholarly sources and also in popular books and magazines, e.g., Ōmori Minoru, *Sengo hishi*, vol. 5, *Makkāsā no kenpō* (Kōdansha, 1975), pp. 244–64. C. L. Kades and Komori Yoshihisa, " 'Kōsenken' hōki wa muyō datta," *Gendai*, 15, 8 (Aug. 1981), 52–83.

58. See Dower, "Occupied Japan as History," pp. 502–3. Because English was the lan-

guage of GHQ-Japanese relations, even some Japanese government documents are available in English, e.g., reports of the Economic Stabilization Board, in the National Planning Agency in Tokyo. Occupation officials also translated vast quantities of materials for their own use, e.g., transcripts of Diet sessions (SCAP, *Official Gazette Extra*) and extensive translations from the press (SCAP, Allied Translator and Interpreter Section [ATIS], *Press Translations and Summaries: Japan* [Tokyo: 5 Nov. 1945–22 Aug. 1949]). The 55 monographs in the occupation's official history often contain Japanese material (SCAP, Statistics and Reports Sections, *History of the Non-military Activities of the Occupation of Japan* [Tokyo: SCAP, 1952]). See Ward and Shulman, *The Allied Occupation of Japan, 1945–52,* pp. 123–37.

59. For an example of the subject/object category and how it is changing, see Shisō no kagaku kenkyūkai, ed., *Kyōdō kenkyū Nihon senryōgun: sono hikari to kage,* 2 vols. (Gendaishi shuppankai, 1978). For substantial attention to Japanese materials, Tōkyō daigaku shakai kagaku kenkyūjo, *Sengo kaikaku,* is of great value.

60. Dower, *Empire and Aftermath,* pp. 1, 273–492; in Japanese, the third volume of a recent biography which treats the postwar years: Inoki Masamichi, *Hyōden: Yoshida Shigeru* (Yomiuri shinbunsha, 1981).

61. Dower, *Empire and Aftermath,* pp. 292–308, notes 44–46; on the very early period and the Higashikuni cabinet, James William Morley, "The First Seven Weeks," *The Japan Interpreter,* 6, 2 (Sept. 1970), 151–64; for MacArthur-Yoshida letters, Sodei Rinjirō, "Makkāsā-Yoshida ōfuku shokan," part 1, *Hōgaku shirin,* 77, 4 (March 1980), 91–132.

62. Recently made public, but not yet fully accessible materials include *Ashida Hitoshi nikki* and *Hatoyama Ichirō Nikki.* See Kokuritsu kokkai toshokan, ed., *Gikai kaisetsu kyūjūnen kinen gikai seiji tenjikai mokuroku* (Kokuritsu kokkai toshokan, 1980).

63. For the bureaucratic reforms that were attempted, see T.J. Pempel, "The Tar Baby Target: Reforms of the Japanese Bureaucracy under the American Occupation," in Ward and Sakamoto, eds., *Democracy and Planned Political Change;* Gary D. Allinson, "Spoil Not The System: Civil Service Reforms and the American Occupation," in Thomas W. Burkman, ed., *The Occupation of Japan: Educational and Social Reforms* (Norfolk: MacArthur Memorial 1981); Ide Yoshinori, "Sengo kaikaku to Nihon kanryōsei: Kōmuin seido no sōshutsu katei," in *Sengo kaikaku,* vol. 3, *Seiji katei,* Tōkyō daigaku shakai kagaku kenkyūjo, ed., pp. 143– 229. For the occupation's promotion of bureaucracy, Hollerman, "International Economic Controls in Occupied Japan," p. 707. For occupation period origins of the political, financial, and bureaucratic "Japan, Inc.," see Dower, *Empire and Aftermath,* p. 8 and *passim.*

64. See Pempel, "The Tar Baby Target," and Amakawa Akira, "Senryō seisaku to kanryō no taiō," in Shisō no kagaku kenkyūkai, ed., *Kyōdō kenkyū Nihon senryōgun: Sono hikari to kage,* vol. 1, pp. 215–22.

65. Amakawa, "Senryō seisaku to kanryō no taiō," pp. 215–46; Amakawa, "Chihō jichi seido no kaikaku," in *Sengo kaikaku,* vol. 3, *Seiji katei,* Tōkyō daigaku shakai kagaku kenkyūjo, ed., pp. 231–86; Amakawa, "Senryō shoki no seisaku jōkyō: Naimushō to minseikyoku no taiō," *Shakai kagaku kenkyū,* 26, 2 (1975). On the land reform bill, Yoshida Katsumi, "Nochi kaikakuhō no rippō katei," in *Sengo kaikaku,* vol. 6, *Nōchi kaikaku,* pp. 137–80; for recently published primary materials, Nōchi kaikaku shiryō hensan iinkai, ed., *Nōchi kaikaku shiryō shūsei* (Nōsei chōsakai, 1974). On the first electoral reform, Soma Masao, "Senkyō seido no kaikaku," in *Sengo kaikaku,* vol. 3, *Seiji katei,* pp. 91–141.

66. Amakawa, "Chihō jichihō no kōzō," in Nakamura, ed., *Senryōki Nihon no keizai to seiji,* pp. 119–76.

67. "New life" *(shinsei),* a common expression among intellectuals in the fall of 1945, was also the title of the most widely read literary journal at that time; it began publication in

November and sold 130,000 copies the first day. "Bloodless revolution," or a variant, frequently appeared in political discourse of the same time, e.g., *Asahi shinbun,* Jan. 6. 1946.

68. Available in English translation are Takemae, "Reformist Parties and Mass Movements," and Uchida Kenzō, "Formation and Changes in Japan's Postwar Conservative Parties," in Ward and Sakamoto, eds., *Democracy and Planned Political Change.* On postwar reconstruction of the parties, Itō Takashi, "Sengo seitō no keisei katei," in Nakamura, ed., *Senryōki Nihon no keizai to seiji,* pp. 87–117; for documents on the same subject, Awaya Kentarō, ed., *Shiryō Nihon gendaishi,* vol. 3, *Haisen chokugo no seiji to shakai,* vol. 2 (Ōtsuki shoten, 1981), pp. 4–166. For the occupation and the parties, *ibid.,* pp. 306–34; and Sodei Rinjirō, "Makkāsā—Katayama—Ashida ōfuku shokan," *Hōgaku shirin,* 78, 1–2 (Jan. 1981), 73–97. Kamiyama Shigeo, ed., *Nihon kyōsantō sengo jūyō shiryōshū* (San'ichi shobō, 1971); personal accounts include Kameyama Kōzō, *Sengo Nihon kyōsantō no nijū chōbō* (Gendai hyōronsha, 1978); Hakamada Satomi, *Watakushi no sengoshi* (Asahi shinbunsha, 1978). On the Socialist Party, Nihon Shakaitō, ed., *Nihon Shakaitō no sanjūnen,* 3 vols. (Shakai shinpōsha, 1975), Narita Kiichiro, "Sengo Nihon ni okeru shakai minshushugi no keisei," *Minshūshi kenkyū,* 14; on the progressive party cabinets of 1947–1948, Takahashi Hikohiro, "Shakaitō shuhan naikaku no seiritsu to zasetsu," *Iwanami kōza Nihon rekishi,* vol. 22, *Gendai* 1, pp. 265–302; Shibayama Toshio, "Katayama naikakuki no seiji jōsei," and Yamada Takeo, "Ashida naikakuki no seiji jōsei," *Rekishi hyōron,* 298 (Feb. 1975), 3–34; for essays on the progessive parties, Takahashi Hikohiro, *Nihon no shakai minshushugi seitō* (Hōsei daigaku shuppan kyoku, 1972). For a journalistic account of the conservative parties, Tominomori Eiji, *Sengo hoshutōshi* (Nihon hyōronsha, 1977).

69. Matsuo Takayoshi, "Kyūshihai taisei no kaitai," *Iwanami kōza Nihon rekishi,* vol. 22, *Gendai* 1, pp. 110–14. Also on the united front, see Kanda Fuhito, "Tōitsu sensenron," in *Taikei Nihon gendaishi,* vol. 5, *Senryō to sengo kaikaku,* Kanda, ed., pp. 96–146; Masujima Kō, ed., *Nihon no tōitsu sensen,* 2 vols. (Ōtsuki shoten, 1978).

70. Kanda, "Tōitsu sensenron," p. 137.

71. For one of the rare studies in English on popular movements in this period, see Joe B. Moore, *Production Control and the Postwar Crisis of Japanese Capitalism, 1945–1946* (Madison: University of Wisconsin Press, forthcoming); also, for a related presentation, Moore, "From Industrial Unionism to Enterprise Unions: Worker Control during the Occupation of Japan," in Moore, ed., *Japan under American Rule.* See also Kuriki Yasunobu, "Keizai kiki to rōdō undō," in *Iwanami kōza Nihon rekishi,* vol. 22, *Gendai* 1, pp. 221–64; Yamamoto Kiyoshi, *Sengo kiki ni okeru rōdō undō* (Ochanomizu shobō, 1977); and Tōkyō daigaku shakai kagaku kenkyūjo, *Sengo kaikaku,* vol. 5, *Rōdō kaikaku, passim.*

72. Kuriki, "Keizai kiki to rōdō undō," p. 252. For the farmers' part in these movements, see Tanaka Manabu, "Nōchi kaikaku to nōmin undō," in *Sengo kaikaku,* vol. 6, *Nōchi kaikaku,* Tōkyō daigaku shakai kagaku kenkyūjo, ed., pp. 263–88.

73. Kanda, "Tōitsu sensenron," pp. 100–106.

74. Among the many other groups active at the time were the liberal Minpō group around Matsumoto Shigeharu and the constitution research group (Kenpō kenkyūkai), both of which advocated constitutional monarchy. Kanda, pp. 116–7; for a general account of the period, Ishida Takeshi, "Sengo minshu kaikaku to kokumin no taiō," *Iwanami kōza Nihon rekishi,* vol. 22, *Gendai* 1, pp. 129–73.

75. Ray Moore is working on the interaction between nongovernmental Japanese groups and SCAP in relation to educational reform. For the "Hattori group" and rearmament, Hata, *Shiroku Nihon saigunbi,* pp. 156–75. For the Japan lobby contacts, Roberts, "The 'Japan Crowd,' " pp. 396–411; for Japanese business pressure on the anti-monopoly bill, Miwa Ryō-

ichi, "1949-nen no dokusen kinshihō kaisei," in Nakamura, ed., *Senryōki Nihon no keizai to seiji,* pp. 223–66.

76. For "clientele," Ward, "Reflections on the Allied Occupation," pp. 528–32; for the lack of Japanese cooperation, Bronfenbrenner, "The American Occupation of Japan," p. 15; for the resistance of the old guard, a standard explanation in Japanese scholarship, see, in English, Bisson, *Prospects for Democracy in Japan* (1949) and *Zaibatsu Dissolution in Japan* (1954), discussed in Howard B. Schonberger, "T.A. Bisson and the Limits of Reform in Occupied Japan," *Bulletin of Concerned Asian Scholars,* 12, 4 (Oct.-Dec. 1980), 29–34. Schonberger also had access to Bisson's unpublished letters, "Reform Years in Japan 1945–47: An Occupation Memoir."

77. Some details of the daily liaison between the Japanese bureaucracy and GHQ can now be gleaned from recently published records of one of the Japanese involved, Gaimushō, ed., *Shoki taiNichi senryō seisaku: Asakai Kōichi hōkokusho* (Mainichi shinbunsha, 1979).

78. On occupation organization, Ralph Braibanti, "Administration of Military Government in Japan at the Prefectural Level," *American Political Science Review,* 43 (April 1949), 250–75.

79. Okada Akira, "Senryōki ni okeru chihō jichitai no kōhō soshiki no sōsetsu katei—Saitama-kenka no shichōson hōdō iinkai no jirei o chūshin to shite," *Shakai rōdō kenkyū,* 26, 3–4 (1980).

80. Satō Genji, *Senryōka no Yamagata-ken kyōikushi* (Yamagata: Yamagata Senryōka no Yamagataken kyōikushi shuppan kyōsankai, 1980), pp. 90–100, 188–92, 353–58.

81. For education reform, see Toshio Nishi, *Unconditional Democracy: Education and Politics in Occupied Japan* (Stanford, Calif.: Hoover Institution Press, 1982), pp. 141–241; Burkman, ed., *The Occupation of Japan: Educational and Social Reform,* which includes essays on entrance examination reform (Frost), decentralization (Wray), the first U.S. education mission (Beauchamp), Yokohama schools in 1945–1946 (Graebner), presurrender education planning (Mayo), curriculum reform (Todd), and an essay on sources (Satō). Harry Wray, "Trilateral Relationship: SCAP, the Ministry of Education, and the Japanese Education Reform Committee," in Moore, ed., *Japan under American Rule.* The standard source in Japanese is Kaigo Tokiomi, ed., *Sengo Nihon no kyōiku kaikaku,* 10 vols. (Tōkyō daigaku shuppankai, 1975); for documents, Miyahara Seiichi et al., *Shiryō Nihon gendai kyōikushi,* vol. 1, *1945–1950* (Sanseido, 1974); Ikazaki Akio and Yoshihara Kōichirō, eds., *Sengo kyōiku no genten,* vols. 1–3 (Gendaishi shuppankai, 1980).

82. See the four volumes produced by the collaborative research of Shisō no kagaku kenkyūkai, which stress the views of the occupied rather than of the occupiers: *Kyōdō kenkyū: Nihon senryō* (Tokuma shoten, 1972) and *Kyōdō kenkyū Nihon senryōgun: sono hikari to kage,* 2 vols., plus a supplementary volume entitled *Kyōdō kenkyū: Nihon senryō kenkyū jiten,* a dictionary of occupation names and terms (Tokuma shoten, 1978). For documents, Awaya Kentarō, *Shiryō Nihon gendaishi,* vol. 2, *Haisen chokugo no seiji to shakai,* vol. 1. Included here are excerpts from the United States Strategic Bombing Survey, "The Effects of Strategic Bombing on Japanese Morale" (Washington, D.C., 1947), which is of course from the English original. See Gordon Daniels, ed., *A Guide to the Reports of the United States Strategic Bombing Survey* (London: Boydell and Brewer, 1981). Also, for Japanese public opinion surveys assembled by SCAP, see Civil Information and Education Section, Public Opinion and Sociological Research Division, *Current Japanese Public Opinion Surveys* (Tokyo: SCAP, 29 May 1948–19 March 1949) and *Survey Series* (22 Jan. 1949–2 Feb. 1951); this last also contains surveys conducted by SCAP. In general, Japanese sources for occupation period social history are vast and varied, from diaries to newspapers to official documents; the published collections

represent only a sampling of the available material. As noted above, some of this is accessible in English.

83. Awaya, *Shiryō Nihon gendaishi,* vol. 2, pp. 227–309. Awaya's argument on the popular understanding of unconditional surrender is partly a criticism of Etō Jun's insistence that the Japanese were compelled through force and censorship to misconstrue a surrender that was by the *terms* of the Potsdam Declaration in fact conditional (*ibid.*, pp. 461–71). For popular reactions, see also Hayashi Shigeru et al., eds., *Nihon shūsenshi,* 3 vols. (Yomiuri shinbunsha, 1963); Awaya, pp. 4–137; Yasuda and Fukushima, *Shōwa nijūnen hachigatsu jugonichi;* Shisō no kagaku kenkyūkai, ed., *Kyōdō kenkyū: Nihon senryō,* pp. 19–20. In English, the U.S. Strategic Bombing Survey cited above contains descriptions of Japanese reactions gathered from October to December 1945.

84. Awaya, pp. 302, 310–31.

85. Awaya, pp. 384–432, 492–96, 297–99. For an interesting U.S. poll of Japanese residents in Peking on similar subjects, Department of State, Office of Research and Intelligence, "Survey of Political Opinions of Japanese in Pei-P'ing," April 30, 1946, in OSS/State Department Intelligence and Research Report, II, *Postwar Japan, Korea and Southeast Asia* (University Publications of America Microfilm, 1977), translated in Awaya, vol. 3, pp. 352–83.

86. Awaya, pp. 219 ff, 302–304, 334–64, and *passim.*

87. Shisō no kagaku kenkyūkai, ed., *Kyōdō kenkyū: Nihon senryō,* pp. 25–6.

88. "8.15—Sengo hitei no fūchō ni kōshite," *Asahi jānaru,* Aug. 11–18, 1978, pp. 15–18.

89. Hidaka Rokuro, " 'Messhi hōkō' kara 'mekkō hōshi' made," *Asahi jānaru,* Aug. 17–24, 1979, pp. 10–17.

90. Kojima Nobuo, "The American School," translated in Howard Hibbett, ed., *Contemporary Japanese Literature* (New York: Knopf, 1977), pp. 119–44.

91. Takemae, "Sengo demokurashii to eikaiwa: 'Kamu kamu eigo' no yakuwari," in his *Senryō sengoshi,* pp. 316–44.

92. E.g., Homma Nagayo, "Nihon bunka no Amerikaka: raifu sutairu to taishū bunka," in Hosoya Chihiro and Saitō Makoto, eds., *Washington taisei to nichibei kankei* (Tōkyō diagaku shuppankai, 1978), pp. 603–30.

93. For a brief overview of American images of Japan, see Sheila K. Johnson, *American Attitudes toward Japan, 1941–1975* (Washington: American Enterprise Institute, 1975).

94. For the photographs and the press (August 27–30, 1945), Fukushima Jūrō, "Senryō shoki ni okeru shinbun ken'etsu," in *Kyōdō kenkyū Nihon senryōgun: sono hikari to kage,* vol. 1, Shisō no kagaku kenkyūkai, ed., p. 121; Awaya, *Shiryō Nihon gendaishi,* vol. 2, pp. 370–72. Also, on occupation censorship, Matsuura Sōzō, *Senryōka no genron dan'atsu,* rev. ed. (Gendai jānarizumu shuppankai, 1974); a vignette on film, Iwasaki Akira, "The Occupied Screen," *Japan Quarterly,* 25, 3 (July-Sept. 1978), 302–22; and a bibliography on media policy, Hōsō hōsei rippō katei kenkyūkai, ed., *Shiryō: senryōka no hōsō rippō* (Tōkyō daigaku shuppankai, 1980), pp. 537–634. For the constitution, Takayanagi, Ohtomo, and Tanaka, *Nihonkoku kenpō seitei no katei,* vol. 1, pp. 320 ff.

95. Shisō no kagaku kenkyūkai, ed., *Kyōdō kenkyū: Nihon senryō,* p. 590.

96. For a sampling of MacArthur's statements, SCAP, *Political Reorientation of Japan,* vol. 2, pp. 736–89; for Article Nine, see note 30.

97. *Political Reorientation of Japan,* vol. 2, p. 741. For a typical presentation of the *godai kaikaku,* Ōe Shinobu, *Nihon no rekishi,* vol. 31, *Sengo kaikaku* (Shōgakkan, 1976), pp. 111–12.

98. *Political Reorientation cf Japan*, vol. 2, pp. 776, 741.

99. Koseki Shōichi, "Senryōshi kenkyū no genjō to kadai," *Rekishigaku kenkyū*, 489 (Feb. 1981), p. 58; Takemae, *Amerika tainichi rōdō seisaku no kenkyū*, pp. 3–4, 362–68.

100. Kinoshita Hanji, "Kyūshihaiso no kaitai to fukkatsu," in *Sengo Nihon no seiji katei*, ed. Nihon seiji gakkai (Iwanami shoten, 1953), p. 85; Edwin O. Reischauer, *The Japanese* (Cambridge: Harvard University Press, 1977), p. 105.

101. Shindō Eiichi, "Hoshuka no naka no sengoshizō," *Asahi shinbun*, Sept. 12, 1980, evening edition; the paper in question was Peter K. Frost, "Changing Gears: Reverse Course in Occupation Historiography," in Moore, ed., *Japan under American Rule, 1945–52;* for other Japanese responses, see note 25.

102. Kinoshita, "Kyūshihaiso no kaitai to fukkatsu," p. 84.

103. Williams, *Japan's Political Revolution under MacArthur*, p. 208.

104. Dower, "The Superdomino in Postwar Asia," p. 113.

105. For examples of this chronology, see Kanda Fuhito, "Tōitsu sensenron," pp. 97–106; Takemae, *Amerika tainichi rōdō seisaku no kenkyū*, pp. 12–16, 17–20; on the red purge, Takemae, *Senryō sengoshi*, pp. 185–221. In contrast, English sources rarely treat the red purge, though mention is made in Hans Baerwald, *The Purge of Japanese Leaders under the Occupation* (Berkeley: University of California Press, 1959), pp. 78–106; and Ivan Morris, *Nationalism and the Right Wing in Japan: A Study of Postwar Trends* (New York: Oxford University Press, 1960), pp. 105 ff.

106. For a comprehensive summary, see Hata, *Shōwa zaiseishi*, pp. 311–409. Royall's speech, which has figured prominently in Japanese accounts, is reprinted in V. P. Dutt, *East Asia: China, Korea, Japan, 1947–50* (New York: Oxford University Press, 1958), pp. 631–37. For examples of the general narrative, see Rekishigaku kenkyūkai, ed., *Taiheiyō sensōshi*, vol. 6, *Sanfuranshisuko kōwa* (Aoki shoten, 1973), and Fujiwara Akira, ed., *Reisenka no Nihon, Taikei Nihon gendaishi*, vol. 6 (Nihon hyōronsha, 1979).

107. See, e.g., Sasaki Ryūji, "Reisen no gekika to senryō seisaku no tenkan," *Iwanami kōza Nihon rekishi*, vol. 22, *Gendai 1*, pp. 340–79.

108. For presentations of the changes in economic policy, see Hata, *Shōwa zaiseishi*, pp. 363–516; Nakamura, "SCAP to Nihon," pp. 3–24. For the impact on Japanese capitalism, Tamagaki Yoshinori, "Nihon shihonshugi no saiken," *Iwanami kōza Nihon rekishi*, vol. 23, *Gendai 2*, pp. 51–93; Katō Toshihiko, "Kaikakuki no Nihon keizai," *Sengo kaikaku*, vol. 7, pp. 3–32.

109. Hayakawa, "Kankō rōshi kankei no seisei to hatten," in *Sengo kaikaku*, vol. 5, pp. 309–54; Takemae Eiji, "1949-nen rōdōhō kaisei zenshi," in Nakamura, ed., *Senryōki Nihon no keizai to seiji*, pp. 301–38.

110. Hayakawa, pp. 350–52; Takemae, pp. 326–28.

111. "American Labor's Cold War in Occupied Japan," *Diplomatic History*, 3, 3 (Summer 1979), 249–72.

112. See Dower, *Empire and Aftermath*, pp. 333–41, and Ōkochi Kazuo, *Sengo Nihon no rōdō undō* (Iwanami shinsho, 1961).

113. See Dower, "The Eye of the Beholder," pp. 16–17; Dower, "Occupied Japan and the American Lake, 1945–1950," pp. 146–73; G. Kolko, *The Politics of War*, pp. 543–48; Jon Halliday, *A Political History of Japanese Capitalism* (New York: Pantheon, 1975), pp. 161–70; J. and G. Kolko, *The Limits of Power*, pp. 301–303; Bix, "Japan: The Roots of Militarism," pp. 320–21.

114. J. and G. Kolko, *The Limits of Power*, pp. 301–303; Dower, "Occupied Japan and the American Lake, 1945–1950," p. 175.

115. Igarashi also discusses the impact of factors outside the cold war framework, such as U.S. domestic economic and political considerations. "Tainichi kōwa no teishō to tainichi senryō seisaku no tenkan," *Shisō,* 628 (Oct. 1976), 1–42; Igarashi, "Tainichi kōwa no teishō to hankyōkan no isō," *Kokusai mondai* (July 1976); Igarashi, "Tainichi senryō seisaku no tenkan to reisen," and "Jyōji Kenan to tainichi senryō seisaku no tenkan," in Nakamura, ed., *Senryōki Nihon no keizai to seiji,* pp. 25–86.

116. Hata, *Shōwa zaiseishi,* pp. 351, 381n1.

117. See Eleanor Hadley, *Antitrust in Japan* (Princeton: Princeton University Press, 1970). Also on *zaibatsu* dissolution, Shibagaki Kazuo, "Zaibatsu kaitai to keizai fukko," *Iwanami kōza Nihon rekishi,* vol. 22, *Gendai* 1, pp. 306–308; Shibagaki, "Zaibatsu kaitai to shūchū haijo," *Sengo kaikaku,* vol. 7, pp. 33–107; Ōkurashō zaiseishi shitsu, ed., *Shōwa zaiseishi,* vols. 2, 12. For an argument that the deconcentration efforts were not as inconsequential as is usually claimed, see Uekusa Masu, "Senryōka no kigyō bunkatsu," in Nakamura, ed., *Senryōki Nihon no keizai to seiji,* pp. 203–21.

118. Hadley, p. 142.

119. Schonberger, "General William Draper," in Moore, ed., *Japan under American Rule, 1945–52.*

120. For examples of the factors usually adduced, see Nakamura, "SCAP to Nihon," pp. 13–14, and Igarashi, "Tainichi senryō seisaku no tenkan to reisen," p. 50, both in Nakamura, ed., *Senryōki Nihon no keizai to seiji,* a volume whose various essays nearly all touch on the "policy change" in one way or another; see Introduction, pp. i–ii. Also, Kozo Yamamura, *Economic Policy in Postwar Japan: Growth versus Economic Democracy* (Berkeley: University of California Press, 1967), pp. 21–38. One writer who does mention the "termination of war" expenditures is Martin Bronfenbrenner, in "Inflation Theories of the SCAP Period," *History of Political Economy,* 7, 2 (Summer 1975), 148–49.

121. See Dower, *Empire and Aftermath,* pp. 458–59, 473–80.

122. Dick K. Nanto, "The Dodge Line: A Reevaluation," in Redford, ed., *The Occupation of Japan: Economic Policy and Reform,* p. 51. Bronfenbrenner himself speculates that had the Korean War not intervened, Japan's economy would have recovered anyway, though more slowly. *Ibid.,* p. 73. But most Japanese sources still attribute the recovery to the Korean War which ended the "Dodge depression." Suzuki Takeo, *Kin'yū kinkyū sochi to Dojji Rain* (Seimeikai shuppanbu, 1970). On Japanese economic planning during this period, see Haruhiro Fukui, "Economic Planning in Postwar Japan: A Case Study in Policy Making," *Asian Survey,* 12, 4 (April 1972), 327–48.

123. See Shisō no kagaku kenkyūkai, ed., *Kyōdō kenkyū: Nihon senryō,* pp. 30–31.

124. "Gyakkōsu," *Yomiuri shinbun,* Nov. 2–Dec. 2, 1951.

125. Dower, *Empire and Aftermath,* pp. 415–16; Ishida Takeshi, "Sengo kaikaku to soshiki oyobi shōchō," in Tōkyō daigaku shakai kagaku kenkyūjo, ed., *Sengo kaikaku* (Tōkyō daigaku shuppankai, 1974), vol. 1, pp. 211–12.

126. Nakamura Masanori, " 'Gyakkōsu' to senryō kenkyū," *Sekai* (June 1981), p. 22.

127. E.g., Wada Haruki, "Sobieto renpo no tainichi seisaku," in Tōkyō daigaku shakai kagaku kenkyūjo, ed., *Sengo kaikaku* vol. 2, pp. 33–89; Takeda Kiyoko, *Tennōkan no sōkoku: 1945-nen zengo* (Iwanami shoten, 1978); Hosoya Chihirō, "Jōji Sansomu to sengo Nihon," *Chūō kōron,* 1062 (Sept. 1975); for an English summary, see "George Sansom: Diplomat and Historian," in Ian Nish and Charles Dunn, eds., *European Studies on Japan* (Tenterden, Kent: Paul Norbury Publications, 1979), pp. 113–19; Bamba Nobuya, "Senryō to Nōman," *Shisō,* 634 (April 1977).

128. E.g., on the German occupation, Tezuka Kazuaki, "Taidoitsu senryō seisaku no

keisei to 'tenkan'," in Nakamura, ed., *Senryōki Nihon no keizai to seiji,* pp. 383–430; Totsuka Hideo, "Nishi doitsu ni okeru sengo kaikaku," in Tōkyō daigaku shakai kagaku kenkyūjo, ed., *Sengo kaikaku* vol. 2, pp. 91–152; for suggestions for more adventurous comparisons, Shisō no kagaku kenkyūkai, ed., *Kyōdō kenkyū: Nihon senryō,* p. 72; Takemae, *Senryō sengoshi,* p. 395.

129. Nakamura suggests that the conflict of opinion within the occupation bureaucracy over the proper economic course for Japan from 1946 to 1948 resembled the debates between the prewar reformist intellectuals and the military over how to create an ideal state in their own image in Manchuria. *Senryōki Nihon no keizai to seiji,* p. 13. For examples of critical references, see Fujiwara Akira, "Gendaishi josetsu," in *Iwanami kōza Nihon rekishi,* vol. 22, *Gendai 1,* p. 22; Ienaga Saburō, *The Pacific War: World War II and the Japanese* (New York: Pantheon, 1978), pp. 236–45.

130. See Miyasato Seigen, "Amerika no tai Okinawa seisaku no keisei to hatten," in Miyasato, ed., *Sengo Okinawa no seiji to hō* (Tōkyō daigaku shuppankai, 1975), pp. 3–116; Ōta Masahide, *Kindai Okinawa no seiji kōzō* (Chikuma shobō, 1972); Ōta, "Senryō ka no Okinawa," in *Iwanami koza Nihon rekishi,* vol. 23, *Gendai 2,* pp. 291–342; Ōta, " 'Sengo kaikaku' to Okinawa no bunri," *Sekai,* 401 (April 1979), 52–63; Arasaki Moriteru, *Sengo Okinawa shi* (Nihon hyōronsha, 1976); Higa Mikio, "Amerikagawa kara mita Okinawa," *Sekai,* 401 (April 1979), 64–74; Kano Masanao, "*Konnichi no Ryūkyū* o tōshite mita zai-Okinawa Amerika gun no bunka seisaku," *Nihon rekishi,* 375 (Aug. 1979), 1–18. Kano is presently working on a history of the American occupation of the Ryūkyūs. For a recent example of the way Okinawa is used in a general narrative history of the occupation, see Ōe Shinobu, *Sengo henkaku, Nihon no rekishi,* vol. 31, which begins and ends with sections on Okinawa. See also Frederick F. Shiels, *America, Okinawa, and Japan: Case Studies from Foreign Policy Theory* (Washington, D.C.: University Press of America, 1980), pp. 53–148; Watanabe Akio, *The Okinawa Problem: A Chapter in Japan-U.S. Relations* (Melbourne: Melbourne University Press, 1970), pp. 3–30; Mark Selden, "Okinawa and American Security Imperialism" in Selden, ed., *Remaking Asia: Essays on the American Uses of Power* (New York: Pantheon, 1974), pp. 279–304; Shindo Eiichi, "Bunkatsu sareta ryōdo," *Sekai,* 401 (April 1979), 31–51; Shindo, "Divided Territories and the Origins of the Cold War," in Moore, ed., *Japan under American Rule.*

131. For relevant aspects of U.S. policy toward East Asia, see John Lewis Gaddis, "Korea in American Politics, Strategy, and Diplomacy, 1945–1950," in Nagai Yōnosuke and Iriye Akira, eds., *The Origins of the Cold War in Asia* (New York: Columbia University Press, 1977), pp. 277–98; William Whitney Stueck, Jr., *The Road to Confrontation: American Policy toward China and Korea, 1947–1950* (Chapel Hill: University of North Carolina Press, 1981). For a popular view, see James C. Thomson, Jr., Peter W. Stanley, and John Curtis Perry, *Sentimental Imperialists: The American Experience in East Asia* (New York: Harper and Row, 1981), pp. 203–52.

132. Schaller and Elston, "Securing the Great Crescent," in Moore, ed., *Japan under American Rule.* See also Schaller, "Securing the Great Crescent: Occupied Japan and the Origins of Containment in Southeast Asia," *Journal of American History,* 69, 2 (Sept. 1982) and a forthcoming volume of the same title, to be published by Oxford University Press; Borden, "The United States and Japan in Southeast Asia, 1947–1955," in Moore, ed., *Japan under American Rule.* Both Borden and Schaller have drawn on a wide variety of sources, both government and private, many of them unused in scholarship until now. Saitō Takashi, "Amerika no taigai seisaku to Nihon senryō," *Sengo kaikaku,* vol. 2, pp. 3–32. For examples of views of younger Japanese scholars, see Miyazato Seigen, "The Truman Administration and

Indochina," *The Japanese Journal of American Studies* (1981); Yoshida Morio, "Dai nijisekai taisen no shūketsu to Amerika no tō Ajia shihai," *Nihonshi kenkyū,* 187 (March 1978), 135–62; Yamagiwa Akira, "Amerika no sengo kōsō to Ajia: tainichi senryō seisaku o minaosu," *Sekai,* 371 (Sept. 1976), 51–73.

133. An NSC draft of December 23, 1949, based on NSC 48. Dower, "The Superdomino in Postwar Asia," p. 105.

134. Nancy Bernkopf Tucker, "Sino-Japanese Trade in the Postwar Years: Politics and Prosperity," and Michael Schaller, "The U.S. Occupation of Japan and Regional Integration," papers presented at Organization of American Historians meeting, Philadelphia, March 1982.

135. Borden, *The Pacific Alliance.*

136. Much of this work is currently in progress, although there are a number of published writings, e.g., Yamagiwa Akira, "Chōsen sensō to sanfuranshisuko kōwa jōyaku," in *Iwanami kōza Nihon rekishi, Gendai* 1, pp. 381–417. On the Korean War, Nagai Yōnosuke, "The Korean War," *The Japanese Journal of American Studies* (1981); Koseki Shōichi, "Chōsen sensō to Nihon saigunbi," *Rekishi hyōron,* 367 (June 1980), 37–50; Wakui Hideyuki, "Chōsen sensō to Nihon dokusen shihon no fukkatsu," *Rekishi hyōron,* 357–62 (Jan.-June 1980), 51–62; a forthcoming volume by Okonogi Masao will provide a full-length study of the Korean War. On the peace treaty, Nishimura Kumao, *San Furanshisuko heiwa jōyaku* (Kajima kenkyūjo shuppankai, 1971); Igarashi Takeshi, "American-Japanese Peacemaking and the Cold War, 1947–1951," *Amerika kenkyū,* 13 (1979), 166–87. Aoki Tetsuo, "Sanfuranshisuko taisei no seiritsu," in *Taikei Nihon gendaishi,* vol. 6, *Reisenka no Nihon,* ed. Fujiwara, pp. 207–43; Aoki, "Kōwa–dokuritsu ni yoru seiji kōzō to tenkan," *Rekishi hyōron,* no. 384 (April 1982), pp. 24–37. For a comprehensive diplomatic history of U.S.-Japan relations during the occupation but before the treaty issue, see Suzuki Tadakatsu, *Shūsen kara kōwa made, Nihon gaikoshi,* vol. 26 (Kajima kenkyūjo shuppankai, 1973). Earlier works include Frederick Dunn, *Peacemaking and the Settlement with Japan* (Princeton: Princeton University Press, 1963), and Bernard Cohen, *The Political Process and Foreign Policy: The Making of the Japanese Peace Settlement* (Princeton: Princeton University Press, 1957). Also, R. K. Jain, *Japan's Postwar Peace Settlements* (Atlantic Highlands, N.J.: Humanities Press, 1978).

137. For a representative treatment, see Fukushima Shingo, "Nichibei anpō taisei to sai-gunbi," *Iwanami kōza Nihon rekishi,* vol. 23, *Gendai* 2, pp. 1–49. On rearmament, Hata Ikuhiko, *Shiroku Nihon saigunbi;* Koseki Shōichi, "Reisen seisaku ni okeru Nihon saigunbi no kihonteki seikaku," in Rekishi kagaku kenkyūkai, ed., *Sekaishi ni okeru chiiku to minshū— 1979 nendo rekishigaku kenkyūkai taikai hōkoku* (Aoki shoten, 1979); Koseki, "Chōsen sensō to Nihon saigunbi," *Rekishi hyōron,* 362 (June 1980), 37–50; James E. Auer, *The Postwar Rearmament of Japanese Maritime Forces, 1945–1971* (New York: Praeger, 1973); Martin E. Weinstein, *Japan's Postwar Defense Policy, 1947–1968* (New York: Columbia University Press, 1971).

138. Roger Dingman, "Reconsiderations of the U.S.-Japan Security Treaty," *Pacific Community,* 7 (July 1976), 471–94; Dingman, "Strategic Planning and the Policy Process: America Plans for War in East Asia, 1945–1950," *Naval War College Review* (Nov.-Dec. 1979), pp. 4–21; Dingman, "The U.S. Navy and the Cold War: The Japan Case," in Craig L. Symonds, ed., *New Aspects of Naval History* (Annapolis: Naval Institute Press, 1981), pp. 291–312; for an analysis of the "Yoshida letter" in the context of Anglo-American alliance politics, Dingman, "The Anglo-American Origins of the Yoshida Letter, 1951–1952," in David J. Lu, ed., *Perspectives on Japan's External Relations* (Lewisburg, Pa.: Center for Japanese Studies, Bucknell University, 1982), pp. 26–107. In Japanese, "Yoshida shokan (1951-nen) no kigen: Nihon o meguru eibei no kōsō," Amakawa Akira, tr., in *"Reisen"—sono kyokō to*

jitsuzō, ed. Nihon kokusai seiji gakkai (Yūhikaku, 1975), pp. 121–40. Dingman, "Theories of, and Approaches to, Alliance Politics," in *Diplomacy: New Approaches in History, Theory, and Policy* (New York: Free Press, 1979), pp. 245–66. Dingman is now working on a full-length study of the peace settlement, which draws on British, Canadian, Australian, and Philippine, as well as Japanese and American, archives. It is entitled *Peace in the Pacific: Making Peace with Japan, 1941–1952.* See also Hosoya Chihiro, "The Road to San Francisco: The Shaping of American Policy on the Japanese Peace Treaty," *The Japanese Journal of American Studies,* no. 1 (1981). Hosoya is preparing a full-length study on the subject in Japanese.

139. See Michael Y. Yoshitsu, *Japan and the San Francisco Peace Settlement* (New York: Columbia University Press, 1983); Hosoya Chihiro, "Japan's Response to U.S. Policy on the Japanese Peace Treaty: The Dulles-Yoshida Talks," *Hitotsubashi Journal of Law and Politics* 10 (December 1981), 15–27; also, Nishimura Kumao, *San Furanshisuko heiwa jōyaku* (Kajima kenkyūjo shuppankai, 1971).

140. For a provocative thesis that asserts the convergence of Japanese and American postwar policy on the pattern of "the shared Wilsonian internationalism of the 1920s," see Iriye Akira, *Power and Culture: The Japanese-American War, 1941–1945* (Cambridge: Harvard University Press, 1981); in Japanese, *Nichi-Bei sensō* (Chūō kōron, 1978).

141. E.g., Roger W. Buckley, *Occupation Diplomacy: Britain, the United States and Japan* (Cambridge: Cambridge University Press, 1982); also, Buckley, "Britain and the Emperor: The Foreign Office and Constitutional Reform in Japan, 1945–46," *Modern Asian Studies,* 12, 4 (1978), 553–70; Ian Nish, ed., *Anglo-Japanese Alienation, 1919–1952* (Cambridge: Cambridge University Press, 1982) contains essays by Akira Iriye on wartime Japanese planning for postwar Asia, Akio Wantanabe on Japanese views of the United Kingdom, 1945–1952, and Gordon Daniels on Britain's view of postwar Japan, 1945–1949; D. C. Watt, "Britain and the Cold War in the Far East," in Nagai and Iriye, eds., *The Origins of the Cold War in Asia,* pp. 89–122; Roger J. Bell, *Unequal Allies: Australian-American Relations and the Pacific War* (Melbourne: Melbourne University Press, 1977), pp. 144–232; also, Bell, "Australian-American Disagreement over the Peace Settlement with Japan," *Australian Outlook,* 30, 2 (Aug. 1976), 238–62. For other Australian materials, see the Shulman supplementary bibliography. The New Zealand Ministry of External Affairs official history of peacemaking with Japan will be published in 1983. Christopher Thorne touches on the postwar order in *Allies of a Kind: The United States, Britain and the War Against Japan, 1941–1945* (New York: Oxford University Press, 1978), pp. 654–71.

142. Iriye, "Continuities in U.S.-Japanese Relations, 1941–49," in Nagai and Iriye, eds., *The Origins of the Cold War in Asia,* and Yamamoto Mitsuru, "The Cold War and U.S.-Japan Economic Cooperation," *ibid.,* pp. 408–25. This volume contains several valuable essays from different international perspectives. See also Iriye, *The Cold War in Asia: A Historical Introduction* (Englewood Cliffs, N.J.: Prentice-Hall, 1974); and Nagai Yōnosuke, *Reisen no kigen* (Chūō kōronsha, 1978). For Japanese Marxist and new left perspectives on the cold war, see, e.g., Takita Ryōsuke, *Gendai Amerika gaikōron* (Nihon hyōronsha, 1978); Amerika wakashu kenkyūkai gendaishi guruppu, " 'Yaruta gaikō' kara Torūman dokutorin e," *Rekishigaku kenkyū,* 386 (July 1972), 11–24; and Yui Daizaburō, "Teikokushugi sekai taisei no saihen to 'reisen' no kigen—Torūman dokutorin to eibei kankei o tegakari to shite," *Rekishigaku kenkyū,* supplement, 1974.

143. Herblock, *The Washington Post,* March 1951. Reprinted in Herbert Block, *The Herblock Book* (Boston: Beacon Press, 1952), p. 204.

144. John Lewis Gaddis, *Strategies of Containment: A Critical Appraisal of Postwar American National Security Policy* (New York: Oxford University Press, 1982), p. 39.

145. E.g., Feis, *Contest over Japan* (New York: Norton, 1967).

146. Borden, *The Pacific Alliance,* ch. 1.

147. For the German instance, see Edward N. Peterson, *The American Occupation of Germany: Retreat to Victory* (Detroit: Wayne State University Press, 1977), pp. 138 ff.

148. See Ōuchi Tsutomu, "Sengo kaikaku to kokka dokusen shihonshugi," and Ōishi Kaichirō, "Sengo kaikaku to Nihon shihonshugi no kōzō henka," in Tōkyō daigaku shakai kagaku kenkyūjo, ed., *Sengo kaikaku,* vol. 1, pp. 3–98.

149. Hata Ikuhiko and Sodei Rinjirō, *Senryō hishi* (Asahi shinbunsha, 1977), pp. 211–12.

150. John W. Dower, *Occupied Japan, 1945–1952* (New York: Pantheon, forthcoming).

151. John W. Maki, tr. and ed., *Japan's Commission on the Constitution: The Final Report* (Seattle: University of Washington Press, 1980), pp. 221–25.

152. See, e.g., Fujiwara Akira, "Shinkenpō taisei," in *Taikei Nihon gendaishi,* vol. 5, *Senryō to sengo kaikaku,* Kanda Fuhito, ed. (Nihon hyōronsha, 1979), pp. 5–7, 148–86. Also, Haruhiro Fukui, "Twenty Years of Revisionism," in Dan Henderson, ed., *The Constitution of Japan: Its First Twenty Years, 1947–67* (Seattle: University of Washington Press, 1968), pp. 41–70.

153. See, e.g., Yoshida Morio, "Nihon no kōfuku to shinkenpō: Etō Jun '*Mō hitotsu no sengoshi*' ninshiki hihan," *Rekishi hyōron,* 353 (Sept. 1979). Other similar issues include aspects of the "symbol emperor system" and war responsibility (see note 34), the war crimes trial, the bomb, and rearmament. See, e.g., Arai Shinichi, "Tennō no sensō sekinin mondai to Amerika," in Fujiwara and Matsuo, eds., *Ronshū gendaishi* (Chikuma shobō, 1976), pp. 363–86; Awaya Kentarō, "Sensō hanzai saiban to gendai shi kenkyū," *Rekishigaku kenkyū,* 453 (Feb. 1978), 17–27. On the war crimes trial in English, Richard Minear, *Victor's Justice: The Tokyo War Crimes Trial* (Princeton: Princeton University Press, 1971); Philip Piccigallo, *The Japanese on Trial: Allied War Crimes Operations in the Far East, 1945–1951* (Austin: University of Texas Press, 1979). Also, the proceedings have now been printed: R. John Pritchard and Sonia Zaide Pritchard, comps. and eds., *Toyko War Crimes Trial,* 27 vols. (New York: Garland, 1980). The judgment alone is available as: B.V.A. Röling and C.F. Rüter, eds., *The Tokyo Judgment: The International Military Tribunal for the Far East (IMTFE), 29 April 1946–12 November 1948,* 2 vols. (Amsterdam: APA-University Press, 1977).

154. Dower, *Empire and Aftermath,* pp. 277–78.

155. See Amakawa Akira, " 'Nihon senryō' kenkyū no tenbō," *Kokka gakkai zasshi,* 88, 4–5 (May 1975), 378–79.

156. See "Handō ideorogii ronsō," *Rekishi hyōron,* 364 (Aug. 1980), 8–9; Tōkyō rekishi kagaku kenkyūkai, *Tenkanki no rekishigaku* (Gōdō shuppan, 1975), pp. 13ff. The historian criticized for linking the prewar with the postwar is Itō Takashi. See also Shigeyama Toshio, "Handō ideorōgu ni yoru rekishi no kakikae to sono hōhō ni tsuite," *Rekishi hyōron,* 353 (Sept. 1979), 25–34; Yamaguchi Keiji and Matsuo Shōichi, *Sengoshi to handō ideorogii* (Shin Nihon shuppansha, 1981).

157. Dower, *Empire and Aftermath,* p. 311.

158. Charles S. Maier, "The Two Postwar Eras and the Conditions for Stability in Twentieth-Century Western Europe," *American Historical Review,* 86, 2 (April 1981), 328.

EIGHT

Korean–American Relations: A Century of Contact and Thirty-Five Years of Intimacy

by BRUCE CUMINGS

KOREAN-AMERICAN RELATIONS is not a field where scholars can gather for conferences to assess the work of the previous decade, unfortunate as that may be for intellectual exchange and the chance to get away for a pleasant weekend. Content with small victories in each decade, people who work on Korea perhaps should hold bicentennials to discuss really important milestones of scholarship.

In the early period of Korean-American relations, from 1876 to 1910, the United States played a minor role in opening the Hermit Kingdom to intercourse with the Western world, which meant altering Korea's ancient position within the Chinese world order. On this latter topic there is much good and interesting scholarship. What links this early period with the post-1945 era of heavy American involvement in Korea? Maybe nothing more than a set of images of Korea formed in the early period and continuing down to 1945 and thereafter, when images influenced policy. But this set of images does tell us much about Americans in alien lands.

The major part of this essay surveys the literature on the origins of the current Korean-American relationship, in the period 1945–1953. From this point on, no Asian nation has been in more intense, sustained, and conflictual relations with the United States than Korea. We can witness in the early postwar period the origins of our era and the peculiar problems that it bequeathed.

THE EARLY PERIOD

John Fairbank remarked in 1972 that Tyler Dennett's *Americans in Eastern Asia* "set a nationalistic style in 1922 which has persisted ever since" in the literature.[1] By that he meant too many historians have ignored the British archives. In the case of the early literature on Korean-American relations we find a different sort of nationalistic style: an assumption that one can understand Korean-American interaction by studying the American record, and sometimes perhaps the Chinese or Japanese record, but that the Korean record is unimportant—and not only the historical record, as historians have rendered it, but the actions of Koreans themselves. The assumption is that Korea gets things done to it, so one should look at the doers. Thus there exists in much of the literature on Korean-American relations an overestimation of the capacities of the powers to effect changes in Korea, and an underestimation of the abilities of Koreans to act and react in a situation where foreigners, since the opening of Korea, held most of the cards.

The result in the literature is that not until 1945 did a book appear that took seriously the capabilities of Koreans and particularly the intricacies of Korea's interaction with China as a subject worthy of study in its own right. M. Frederick Nelson's *Korea and the Old Orders in Eastern Asia* [2] displayed a subtle, if idealized, appreciation of the reciprocal interaction between Korea and China, which made this the most important case in China's tributary system, and the delicate manner in which the system functioned to make China less than a suzerain and Korea more than a dependency. Alone to his time, Nelson understood that Korea's relations with China were embedded in a history stretching back to antiquity and a world order that had much to recommend it. His discussion of the Chinese world order remained unsurpassed in the literature for many years.

From Nelson forward there is another long drought in the literature, ending only in the mid-1970s with three books of impeccable scholarship that explode the comfortable assumption that one can get the story without looking at the Korean side of it. James B. Palais, Martina Deuchler, and Key-Hiuk Kim show that there is much to learn from filling in the empty space that has been Korea in the general literature.[3]

Until 1945 and Nelson the entire literature on East Asian–American relations treated Korea as an afterthought, important to something else, perhaps, but not important enough to subject to close scrutiny. An exception would be Tabohashi's magisterial study, completed in 1941 but inaccessible to those who cannot read the classical language; also perhaps a couple of articles by T. F. Tsiang and others.[4] Dennett's pathbreaking work has the virtue of at least postulating a trinity in East Asia, but Korea appears first on page 407, followed by a narrative that shows little comprehension of Korea's tributary relations with China and none of the internal scene in Korea. Basing himself entirely in Western concepts of sovereignty, Dennett argues that China in 1876 (when Korea was opened) "had no valid claim to Korea," since China "exercised no administrative functions" and had repeatedly "denied any control of Korean affairs."[5] He does not stop to ask if perhaps the Koreans felt a claim on China, or if both might be happy with a relationship of formal hierarchy and substantive autonomy. Korea's seclusion policy Dennett finds "blind and irrational."[6] Yet this policy had the virtue of having worked for Korea for the three centuries since the Hideyoshi invasions, and of having staved off the imperial impact such that Korea was the last Asian nation to be opened. Dennett is right to have seen the 1882 treaty with the United States as "the instrument which set Korea adrift on an ocean of intrigue," but he fails to understand Li Hongzhang's (Li Hung-chang) motives and states that Li "failed to accomplish his purpose."[7] The purpose was precisely to place Korea on an ocean of intrigue, but not so that it would drift; the United States and other powers would involve themselves in Korea's fate and therefore hamstring Japan and maintain Korea's autonomy.

Much like Fred Harvey Harrington after him, Dennett inflates Horace Allen's personal influence, arguing that within months of Allen's arrival "American influence in Seoul was easily paramount."[8] It is possible to ask if American influence in Seoul has *ever* been paramount when compared to that of China or Japan, but certainly this is an exaggeration of U.S. potency in the mid-1880s. Later in the book Dennett comes closer to the truth when he argues that the activities of a handful of missionaries, diplomats, and businessmen (sometimes all wrapped up in the same person, as with Allen) led to "a very strong unofficial American influence"[9]—although he again confuses individuals with the nation. Even then, such influence paled before that exercised by China and Japan. Dennett concludes that U.S. policy toward Korea to 1900 "while not properly open to the charge of having betrayed the Koreans, was certainly lacking in political sagacity and was most deficient in its contempt for general cooperation. Statesmanship was nowhere apparent."[10] What policy? Can one credit the United States with having had a policy toward Korea? The 1882 treaty was negotiated by an impulsive naval officer and a shrewd Chinese (Shufeldt and Li), mainly at Li's instance. Most American presidents were unaware of the "good offices" clause, since it was standard for such treaties at the time. In the 1890s the Philippines were more important; in the 1900s Japan was more important. Korea was but an afterthought. True, statesmanship may have been nowhere apparent, but few have done more with less than Horace Allen. Dennett shows more understanding in another book, when he says that the 1882 treaty "may truly be claimed as an act of absent-mindedness."[11]

In *Roosevelt and the Russo-Japanese War,* however, Dennett's intent is to justify Roosevelt's *realpolitik* in supporting Japan's annexation of Korea, and so he makes less of the American role in Korea than he did in *Americans in Eastern Asia.* Dennett echoes Roosevelt's judgment that Korea was "long a derelict state"; 1905 was the time it should be "towed into port and secured." Korea's history would "admit of no other conclusion." The Taft-Katsura memorandum "was not a sacrifice of Korea for the sake of the Philippines"; instead, Korea was betrayed "not by President Roosevelt but by her own Emperor and for the most sordid of motives."[12] Korea was not Roosevelt's to betray, of course, but Korea's history might admit of conclusions other than that Japan should swallow it. Even assuming that Koreans were not governed well by Western standards, why was it necessary that the Japanese should govern the Hermit Kingdom, which had never bothered anyone outside its borders?

William Sands' memoir appeared a few years after Dennett's work.[13] The memoir is unreliable historically, since Sands was not in a position to observe high politics and was unacquainted with the archives or scholarship. But the book does offer local color and interesting asides drawn from the decades on either side of the turn of the century. Sands was the first to observe what has become a tradition in Korean-American relations: the abstractions of Washington policy versus the realities of the scene in Korea, both usually running on different tracks. Sands says he and a few other American diplomats "only guessed at home policy" in "so remote a spot." In such circumstances those on the scene accumulate power and sometimes can sway events. Allen and a tiny number of missionaries interested in converts and businessmen interested in profits parlayed America's small official stake into big personal stakes: Americans obtained the first railroad and gold mine concessions (not giving up the latter until 1939), had interests in Seoul's streetcar and electric services, and ran several schools and hospitals that imparted Western learning, medical and otherwise. The comforts deriving from small representation of a big power were there as well: "Life was easy at Seoul. One kept far too many servants. . . . The two first must be Chinese; the coolie might be a native."[14] Sands' overall judgment on Allen and a few other Americans was closer to the mark than Dennett's defensiveness about Roosevelt and his wistful notion that the Koreans liked Americans better than other imperialists: Such Americans "had all of what history writers today are fond of calling the machinery of imperialism without the motive power of imperialism."[15]

A. Whitney Griswold turns the bright glare of unsentimental history upon American policy during the Roosevelt years (the only time before the 1940s when U.S. policy made any difference in regard to Korea—and the difference was not much). Roosevelt comes off utterly different than Dennett would have him. A dabbler in old world *realpolitik*, Griswold finds him, being trumped across the board by the Germans, Japanese, and others. To Griswold the Taft-Katsura memorandum was indeed a trade-off of the Philippines for Korea, but apart from that he has almost nothing to say about Korea in U.S. policy.[16] In a book about U.S. Far Eastern policy, which was subordinate to policy toward Europe, which was in turn subordinate to the general business of Americans at home, this is probably an appropriate epitaph for the Korean-American relationship to 1910. There just was not much to it.

Still, there was that strange character who represented by himself the three impulses of Americans in Asia in the nineteenth century: Horace Allen—missionary, diplomat, and concessionaire not above taking a bribe for his efforts. Fred Harvey Harrington has a field day with this fellow, but at the expense of making us think that Allen really was important in the events of the period (Nelson barely mentions Allen). Harrington has Allen taking part in court intrigue for twenty years after 1885, perhaps even "spending half his time" at it,[17] but it would be difficult to find one significant event that was swayed by Allen rather than by the Chinese, the Japanese, or the Koreans themselves. Yet, where Allen did make an impact—on the first concessions that King Kojong gave out—Harrington's historical skills take wing. The chapters "Selling Chosen's Charms" and "A Cripple Creek All of Our Own" are gems, even if the concessions proved insignificant for American interests in the longer run—or, as Harrington put it, "so ran the path of an economic imperialist who lacked the backing of his government and his home country's financiers." Harrington's conclusion was both right and wrong: "The gospel and the dollar are the keys to Horace Allen's life [yes] and to American diplomacy in Chosen [no]."[18] Again, there was no "American diplomacy."

In recent years Koreans have written much on the early period in the Korean-American relationship. Some of it is valuable, such as the multivolume series of reprinted documents put out under the auspices of the Asiatic Research Center of Korea University.[19] This monumental effort will keep scholars busy for years, although a brief perusal of the many volumes suggests again that there is much to say about Korean diplomacy in general, but little that is new about Korean-American relations. Interpretive studies by historians of both South and North Korea are less satisfying. Both use the present to criticize the past, so that the northern historians read ultimate perfidy into every American action, from the bumbled voyage of the *General Sherman* in 1866 to the small-potatoes ventures of Allen; the southerners treat the Americans kindly while lamenting that they never did enough to keep Korea out of Japan's hands. It is interesting, however, to read a recent multivolume DPRK effort which finds use in citing Dennett, William Griffis' *Hermit Kingdom,* Foster Rhea Dulles' *America in the Pacific,* and various volumes of the *Foreign Relations of the United States.* Once one gets past the rhetoric, the book is useful both for what it does say and for what it does not. It also shows the marks of the major effort at historical rewriting that has gone on since the mid-1960s. We find that Kim Il Sung's great-grandfather led those Koreans who burned the *General Sherman* near P'yŏngyang, for example.[20] One will not find evidence of this in the documents put out by the South.

South Korean works by Kim Hyŏn-gil, Sin Ki-sŏk, Sin Kuk-ju, and No Kye-hyŏn[21] are gentler with the Americans but, apart from that difference, show many of the same animuses as the northern literature. The Yi dynasty is seen as hopelessly inept, toadying to China or other foreign powers; the Japanese are imperialists bent from Meiji onward (if not earlier) to conquer Korea, and their imperialism is fundamentally motivated by a capitalist mode of production; the nationalism of the present in both North and South is read back into the past so strongly that if unification ever arrives one will be able to merge the two views on the nineteenth century by rewriting the American section and then dotting some i's and crossing some t's.

There remains much to be said about Korea in the late nineteenth century and several scholars with the linguistic virtuosity required to fathom the period are saying it. Palais' book ostensibly surveys Korea just before its opening by the Kanghwa Treaty of 1876, but it is the first thorough study in English of the structure and function of the Yi dynasty. One of its foci is the *Taewŏn'gun,* Korea's de facto leader from 1864 to 1873, a strong patriot who successfully held off foreign power and a reformer who proved that Korea's agrarian-bureaucratic system could be adaptable and supple in responding to domestic problems, even if it was too weak to resist the full brunt of foreign power. Palais' account will immediately remind China historians of Mary Wright's discussion of the alpenglow of the Qing dynasty, the Tongzhi Restoration. In the published volume there is but one chapter on the diplomacy leading up to the Kanghwa Treaty, but in the dissertation from which the book is drawn there are hundreds of pages.[22] No one who reads Palais' work will be able to argue again that Korea was merely a passive supplicant in the diplomacy of the late nineteenth century.

Kim's study, *The Last Phase of the East Asian World Order,* places diplomacy front and center. It argues for both the adaptability and the centrality of tradition to the foreign policy behavior of Korea, Japan, and China in the two decades from 1860 to 1880. Korea reasserted its traditional seclusion policy, here defined more sharply as "exclusionism," and was successful in so doing for most of the period, even if its victories eventually proved Pyrrhic. China took vigorous action to reassert a long-dormant interest in Korea. Perhaps most provocative is Kim's interpretation of Japanese behavior: He suggests that Japan after Meiji sought not something new in Korea, but a reassertion of a fictive tributary relationship thought to have existed long in the misty past. Thus, he argues, the East Asian world order was undone not so much by the clash of East and West as that of East and East: "An emerging rivalry between China and Japan" was the main cause of the disruption of this world order where it had been most important, that is, in northeast Asia.

Kim's account of Korean exclusionism is the best in the literature and provides a way of understanding the seemingly strange behavior of North Korea today and especially its relationship with China. North Korea cloisters even socialist-bloc diplomats in P'yŏngyang and restricts their travel in the interior; the Yi dynasty did the same to Qing diplomats. North Korea uses a highly moral set of prescriptions and proscriptions to evaluate the rest of the world, arguing continually for the worth of its *"chuch'e"* (self-reliance) doctrine as opposed to the worthlessness or decadence of all other doctrines. One thinks they would not disagree with the words of State Councillor Hong Sun-mok, quoted by Kim: "Every corner of the world today has been contaminated by a dark and evil spirit; only our country remains clean. This is because we have guarded our land with propriety and justice" (p. 64). Then, as now in North Korea, the Koreans put all foreign powers at arm's length, or wanted to: They found it possible only with China to drop the guard for an occasional embrace. Traditionally (and now) Koreans have seen China as a problem, but less of a problem than other powers. Chinese benign neglect has been reciprocated by a grudging Korean respect, if not love.

Kim argues that Japanese development after Meiji only increased the traditional contempt Koreans felt for Japanese as inferiors more removed than Korea from the splendors of Chinese culture. Japan's adoption of Western dress, armaments, and industries only reinforced the Korean sense that these were lesser people, taken with barbarian baubles and toys. Korea "will always adhere to the way of the Sages," said Kim Ki-su, "and will never seek excellence in clever skills and evil arts" (p. 259). Key-Hiuk Kim appreciates the subtleties as well as the crudities of Korea's "low determines high" diplomacy. The Taewŏn'gun "professed an undying devotion to China without any intention of following the Chinese lead"; Korean officials curtly refused even to read documents brought by Japanese emissaries, quibbling endlessly over initial wording. How could the Japanese refer to their leader as "emperor," when there was only one of those and he was in China? For a time such exasperating techniques worked well in keeping foreigners out of Korea.

Kim makes a major contribution in his discussion of Korea's place in the Chinese world order, saying that China's role rarely went beyond "ceremonial diplomacy," leaving Korea "for all practical intents and purposes . . . completely independent in the management of its own affairs." The "basic norm and principle" of Chinese policy was "non-interference." He takes the analysis back to the Ming and up to the period of strong Chinese influence in the 1880s. The book also has the best discussion in English of America's "little war with the heathen" over the *General Sherman*. Following Frederick Foo Chien,[23] Kim suggests that Korea was not really opened by the Kanghwa Treaty: Instead, the treaty represented, at least from the Korean side, a restoration of traditional relations with Japan from before the Tokugawa seclusion.

If China pursued only ceremonial diplomacy in Korea, some will ask, then what was Yuan Shikai (Yuan Shih-k'ai) doing there in residency? Kim suggests that Chinese behavior in the 1880s was less a reassertion of traditional interest than a metamorphosis into nineteenth-century balance-of-power thinking that had no precedent in the previous Sino-Korean relationship. If Japan came into Korea in the 1870s under the impact of the "new learning," then so did China in the 1880s.

It is here that the 1882 treaty with the United States becomes important. China, under Li Hongzhang's foreign policy leadership, adopted what Kim calls "treaty-system diplomacy" to keep Korea out of the hands of Japan and Russia. Korea should develop diplomatic and commercial relations "with those Western powers whose interest in East Asia was chiefly in trade, not in territorial aggrandizement" (p. 277). The United States was the best candidate, a Chinese counselor in Tokyo argued in an important memorandum entitled "A Strategy for Korea." He suggested that the Americans have "always upheld justice" and "never permitted the European powers to freely perpetrate their evil deeds." Chief State Councillor Yi Ch'oe-ŭng had been thinking along the same lines in Seoul, and so recommended to the king that it was not bad policy to have a treaty with the United States. So the treaty was signed, to be followed shortly by identical treaties with Great Britain and Germany. Thus Kim concludes:

From beginning to end, Korea's first treaties with Western powers had been masterminded and negotiated by China under its new 'treaty-system policy' for Korea. Departing from its tradition of non-interference in Korean affairs, the Ch'ing government intervened in Korea's foreign affairs and virtually took over the entire conduct of its foreign policy. (p. 316)

As for the United States, supremely indifferent about and irrelevant to the conclusion of this little treaty, it might have learned a lesson. Those who display their beneficence from afar get rewards that escape those who meddle in others' affairs. The United States had "upheld justice" only in the sense in which not-doing is doing (*wuwei er chih*).

Deuchler's book arrives at conclusions similar to Key-Hiuk Kim's, although they are less forcefully announced.[24] Her study also is based on thorough reading of the documents, and it fills out Kim's account of the diplomatic maneuvering over Korea with a discussion of the economic history of the period, particularly the opening of several ports, the beginning of trade, inflow of Japanese commerce, and the interesting if halting attempts at "self-strengthening" carried out under King Kojong's aegis. The book is limited to the decade 1875–1885, but this allows for a thorough discussion of the U.S.–Korean Treaty. Deuchler argues that traditionally "the Sino-Korean relationship was dominated by China; the Korean-Japanese relationship was dominated by Korea" (p. 4). With China things remained this way through the 1880s. It was China that brought Korea into the Western system of unequal treaties. But by that time Japan had begun to create an informal empire with its developing economic activity in Korea. Japan may not have opened Korea formally in 1876, but in the aftermath all of the usual effects of such "opening" in late nineteenth-century Asia were visible. Korea may have seen the Kanghwa Treaty as a continuation of its seclusion policy, as Kim and Deuchler argue, but "the Koreans had to give in to the Japanese step by step. Against their will, a new era had started."[25] Like the Kim book, Deuchler's analysis of the seclusion policy suggests comparisons with today's North Korea: "Seclusion was . . . a positive concept as far as the Koreans were concerned. It was the expression of a self-sufficient system . . ." (p. 5).

A final addition to the literature on the early period is C. I. Eugene Kim and Han-kyo Kim, *Korea and the Politics of Imperialism, 1876–1910.*[26] It has the virtue of covering a longer period than the previous three studies and is a most useful book in the classroom. But it is deficient in its command of the sources, overlooking both good Korean-language secondary works and major collections of official documents. The authors also overdo their argument that Yi dynasty leaders were inured to relying on outside power and failed to see the coming catastrophe of national obliteration. Happily this volume is at its best on the period 1890–1910, which the others do not treat, and therefore all four can be read together. When one does so, the depiction of old Korea in the maelstrom of late nineteenth-century imperialism will have to change in the general literature on East Asian–American relations.[27]

What remains to be done on the early period of the Korean-American relationship? Individuals such as Lucius H. Foote and George C. Foulk could be studied, but one would run the risk again of taking the activities of one person for American policy.[28] Unbeknownst to the United States, some Korean reformers and liberals took American models as their guide, such as Sŏ Chae-p'il (Philip Jaisohn) and other members of the Independence Club (1896–1898). Vipin Chandra, Clarence Weems, and Shin Yong-ha have studied them.[29] American missionary activities brought big results from a small effort, and more might be done here.[30] There will always remain the question, however, of what it all meant when the American government was generally uninvolved. Korea existed within the orbit of China and Japan; after that there was Russia. Much remains to be done on these relationships, in particular, a volume or volumes that would integrate our understanding of China, Japan, and Korea on the one hand and the Western imperial impact on the other. Such work might account for the different domestic situations of the three East Asian countries and seek a coherent theoretical or analytical model that would allow for comparison with the imperial impact in other parts of the globe. But that is not necessarily something to be done under the rubric of Korean-American relations.

We can say something more, however, about this relationship by examining the attitudes and assumptions that began appearing in the literature in the early period and that continue, in modified form, today. Here is the thread tying the disinterested and vague gropings of the early period to the onset of a major relationship after 1945.

IMAGES

When do we first find the distinction between East and West—that strange assumption that distinguishes us from them, which makes no sense if one stands in a spot on the globe where "East" is West or "West" is East? In Aristotle's *Politics,* the classic authority of antiquity, Asians are referred to as "more servile than Greeks; hence they endure despotic rule without protest." The idea of bifurcation, with the judgment that West is superior, seems to be there from the start. Perry Anderson argues that the distinction "starts with the emergence of feudalism, in that historical era when the classical relationship of regions within the Roman Empire—advanced East and backward West—began for the first time to be decisively reversed."[31] With Montesquieu in the eighteenth century we have the first systematic account, arguing that the Asiatic states have no private property, no hereditary nobility, and thus an "egalitarian servitude" among the mass. The East also has no legality, it is unchanging, and its mode of production is determined by climate. Adam Smith, Hegel, and Marx elaborated on such ideas, producing the full-blown notion of the Asiatic Mode of Production. Equality without freedom signals despotism, says Hegel; no internal dynamic to Asian society gives it a "vegetable existence." For Marx, it all adds up: No private property means no enterprising class; no bourgeoisie therefore means no capitalism; no capitalism means no dynamism, and thus Asia vegetates in the teeth of time. Or, as Anderson summarizes:

Marx's sketch of what he believed to be the archetypal Asian social formation included . . . the absence of private property in land, the presence of large-scale irrigation systems [etc.] . . . and the domination of a despotic state machine. . . . Between the self-reproducing villages 'below' and the hypertrophied state 'above,' dwelt no intermediate forces.[32]

Japan was in the East, but it was always thought to be an exception. Again Marx: "Japan with its purely feudal organization of landed property and its developed *petite culture,* gives a much truer picture of the European middle ages than all our history books."[33] Japan had feudalism, not Oriental despotism. Japan subsequently developed capitalism. Japan became the only Asian state indigenously first to confront the West and then to conquer a Western power. Japan seems to be an honorary member of the "West" in the East. Japan seems to do it *our* way.

We may say that from antiquity the West has measured the East by the degree to which it seems to diverge from the path of Western historical development. This path—whether for Marxists or for non-Marxists—has such a call on our attentions that we presume it to be the normal path, the accepted path, the best path. The image is so deeply ingrained that in 1981 David Landes, a highly respected economic historian of Europe, could give a lecture in which he asserted that the source of all dynamism, energy, innovation, science, and new technique in the modern world has been Western Europe, with Japan cast in the role of copycat and China so vast, so alien, that all external impulses for change "melt into the yellow sea" of China's vast population. What does all this have to do with Korean-American relations?

There is something in the literature on Korea, beginning with the first Western and American contacts and continuing in different forms down to the present, that strikes the reader first and most forcefully: the decidedly unfavorable impression that Americans bring out from Korea. Particularly where its political institutions are concerned, all find Korea wanting. This extends well into the scholarly literature, but it is always more palpable in what Marilyn Young calls "the *dailiness*" of the foreign impact.[34] "Korea is 900 years behind us," a pharmacist who had fought in Korea told me as I bought supplies for a year's stay there. At the end of that year, as my plane taxied down the tarmac bound for San Francisco, a young American soldier in the seat behind regaled the whole plane with his cries of relief at finally exiting "this hellhole that God forgot."

In old Korea, missionaries, traders, naval officers, and scholars measured the presumed distance between their idealized image of the West and their perception of Korean realities and found it immense, unfathomable, unbridgeable. Sometimes the yardstick was not the West but Japan; again Korea came up short. In this perception of alien, distant, and depraved Korea we find an extreme example of Edward Said's "Orientalism," a complex of attitudes and assumptions extending from the ignorant traveler to the learned expert that defines the Oriental by what he is *not*.[35] We can also discern a theme that continues in the Korean-American relationship today. Much of the literature has concerned itself with the chasm between what seems to be and what ought to be. In turn, this has affected the circumstances of Korea's entrance into the modern world and even diplomacy at the highest level.

The literature by early American travelers and missionaries betrays an image of Koreans mired in an ooze of decadence almost with the turning of every page. At least for missionaries, such depravity suggested much work for many people in turning this sow's ear into a silk purse, or as L. H. Underwood put it, making Korea "a polished shaft in God's quiver in conquering [China] . . . for His kingdom."[36] Even here, as with the diplomacy discussed earlier, Korea is important primarily with reference to something else. Until the turn of the century, of course, it would be difficult to say that negative American images made much difference, since the United States did not make much difference. But as Korea moved finally to loss of its independence, such attitudes began to affect policy.

Our starting point is George Kennan, sometime advisor to Teddy Roosevelt and elder cousin to the contemporary scholar/diplomat of the same name. In 1905 he wrote:

The first impression that the Korean people make upon an impartial and unprejudiced [sic] newcomer is strongly and decidedly unfavorable. In the fantastic and unbecoming dress of the Ming Dynasty, which they all wear, they look so much like clowns in a circus . . . . [The laborers] do not compare at all favorable with the neat, industrious laborers of Japan. Generally speaking, the whole Korean population seems to be lacking in dignity, intelligence, and force . . . . They are the rotten product of a decayed Oriental civilization.[37]

Yes, to a Westerner the traditional Korean dress was unbecoming, even if it had little to do with the Ming. But clowns? No dignity? Rotten?

A Yale professor and friend of Itō Hirobumi, George Trumbull Ladd, found at about the same time that Korea was full of "drunkenness and gluttony," "enforced ignorance, sloth and corruption." The Koreans, he observed, were "a slow-moving, stubborn, and stupid crowd." Not above a crude play on words, Ladd asserted that "The Seoul of the people is disgustingly filthy and abjectly squalid." One of Korea's greatest modernizers and early nationalists, Yun Ch'i-ho, was "unfitted . . . for any of the responsibilities of leadership." Were the firm hand of Itō to be withdrawn, Koreans would immediately give themselves over to "violence, lust, and thriftlessness."[38]

Not only these apologists for imperialism but also Sidney and Beatrice Webb (admittedly not the most discerning of Fabians in foreign lands) found that the Japanese "shame our administrative capacity . . . shame our inventiveness . . . shame our leadership," but the Koreans are "a horrid race" (as are the Chinese), "lowly verte-brates" who "show us, indeed, what homo sapiens can be if he does not develop."[39] Japanese, then as now, seemed just so much more like us, in what they did if not in what they were, and so in Western eyes being modern for Korea has often meant being more like Japan. Breathing through this literature is the Western and American sense of dynamic industry and distant conquests typical of the turn of the century and characteristic of our virile president then. Although other considerations probably determined Roosevelt's support for Japan's annexation of Korea, his decision had at least something to do with this complex of attitudes and images. How could the United States do anything for an indolent and decayed Korea, which in Roosevelt's words could not strike a blow in its own defense? (Never mind the three years of scattered insurgency by the *Ŭibyŏng* or Righteous Army that inaugurated Japanese rule.)

Tyler Dennett, writing in a calmer period and with more detach-ment, still argued that "Korea lacked the vitality which alone makes possible the exercise of sovereignty. The Korean government was a vine, not a very lovely one either, which trailed in the dust unless it could cling to some stronger power for support. Of independence there was nothing save a pitifully feeble cry of desire."[40] Sands had a bit better image of Koreans, perhaps because he had spent some time cultivating Korea reformers and liberals with the hope of getting an "American party" off the ground. But he too found little to crit-icize in Itō's rule and stated that "the worst thing Koreans ever did for themselves" was for patriots to have killed Itō and the American adviser, Durham White Stevens.[41] The assassins are lionized in North and South Korea today.

In the literature there is the image, also, of American mission-aries encouraging Korean nationalists to resist the Japanese before and throughout the colonial period. Ladd reserved some of his invec-tive for such bleeding-heart Americans, whereas Dennett argued that "most of the missionaries" were "uncompromising champions" of Korean independence.[42] It would be more accurate to say that the missionaries supported Koreans who were nationalists in their own image, that is, Christians and democrats. During the harsh first de-cade of colonial rule such a distinction was not problematic because

Korean resisters were patriots pure and simple and sought support from a distant United States and resident missionaries. But in the aftermath of the March 1 Independence Movement in 1919, Koreans diverged into several streams of nationalism: gradualists, cultural nationalists, radical or revolutionary nationalists, and armed resisters. Such splits prefigured those that emerged full-blown in 1945, and in the 1920s we find missionaries preferring those who took the moderate path of careful preparation and tutelage of fellow Koreans toward the distant end of independence. Bishop Herbert Welch, an American Episcopalian writing in 1920, argued that "the most intelligent and far-seeing nationalists are persuaded that there is no hope of speedy independence, and that they must settle down for a long period to build up the Korean people, in physical conditions, in knowledge, in morality, and in the ability to handle government concerns."[43] Such advocacy was in keeping both with nonviolent conceptions of resistance and with support of Baron Saito's "cultural rule" after 1920, a happy coincidence which allowed the missionaries to continue working with native nationalists and to sustain the comfortable, even luxurious living standard that less pious observers were wont to comment upon.[44]

Among various other Korean nationalists the twin experiences of the coming to power of the Bolsheviks in Russia and the dashing of fond, if naive hopes for Wilsonian intervention to save Korea at Versailles led to new hopes in Russia and disillusionment with the United States. We see this in, for example, Yŏ Un-hyŏng and Kim Kyu-sik, two Koreans who attended American missionary-run schools before the Japanese period. Kim received a degree from Roanoke College and Yŏ's brother graduated from Wooster College. But in the early 1920s they turned first to the Russian revolution and thence to the Chinese in search of Korean salvation.[45] Kim San, another Korean who went to China, wrote that the "American group," which he thought was led by Syngman Rhee, were all "gentlemen," most Christians. "Most of them spoke good English. They actually expected to get Korean independence by being able to speak persuasive English! They would not even help the terrorists in their program for demoralizing the Japanese."[46] It was, however, this same group that became the repository of missionary hopes for an independent, but

American-aligned, Korea. And there remained always individual missionaries who did not support even the moderates, so convinced were they that Japanese tutelage held the best prospect of a modern Korea.

By the 1940s we find several competing images of Koreans, which tended to shift with changing images of Japan. After the United States learned what it felt like to be aggressed upon by Japan, only a die-hard like Hugh Byas could argue that Korea should remain Japan's after the war ended.[47] The dominant tendency was to stress the harsh features of Japanese rule, leading Andrew Grajdanzev and others to argue for a thorough extirpation of Japanese influence and a general purging of Koreans who had done Japanese bidding. Japan specialists in the State Department in 1945 thought that Korea should be subject to the same thorough reforms (purging of the administration, breaking up the national police, etc.) that were planned for postwar Japan.[48] The paradox here was that the same "American group" that had emerged in the 1920s was by the 1940s a collaborationist body, having been subjected to intense Japanese pressures to support the war effort and the Greater East Asia Co-prosperity Sphere. In this manner the colonial authorities destroyed the fruits of a generation of gradualist and moderate efforts, stripping new elites of their legitimacy in the eyes of other Koreans. A thorough purging would therefore eliminate a pro-American group.

The leader of that group in exile, Syngman Rhee, had so alienated the State Department with his repeated insults and wild charges that it tried to block his return to Korea after liberation. Among other things, Rhee had suggested in 1944 that communists or their sympathizers in the State Department had blocked recognition of the Chongqing-based "Korean Provisional Government" (KPG), and in 1945 that Korea was yet another victim of the "Yalta sellout." Stanley K. Hornbeck was the first to deny Rhee recognition and to declare him virtually unknown among the home population, in 1942; later Hornbeck expressed admiration for a group of Koreans who were willing to take up arms against the Japanese without waiting for U.S. help, that is, Manchurian guerrillas such as those led by Kim Il Sung.[49]

Such attitudes were even stronger in Chongqing, where Ambassador Clarence Gauss, John S. Service, and others who dealt with the KPG exiles thought them to be unrepresentative of Koreans generally, riven by factions, and even less willing than the Kuomintang to push the war effort against Japan. Perhaps the following colloquy between Cho (Tso) So-ang of the KPG and Gauss in May 1944 captures the situation best:

> TJO: With recognition [of the KPG] we might be able to prevent Koreans from being drafted into the Japanese Army.
> GAUSS: How?
> TJO: Well, what would you suggest as a possible action?
> GAUSS: Have any Koreans been able to obtain military intelligence on Korean [sic], Manchuria, or Japan and pass it on to the UN?
> TJO: No.
> GAUSS: Has there been any attempt to do it?
> TJO: No. But that is difficult without money. There might be opportunities for propaganda because a recent man who reached Chungking from Korea reported that at home there is no knowledge of the Cairo Declaration and little of the KPG.

Cho went on to say that although the KPG had only about 500 unarmed men willing to fight, there were large numbers of partisans in Manchuria—meaning again, Kim Il Sung's forces and others.[50]

Such experiences reinforced State Department judgments that Koreans would not be able to run their own affairs at war's end, something FDR, for different reasons, had already concluded. The Cairo Declaration, issued December 1, 1943, pledged the United States, China, and Great Britain to Korean independence, but with the proviso, "in due course." Roosevelt wanted a multilateral administration in Korea and Indochina that would end unilateral colonialism, contain the Soviets and revolutionary nationalism, and open the door to U.S. influence and commerce. He justified the delay in granting Korean independence (which he at times put at forty or fifty years) by reference to the Philippine experience.[51]

We need not go into the fate that befell trusteeship and the alternative plans for a separate southern administration that emerged quickly after the Americans landed in Korea, except to note that William Langdon, author of the alternative plan and a foreign service

officer with previous experience in Korea, argued that Korean infirm-
ities could in a sense be virtues:

The old native regime internally was feudal and corrupt but the record shows that it was the best disposed toward foreign interests of
the three Far Eastern nations, protecting foreign lives and property
and enterprises and respecting treaties and franchises. I am sure
that we may count on at least as much from a native government
evolved as above.[52]

Similar attitudes came from other sources in the 1940s, such as
George Frost Kennan. He did not have much to say about Korea
during his tenure as head of the Policy Planning Staff (PPS) from
1947 to 1950, but what he did say was striking. And it was well
within the tradition of American diplomacy toward Korea. Kennan's
thinking about the reverse course in Japan set him to thinking about
Korea. In September 1947 the PPS laid out the basic policy leading
to an economically revived Japan, friendly to the United States; Kennan thought Japan (not China or Korea) should have the highest call
on limited American resources. Once the policy was accomplished,
and assuming interim aid to keep South Korea out of Soviet hands,
he hoped that Japan would again serve as the balance to Russia in
northeast Asia.

The best statement of Kennan's view came in a paper in 1949:
"The day will come, and possibly sooner than we think, when realism will call upon us not to oppose the re-entry of Japanese influence
and activity into Korea and Manchuria. This is, in fact, the only
realistic prospect for countering and moderating Soviet influence in
that area. . . ." He then cited Teddy Roosevelt's views in 1905,
sanctioning Japan's position in Korea and reinforced by the elder
George Kennan's opinion of Korean failings.[53] Kennan saw East Asia
much as turn-of-the-century observers had: Japan had a modern industrial structure and could be admired and defended; Korea and China
now as then had incontinent regimes and were weak points in the
containment line. Except for Japan, Asian government was for Kennan a contradiction in terms, Asia being the far periphery of a high
civilization that radiated outward from Western Europe, with the

eastward projection having a decidedly downhill trajectory: the first drop was in Eastern Europe, the second in Russia (most of whose vices were Oriental), the third (and here one began to scrape bottom), China and its little brother Korea.

On China Kennan arrived at the right policy for the wrong reasons: nonintervention in the Chinese civil war, because China was "a country with a marvelous capacity for corrupting not only itself but all those who have to do with it. . . . You can help any government but one which does not know how to govern." [54] Korea had the same internal problem, but Japan was nearby and that made a difference.

Such thinking pops up again in an unlikely place: Kennan's draft of a speech for Dean Acheson to be given at the National Press Club on January 12, 1950. [55] After tracing the "xenophobic," "exotic," and "despotic" character of Asian regimes, Kennan writes, "Military balance in northern Asia, as Theodore Roosevelt clearly saw, lay with Russia and Japan. You could not lay prostrate Japan without creating vast alteration in that balance to favor of Russia." Acheson did not use the draft, needless to say, although the one he did use got him into only slightly less hot water than this one would have. The logic of Kennan's position suggested a withdrawal of American power from Korea, through a substitution of Japanese power. Ludicrous from the standpoint of 1950, it has been a key element of American planning in every American administration since 1960. Kennedy wanted Japanese economic influence back in, and Nixon and Carter pushed Japan slowly toward a military role. The problem, of course, is that such thinking runs contrary to the views of the majority of Koreans, whether in 1905, 1950, or 1981.

In the occupation of Korea Americans and Koreans were first thrown together in "dailiness," and the interaction was not entirely happy. Hodge instructed his troops as they embarked from Okinawa in September 1945 to beware of crooked deals and underhanded duplicity by Koreans, no doubt drawing on his image of Chinese laundrymen or Chinatowns in the United States. Officers in the occupation initially decided to use the acronym USAMGOK (U.S. Military Government of Korea) but changed it to USAMGIK (*in* Korea) because the former "ended in three letters that sounded like 'gook,' "

and too many Americans used that term to refer to Koreans. A. Wig-
fall Green, a senior officer in the Occupation, begins his quite useful
memoir of the period as follows:

Korea, to some Americans, is a land of gooks. Everyone knows
vaguely, but not specifically, what a gook is. Perhaps a gook is anyone other than a North American, but he is, more especially, an Oriental. . . . Gook is sometimes used to belittle; but it is also used to
express familiarity and even fondness. . . . Korea is a land of gooks;
the Korean is a gook. He is incomprehensible because his thought
processes are different . . . he belongs to another world.[56]

Americans still measure Korea by what it ought to be and what
it is not. One of the best books on Korea, which also can be read as
a text on Korean-American relations, is Gregory Henderson's *Korea:
The Politics of the Vortex.*[57] Henderson began his career as a foreign
service officer, rose to cultural attaché, and then moved into the academic field of Korean studies. His is the most stimulating book on
Korea is many years. But in what he finds and recommends, the
reader can discern the same Eurocentrism that underlies the theory of
the Asiatic Mode and the conception of Oriental despotism. Korea
lacks intermediate groups, plural associations, viable political parties,
a balance of power between center and locality, and the rootedness
that comes with stable loyalties and an upper class that breeds the
proper values. Thus Koreans confront each other in anomic disarray,
incapable of forming groups that last and a politics that can be recommended. The center dominates society; if not despotic it is at least
too strong, setting off a scramble of "atomistic striving" to gain the
rewards of Seoul. Korea seems thus to be a "mass society" and in
dire need of remedial help. What are the remedies? Pluralism, a cast-
ing down of power, decentralization, checks and balances, the creation of alternative centers of influence in economy and society that
draw people off from the whooshing vortex. Like the mass society
literature in modern sociology that Henderson draws upon, this is a
vision of social and political pathology: something is rotten in Korea.
Ironically, it would be hard to find an American more devoted to
things Korean than Henderson.

Henderson is not, however, guilty of a fault that surfaces in the most recent literature on South Korea, studies (mostly by economists and policymakers) of "the miracle on the Han." Unquestionably South Korea's economic prowess in the past fifteen years is worthy of praise. The problem is that the praise so often goes hand in hand with inattention to or ignorance about the costs of such growth. Moreover, there has been no miracle. A long view of Korea's twentieth-century development would suggest that the recent growth is not surprising, given that Korea was never so desperate as depicted in the early literature. Korea long had the basic prerequisites of nationhood, and it had begun modernization not in 1961 but before the turn of the century. Furthermore, its colonial master had not been a Portugal, content for four hundred years to stitch a little modern fringe along the coasts of its colonies, but Japan, which saw Taiwan, Korea, and Manchuria as integral parts of its major agrarian and industrial strategies of the 1920s and 1930s. When Westerners speak in terms of "miracles" in the developing world they often betray their own subliminal assumptions about the inferior capabilities of non-Westerners. That is, the early view of Korea's torpid indolence and depravity would not predict later economic success: thus either a miracle occurred, or the early and the later views are both wrong.

THE KOREAN-AMERICAN RELATIONSHIP BEGINS

On a beautiful, late summer day in September 1945, the command ship *Catoctin* (the same one that brought Roosevelt to Yalta) anchored off the shore of Inch'ŏn and sent units of the Twenty-fourth Corps of the U.S. Tenth Army through the treacherous tides of the harbor in landing craft. Sixty-three years after the U.S.–Korean Treaty of Amity was signed in the same place, American power had finally reached Korea. A few days earlier General Douglas MacArthur had presided over the Japanese surrender on the *U.S.S. Missouri*. Those in attendance watched as the Japanese foreign minister, Mamoru Shigemitsu, limped aboard to sign the instruments of surrender. Why was he limping? His leg had been blown off in Shanghai in 1932 by Korean associates of Kim Ku, a Korean nationalist in China. It was a perfect symbol of the failed Japanese effort in Korea: Koreans had remained incorrigibly Korean throughout almost four decades of imperial rule.

Five years later nearly to the day, MacArthur directed a second landing at Inch'ŏn, destroying the North Korean calculus of victory. One act of hubris ended and another began, as MacArthur marched toward the Yalu. When the Chinese delivered their chastisement, American policy was kicked back to a point from which it has yet to diverge, that is, the demilitarized zone that continues to bisect Korea.

We thus may take these two Inch'ŏn landings as the alpha and the omega of U.S. policy toward Korea, although each represented the preemption of previous policy. When General John Reed Hodge landed in 1945, Washington's policy favored multilateral great-power administration of a unified Korea. Here was the residue of Rooseveltian internationalism six months after he had died. Hodge, however, favored containment, and we may see in him a premature cold warrior. His early preemptive actions, designed to create an anticommunist bulwark in the South, later won favor as Washington came around to its own containment policy. MacArthur, in turn, was thought to have preempted containment for the only application of rollback in the postwar period, but this was too much for China. Containment, thus, was and is the policy preferred by Americans.

In much of the existing literature on the period 1945–1953, however, the dominant assumption is that two dates count, 1945 and 1950, and never the twain shall meet. The year 1945 inaugurated a murky, ill-understood period of chaos as Koreans scrapped among themselves over obscure issues, Russia moved inexorably toward the establishment of a satellite state, and the United States fumbled and bumbled so badly that one wonders if it had any policy at all. In any case, the three years of American occupation are of little moment in understanding the thunderclap that came in June 1950, inaugurating an entirely new set of issues. Few credit the idea that 1950 simply continued 1945 by other means, that the issues were the same and not new, and that the opening of conventional fighting represented a denouement of the previous five years rather than a beginning.

Robert Dallek has a different idea, that we take what Koreans did in this period seriously. He argues that what is "most striking" in the literature is "the shortcoming of which [the authors] complain—the failure to take account of indigenous forces. . . . We need to know how traditional Korean political, economic, and social patterns affected what the United States did."[58] It is surely impossible to understand the period without understanding what Koreans were thinking and doing. The best way to accomplish this is to go beyond the English language material. And those who write on postwar American policy in Korea should utilize the new English language materials now available: the archival files of the occupation and the extensive mission reports by embassy personnel in the period 1948–1950. Yet, as we shall see, the history of the period is still written from the Washington side alone. In other words, there remains a deeply rooted assumption that what happened in Washington (or Moscow) is what really counted. It is like analyzing American policy toward China without considering the simultaneous social revolution.

With this as preface we can ask, what remains useful in the literature and what more needs to be done? First, there is what one might call a classic literature,[59] done mostly in the early postwar period and still revelatory. E. Grant Meade's *American Military Government in Korea* will always reward a careful reading. Although it covers primarily one province for one year (South Chŏlla in 1945–1946), the account can be generalized to other provinces. It is based on Meade's own experience, interviews with other participants, and extensive use of various occupation internal reports. It was this book that first led me to examine the "people's committees" that emerged throughout the peninsula in 1945.

George McCune was the only trained Korea specialist in the State Department in 1945. Illness robbed him, and U.S. policy, of the chance to make a difference in the late 1940s. But his *Korea Today* uses the then best available public documents to present a critical but complex and scrupulously fair account of the occupation. He also wrote a number of articles (listed in the book's bibliography) that remain required reading. He represented a liberal, internationalist position on Korea held by several at State, including John Carter Vincent and Hugh Borton. McCune's position, however, was filled out with thorough knowledge of Korea, giving him an informed heart that makes his judgments nearly always on the mark.

Mark Gayn and Richard Lauterbach each devote about a hundred pages to Korea in their journalists' memoirs of the period. Gayn's *Japan Diary* was for decades the only source on a significant and unstudied rebellion that spread throughout much of southern Korea in the autumn of 1946. Long thought to be excessively critical, this account proves accurate when one reads original sources in the occupation files. Lauterbach renders in English a number of apocryphal stories about Koreans, for example, that the northern military leader Mu Chŏng was "chief of staff" in the Chinese Eighth Route Army, and that the nationalist Kim Ku strangled the killer of Queen Min (1896) with his bare hands. But the account provides interesting color, useful portraits of Koreans and Americans, and an appropriately sardonic humor. For more color see Irma Materi's *Irma and the Hermit,* a funny and often revealing account of American compound life in Seoul and of the Koreans she and her husband (Joseph Materi, an advisor to the Korean National Police) knew. Along with Green's *Epic of Korea,* these are the only book-length memoirs of the occupation by participants, although John Caldwell's two books are based mostly on the year or so he spent in Korea and also have interesting anecdotes.

Robert Oliver's two books on Syngman Rhee (one a classic, one new) are indispensable for understanding both Rhee's successes in coming out on top in 1945–1946 and 1950 and the important viewpoint of conservative Americans and Republicans who constituted a small "Korea lobby" on the model of the China lobby. Both books quote from Rhee's extensive correspondence with Oliver, his advisor. Unfortunately, this correspondence is available now only to approved scholars and therefore one must rely on what Oliver chooses to say.

There are a few other reminiscences (e.g., E. A. J. Johnson's *American Imperialism in the Image of Peer Gynt* [60]), but the major participants—Hodge, Major General Archibald Arnold, General Archer Lerch, Leonard Bertsch, Arthur Bunce, H. Merrell Benninghoff, William Langdon—left no memoirs and, to my knowledge, no private papers. M. Preston Goodfellow, an important backer of Rhee, did deposit his papers, including a significant correspondence with Hodge, at the Hoover Institution. Twenty-fourth Corps historian Albert Keep's journal, in the occupation archival materials, also records many of Hodge's reactions to Korea and the first year of the occupation.

Two general accounts of Korean-American relations in the 1940s, although published before much of the documentation was declassified, are well worth the reader's time.[61] Carl Berger's *Korea Knot* is split about half and half between the occupation and the Korean War; the section on the occupation is considerably more interesting. Berger was the first to document Hodge's opposition to trusteeship. Berger betrays little knowledge of the Korean scene, however, particularly in his judgments of Korea's "great leader," Syngman Rhee. Soon Sung Cho's study is a thoroughly documented, scholarly, and usually judicious treatment of the decade of the 1940s, written from the point of view of a South Korean nationalist who, in essence, wished that the United States had done much more rather than much less for his half of Korea. U.S. policy, for Cho, lurches from half-hearted commitment to Korean independence to blind ignorance of Korea to various and sundry mistakes, finally to firm defense of the ROK in 1950. Cho calls for more firmness and consistency from the United States and locates much of the blame for failed policy on the military.

Short of immersion in the archives, a number of published and unpublished, official and unofficial, studies of the occupation are now available.[62] Leonard Hoag, a scholar who taught at the University of Vermont, prepared a thorough manuscript on the period 1941–1946 for the Office of the Chief of Military History, which decided not to published it. It is solidly based in occupation archival materials, even if it makes sparing use of State Department records. Hoag finds, among other things, that Hodge and his Korean supporters were mainly responsible for undoing the Moscow agreements on Korea negotiated in late December 1945. Richard Robinson and Stewart Meacham, officers in the occupation, both wrote unpublished studies of the period. Robinson's is much more extensive, but both are highly critical of American policy. They document the widespread suppression of left-wing forces from 1945 to 1948. Robinson argues that the Soviet-American Joint Commission meetings in 1946 broke down after the American side cynically manipulated the "free speech" issue to discredit the Russians and forestall real negotiations, while Meacham provides a devastating account of the problems of labor under military government.

The occupation viewpoint is given in a massive, three-volume manuscript entitled "History of the U.S. Armed Forces in Korea," completed in 1947 and 1948 by military historians. It cannot be called an official source because it was never approved for publication, but it is extraordinarily detailed and useful. No one should write on the occupation without digesting it. The chapters vary in quality, since they were written by different people; some accounts are expurgated and read like public affairs briefings while others tell all sides of the story. The information on what Koreans were doing must be balanced by Korean sources, however, or one will be entirely misled about Korean politics. Portions of the manuscript represent briefs for the military in its conflicts with the State Department. For example, the authors argue that Hodge received no political directives from Washington until early 1946: this is the best they can do with Hodge's periodic insubordination, and other sources prove that he did get the directives. Scholars interested in research on specific aspects of the occupation might begin with one of the long chapters in this study, e.g., agriculture, police affairs, justice, and then follow the footnotes as a guide to where to find the original documents in the archives.

State Department files are now open through the end of 1949 and we have the 1950 and 1951 *Foreign Relations of the United States* volumes for Korea. Needless to say, Washington's policy cannot be understood without using these materials, but they are thin on the internal situation in 1945–1948 when State had slim representation in Seoul. The mission reports, 1948–1950, have excellent materials on Korean politics and economics. In its own way State has also shaped the documentation in its published volumes to support its side in bureaucratic conflicts, although in a much more sophisticated manner than the military branches. Neither side should be read alone.

Robert K. Sawyer's study is the only one on the American role in creating a southern military force and on the Korean Military Advisory Group, which succeeded the occupation in 1948. It is very useful on the Japanese military background of most high officers in the ROK Army, and on guerrilla warfare in the South. Sawyer could have said much more than he did on the conflict along the thirty-eighth parallel in 1949 and 1950, judging from his now declassified on-scene reports. C. Clyde Mitchell was a high officer in the New Korea Company—the renamed Oriental Development Company—and his report (which later formed the basis for his Harvard dissertation) is essential reading on the occupation's faltering attempts at land reform.

The Army G-2 study, "History of the North Korean Army," is full of unvarnished cold war rhetoric but is one of the few places where one can document the origins of the northern military, especially its Manchurian and Chinese connection that is so important for understanding North Korean politics. Military historians writing on the assumption of monolithic Soviet-Chinese unity found it unproblematic that upwards of thirty thousand Koreans who fought with the Eighth Route Army were transferred back to Korea roughly coterminous with Stalin's pullout of Soviet armed forces. In fact this sequence of events was the beginning of the end of Moscow's dominance in P'yŏngyang. The State Department's official study of the assumption of power by communists in the North also provides useful insights once one gets past the rhetoric. It is based on extensive use of POW interview transcripts and very partial use of captured Korean-language materials. The latter are now available in several thousand archival boxes in Washington and are so good that it is now possible to do well-documented history on the origins of the socialist state in the North.[63] Few scholars have been into these materials as yet.

There are a handful of useful Russian-language studies of the late 1940s in Korea,[64] but in general the circumstances of Soviet-American conflict, the Korean War itself, and the many subsequent difficulties in the Soviet–North Korean relationship all combine to mute the Soviet side. The Soviet magazine *New Times* published many articles on Korea and U.S. policy in the late 1940s.

Koreans or Korean-Americans who publish in the United States, such as Soon Sung Cho, Chong-sik Lee, and Dae-sook Suh,[65] can write with relative freedom on the 1940s, although there are usually distinct outer limits on their criticisms of U.S. and South Korean policy. Unlike the situation in the China field, there is no sympathy or empathy for the communist side. It will be interesting to see what a second generation of Korean scholars in the United States has to say about the period; thus far all the accounts have been written by emigrés to the United States from Korea in the postwar years. Suh and Lee have done much to build the field of twentieth-century Korean studies, and their books should be read by anyone studying the Korean-American relationship. Suh has one chapter on the North in the 1940s, but he details the background of the left-right splits that emerged first in the 1920s and represented themselves in the 1940s in the northern and southern sides of the civil conflict. Lee and Scalapino's *Communism in Korea* covers the entire history of Korean communism from 1918 to the 1970s, with one chapter each on the North 1945–1950 and the southern left during the occupation. The speculative account of the North Korean decision to attack in June 1950 is particularly interesting. The authors carefully note that many aspects of the decision remain "shrouded in mystery." In spite of the extensive use of Korean-language materials, the account of the period 1945–1953 is weakly documented. It relies too heavily on emigré accounts and journalistic sources, with almost no attention to the fairly voluminous American intelligence reports compiled on the North in 1945–1950, and little grasp of U.S. policy. There is also, at times, an obvious intent to discredit Kim Il Sung and the communists wherever possible. Nonetheless, the book must be read.

Korean scholars who work in Korea, North and South, cannot study the late 1940s without careful clearance by state authorities. In one case, a Korean who wrote a critical dissertation on the period was hauled into the Korean Central Intelligence Agency and tortured while his interrogators read to him from his dissertation. In North Korea today it is impossible to discuss the period without featuring quotations from Kim Il Sung on almost every page. Both sides continually erase and distort history. The frontispiece in the major South Korean history of the war has characters in Park Chung Hee's calligraphy saying, "destroy communism," while northern war histories pay homage to the eternal benevolence of the fatherly leader (Kim Il Sung, the same fellow who sponsored the disastrous assault in 1950). Collections of documents, newspapers, and magazine articles from the 1940s are reprinted after names of certain important people are cropped out. Interesting accounts have been published in the South, however, during brief periods when current orthodoxy has been cast down—mainly during the Chang Myun regime in 1960–1961, and the six months after the assassination of Park Chung Hee in November 1979.[66]

The result is that scholars must use Korean accounts with great care, and the best methodology is to seek out materials published before June 1950. Fortunately, there are many of the latter. In English, an entire run of the *Seoul Times* from 1945 to 1948 is available at the Library of Congress; the *Voice of Korea,* published during the same period in Washington, D.C. by Kim Young-jeung, is also useful.

Mary Wright gathered and deposited at the Hoover Institution an excellent collection of Korean books and magazines from the late 1940s. The library collection on Korea at the University of Washington is also quite good on the period. Yearbooks in Korean for 1947 and 1948 are full of information, and a particularly valuable yearbook was published in 1946 by southern leftists.[67] A variety of biographies about or memoirs by important Korean political leaders exist, including several on Yŏ Un-hyŏng, the moderate-left leader of the Korean People's Republic in 1945–1946. Other figures covered include Cho Pyŏng-ok, Song Chin-u, Kim Kyu-sik, Kim Ku, Pak Hŏn-yŏng, and of course Syngman Rhee. Rhee's sidekick, Ben Limb, has published several accounts written from Rhee's viewpoint.

Among official Korean histories and compilations, the most useful is the seven-volume collection on the period 1945–1948.[68] Despite its size, much has been left out including nearly everything published in the 1940s that was left of center. Next best is the southern history of the war, which begins in 1945 and provides a full account of the development of the southern military.[69] The North has published several versions of its *History of the Just Fatherland Liberation War,* including an English version in 1957. There are general histories of the period 1945–1953 as well; the best rule of thumb is to use volumes published before the mid-1960s, when the developing focus on Kim Il Sung caused a general rewriting of history. The North Korean "white paper" on the war, *Facts Tell,* is a pathetic attempt to forge documents in broken English to prove that the United States started the war. A most useful source on the North is the *Cen-*

tral Yearbook, published every year or so beginning in 1949. Some volumes are available in English translation from Joint Publications Research Service.

Kim Se-jin's collection of documents on Korean-American relations from 1943 to 1976 is a disappointment.[70] Done under official sponsorship, it misses most of the important declassified documentation from the American side, has none from the Korean side, and contents itself with reproducing documents that were mostly public to begin with. Kim Chum-gon's official study of the Korean War is the best English source for the southern interpretation, and it has interesting information on the guerrilla struggle in the South.[71]

A genuinely "revisionist" literature on the period 1945 to 1953 has existed for some time, anchored by I. F. Stone and D. F. Fleming.[72] These authors argue that the United States bears the major responsibility for the division of Korea and the outbreak and course of the Korean War (or at least the second Korean War, that is, post-Inch'ŏn). Stone's thesis—more of an hypothesis—is that Rhee, MacArthur, Chiang Kai-shek, and perhaps John Foster Dulles may have connived in a conspiracy of silence in 1950. Knowing that the attack was coming, they fell silent so that the civil aspect of the Korean conflict would fade into the background and the international aspect would manifest itself in a conventional assault across an "international" boundary that could be blamed on Stalin. Instead of provoking fighting along the 38th parallel, as it did throughout the summer of 1949, the South would take a body blow, reel with it, and get the full American support it so desperately needed. Stone also has some interesting speculations on the soybean market, Republican politics, and the delayed settlement at P'anmunjŏm.

Fleming mines all the published material on the period 1945–1953, providing a highly critical account of the occupation and an interpretation of the war that is not far from Stone's. Fleming's is still the fullest and best of the revisionist accounts published before the documents became available; there remain many interesting hypotheses that can be followed up in the new materials.

After Fleming and Stone an involution occurred, as one revisionist after another milked the same literature that had been around since the mid-1950s. Horowitz's account is just a hair away from plagiarism of Fleming, Burchett's work shows a sloppy disrespect for the historical record, and Gupta makes much ado about nothing in his attempt, once again, to show that the South actually attacked first on June 25. Halliday has done better in using the existing sources; his 1973 essay is particularly interesting. In general, however, this effort is at a dead end unless one is willing to do primary research oneself. The Kolkos began this in *The Limits of Power,* and they were among the first to note the essential unity of 1945–1950: the unbroken chain linking liberation from the Japanese with the war. Simmons's study is mildly revisionist, at its best in pursuing strains within the presumed communist monolith in 1950. His argument that factional conflicts in the northern leadership touched off the 1950 attack is new in English, but old in the Korean literature. A Korean in Japan, Kim Sam-gyu, argued this thesis within months of the outbreak of the war. Simmons also seems at times to take a molehill of evidence and turn it into a mountain of speculation: This is particularly true of his argument that the Russians were actually trying to keep the Chinese *out* of the United Nations in 1950.

At this writing it is possible to remove Dulles from whatever scheming was going on in 1950, since his papers at Princeton give no suggestion that he had anything to do with Rhee or MacArthur before the war. Of Rhee and MacArthur, however, it is impossible to disprove Stone's thesis—or to prove it, for that matter. Rhee's papers are still jealously guarded by his wife in Hawaii and the Korean authorities in Seoul, and the MacArthur archive has no record of the many private meetings Rhee and MacArthur held in the period 1945–1950. We now know, also, that MacArthur excluded the Central Intelligence Agency from Korea until after the war began; his own regular G-2 reports document the North Korean buildup but show no evidence of drawing in MacArthur's attentions. The same can be said of scattered documents available from the files of the separate intelligence operation in Korea run by Willoughby.

The important manuscript by Harold Noble[73] would seem to refute decisively the idea that Rhee saw it all coming, since Noble has him in a panic after June 25. But both Noble and the extensive annotations by Frank Baldwin underestimate Rhee's ambition, his manipulative skills, and his unsurpassed acting talents. Both Rhee and

MacArthur were willful, calculating gamblers who saw themselves as men of destiny. The jury should still be out on both of them.

A number of new studies of the period 1945–1953 should be mentioned.[74] William Stueck's book is based on new documentation from the Washington side and is the first study systematically to compare China policy with Korea policy in the period 1947–1950. The book contains many new discoveries, especially about the march north in 1950, but the dominant impression is the degree to which Stueck has bolstered the existing conventional interpretations with new materials. Stueck also stretches to the limit a methodology assuming that one can get the story in Washington without looking intensively at the Korean or Chinese side. The author simply is not much interested in what the Asians were doing in the period. A volume edited by Yōnosuke Nagai and Akira Iriye has the great virtue, like Stueck's, of placing Korea within the general concerns of American–East Asian relations in the late 1940s. In one of the book's three articles on Korea, Robert Slusser offers the only English-language effort to ascertain Stalin's goals in Korea; his method leads him to make of Stalin's mute posture on Korea policy a series of pregnant silences: his wordlessness was studied and calculated. Unfortunately, by its nature such a method cannot prove anything. John Lewis Gaddis' effort assays Washington's Korea policy, but it does not get very far because Gaddis takes what Washington said for policy, rather than looking at what was actually happening in Korea. His argument that the United States had no intention of setting up a "rightist, undemocratic regime" in South Korea simply cannot be sustained when looked at from the Seoul side, except in the sense that Americans did not want an undemocratic regime if they could get something else. But in Korea, as in so much of the Third World, the United States had a choice between revolution and reaction and chose the latter. Okonogi Masao's article is far too brief, but very good in exploiting multilingual sources to argue for the civil origins of the Korean War.

Among recent dissertations on the period, or ones in preparation, the following are especially useful. John Merrill is completing the first study of the internal war that set the stage for the conventional war of 1950, using new documentation and Korean sources as well. Mark Paul argues for the importance of the Potsdam Conference in pushing the United States away from diplomacy and toward intervention in Korea, with the atomic bomb making a major difference in the American decision to abjure diplomacy. John Kotch was the first to detail "Operation Everready," the 1953 scheme to move against Rhee (with a coup, if necessary) in case he continued sabotaging the P'anmunjŏm settlement. James Matray has surveyed the entire period in a valuable two-volume dissertation, again mostly from Washington's angle. One of the best is William Morris' careful study of the trusteeship question; he also has great material on Rhee's tempestuous battles with State Department officers. Earlier dissertations by Won-sul Lee and Han-mu Kang are still worth reading. Finally, Professor Ch'oe Sung-il of Korea University has produced a fine study of the American liberation of Korea, written in Japanese and utilizing a wide array of Asian-language sources.

One final exercise may serve to make the point that the story of the period 1949–1953 cannot be told without grasping the Korean end—the tail of the dog, true, but one that often wagged the dog. What do two scholars whose general work is beyond reproach do when they try to figure out Korea?[75] Writing in 1973, Ernest May argues that the Munich analogy governed Truman's "reversal" in the moment of crisis in 1950, after the United States had decided to avoid military involvement in Korea. Fair enough, this analogy was important, and May did not have access to documentation that might suggest otherwise. But then he writes that before the war with Japan ended, the United States "had not planned" to occupy southern Korea, and trusteeship involved "no occupation by foreign troops." This is mistaken. He argues that Koreans could not understand the Cairo proviso, "for their language had no character for 'in due course.' " Actually, the Koreans translated the proviso as *sangdanghan sigi e,* "at any appropriate time," which was exactly the phrase Roosevelt used at Cairo, with the British providing the extra flourish in the final wording. May's next sentence: "Hundreds of politicians and political organizations offered to form governments." In fact, from the beginning the occupation perceived only two important organizations, the Korean People's Republic and the Korean Democratic Party. According to May, "Hodge made haphazard choices among these volunteers." In fact, Hodge began choosing systematically from the right the day after he landed. Later, Hodge and the military in general are said to have wanted out of Korea as soon as possible, but were opposed by the State Department. This judgment is closer to the mark in regard to the military, if not to Hodge. But it was not until April 1947 that the military—meaning Secretary of War Robert Patterson—made an argument for pulling out of Korea, and it is not clear that this particular conflict involved more than the War Department being tired of State's carping about an under-funded, over-critized occupation that no one could be happy with.

May's chapter on Korea soars when he talks about Washington, especially the historical analogies that Truman and his advisors made between Korea and Munich. But on the Korea side May was victimized by the existing literature and its depiction of a bumbling Uncle Sam who never quite knew what he wanted in Korea.

Russell Buhite argues for a category of national interest that would encapsulate China, Korea, and Taiwan in the early postwar period: Clearly not vital interests, all were just as clearly not peripheral. His suggestion that we need something in-between (''major'' interests) is a good one. On Korea, however, he makes a number of judgments that cannot be sustained: (1) that the "primary American objective" in 1945 was "a free, independent, and democratic Korea"; in fact, the objective was to delay Korean independence until a Korea or a part of Korea friendly to the United States could be assured. (2) In the fall of 1945 the Soviets sought predominant influence throughout Korea by using "a Communist committee in the South"; in fact, southern leftists, and the KPR, were indigenous forces often at odds with Kim Il Sung and the Russians. (3) U.S. policy is seen to be monolithically pursuing trusteeship in 1945–1946, only to be frustrated by Soviet intransigence; actually trusteeship was Washington's policy. Hodge wanted none of it, and so undid the policy just after it had been agreed upon in Moscow. Other objections might be raised on this article without affecting the overall conclusions, which seem correct. The point is not to denigrate either May or Buhite, but to show that even the best historians cannot do much with an existing literature that assumes the whole story can be learned from Washington's side.

Other literature on the Korean War is simply too voluminous to discuss here. Readers might be referred to Carroll Blanchard's extensive bibliography, which is particularly useful on the obscure (to scholars) military periodical literature.[76] In the American literature there is a paucity of studies that depict what the war meant to the Korean people themselves. This was a nasty, dirty war, with all sides guilty of continuing atrocities. The American prosecution of the war, unlike the one in Vietnam, went on in the general absence of effective scrutiny by an informed public, and thus we find little comment on the daily use of napalm against civilian targets, the carpet bombing of North Korea, the breaking of dikes from the air that caused massive loss of civilian life, or the threats to use atomic weapons against an enemy that possessed none itself. This experience is not forgotten in North Korea. In some ways the northern society was so fractured by the effects of the war that some of the current pathologies of the system can still be traced to it—for example, the monumental cult of Kim, combined with the general purging and scapegoating of other elements (the southern communist leadership especially) when the failed attempt at armed unification brought a holocaust upon the North.

THE RECENT PERIOD

Almost three decades have passed since the war ended, but it is difficult to say that advances have been made in the study of Korean-American relations. For one thing, despite fits and starts in other directions, U.S. policy remains fundamentally what it was in 1953: harsh confrontation along the demarcation line, a tripwire deterrent which thus far has staved off another war but carries always the possibility that one might occur through an incident or miscalculation, and general American support for the southern side with no moves toward accommodation with or recognition of the North. The year 1980 brought home how close we still are to 1950. During the rebellion in Kwangju and much of South Chŏlla province in May there was a possibility of war, with the United States dragged in again; fortunately, North Korea sought no advantage from the turmoil. Since

May 1980 the United States has displayed awesome military force in Korea and its environs (frequent visits by ships of the Seventh Fleet, months-long military exercises, trial bombing runs by B-52s from Guam), comparable to Soviet behavior in and around Poland in the same period.

In the absence of documentation on the post-1953 period it is difficult to write history; thus the vast majority of the policy-related literature has a half-life of about a year as events quickly overtake one's analysis.[77] To cite one example, when President Carter proclaimed the troop withdrawal in 1977 a spate of articles, pamphlets, and books appeared seeking to justify the policy. Almost as soon as they appeared the policy was reversed, and so cogent argument went for naught. Indeed, some of the same people arguing for the troops to come out in 1978 argue for them to stay in now.

There are some useful studies, however.[78] Kim Kwan-bong's book on the negotiations leading up to the normalization of relations with Japan in 1965 documents the considerable American pressure brought to bear to get that result. The "Koreagate" investigation of Korean-American relations produced the best source on the 1960s, and in its footnotes one can find a number of still-classified government studies that might be obtained under the Freedom of Information Act. Selig Harrison's *The Widening Gulf* has several chapters on Korea that break new ground, particularly in the discussion of Korean nationalism in North and South and the continuing salience of the unification issue. A 1972 Senate Foreign Relations Committee study of Korea and the Philippines is especially good on Nixon administration policies. Among the more recent policy-related books, the best are volumes by Nathan White, William Barnds, and Fuji Kamiya and Franklin B. Weinstein. Each presents the full range of issues as Washington policymakers, or those well-connected in Washington, see them.

Since 1965 South Korea has distinguished itself in economic development, making for a new field in Korean-American relations. Unfortunately, almost all of the studies of this phenomenon have been by economists, who refuse to assess the political consequences of economic development, either for the internal politics of Korea or for the relationship with the United States. It is possible to argue that the success of this program has both given the relationship a different stake than it had before and led to increasing difficulties in Washington's relations with Seoul. For example, conflict over export quotas to the American market has been endemic since the early days of the Nixon administration; in June 1978 I heard a State Department official argue that one goal of U.S. policy in Korea should be "managing the articulation of Korea with the world economy," so that "we don't get another Japan there." In this respect the Nixon administration's policy toward Korea deserves much more study than it has been given. Nixon is the only president since 1953 to make important changes in the relationship. Nixon alone was able to withdraw a division of troops, something which eluded Carter; Nixon also excluded Korean politics from his considerations, unlike Kennedy and Carter, enabling Park to restructure the state along formal authoritarian lines, thus putting an end to electoral politics and a viable National Assembly and vastly increasing the scope of the state in the economy. Nixon was tough in economic negotiations, and, of course, opened a major relationship with P'yŏngyang's ally, China. It was this experience with Nixon that led the Koreans to seek influence in American politics through the multivariate activities of the Koreagate crowd, in turn leading to a major crisis in Korean-American relations. Economic conflict also continued as a current during the Carter years, until the ROK economy nosedived in 1979. Suddenly the competitive threat posed by Korea disappeared, and Washington was concerned with getting the Koreans back on their feet.

The other major change in the 1970s was in the strategic relationship that had held in Northeast Asia since 1945. The opening to China was a deep shock in the South, and it underlined the North's inability to obtain joint Sino-Soviet backing in its conflict with the ROK. Both Koreas watched as their big-power guarantors went their own way. North Korea reacted rather nimbly in the new circumstances, breaking out of isolation to the point where almost 110 nations now recognize the DPRK. North Korea has been active in the Non-Aligned Movement, and it has also reached out to the United States by inviting private visits by prominent Americans and, in the period 1977–1980, trying to cultivate liberal elements in the Carter administration. The DPRK is also part of the Korean-American relationship, as thousands of Americans have learned while stationed along the demilitarized zone. Much of the society is still structured by reference to a constant threat from American imperialism. The experience of recent years has made clear that North Korea wants a change, but Washington has not responded for fear of destabilizing Seoul. It is likely that some sort of U.S.–DPRK relationship will develop in the 1980s, however, simply because the strategic calculus has changed so much since 1971.

CONCLUSIONS

Korea and America have been linked in two periods: loosely, in the years from 1882 to 1905; tightly in the years from 1945 to 1981. In between was a four-decade-long hiatus as Japan structured the peninsula's relation to the rest of the world. The Korean-American relationship is now into its fourth decade as well. I have a strong sense that in its present form it will not last much longer than did the Japanese parenthesis. Why should this be the case?

First, and most obviously, a look at the strategic realities of Northeast Asia in the 1980s suggests that the fault lines of great power conflict no longer cut across the Korean peninsula. America's newfound friend, China, is P'yŏngyang's closest ally. The Soviet Union has less influence in East Asian nations than at any time in the postwar period, perhaps in the past century, and North Korea is no exception. Neither China nor the Soviet Union will sponsor North Korean adventurism; thus the United States defends against a small power with purely local concerns. It seems unlikely that Washington would back South Korea if this backing were to be at the sacrifice of its relationship with China. In any case, withdrawal of American ground forces has been on the agenda of two of the past three presidents. Thus it may be that the next decade will witness Korea's return to some sort of regional interconnectedness with its Asian neighbors, as strategic realities come to dominate.

Second, the recent economic stake in South Korea may not be enough to sustain the American connection. Japan is the ROK's natural economic partner, and by far its biggest one. Assuming that its economy recovers, South Korea will continue to be one of a handful of logical points at which to receive Japanese declining industry— meaning, paradoxically enough, automobiles in the mid- to late-1980s. With China beginning to export textiles and light industrial items, and assuming a continuing outward orientation to the market economies, it may in time threaten South Korea's economic program. In any case China will be a much more attractive market and may soon hold competitive advantages over the ROK. So the economic stake does not seem enough to sustain such a large U.S. commitment to Korea.

There are other, more subtle reasons why the relationship may undergo fundamental change. As suggested earlier in this paper, the United States has never had the sustained, structuring impact on Korea that China had over centuries and that Japan had in forty years of intense colonial rule. This also argues for an eventual reintegration of the peninsula with the East Asian region. The character of the Korean-American relationship itself is another reason. Parts of this paper probably make painful reading for Koreans, it being so clear that Korea has never mattered much to Americans for its intrinsic interest or characteristics, but only as it relates to some broader concern. Indeed, one can question whether it is proper to speak of mutuality in this relationship at all, since the influence has been so strongly one-way, and since it is hard to argue that Korea, or South Korea, has been an autonomous actor vis-à-vis the United States. An American still commands the ROK military forces, for example. This has to make the relationship different than that with China or Japan.

In the final analysis the United States will be motivated by the same broader concerns that have shaped its relationship with Korea over the past century: national interest, and the more important connections with China and Japan. South Korea will slowly be placed at arm's length. Korea will once again move in the orbit of East Asia, and the Korean-American relationship as described herein will appear as a four- or five-decade-long anomaly.

NOTES

1. Fairbank, "America and China: The Mid-Nineteenth Century," in Ernest R. May and James C. Thomson, Jr., eds., *American–East Asian Relations: A Survey* (Cambridge: Harvard University Press, 1972), p. 31.

2. (New York: Russell & Russell, 1967; orig. Louisiana State University Press, 1945).

3. Palais, *Politics and Policy in Traditional Korea* (Cambridge: Harvard University Press, 1975); Deuchler, *Confucian Gentlemen and Barbarian Envoys: The Opening of Korea, 1875–1885* (Seattle: University of Washington Press, 1977); Kim, *The Last Phase of the East Asian World Order: Korea, Japan, and the Chinese Empire, 1860–1882* (Berkeley: University of California Press, 1980).

4. Tsiang, "Sino-Japanese Diplomatic Relations, 1870–1894," *Chinese Social and Political Science Review*, 17 (April 1933); Harold J. Noble, "The U.S. and Sino-Korean Relations, 1885–1887," *Pacific Historical Review*, 2 (1933).

5. Dennett, *Americans in Eastern Asia* (New York: Macmillan, 1922), p. 451.

6. *Ibid.*, p. 452.

7. *Ibid.*, p. 460.

8. *Ibid.*, p. 478.

9. *Ibid.*, p. 569.

10. *Ibid.*, p. 679.

11. Dennett, *Roosevelt and the Russo-Japanese War* (New York: Doubleday, 1925), p. 103. In *Americans in Eastern Asia* Dennett says it a bit differently: The 1882 treaty was "by far the most important political action undertaken by the U.S. in Asia until the occupation of the Philippines in 1898" (p. 450).

12. *Ibid.*, pp. 111, 115, 305–6.

13. William Franklin Sands, *Undiplomatic Memories* (New York: McGraw-Hill, 1930).

14. *Ibid.*, p. 99.

15. *Ibid.*, p. 220.

16. Griswold, *The Far Eastern Policy of the United States* (New York: Harcourt, Brace, 1938), ch. 3.

17. Harrington, *God, Mammon and the Japanese: Dr. Horace N. Allen and Korean-American Relations, 1884–1905* (Madison: University of Wisconsin Press, 1944), p. 44.

18. *Ibid.*, pp. 182, 205.

19. Asea munje yŏn'guso, *Ku Han'guk oegyo munsŏ* [Documents on the foreign relations of old Korea], 21 vols. (Seoul: Asea munje yŏn'guso, 1966–1973). There are other, less imposing, collections of documents. Interested readers should consult the bibliographies in Palais, *Politics and Policy;* Deuchler, *Confucian Gentlemen;* Kim, *Last Phase.*

20. Academy of Social Sciences, *Mi-Il cheguk chuŭi ŭi kongmo kyŏlt'ak e ŭihan Chosŏn ch'imnyak-sa* [History of aggression against Korea by the conspiracies of American and Japanese imperialism] (P'yŏngyang: Sahoe kwahak ch'ulp'an-sa, 1974), 2 vols., pp. 9, 11, 24–25, 86, 343. Apparently there are two additional volumes covering the period to 1945.

21. Kim, *Ku Han'guk chukwŏn sangsil kwajŏng e issŏssŏ ŭi oegyo kwan'gye* [Diplomatic relations regarding Korea's loss of sovereignty] (Seoul: n.p., 1962); Sin Ki-sŏk, *Hanmal oegyo-sa yŏn'gu* [Studies in the diplomatic history of the last years of the Yi dynasty] (Seoul: Il-cho'gak, 1967); Sin Kuk-ju, *Han'guk kŭndae chŏngch'i oegyo-sa* [Studies in the modern political and diplomatic history of Korea] (Seoul: Tan'gu-dang, 1965); No, *Han'guk oegyo-sa yŏn'gu* [Studies in Korean diplomatic history] (Seoul: Haemun-sa, 1967). Two exceptions from the

generalizations in the text, because of their excellent scholarship and general objectivity, are Pak Il-gun, *Kŭndae Han-Mi oegyo-sa* [History of modern Korean-American relations] (Seoul: Pagu-sa, 1968), covering mostly the period 1866–1888 and dealing in particular with the question of Korea's relationship to the Qing; and Yi Hyŏn-jong, *Han'guk kaehangjang yŏn'gu* [Studies on the opening of Korean trading ports] (Seoul: Ilcho'gak, 1975), a thoroughly researched account of the successive opening of ports, foreign commerce, foreign settlements, and extraterritoriality in late nineteenth-century Korea.

22. James B. Palais, "Korea on the Eve of the Kanghwa Treaty, 1873–1876" (Ph.D. diss., Harvard University, 1968), pp. 490–605.

23. *The Opening of Korea: A Study of Chinese Diplomacy* (n.p.: Shoe String Press, 1967). This is a well-documented account of the period 1876–1885, told mostly from the Chinese side.

24. Deuchler, *Confucian Gentlemen.*

25. *Ibid.,* p. 51.

26. (Berkeley: University of California Press, 1967).

27. The reader should also be aware of Hilary Conroy's fine study, from the Japanese side, *The Japanese Seizure of Korea, 1868–1910* (Philadelphia: University of Pennsylvania Press, 1960), which was discussed in May and Thomson's *American-East Asian Relations.* Also see collections of documents on the early period in English: George M. McCune and John A. Harrison, eds., *Korean-American Relations: Documents Pertaining to the Far Eastern Diplomacy of the United States, I, The Initial Period, 1883–1886* (Berkeley: University of California Press, 1951), and the subsequent volume, edited by Spencer Palmer, *The Period of Growing Influence, 1887–1895* (1963).

28. Foote was the first minister from the United States, arriving in May 1883; Foulk, U.S. Naval attaché, arrived in 1884 and soon became a key aide to Foote. Foulk accompanied the first Korean mission to the United States on its return journey. His papers are held at the New York Public Library.

29. Chandra, "Nationalism and Popular Participation in Government in Late 19th Century Korea: The Contribution of the Independence Club (1896–1898)" (Ph.D. diss., Harvard University, 1977); Weems, "The Korean Reform and Independence Movement" (Ph. D. diss., Columbia University, 1954); Shin, *Tongnip hyŏphoe yŏn'gu* [Studies on the Independence Club] (Seoul: Ilcho'gak, 1976).

30. See Spencer J. Palmer, *Korea and Christianity: The Problem of Identification with Tradition* (Seoul: Royal Asiatic Society, 1967); also L. G. Paik, *The History of Protestant Missions in Korea* (P'yŏngyang: n.p., 1927).

31. Anderson, *Passages from Antiquity to Feudalism* (London: NLB, 1974), p. 16.

32. Perry Anderson, *Lineages of the Absolutist State* (London: NLB, 1974), p. 483. I draw on his discussion of the Asiatic Mode of Production (pp. 462–549).

33. Karl Marx, *Capital* (New York: International Publisher's edition, 1967), vol. 1, p. 718n.

34. Young, "The Quest for Empire," in May and Thomson, eds. *American–East Asian Relations,* p. 138.

35. Edward Said, *Orientalism* (New York: Vintage Books, 1979).

36. L. H. Underwood, *Fifteen Years Among the Topknots* (New York: American Trust Society, 1904), p. 269.

37. Kennan, "Korea, A Degenerated State," *Outlook,* October 7, 1905.

38. Ladd, *In Korea with Marquis Ito* (New York: Scribner's, 1908), pp. 26, 28, 34, 36, 39.

39. Colin Holmes and A. H. Ion, "Bushidō and the Samurai: Images in British Public Opinion, 1894–1914," *Modern Asian Studies,* 14, 2 (1980), 320; also J. M. Winter, "The Webbs and the Non-White World: A Case of Socialist Racialism," *Journal of Contemporary History,* 9, 1 (January 1974).

40. *Americans in Eastern Asia,* p. 495.

41. *Undiplomatic Memories,* pp. 121, 227.

42. *Roosevelt and the Russo-Japanese War,* p. 106.

43. Quoted in Alleyne Ireland, *The New Korea* (New York: Dutton, 1926), p. 70.

44. H. B. Drake wrote, "What strikes the outsider . . . is the almost luxurious style in which the missionaries live." *Korea of the Japanese* (New York: Dodd Mead, 1930), p. 165.

45. See Kim Kyu-sik's elegant essay, "The Asiatic Revolutionary Movement and Imperialism," in Dae-sook Suh, *Documents on the Korean Communist Movement 1918–1948* (Princeton: Princeton University Press, 1970).

46. Nym Wales and Kim San, *Song of Ariran: A Korean Communist in the Chinese Revolution* (1941; reprint ed., San Francisco: Ramparts Press, 1972), p. 114. This book is the only window in English opened upon the lives of Korean revolutionaries, of whom there were many.

47. Byas, *Government by Assassination* (New York: Knopf, 1942). Byas argues that "to thrust self-government on Korea . . . would be a cruel gift," and urges a Japanese mandate in Korea after the war (pp. 359–60).

48. Grajdanzev, *Modern Korea* (New York: Institute of Pacific Relations, 1944), pp. 276–90; among many other State Department documents, see "Basic Initial Directive to the Commander-in-Chief, U.S. Army Forces Pacific, for the Administration of Civil Affairs in Those Areas of Korea Occupied by U.S. Forces," *Foreign Relations of the United States* (1945), vol. 6, pp. 1073–91.

49. See my *Origins of the Korean War: Liberation and the Emergence of Separate Regimes* (Princeton: Princeton University Press, 1981); also William George Morris, "The Korean Trusteeship, 1941–1947: The U.S., Russia, and the Cold War" (Ph.D. diss., University of Texas, 1974).

50. Quoted in Morris, "The Korean Trusteeship," p. 32.

51. Cumings, *Origins of the Korean War,* ch. 4.

52. Langdon, cable to Secretary of State, *Foreign Relations of the United States* (1945), vol. 6, pp. 1129–33.

53. RG59, Policy Planning Staff file, Kennan memo to Dean Rusk, October 6, 1949, box 13, orig. classification "top secret."

54. "China," February 1948, George F. Kennan Papers, Princeton University, box 23.

55. January 9, 1950, *ibid.,* box 24.

56. Green, *The Epic of Korea* (Washington: Public Affairs Press, 1950), p. 7.

57. (Cambridge: Harvard University Press, 1968); see also my review, "Is Korea a Mass Society?" *Occasional Papers on Korea* (Seattle: University of Washington, 1974).

58. Robert Dallek, "The Truman Era," in May and Thomson, eds., *American-East Asian Relations,* p. 364.

59. E. Grant Meade, *American Military Government in Korea* (New York: King's Crown Press, 1951); George McCune, *Korea Today* (Cambridge: Harvard University Press, 1950); Mark Gayn, *Japan Diary* (New York: William Sloane Associates, 1948); Richard Lauterbach, *Danger from the East* (New York: Harper, 1947); Irma Materi, *Irma and the Hermit* (New York: Norton, 1949); John C. Caldwell, *The Korea Story* (Chicago: Henry Regnery, 1952); Caldwell, *Korea: Second Failure in Asia* (Washington, D.C.: Public Affairs Press, 1951);

Robert T. Oliver, *Syngman Rhee: The Man Behind the Myth* (New York: Cornwall Press, 1955); Oliver, *Syngman Rhee and American Involvement in Korea* (Seoul: Panmun Books, 1979).

60. (Minneapolis: University of Minnesota Press, 1971).

61. Carl Berger, *The Korea Knot: A Military-Political History* (Philadelphia: University of Pennsylvania Press, 1957); Soon Sung Cho, *Korea in World Politics, 1940–1950* (Berkeley: University of California Press, 1967).

62. Leonard C. Hoag, "American Military Government in Korea: War Policy and the First Year of Occupation, 1941–46," draft ms. produced under the auspices of the Office of the Chief of Military History, 1970; Richard D. Robinson, "Betrayal of a Nation" (Massachusetts Institute of Technology, 1960); Steward Meacham, "Labor Report" (Seoul: USAMGIK, 1948); "History of the U.S. Armed Forced in Korea," 3 vols. (Seoul, Tokyo: Office of Chief of Military History, 1947, 1948); Robert K. Sawyer, *Military Advisors in Korea KMAG in Peace and War* (Washington, D.C.: Office of the Chief of Military History, 1962); C. Clyde Mitchell, *Final Report and History of the New Korea Company* (Seoul: National Land Administration, 1948); "History of the North Korean Army" (Tokyo: Office of the Chief of Military History, Far East Command, G-2 Section, 1952); Department of State, *North Korea: A Case Study in the Techniques of Takeover* (Washington, D.C.: Department of State, 1961).

63. Record Group 242, "Captured Enemy Documents," National Records Center.

64. For the fullest treatment see George Ginsburgs, *Soviet Works on Korea, 1945–1970* (Los Angeles: University of Southern California Press, 1967).

65. Dae-sook Suh, *The Korean Communist Movement, 1918–1948* (Princeton: Princeton University Press, 1967); Robert Scalapino and Chong-sik Lee, *Communism in Korea,* 2 vols. (Berkeley: University of California Press, 1972). For an excellent review of this and other literature, see Samuel Kim, "Research on Korean Communism: Promise vs. Performance," *World Politics* 32, 2 (Jan. 1980).

66. See for example Han T'ae-su, *Han'guk chŏngdang-sa* [History of Korean political parties] (Seoul: Sin t'aeyang-sa, 1961). A collection of essays entitled "Haeband" [Liberation], published in early 1980 in manuscript form, is very critical of the American occupation.

67. Minjujŭi minjok chŏnsŏn, *Chosŏn haebang illyŏn-sa* [History of the first year of Korea's liberation] (Seoul: Munu-sa, 1946).

68. Kuksa p'yŏnch'an wiwŏnhoe, *Taehan min'guk-sa* [History of the Republic of Korea], 7 vols. (Seoul Kuksa p'yonch'an wiwonhoe, 1970–1974).

69. Kukbang-bu, *Han'guk chŏnjaeng-sa* [History of the Korean War], 10 vols. (Seoul: Kukbang-bu, 1966–1970).

70. Kim Se-jin, ed., *Documents on Korean-American Relations, 1943–1976* (Seoul: Research Center for Peace and Unification, 1976); in Korean see *Han'guk oegyo ŭi isimnyŏn* [Twenty years of Korean diplomatic history] (Seoul: ROK Ministry of Foreign Affairs, 1967, 1971), covering the period 1948–1970. This is a good reference source on diplomatic agreements, treaties, trade negotiations, etc.

71. Kim Chum-gon, *The Korean War* (Seoul: Kwangmyong Publishing Co., 1973).

72. Stone, *The Hidden History of the Korean War* (New York: Monthly Review Press, 1952); Fleming, *The Cold War and Its Origins, 1917–1960,* 2 vols. (New York: Doubleday, 1961); David Horowitz, *The Free World Colossus* (New York: Hill and Wang, 1965); Wilfred Burchett, *Again Korea* (New York: International Publishers, 1968); Karunakar Gupta, "How Did the Korean War Begin?" *China Quarterly,* 52 (Oct.–Dec. 1972); Jon Halliday, "What Happened in Korea? Rethinking Korean History, 1945–1953," *Bulletin of Concerned Asian Scholars,* 5, 3 (1973); Joyce Kolko and Gabriel Kolko, *The Limits of Power: The World and*

United States Foreign Policy, 1945–1954 (New York: Harper & Row, 1972); Robert Simmons, *The Strained Alliance: Peking, P'yŏngyang, Moscow and the Politics of the Korean Civil War* (New York: Free Press, 1975).

On standard, scholarly accounts of the Korean War such as those by Allen S. Whiting, Glenn Paige, and others, see Dallek, "The Truman Era."

73. Noble, *Embassy at War,* Frank Baldwin, ed. (Seattle: University of Washington Press, 1975).

74. Stueck, *The Road to Confrontation: American Policy toward China and Korea, 1947– 50* (Chapel Hill: University of North Carolina Press, 1981); Nagai and Iriye, eds., *The Origins of the Cold War in Asia* (New York: Columbia University Press, 1977); Merrill's dissertation is being completed at the University of Delaware, Paul's at Stanford University; Kotch, "The Origins of the American Security Commitment to Korea" (Ph.D. diss., Columbia University, 1975); Matray, "American Foreign Policy in Korea, 1941–1950" (Ph.D. diss., University of Virginia, 1977); Morris, "Korean Trusteeship." Two dissertations I have not been able to read yet are Charles Dobbs, "American Foreign Policy, the Cold War, and Korea: 1945–1950" (Indiana University, 1978), and Kenneth R. Mauck, "The Formation of American Foreign Policy in Korea, 1945–1953" (University of Oklahoma, 1978). Ch'oe Sung-il's Tokyo University dissertation (1971) is available at the University of Washington. Finally, see Won-sul Lee, "The Impact of U.S. Occupation Policy on the Socio-Political Structure of South Korea, 1945–48" (Ph.D. diss., Western Reserve University, 1961), and Han-mu Kang, "The U.S. Military Government in Korea, 1945–1948" (Ph.D. diss., University of Cincinnati, 1970). See articles by Merrill, Stueck, Kotch, Paul, and Matray in Bruce Cumings, ed., *Child of Conflict: The Korean-American Relationship, 1945–53* (Seattle: University of Washington Press, 1983).

75. Ernest May, *'Lessons' of the Past: The Use and Misuse of History in American Foreign Policy* (New York: Oxford University Press, 1973); Russell Buhite, " 'Major Interests': American Policy Toward China, Taiwan, and Korea, 1945–1950," *Pacific Historical Review,* 47, 3 (August 1978).

76. Carroll H. Blanchard, Jr., *Korean War Bibliography and Maps of Korea* (Albany, N.Y.: Korean Conflict Research Foundation, 1964).

77. I include myself in this criticism. I argued in 1977 that the USSR and China would repair the Sino-Soviet split shortly.

78. Kim Kwan-bong, *The Korea-Japan Treaty Crisis and the Instability of the Korean Political System* (New York: Praeger, 1971); Subcommittee on International Organizations of the Committee on International Relations, U.S. House of Representatives, *Investigation of Korean-American Relations,* 6 vols. (Washington, D.C.: U.S. Government Printing Office, 1978); Selig Harrison, *The Widening Gulf* (New York: Free Press, 1978); Senate Foreign Relations Committee, *Korea and the Philippines* (Washington, D.C.: U.S. Government Printing Office, 1972); William Barnds, ed., *Korea and the Major Powers in East Asia* (New York: Council on Foreign Relations, 1978); Nathan White, *U.S. Policy Toward Korea* (Boulder, Colo.: Westview Press, 1979); Franklin B. Weinstein and Fuji Kamiya, eds., *The Security of Korea* (Boulder, Colo.: Westview Press, 1980).

Index

Studies of the East Asian Institute

THE LADDER OF SUCCESS IN IMPERIAL CHINA, by Ping-ti Ho. New York: Columbia University Press, 1962.

THE CHINESE INFLATION, 1937-1949, by Shun-hsin Chou. New York: Columbia University Press, 1963.

REFORMER IN MODERN CHINA: CHANG CHIEN, 1853-1926, by Samuel Chu. New York: Columbia University Press, 1965.

RESEARCH IN JAPANESE SOURCES: A GUIDE, by Herschel Webb with the assistance of Marleigh Ryan. New York: Columbia University Press, 1965.

SOCIETY AND EDUCATION IN JAPAN, by Herbert Passin. New York: Teachers College Press, Columbia University, 1965.

AGRICULTURAL PRODUCTION AND ECONOMIC DEVELOPMENT IN JAPAN, 1873-1922, by James I. Nakamura. Princeton: Princeton University Press, 1966.

JAPAN'S FIRST MODERN NOVEL: UKIGUMO OF FUTABATEI SHIMEI, by Marleigh Ryan. New York: Columbia University Press, 1967.

THE KOREAN COMMUNIST MOVEMENT, 1918-1948, by Dae-Sook Suh. Princeton: Princeton University Press, 1967.

THE FIRST VIETNAM CRISIS, by Melvin Gurtov. New York: Columbia University Press, 1967.

CADRES, BUREAUCRACY, AND POLITICAL POWER IN COMMUNIST CHINA, by A. Doak Barnett. New York: Columbia University Press, 1967.

THE JAPANESE IMPERIAL INSTITUTION IN THE TOKUGAWA PERIOD, by Herschel Webb. New York: Columbia University Press, 1968.

HIGHER EDUCATION AND BUSINESS RECRUITMENT IN JAPAN, by Koya Azumi. New York: Teachers College Press, Columbia University, 1969.

THE COMMUNISTS AND CHINESE PEASANT REBELLIONS: A STUDY IN THE REWRITING OF CHINESE HISTORY, by James P. Harrison, Jr. New York: Atheneum, 1969.

HOW THE CONSERVATIVES RULE JAPAN, by Nathaniel B. Thayer. Princeton: Princeton University Press, 1969.

ASPECTS OF CHINESE EDUCATION, edited by C. T. Hu. New York: Teachers College Press, Columbia University, 1969.

DOCUMENTS OF KOREAN COMMUNISM, 1918-1948, by Dae-Sook Suh. Princeton: Princeton University Press, 1970.

JAPANESE EDUCATION: A BIBLIOGRAPHY OF MATERIALS IN THE ENGLISH LANGUAGE, by Herbert Passin. New York: Teachers College Press, Columbia University, 1970.

ECONOMIC DEVELOPMENT AND THE LABOR MARKET IN JAPAN, by Kōji Taira. New York: Columbia University Press, 1970.

THE JAPANESE OLIGARCHY AND THE RUSSO-JAPANESE WAR, by Shumpei Okamoto. New York: Columbia University Press, 1970.

IMPERIAL RESTORATION IN MEDIEVAL JAPAN, by H. Paul Varley. New York: Columbia University Press, 1971.

JAPAN'S POSTWAR DEFENSE POLICY, 1947-1968, by Martin E. Weinstein. New York: Columbia University Press, 1971.

ELECTION CAMPAIGNING JAPANESE STYLE, by Gerald L. Curtis. New York: Columbia University Press, 1971.

CHINA AND RUSSIA: THE "GREAT GAME," by O. Edmund Clubb. New York: Columbia University Press, 1971. Also in paperback.

MONEY AND MONETARY POLICY IN COMMUNIST CHINA, by Katherine Huang Hsiao. New York: Columbia University Press, 1971.

THE DISTRICT MAGISTRATE IN LATE IMPERIAL CHINA, by John R. Watt. New York: Columbia University Press, 1972.

LAW AND POLICY IN CHINA'S FOREIGN RELATIONS: A STUDY OF ATTITUDES AND PRACTICE, by James C. Hsiung. New York: Columbia University Press, 1972.

PEARL HARBOR AS HISTORY: JAPANESE-AMERICAN RELATIONS, 1931-1941, edited by Dorothy Borg and Shumpei Okamoto, with the assistance of Dale K. A. Finlayson. New York: Columbia University Press, 1973.

JAPANESE CULTURE: A SHORT HISTORY, by H. Paul Varley. New York: Praeger, 1973.

DOCTORS IN POLITICS: THE POLITICAL LIFE OF THE JAPAN MEDICAL ASSOCIATION, by William E. Steslicke. New York: Praeger, 1973.

JAPAN'S FOREIGN POLICY, 1868-1941: A RESEARCH GUIDE, edited by James William Morley. New York: Columbia University Press, 1973.

THE JAPAN TEACHERS UNION: A RADICAL INTEREST GROUP IN JAPANESE POLITICS, by Donald Ray Thurston. Princeton: Princeton University Press, 1973.

PALACE AND POLITICS IN PREWAR JAPAN, by David Anson Titus. New York: Columbia University Press, 1974.

THE IDEA OF CHINA: ESSAYS ON GEOGRAPHIC MYTH AND THEORY, by Andrew March. Devon, England: David and Charles, 1974.

ORIGINS OF THE CULTURAL REVOLUTION, by Roderick MacFarquhar. New York: Columbia University Press, 1974.

SHIBA KŌKAN: ARTIST, INNOVATOR, AND PIONEER IN THE WESTERNI-ZATION OF JAPAN, by Calvin L. French. Tokyo: Weatherhill, 1974.

EMBASSY AT WAR, by Harold Joyce Noble. Edited with an introduction by Frank Baldwin, Jr. Seattle: University of Washington Press, 1975.

REBELS AND BUREAUCRATS; CHINA'S DECEMBER 9ERS, by John Israel and Donald W. Klein. Berkeley: University of California Press, 1975.

HOUSE UNITED, HOUSE DIVIDED: THE CHINESE FAMILY IN TAIWAN, by Myron L. Cohen. New York: Columbia University Press, 1976.

INSEI: ABDICATED SOVEREIGNS IN THE POLITICS OF LATE HEIAN JA-PAN, by G. Cameron Hurst. New York: Columbia University Press, 1976.

DETERRENT DIPLOMACY, edited by James William Morley. New York: Columbia University Press, 1976.

CADRES, COMMANDERS AND COMMISSARS: THE TRAINING OF THE CHINESE COMMUNIST LEADERSHIP, 1920-45, by Jane L. Price. Boulder, Colo.: Westview Press, 1976.

SUN YAT-SEN: FRUSTRATED PATRIOT, by C. Martin Wilbur. New York: Columbia University Press, 1976.

JAPANESE INTERNATIONAL NEGOTIATING STYLE, by Michael Blaker. New York: Columbia University Press, 1977.

CONTEMPORARY JAPANESE BUDGET POLITICS, by John Creighton Campbell. Berkeley: University of California Press, 1977.

THE MEDIEVAL CHINESE OLIGARCHY, by David Johnson. Boulder, Colo.: Westview Press, 1977.

ESCAPE FROM PREDICAMENT: NEO-CONFUCIANISM AND CHINA'S EVOLVING POLITICAL CULTURE, by Thomas A. Metzger. New York: Columbia University Press, 1977.

THE ARMS OF KIANGNAN: MODERNIZATION IN THE CHINESE ORD-NANCE INDUSTRY, 1860-1895, by Thomas L. Kennedy. Boulder, Colo.: Westview Press, 1978.

PATTERNS OF JAPANESE POLICYMAKING: EXPERIENCES FROM HIGHER EDUCATION, by T. J. Pempel. Boulder, Colo.: Westview Press, 1978.

THE CHINESE CONNECTION, by Warren Cohen. New York: Columbia University Press, 1978.

MILITARISM IN MODERN CHINA: THE CAREER OF WU P'EI-FU, 1916-1939, by Odoric Y. K. Wou. Folkestone, England: Wm. Dawson & Sons, 1978.

A CHINESE PIONEER FAMILY, by Johanna Meskill. Princeton: Princeton University Press, 1979.

PERSPECTIVES ON A CHANGING CHINA: ESSAYS IN HONOR OF PROFES-SOR C. MARTIN WILBUR, edited by Joshua A. Fogel and William T. Rowe. Boulder, Colo.: Westview Press, 1979.

THE MEMOIRS OF LI TSUNG-JEN, by T. K. Tong and Li Tsung-jen. Boulder, Colo.: Westview Press, 1979.

UNWELCOME MUSE: CHINESE LITERATURE IN SHANGHAI AND PEKING, 1937-1945, by Edward Gunn. New York: Columbia University Press, 1979.

YENAN AND THE GREAT POWERS: THE ORIGINS OF CHINESE COMMUNIST FOREIGN POLICY, 1944-1946, by James Reardon-Anderson. New York: Columbia University Press, 1980.

UNCERTAIN YEARS: CHINESE-AMERICAN RELATIONS, 1947-1950, edited by Dorothy Borg and Waldo Heinrichs. New York: Columbia University Press, 1980.

THE FATEFUL CHOICE: JAPAN'S ADVANCE INTO SOUTHEAST ASIA, 1939-1941, edited by James W. Morley. New York: Columbia University Press, 1980.

TANAKA GIICHI AND JAPAN'S CHINA POLICY, by William F. Morton. Folkestone, England: Dawson, 1980; New York: St. Martin's Press, 1980.

THE ORIGINS OF THE KOREAN WAR: LIBERATION AND THE EMERGENCE OF SEPARATE REGIMES, 1945-1947, by Bruce Cumings. Princeton: Princeton University Press, 1981.

CLASS CONFLICT IN CHINESE SOCIALISM, by Richard Curt Kraus. New York: Columbia University Press, 1981.

PRIVATE ACADEMIES OF THE TOKUGAWA PERIOD, by Richard Rubinger. Princeton: Princeton University Press, 1982.

EDUCATION UNDER MAO: CLASS AND COMPETITION IN CANTON SCHOOLS, 1960-1980, by Jonathan Unger. New York: Columbia University Press, 1982.

NEW FRONTIERS IN AMERICAN-EAST ASIAN RELATIONS: ESSAYS PRESENTED TO DOROTHY BORG, edited by Warren I. Cohen. New York: Columbia University Press, 1983.